Wakefield Press

Sir Josiah Symon KCMG KC

Ian Hancock has written extensively on the political history of Uganda and of Southern Rhodesia/Rhodesia/Zimbabwe; and taught courses on imperial, colonial and African history at Monash University and on African, Australian and British history at the Australian National University.

He has published many entries on Liberal Party figures for the *Australian Dictionary of Biography*, including one on former Prime Minister Harold Holt. He has also published full-length biographies of former Prime Minister Sir John Gorton, former NSW Premier Nick Greiner, former federal Attorney-General and long-term leader of the NSW Bar Tom Hughes, and of Gorton's controversial and trail-blazing staffer, Ainsley Gotto. He is presently completing a co-authored biography of a Public Service mandarin, Sir Frederick Wheeler, who had major confrontations with Gough Whitlam and Malcolm Fraser.

Sir Josiah Symon with his wife Nell, c. 1896

Sir Josiah Symon KCMG KC

A Biography

IAN HANCOCK

Wakefield Press

Wakefield Press
16 Rose Street
Mile End
South Australia 5031
www.wakefieldpress.com.au

First published 2023

Copyright © Ian Hancock, 2023

All rights reserved. This book is copyright. Apart from
any fair dealing for the purposes of private study, research,
criticism or review, as permitted under the Copyright Act,
no part may be reproduced without written permission.
Enquiries should be addressed to the publisher.

Cover designed by Stacey Zass
Edited and typeset by Michael Deves, Wakefield Press

ISBN 978 1 74305 974 6

A catalogue record for this
book is available from the
National Library of Australia

Wakefield Press thanks
Coriole Vineyards for
continued support

In gratitude

Elizabeth Symon Dyer

SYMON FAMILY TREE

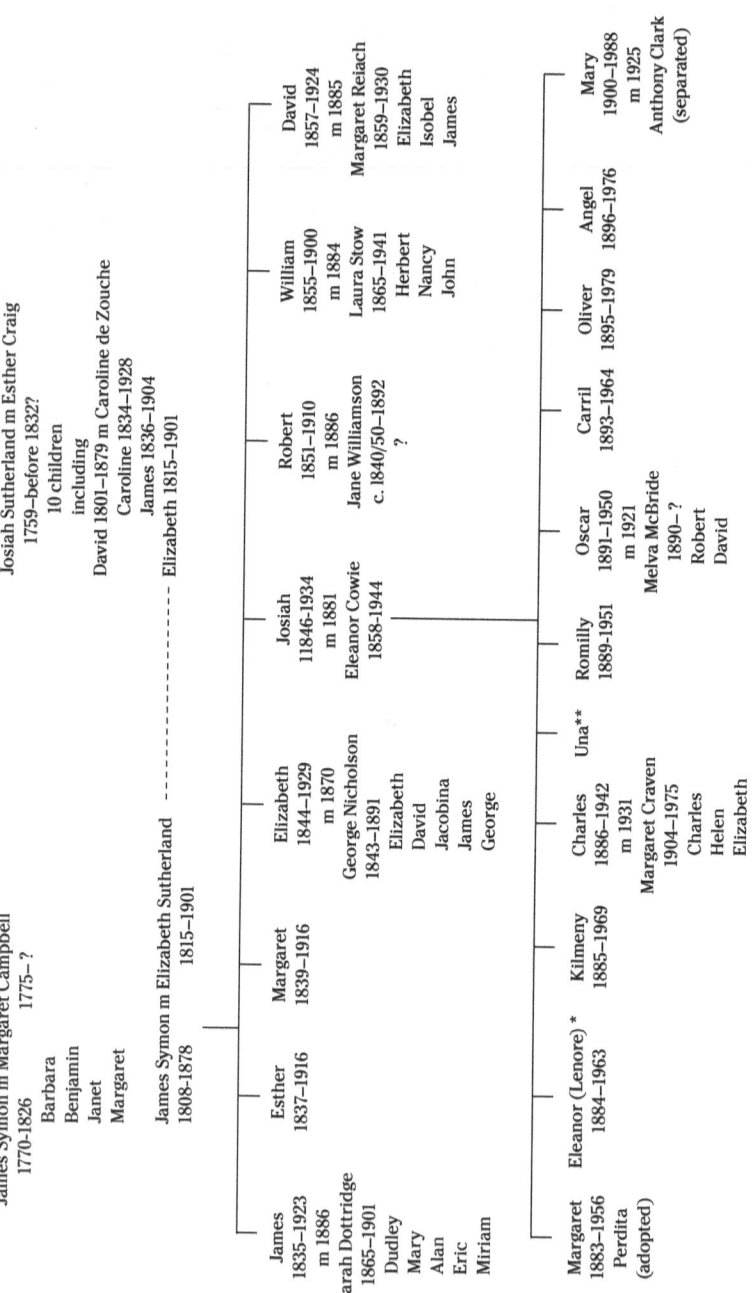

James Symon m Margaret Campbell
1770–1826   1775–?
  Barbara
  Benjamin
  Janet
  Margaret

Josiah Sutherland m Esther Craig
1759–before 1832?
10 children
including
David 1801–1879 m Caroline de Zouche
  Caroline 1834–1928
  James 1836–1904

James Symon m Elizabeth Sutherland
1808–1878   1815–1901

- - - - - - - - - - Elizabeth 1815–1901

James 1835–1923 m 1886 Sarah Dottridge 1865–1901
  Dudley
  Mary
  Alan
  Eric
  Miriam

Esther 1837–1916

Margaret 1839–1916

Elizabeth 1844–1929 m 1870 George Nicholson 1843–1891
  Elizabeth
  David
  Jacobina
  James
  George

Josiah 1846–1934 m 1881 Eleanor Cowie 1858-1944

Robert 1851–1910 m 1886 Jane Williamson c. 1840/50–1892

William 1855–1900 m 1884 Laura Stow 1865–1941
  Herbert
  Nancy
  John

David 1857–1924 m 1885 Margaret Reiach 1859–1930
  Elizabeth
  Isobel
  James

Children of Josiah and Eleanor:

Margaret 1883–1956 Perdita (adopted)

Eleanor (Lenore) * 1884–1963

Kilmeny 1885–1969

Charles 1886–1942 m 1931 Margaret Craven 1904–1975
  Charles
  Helen
  Elizabeth

Una** ?

Romilly 1889–1951

Oscar 1891–1950 m 1921 Melva McBride 1890–?
  Robert
  David

Carril 1893–1964

Oliver 1895–1979

Angel 1896–1976

Mary 1900–1988 m 1925 Anthony Clark (separated)

* Lenore's twin sister, Alison, died two months after her birth in 1884.

** Una died just under five months after her birth in 1888.

Contents

Abbreviations		viii
Preface		ix
1	'a young man of considerable promise'	1
2	'Make good friends of the cook.'	13
3	'this momentous step in my life'	22
4	'I can address a jury as effectively as the best of them.'	36
5	'your dogged determination to succeed did most of the climbing.'	54
6	'There is a first place and you alone occupy it.'	74
7	'it is for the people to say how they shall be governed.'	92
8	'the finest instrument of government that ever was framed'	108
9	'a great paean of triumph in the closely knit union of the race.'	129
10	'I am jealous of the rights of the Commonwealth'	149
11	'he is not fit to be Prime Minister.'	169
12	'this combination has set me free from party'	192
13	'I am really sick of politics & want rest'	214
14	'My boys & girls are all in all to me.'	233
15	'Not a sign or whisper of discontent anywhere'	255
16	'I have had no rest or peace but only worry'	269
17	'I feel it all as a deep personal grief'	285
18	'scandalous, offensive and defamatory'	302
Epilogue		314
Bibliography		322
Notes		329
Index		351

Abbreviations

ACT	Australian Capital Territory
ADB	Australian Dictionary of Biography
AIF	Australian Imperial Force
ANA	Australian Natives' Association
BNC	Brasenose College
CHNS	Carril Hector Nicholson Symon
CJ	Chief Justice
CMG	Companion of St Michael and St George
CLR	Commonwealth Law Reports
CPD	Commonwealth Parliamentary Debates
CPP	Commonwealth Parliamentary Papers
ES&A	English, Scottish and Australian Bank
GCMG	Grand Cross of St Michael and St George
JSS	James Sutherland Symon
JHS	Josiah Henry Symon
JP	Justice of the Peace
KC	King's Counsel
KCMG	Knight Commander of St Michael and St George
LKS	Lesley Kilmeny Symon
MA	Master of Arts
MUP	Melbourne University Press
MP	Member of Parliament
MC	Military Cross
NAA	National Archives of Australia
NDL	National Defence League
NLA	National Library of Australia
P&O	Pacific & Orient
QC	Queen's Counsel
RMS	Royal Mail Service
SLSA	State Library of South Australia
SMH	Sydney Morning Herald
UAP	United Australia Party
UK	United Kingdom

Preface

Sir Josiah Symon KCMG KC was in some ways a vain man, but then he had much to be vain about.

The son of a skilled carpenter, the young Josiah had trained as a primary schoolteacher in Stirling, Scotland, and collected references testifying to his energy and capacity. He arrived in South Australia in 1866 a month shy of 20 years of age, seemingly older than his years although narrow in outlook and limited in experience. In addition to clothing and personal items, he brought with him two boxes of books, a few pounds in cash and the addresses of a near bankrupt uncle in Adelaide and of a wayward hard-drinking cousin who managed a small law firm in Mount Gambier. When he died in 1934 Symon left an estate valued at £220,026/10/2, equivalent in 2020 money terms to $22,256,580.86.[1] And these figures take no account of the large sums previously given to his wife and their children and to various institutions and worthy causes in South Australia and elsewhere in Australia, England and Scotland.

After starting his articles in Mount Gambier and completing them in Adelaide, Symon joined the legal firm of Way & Brook in 1870, headed his own firm of barristers and solicitors from 1876, and for 30 years was the acknowledged leader of the Adelaide Bar. Clerks and junior lawyers considered themselves privileged to join Symon's firm, where they learnt and practised the highest standards of their profession. Symon himself appeared in all jurisdictions and in all branches of the law. His reputation and success rate in the court room discouraged many potential litigants from proceeding against his clients. Several men and at least one woman escaped the death penalty because of Symon's powers of cross-examination and oratory.

Sir Josiah Symon KCMG KC

An ardent federalist in the 1890s, Symon won election to the 1897-8 Constitutional Convention. He led the smaller colonies, chaired its Judiciary Committee, and fought hard for a strong Senate to protect State rights and for a High Court as the final court of appeal. He was rightly proud of his contribution to the achievement and to the form of federation. Joseph Chamberlain, the British Colonial Secretary, who told him in 1900 that Queen Victoria had approved his appointment as KCMG, wrote the following:

> You have rendered eminent services to the cause of Federal unity in Australia both as an advocate of it in the country and in your capacity as a member of the Convention and Chairman of (its) Judiciary Committee.

Symon served in the South Australian House of Assembly (1881-7) and in the Australian Senate (1901-13). He was, albeit briefly, a State and a Commonwealth Attorney-General. He was also a dairy farmer and an orchardist who experimented in environmental protection and owned a highly regarded vineyard that won prizes for its wines which sold well in Australia, Britain and Europe. Symon further supplemented his income by making very profitable investments in West Australian gold mining and through buying and selling in the share markets of London and Australia and in the property market in his home State.

Symon was a voracious reader who built a 'gentleman's library' of more than 10,000 volumes, reflecting a special interest in English law and in the history and literature of the British Isles and of France. Few Scots anywhere were better informed about the works of Sir Walter Scott and Robert Burns. Symon gave lectures and wrote short books and pamphlets on William Shakespeare, and Shakespearean scholars in the northern hemisphere regarded him as one of their fraternity. He collected art and *objets d'art* and either formed, chaired or was the patron of artistic, poetry and literary societies in Adelaide. A highly gifted public speaker, Symon was in demand for special and formal occasions in South Australia and regularly spoke at Robbie Burns' nights and at functions organised by the Australian Natives' Association, the Royal Empire Society, Caledonian societies and Loyal Orange Lodges.

He loved to travel, especially to India, the Continent and North America and, above all, to go 'home', which he variously identified as

Preface

England, Scotland or Britain. Every trip meant making new contacts and renewing established ones, many of them titled and either formerly or presently influential and usually very interesting. They included former governors and governors-general, Indian maharajas, active or retired very senior army and naval officers, cabinet ministers, former and current senior civil servants, leading writers, editors and literary figures, big game hunters, explorers and heads and dons of Oxbridge colleges. New contacts instantly became, in Symon's mind, 'friends'; he would tell his family and others they were men and women 'I know'. In fact, Symon was more widely known and respected outside of Australia than nearly all of his Adelaide contemporaries.

For all his eminence and achievements Symon has usually been ignored, treated cursorily or simply disparaged by historians and commentators.[2] While Symon regarded his work in the 1897–8 Constitutional Convention as his most important contribution to public life, he is customarily rated tenth for the number of words assigned to the ten South Australian delegates to the Convention. Perhaps he was deemed less interesting than his contemporaries. After all, Charles Cameron Kingston was a 'larrikin' and a radical reformer, who was never restrained by the Seventh Commandment. John Downer was a leader in colonial politics and a significant federalist who founded a political dynasty. Patrick McMahon Glynn had a head full of literature and so much Irish charm.

Perhaps Symon never appealed because he was a conservative who sooner or later placed himself on the wrong side of history. He advocated a white Australia even as he favoured importing Tamil labour and admired pro-Empire Indians. Symon remained a free trader when the protective tariff, like the White Australia policy, became a principal plank of the 'Australian Settlement'. He was a passionate conscriptionist during the Great War. Symon wanted the Senate to be the guardian of State rights, and visualised it being composed of the wise and the eminent and becoming an active and dignified contributor to government. Quixotically, he refused to acknowledge, let alone accept, that the Senate in his lifetime had become a second party House, a reward and rest home for party hacks. He never foresaw it providing an opportunity for small parties or single-issue odds and sods to hold governments to account or to ransom.

Ironically, Symon received the most attention when, as Commonwealth Attorney-General, he so hounded the three judges of the High Court over their travelling and other expenses that they held a one-week 'strike' in protest. In the event, the judges got what they wanted: an affirmation of judicial independence and of their right and duty to perambulate around Australia with the assurance of a full reimbursement of expenses. Symon became fair game for those who wanted to censure or to crow. Symon's later critics did not always come to grips with the man himself.

Symon acted on principles and assumptions during the High Court dispute which remind us that the past is indeed 'a foreign country: they do things differently there'.[3] His conservatism is a case in point. Symon thought of himself as an 'independent conservative'. The historian Peter Howell described him as 'a thorough conservative'. Yet within two pages of the same chapter Howell acknowledged Symon to be less than 'thorough'; his conservatism was 'of the more enlightened kind that acknowledges the need for change and does not seek to preserve institutions and practices that have patently outlived their usefulness'.[4] Symon was often ahead of his time. He campaigned for the abolition of appeals to the Privy Council more than 80 years before this was achieved. Symon believed that women should be eligible for Rhodes scholarships fifty years before they were permitted to apply. He campaigned in the 1920s for a women's residential college to be established at the University of Adelaide when there was only one such college in existence in Australia. Symon stood well apart from other conservatives in advocating the abolition of upper houses throughout Australia, including that bastion of toryism, the unreformed Legislative Council in South Australia.

Like so many of his contemporaries, Symon never thought of himself as having a single or exclusive identity. He was a Scot by birth and proud of it, he became partly English by choice and cultural adaptation, regretted that being born outside Australia disqualified him for membership of the Australian Natives' Association and was gratified to belong to what he called the 'British race'. He considered himself to be in equal measure a South Australian, an Australian nationalist and an Empire loyalist. Two of those identities created a recurring tension in his public life between a preference for a strong national government and a commitment to strong

Preface

State governments. Symon was forever advocating or defending one of those elements against the other.

He stood out in public life as a man who brought firm principles to most situations and applied them with little inclination to compromise. As a result, Symon was not always suited to politics. He had a penchant for robust confrontation and vituperation, and 'seemed to fall out with everybody'.[5] Yet, with a few notable exceptions, Symon's fallings out did not last. He was more like the barrister who moved on immediately when a case was concluded. Critics at the time, and more commonly a century later, have not always noticed how Symon easily achieved a reconciliation and too many commentators have been overly shocked or repelled by what at the time was the language of everyday exchanges. He just had a larger vocabulary than most of his opponents.

Josiah Symon grew up with a strong sense of family. As a boy and a young man he cared deeply for his parents and three older sisters and looked up to the brother who was ten years ahead of him. By the time he turned 35 in 1881, Josiah had succeeded his late father as the *de facto* head of the family, become its principal benefactor and was trying to manage the careers of his three younger brothers. In that same year Symon married the woman he adored and by 1900 had fathered twelve children of whom two had died in infancy while one boy was born an 'invalid'. Five years before war broke out in 1914, and during the Great War and its aftermath, Symon became a most attentive father. He gave his four fit sons – all of them returned servicemen – every advantage to prepare them for profitable careers. By the end of the 1920s he accepted they had failed to meet his expectations. The patriarch set about shifting the balance in the family, moved closer to the three older daughters than to any of his sons and treated his third daughter, Kilmeny, as his principal confidante.

The Symon story is worth telling because Symon was at the forefront of so many careers and had such wide interests. His successes and failures, and his connections and disconnections with the present, add to an understanding of the world in which he moved and sought to influence.

Sir Josiah Symon died six years before I was born. There are no contemporaries or even near-contemporaries to interview. In addition to the customary sources, the main ones for this book are the fifty-three tightly-packed and professionally sorted boxes and ten folio cartons of Symon papers in the National Library of Australia (NLA). Deposited by Kilmeny, Symon's literary executor, these papers provide a massive amount of material covering all aspects of his life: his family background, education, teaching, migration, the law, national and state politics, constitutional arrangements, business and financial affairs, the wine industry, literature, philanthropy, book-collecting, wills, travel, and public speaking. In addition, the NLA also holds four boxes of Symon family papers and one box of Elizabeth Dyer's papers. Elizabeth Dyer, a daughter of Sir Josiah's eldest son, Charles, retains several boxes of papers in Adelaide to which the author had access. The NLA also holds a valuable interview with Perdita Eldridge, the adopted daughter of Symon's eldest daughter, Margaret. Some of Perdita's own papers form part of Elizabeth Dyer's collection.

The six boxes of papers containing material relating to Symon's legal career do not offer much beyond an insight into Symon's meticulous approach to preparation and into his arguments with other barristers over professional conduct. Fortunately, the Adelaide press reported virtually every Symon appearance in court thereby providing evidence of his workload, and it covered his criminal cases in detail. There remains, however, a disproportionate emphasis in this book on everything else in Symon's life. That said, Symon treated 'everything else' as very important.

I have several debts. The State Library of South Australia and the Barr Smith Library of the University of Adelaide provided skilled and generous assistance. In particular, I want to thank Carolyn Spooner of the SLSA for her assistance with photographs. The J.S. Battye Library of West Australian History helped me on a particular point. I am once again indebted to the staff at the desk and behind the scenes of the Special Collections Room and the Newspaper Room of the National Library of Australia.

Wilfrid Prest, acting on behalf of Elizabeth Dyer, first brought Symon to my attention, invited me to deliver a lecture in Adelaide for the State Library and the Selden Society and later brought me to the publisher's attention. He and Sabina Flanagan looked after me very well in Adelaide.

Carol Stanley of 'Manoah' kindly showed me over the mansion and the estate which she and her husband now own.

Preface

Various members of the extended Symon family have helped along the way: Perdita Eldridge, Lucas Green, Douglas Nicholson, David Symon, Martin Symon, Neil Symon and Judith Symon. I am especially grateful for the help and advice provided by Christopher Eldridge who also arranged my meeting with his mother, Perdita.

Sebastian Hancock, Graeme Lange, Graham Loughlin, the late John Nethercote, Peter Norman, Greg Taylor and Sophie Torney assisted me at various stages. Justine Buckley, Douglas Craig, Elizabeth Dyer, Joan Ritchie, Paul Santamaria and Susan Sharpe read the entire manuscript and provided acute criticism and very helpful advice.

My greatest debt is to Elizabeth Dyer. She agreed that I should write a biography and provided considerable financial assistance to assist research and publication. She translated Symon's appalling handwriting, gave me full access to the boxes of records at her home where she supplied me with meals, coffee and conversation, edited the manuscript, introduced me to family members, led me through family history and drove me to 'Manoah' and to her grandfather's grave – all the time encouraging me and suggesting lines of enquiry but leaving me to pursue my own interpretations. It has at times been hard for her. Elizabeth's grandfather and some of his relatives, her own father and some of his siblings do not always emerge well in the Symon story, but she is a published historian and biographer accustomed to dealing with awkward and undesirable discoveries.

I am especially grateful to Michael Bollen of Wakefield Press for taking on this project and to Michael Deves of Wakefield for his contributions to the editing and production of the book.

I am entirely responsible for what follows.

Notes: After the early chapters, I generally refer to 'Jo' when writing of Symon's relations with the family, and 'Symon' in his public life. All underlining or emphases within quotations are reproductions of the original.

1
'a young man of considerable promise'

Josiah Henry Symon was born on 27 September 1846 at Wick, Caithness, located in the north-eastern Scottish Highlands. He was the fifth child and second son of James Symon (1808–1878), a master cabinetmaker and joiner, and Elizabeth, née Sutherland (1815–1901).

Family records trace the Symon line to a James Symon who in the late 18th century married one Margaret Campbell. Little is known about this James Symon except that he was a gardener by occupation and probably a member of the Clan Fraser. He and Margaret produced six children, of whom the youngest was the James who became Josiah's father. No details are presently available to show how, where and when Josiah's father acquired his cabinetmaking skills.

Josiah's mother was a descendant – many times removed – of the Sutherlands of Forse, Caithness. Within Elizabeth's family, remoteness from the core did not eliminate a claim to trace their line from the 5th Earl of Sutherland who died around 1370. The Earls of Sutherland made Dunrobin Castle, the most substantial castle in the northern Highlands, the family seat and home of Clan Sutherland. John Sutherland, the 13th Earl, led volunteers attached to the Earl of Loudoun's corps on the side of King George II against 'Bonnie Prince Charlie' at the Battle of Culloden in 1745. When William the 18th Earl of Sutherland died in 1786, there was a contest for the succession between Sir Robert Gordon of Gordonstoun and Captain George Sutherland over who had the better right to the title against the claims of the late Earl's daughter, Lady Elizabeth. The House of Lords determined in favour of the daughter who, as the Countess of Sutherland, married a Leveson-Gower who was subsequently created

Duke of Sutherland. Josiah's mother was now even further removed from the titles but she retained a link with Forse, shared pride in Clan Sutherland and knew that her immediate family were better off materially and socially than the Symons.

Elizabeth's father, Josiah Sutherland, was born in 1759 in Watten, Caithness. He became a wealthy merchant and shipowner and in 1799 married Esther Craig of Wick. Their second son, David (1801–1879), inherited his father's business, managed it for a time in the company of two younger brothers and became well known in the fishing industry. He joined a company in London and emigrated to South Australia in 1840 to become the company's agent for general merchant business. He arrived with his family, servants, household goods and a large quantity of merchandise. David Sutherland immediately prospered. He sat on the Hospital and the Immigration Boards, won election to the House of Assembly (1860–1868) and acquired an estate of 320 acres south of Adelaide which he named 'Dunrobin'. By mid-1866, however, he was in serious financial difficulty: the London company had collapsed, David had made unwise investments, debtors failed on repayments and everything from the weather to markets seemed to turn against him. David remained a fervent free trader and a man of moral rectitude committed to acts of public duty such as serving as an unpaid JP and local councillor. Yet, by the time his nephew Josiah Symon arrived in Adelaide in September 1866, David was almost bankrupt and in the process of trying to sell his estate.

In 1829 David had married Caroline de la Zouche in a Congregational Church in Limerick, Ireland. She was a daughter of a French Huguenot family and David selected South Australia because of its commitment to religious liberty and tolerance. David and Caroline had five children of whom their daughter Caroline and their son James de la Zouche Sutherland figured prominently in Josiah Symon's life in his early days in South Australia.

Josiah's parents had married in 1834 and their first child, James ('Jim') Sutherland Symon, was born in the following year. Jim went to work with Customs in London, possibly to escape family attention, and became a critical figure in Josiah's life as a guardian and mentor. If the Symons had been as well off as the male Sutherlands, Jim might have gone to a university and made more of his wide reading and interest in politics. Three daughters arrived after Jim. Esther, the oldest, became an invalid following an illness. She and Margaret, the sister born immediately after her, earned a living working as milliners and dressmakers in the home they shared. Elizabeth or 'Lizzie' was born in 1844 and married an ironmonger, George or 'Geordie' Nicholson, much loved by the Symon family. Josiah's arrival was not a special event and in terms of upbringing he never became a 'problem' like his three younger brothers. Robert or 'Bob', born in 1851, may have been slightly impaired mentally and behaved erratically in childhood though he did get work as a printer. The two youngest boys – William or 'Bill' born in 1857, and David in 1858 – alternated between roles as mischief-makers and troublemakers. By the time Josiah left school in 1862 he was the bridge between his younger brothers and the older members of the family.

Early in Josiah's life the family moved to Stirling, a growing town in central Scotland. Stirling linked the Highlands and the Lowlands and is situated 26 miles north-east of Glasgow and 37 miles north-west of Edinburgh. Josiah's father had a contract to build the Baptist Church and on completion became its organist and a deacon. Josiah completed his primary schooling in Stirling before enrolling in Stirling High School, with its Latin motto – *Tempori Parendum* – telling students to 'Be Prepared for Your Time'. Established early in the 12th century to train ecclesiastics, the school shifted through many phases and was housed in many different buildings. In 1856 it occupied a specially created building with classrooms set aside for Mathematics, English, Modern Languages, Art and Classics. The school also had a Gymnasium, and an Observatory on the roof. That building is now a hotel. The school continues to list many notable Scots among its former pupils, headed by Henry Campbell-Bannerman, the British Prime Minister (1905–8) who once served in the Gladstone and Rosebery cabinets. Bannerman had left Stirling well before another notable, 'Sir Josiah Symon – Attorney-General of Australia', arrived at the school.

The young Symon's ability was noted before he reached high school. When aged eleven and a few months, he was approached by the relevant authorities who asked him to consider a career in teaching. Since 1846 there had been a significant reform in teacher training in Scotland. Promising recruits were selected at the age of 13 to undertake a five-year apprenticeship as pupil teachers of younger children. Supervised and instructed, they received a stipend of £10 at the age of 13 and annual increments rising to £20 to cover living expenses. Her Majesty's Inspectors tested them in annual examinations. At the conclusion of their apprenticeship they could win Queen's Scholarships tenable at a residential training college where they could obtain certificated status as teachers. The sons and daughters of tradesmen were more likely to be selected for apprenticeships than children of manual workers. A respectable home background and a sound moral character were prerequisites for a pupil teacher because he was expected to 'conduct himself with honesty, sobriety and temperance and not be guilty of any profane or lewd conversation or conduct, or of gambling or any other immorality'.[1] A pupil teacher was also required to attend church every Sunday.

At the age of 12 Josiah was tested for an 'Estimate of Character'. It is unknown who conducted the exercise, whether Josiah was assessed in or out of school and whether his parents had approved the exercise. The 'Estimate' was conducted in accordance with the ideas promulgated by the adherents of phrenology. Active from the late 18th century, phrenologists claimed that by measuring 'bumps' on the skull, corresponding to the shape of the brain beneath it, an investigator could 'discover' an individual's character and potential. An Edinburgh lawyer, George Combe (1791–1855), had experienced a Pauline conversion to the new 'science' and became the critical progenitor of Victorian phrenology. Like Combe, the true believers were often highly educated professionals. In 1826, the 120 members of the Edinburgh Society consisted of physicians, surgeons, teachers, lawyers, military officers, clergymen, merchants, artists, and writers. By then, interest in phrenology had extended to clerks, shopkeepers, and artisans.

Phrenologists divided what they called 'faculties' into two major 'orders'. The first order comprised 'feelings' which were either 'propensities' like 'combativeness' and 'destructiveness' which were shared by men and animals, or 'sentiments' like 'veneration' and 'firmness' which belonged to man alone. The second order consisted of 'intellectual faculties' which extended to external senses such as taste and smell and 'perceptive faculties' such as language.[2]

By the 1840s the 'new science' had been demoted to a 'pseudoscience', and phrenology had become widely ridiculed by 1858 when Josiah Symon's bumps were 'measured'. Nonetheless, the certificate recording the estimate of his character probably deserves attention. A biographer is bound to wonder if Josiah or his family took the estimate seriously. So far, no evidence has emerged either way. It may also be wondered what an upright Scottish family felt about a report suggesting that their son of 12 might have a brain-driven high propensity for 'amativeness'; that is, for 'sexual love or desire'. They need not have worried. The 'reading' was either flawed or Josiah was remarkably disciplined. When he married at the age of 35, he was almost certainly a virgin.

Estimate of Character[3]
of
Josiah H. Symon Nov. 3 1858

Measurement: Circumference: 21; measured 2–22: illegible; Posterior Lobe: 11; Above Caution: 13¾

Scale: 7 ('Primary'), 6 ('Secondary'), 5 ('Tertiary'), 4 ('Fourth Rate'), 3 ('Fifth-Rate'), 2 and 1 ('&c.')

Feelings
- 6 Amativeness, Destructiveness
- 5½ Adhesiveness, Secretiveness
- 5 Alimentiveness, Combativeness
- 4½ Constructiveness
- 4 Philoprogenitiveness, Acquisitiveness

Inferior Sentiments

- 6½ Love of Approbation
- 6 Cautiousness
- 4½ Self-Esteem

Superior Sentiments

- 5½ Benevolence, Veneration, Wit
- 5 Veneration, Hope, Imitation
- 4½ Firmness

Perceptive Faculties
- 6 Individuality, Form, Colouring
- 5 Size, Weight

Perceives the Relations of Objects

- 6 ½ Eventuality
- 5 ½ Locality, Time, Tune
- 4½ Number
- 4 Order, Language

Reflective Faculties
- 6 ½ Casually
- 6 Comparison

Lymphatic 2 Sanguine 2 Fibrous: no result Nervous 3

Josiah joined the teaching service as a 13-year-old pupil teacher. He attended classes at Stirling High School and, under instruction, taught primary school children. Presumably, his parents were pleased. Their second son had a sound future in Scottish society which placed a high value on education and regarded teaching as an honourable and useful profession. Besides, the stipend added to the family's limited budget.

In 1867, Josiah had occasion to reflect upon his time as a pupil teacher. He had learnt that his brother Bill was thinking of following Jo's path. Josiah thought that any benefits were outweighed by 'disadvantages and mischievous tendencies'. The first master-in-charge was very exacting and Josiah felt he made 'rapid strides' in handling the 'truly prodigious' requirements. Whereas the two more senior pupil-teachers 'growled and rebelled', young Symon was held up as a model to the older pupil teachers. Unfortunately, the master-in-charge became seriously ill. His replacement, John Graham, was 'lax and yielding in his discipline, superficial in his knowledge, miserable in Classics and nowhere in Mathematics, and devoid of the energy of body and vigour of will needed to deal with the training of lads of 13 and 14'. Anarchy reigned for almost the remainder of Josiah's contract. He 'became procrastinating, careless of learning, thoughtless and wavering and desultory', and acquired 'evil habits' that were 'almost ineradicable'. Another master took over with just a few months to go, and Josiah might well have recovered his early enthusiasm but, finding that 'anything will do', settled for giving satisfaction. Although Josiah accepted the blame for losing his early eagerness, he considered himself 'too young to strike out for myself in the self-educating principles'. Those who should have coerced him refrained from doing so.

Josiah felt that if Bill had had an uninterrupted tenure under one master he might, by working hard, become a good scholar. Before giving definite advice, however, Jo needed answers to several questions. What did an indenture now entail? What did a pupil teacher gain from the arrangement and was it possible to cancel an apprenticeship? Would it be possible for Bill to take Greek and Latin at a High School so that his higher education did not stagnate? Josiah had just decided on pursuing a career in law. If an indenture did not commit Bill to become a teacher then Jo might earn enough after finishing his articles to send his brother to a college.[4]

'a young man of considerable promise'

After completing his secondary education as Dux of Stirling High School, Josiah received glowing reports from his teachers. John Graham, the subject of Jo's scathing criticisms, spoke warmly of his pupil teacher. His report of 26 January 1862 said he had known 'Mr Josiah Symon' for three years as his pupil teacher. Symon had passed all the annual examinations 'with credit' and had 'gained a very extensive knowledge of ... elementary school instruction'. Graham considered him 'a young man of considerable promise ... of studious & thoughtful disposition, correct in his deportment, and attentive to his duties'. Josiah easily obtained a Queen's Scholarship and entered the next stage of his teacher training.[5]

Josiah Symon was already just over six feet tall, slim and straight-backed, the one physical defect being his poor eyesight caused by a childhood illness. Seemingly older in appearance and manner than his years would suggest, some observers may have wondered if, and when, he was ever 'young'. Josiah added to the image with his serious-mindedness, love of reading history and the classics, and his religious devotion. Nearly 70 years after being 'a lad of 14', Symon published an essay on 'Life' which he had delivered to the Bible class of the Stirling Baptist Church on 11 January 1861. The Rev. (Dr) Culross, the minister of the Church whom Symon described as 'an inspiration', conducted the class.

On 27 January 1863 Jo arrived at the Free Church Training College, Moray House, Edinburgh. Moray was a creation of the 'Great Disruption of 1843'. In that year, the evangelicals constituting more than a third of the 1200 ministers of the General Assembly walked out of the established Church of Scotland to establish the new Free Church of Scotland. They wanted a purified church, freed of state encroachment. Specifically, the evangelicals wanted to end a situation whereby local landowners could impose a minister against the wishes of a majority of heads of family in any congregation. Over 400 teachers in church schools joined the Free Church which set about raising funds to build its own manses, churches and training establishments. In 1846 the Education Committee of the Free Church acquired Moray House in Canongate, Edinburgh. Two years later, a 'Normal and Sessional School' opened at Moray to provide normal classes attended by students training to become teachers. The Education Committee established a curriculum which, in Josiah's time, provided for classes in Religious Knowledge, English, Geography, History, Drawing, Vocal Music, Latin, Greek, Arithmetic, Algebra, Geometry, School Management and Political Economy. Students were also assessed for their attendance, punctuality and home studies as well as for their teaching skills and general conduct.

Importantly, the early Free Church demanded of its adherents a strict approach to morality and observance of the Sabbath. At Moray, Josiah did everything the Church required. It took the voyage to Australia to begin loosening his adherence to rigid codes of behaviour.

Josiah made some rules for himself at Moray. He decided to keep a diary.[6] Fortunately, at this stage of his life his writing had not yet become semi-illegible. His handwriting in a small book was inevitably cramped but is easy enough to follow. His weeks began and ended on a Wednesday. On that day he aimed to write a 'Retrospect' to sum up his week. Periodically he castigated himself for not keeping up. Yet he wrote enough during the week and on Wednesdays to provide an insight into his character, values and expectations.

Reflecting on Wednesday 4 March, Josiah admitted he had not done enough work, 'not so much due to negligence, or idleness, as to a severe indisposition, afflicting and incapacitating me for work during at least three days'. Illness, for him, was a rarity. On the following Wednesday he reported the completion of his 'Normal' work though he felt 'quite disgusted' by 'the little progress made in any subject'. He could have left this retrospect blank but that would break his own rule for keeping the diary. A Royal event rescued him from despair. On 10 March 1863 the eldest son of Queen Victoria and the Prince Consort, the future King Edward VII, married Princess Alexandra of Denmark at St George's Chapel, Windsor. The Bridegroom was aged 17 and the Bride 18. Jo exulted: 'All honour, & happiness to the Royal Pair!!' For nearly four decades Josiah did not have to think again about the man who was to be his King. His increasing affection for the monarch and the Empire rested firmly with Queen Victoria.

Josiah's immediate concern in mid-March was whether he should join the Rector's class in Greek. Jo consulted Jim, as he often did over the next seven years. His older brother urged him to attend, and Jo complied. His diary entries began to allow for compromise. Each retrospect concluded that he had no reason to boast or to be ashamed; he had worked very 'a young man of considerable promise'

hard and long on prescribed work but had little time for other areas such as private mathematical and classical studies and general reading. Josiah worried at the beginning of April that after doing all his required work, 'a lazy indolent feeling' came over him and he did not get on with other subjects. At least he had made progress with Macaulay's *History of England* after two attempts 'to no purpose' and his Greek was improving. Jo also found time to comment on the sermons he heard – more on delivery than on substance – and he regularly wrote home to his mother.

Josiah knew he needed breaks from the routine. As the weather warmed up, Jim suggested Jo might join him in London and together they could study French. Jo made a correct prediction: 'It will not be all play and no work.' He missed family and home and was so pleased to spend a week in Stirling in mid-April.

> It is impossible to find words to describe, the delight, the inward emotion, which I felt on my way to the railway station on Wednesday night & when I saw from the carriage window at Stirling Station, father, Liz, Bob and Bill waiting for me.

He loved sitting by the fireside and listening to all the news, and felt reassured that his father's business 'appears to be prosperous'. The books he took home were left unopened.

Jo assumed the posture of a surrogate parent as he reflected upon his three younger brothers. Bob's hard and dirty work (unspecified) kept him out of mischief and 'I have not yet lost all hopes of Bob, though he is wayward, and occasionally, I found, disobedient'. 'David and Bill are just getting leave to run about too much; though will be the better of it if made to stay at home when a little older.' The older folk were kind as usual and made it hard for him to leave. 'It would be impossible for me to describe everything individually; but ... there is no place like home.' No one could know the pleasure of it 'until he has been away for some time'. On a later visit towards the end of May Jo added a further consideration: 'No kindness is like a mother's or a sister's.' He was, however, even more troubled about one of his brothers. 'Bob I fear much for. In regard to obedience he has apparently grown worse, and father is not by any means acting towards him as he ought, and if care is not taken the result may be worse than looked for.'

There were other available pleasures. Jo recorded how on another visit to Stirling he went to a party on the evening of 7 September. He offered no details but declared being 'never more disgusted at any party in my life. I have not been to many but shd. they all be like this one it is the last I go to.' While it is hard to imagine Josiah attending a night of debauchery in Stirling in 1863 his notion of acceptable 'fun' might have been narrowed by the Free Church of Scotland. Josiah emerges in his diary as a young man already becoming old in temperament. He castigated himself for not doing or completing extra work, and told himself in May to arrange his time more systematically to cover more ground because this state of affairs 'will never do'. At least what he did in the way of 'normal' work was 'pretty respectable ... for any person'. Towards the end of May, Jo believed he found the reason for 'a certain want of determined application'; his mind 'keeps continuously wandering from the point'. Now he had to develop the discipline to overcome this tendency.

Josiah observed his obligations on Sundays and attended morning and afternoon church services. In 1864 he made notes in his diary after each service, usually praising Rev. Johnson's sermons in Edinburgh. He was even more enthusiastic after listening to the Rev. Culross preach at home in Stirling. He continued to be critical of method. The preacher on the 4th Sunday in Lent at St Andrew's Church, Edinburgh, 'had a very good voice: but reads every word'. Josiah's diary entry for Palm Sunday records that while Dr Guthrie, a former Moderator of the Free Church of Scotland, 'is really a splendid preacher', he preferred Dr Landels of London who regularly spoke to packed Baptist congregations around Britain. It is conceivable that Josiah preferred the liberal Baptists to the more fundamentalist Free Church preachers.

In January 1864, at the age of 28 Maurice Paterson took up appointment as Rector of Moray House and remained in the position for 43 years. Paterson presided over Josiah's second and final year at the College. Josiah's career path might have been very different had he arrived at Moray ten years later by which time Paterson had lifted the College from its 'dark ages' as he called the period 1862–72.[7] The curriculum in Josiah's time had been severely restricted and senior students were prevented from studying a chosen subject in any depth. Paterson also took the College into closer contact with Edinburgh 'a young man of considerable promise'

University, a development the young man would have savoured.

Symon finished his two years at Moray and was rated 'Superior' or 'Very Good' in 14 of the 15 subjects, his record in 'Vocal Music' being considered 'Very Fair'. Overall, his place in the class for written examinations was recorded as 'Very Good', his teaching skills as 'Superior' and his general conduct as 'Exemplary'.[8]

Not surprisingly, Symon received supportive references. In November 1864 John Graham repeated his earlier themes while adding two new elements. First, Symon had carried his studies into 'the higher Departments of Knowledge' and obtained 'considerable proficiency' in geometry, algebra, and in the Latin, Greek and French languages. Secondly, Graham felt assured that Symon's 'high moral principles and his ardent disposition' meant he would 'faithfully discharge his duties where his lot may be cast'.[9] James Culross wanted to help. He had heard that the Clifton Bank School at St Andrews was looking for a tutor and Culross was asked about Symon's progress. Culross warned Jo that, all things being equal, the head teacher would prefer 'a university man'. Nevertheless, Culross told Josiah towards the end of 1864 that Clifton Bank offered many advantages: he would be living in a university town, he might be able to attend some university classes and the Rector of the School was 'a Baptist, and a most respectable man in all ways'.

Symon had been a pupil teacher for Neil Heath, the Rector of the Alba Academy in Edinburgh. Heath wrote a suitably warm testimonial, speaking of Symon's 'undoubted promise of becoming an accomplished and successful teacher'. He described Symon as 'quiet, painstaking & perservering' and of 'unimpeachable' character. At the time of writing his reference Heath addressed a separate letter to his pupil teacher;

> He who deserves a testimonial, requires no apologies, besides (here's a piece of advice for you a young man) such highly drawn apologies as those in your letter tend to the very opposite of what you wish. Beware of diffuseness of thought and consider well the advantages resulting from a close, <u>briefly</u> but <u>distinctly</u> expressed [word unclear]. You must leave the flowers and reach the pith. Tell your story shortly, but politely like a man, which you are in the fair way of becoming ... Use your eyes, spare your tongue and be careful of <u>black and white</u>.[10]

As he acquired self-confidence, Symon frequently ignored this seemingly good advice. Josiah could be prolix when writing letters to relatives or responding to arguments or complaints. On his feet, he was rarely brief, judges seldom called on him to conclude an argument and neither the House of Assembly nor the Senate of his era imposed time limits on speeches. Symon was later in demand as a public speaker and his audiences expected or accepted two hours of oratory on a great occasion. Symon was perfectly capable of developing a nuanced argument but was more at home when contrasting good and evil and separating right from wrong. What Neil Heath saw as troubling in 1864 did irritate and frustrate a few observers and victims but the speaker and the writer who thought, wrote and spoke in black and white was more usually admired for his uncompromising delivery and literary 'flowers'.

2

'Make good friends of the cook.'

Josiah's referees in Stirling and Edinburgh wrote and spoke well of his future in elementary education. After receiving two rejections and one unattractive offer he took a twelve-month teaching contract at a Parish School near Glasgow. Two months after completing this contract and receiving excellent teaching testimonials, Josiah boarded a ship for South Australia to start a career in law.

He had applied for the teaching position at the Clifton Bank School, St Andrews, as the Rev. Culross had urged him to do, but the Rector of the school evidently found a suitable 'university man'. Josiah had also applied early in 1865 for a position with John Watson's Institution in Edinburgh, a school founded in 1762. The closing date for submitting applications and testimonials was given as 18 February 1865. When he visited the Institution at 4.00 pm on 13 February to make further enquiries, Josiah learnt that the school had announced the name of the successful appointment at 3.00 pm that day. He promptly wrote to the head of the institution. 'Can you then, Sir, blame my astonishment? Was there not sufficient cause?' Josiah denied being 'prompted by selfish anger, the offspring of personal chagrin & disappointment'. From the very first, he saw his own prospects as 'far from encouraging'. His youth constituted 'an almost insuperable barrier'. Symon took the matter no further; indeed, there was no avenue for doing so. He asked for the return of his testimonials and enclosed a stamp to cover postage.[1]

Josiah had also applied for an advertised teaching position at the Fleetham Street School, Middlesbrough on Tees, North Yorkshire. He received a letter of acceptance, telling him of the requirement to teach either Latin or French, as well as Euclid and Algebra, for five-and-a-half hours a day for a five-day week. The master-in-charge could not afford Symon's requested salary (the figure he sought is not available) but any earnings could be supplemented by ten shillings for private tutoring of seven-and-a-half hours a week. The Moray House graduate was not tempted.

Josiah eventually settled for an appointment closer to home: William Paton's Neilston Parish School in East Renfrewshire, about 12 miles from central Glasgow. It is unclear whether he was sending the education authorities or himself up, or both, but his 1864 diary records the following pending his arrival at the school in 1865:

> His Royal & Most Serene Highness J.H. Symon Grand Vizier to his most noble & sublime Majesty and Potentate of Neilston Intellectual & Educational Domain, Paton, sends greetings to the aforesaid ... and desires authoritatively to inform [you] that, in all the panoply & grandeur becoming his elevated dignified & distinguished position, he will in all likelihood honour them with a visit on Saturday next. He therefore commands due preparation be made.[2]

Symon left the school in the following April. A school inspector wrote on 7 April 1866 of his gratification in witnessing Mr Josiah Symon's energy and ability in performing his duties. The inspector appreciated the discipline of his classes and made special mention of those in Latin and French. William Paton echoed these remarks of the School Inspector and added the following: 'Mr Symon's Moral Character was all that could be desired in the Christian gentleman.' The minister of the parish said Symon 'has been assiduous in the discharge of his professional duties, blameless in his life, and regular in his attendance on the ordinances of religion'.[3]

Josiah was probably disillusioned with the education bureaucracy and the workings of patronage. He might have disliked being judged by stern-faced officials who applied a strict interpretation of the Bible. The Moray experience had taken his education well beyond the boundaries of primary school teaching. In common with so many Scottish emigrants of his time Josiah wanted a career where he could make and implement his own decisions and one where he could widen his mental horizons and obtain a much higher income.[4] Another prospective career may well have stayed in his mind. After the boy read his essay on 'Life' to the Stirling Baptist Bible class the Rev. Culross said he wanted him to become a parson. In 1929 Josiah recalled his reply: 'No; I'm not good enough to be a parson. I'm going to be a lawyer.'[5]

At some stage Josiah had contacted his mother's brother, David Sutherland, and David's son, James, in South Australia. Josiah knew of James' legal practice in Mount Gambier, and no doubt James assured his cousin of his readiness to accept him into the firm to take articles and thereby qualify for admission to the legal profession. The Sutherlands could have assured him that taking articles was a respectable mode of entry for a legal career; a majority of Supreme Court justices in South Australia at that time had begun their legal training as articled clerks.

Josiah would have consulted his older brother Jim, the member of his immediate family he most valued for advice on matters outside the home. Working in London for Customs Jim knew more of the wider world than did the folk in Stirling. Jim also had a high regard for his younger brother's ability and work ethic and understood why Jo could see the limitations of a teaching career. The two men often travelled together for short holidays and talked about Jo's career. On Jim's advice, Jo engaged someone in London to train him to 'anglicise' his accent.[6] Once Jo finally made his decision to emigrate, Jim certainly supported him and lent his brother the money needed for his passage.

Josiah had booked to sail on the *St Vincent*, a composite full-rigged ship of 829 tons. It was built in 1865 for Devitt & Moore, a company owned by two former shipping clerks who over 55 years owned 29 square-rigged sailing ships and two steamships.[7] The *St Vincent* was making its second voyage to South Australia captained again by Alexander Louttit who, like Jo, had been born in Wick but was 12 years older. The rest of the crew, as the emigrant counted and classified them, consisted of four officers or mates, eleven able seamen, four midshipmen or apprentices, a boatswain, a sailmaker, a carpenter and a cook, as well as a doctor. Twenty other passengers joined Josiah on the ship. Fourteen of them belonged to two families whose adult members belonged to the Free Church communion and had long known each other.

The ship also carried a cargo of general merchandise with a declared value of £35,067, including an aviary of English birds – among them, pheasants, blackbirds, thrushes, chaffinches, larks, bullfinches. All save one bird arrived in Adelaide in 'capital' condition.[8] A rat decapitated a pheasant hen on the voyage and, to make the best of this misfortune, the murdered bird was plucked, cooked and served for dinner. The English birds were a private speculation, prized by colonists who admired native birds for their plumage but thought them poor songsters and not particularly useful.

Jo's father and younger brothers saw him off at the Stirling railway station and Jo travelled to London to meet Jim. On Friday 29 June 1866 they went by train to Gravesend where the *St Vincent* lay mid-stream on the Thames. The two men brought on board Jo's luggage consisting of clothes, personal items and his two boxes of books. They proceeded to his berth, set it 'to rights', and Jim stayed on board with Jo overnight. The 'waterman' rowed them ashore the next day and they walked to the station where Jo farewelled 'the last relation whose face I should for many years see in Britain'.[9]

Scheduled to sail on 30 June, the captain waited a day for better weather. Even then, the first hours were among the worst spent on the voyage. Torrential rain and violent winds required the ship to undergo hard tacking at short and sharp intervals. Drenched to the skin, the crew worked without breakfast or dinner, winning the plaudits of nervous passengers. Water swamped Josiah's cabin damaging his books and soaking his mattress and sheets. Eventually the carpenter managed to seal his port window and Josiah squeezed the mattress dry and hung it over his bed. The drama eased when the ship reached The Downs, a sheltered anchorage off the east coast of Kent where the *St Vincent* could wait safely for a fair wind.

Soon after getting under way, Josiah began drawing his own chart and recording the ship's progress in terms of latitude and longitude. He also kept a diary for the voyage which he planned to send home to family and friends.[10] The diarist had no illusions about his readers: what might seem 'noteworthy' to a passenger on a three-month voyage would be viewed with disinterest by those living a busy life on shore. Josiah used 300 words to make that point and, applying Rector Heath's words, used more 'flowers' than the 'pith' required in order to tell his story. He had an advantage over his fellow passengers; he could call upon literary

'Make good friends of the cook.'

assistance from Wordsworth, Coleridge and Tennyson, among others, to enhance his story with suitable quotations. Yet there were many hard facts to tell. Alongside his daily record of the ship's progress he reported on the weather, climate changes and the ship's rituals. He devoted several pages to the ceremonial 'crossing of the line' and paragraphs to passing ships and especially those the passengers and crew considered rivals in the competition to be first to reach somewhere else.

There are two features of the diary which have considerable value to a biographer. First, deliberately and sometimes possibly unconsciously, Symon told his readers how he coped with unfamiliar travel. His brother had given him sound advice when they were in Gravesend: 'Make good friends of the cook.' Following Jim's recommendation, Josiah noted that 'the result was very satisfactory & beneficial'. The cook occasionally slipped him a piece of ham for breakfast, sometimes gave him a loaf of bread, and more than once provided him with preserved salmon. A diary entry for 18 August reads: 'My intimacy with the Cook is of considerable advantage.' On one occasion Jo joined the cook in a birthday dinner with one of the stewards: the three of them ate boiled salmon, which was considered a rare treat, and fresh bread. Jo also made friends with other crew members, particularly those of rank or who had specialist skills. He lent some of Scott's Waverley novels to the third and the fourth mate, played draughts on most days with the ship's doctor and talked frequently with the captain.

Another piece of advice helped him make friends and improved his quality of life. He was told to bring eggs on board packed in salt. The eggs made breakfast of tea and hard biscuit possible to swallow, and Josiah became 'an object of considerable envy' among the other adult passengers. He did 'share them occasionally with those around, as one's generosity is stirred in a very peculiar manner when one sits luxuriating while the remaining sixteen [adults] make the most of a bad matter'. Not all the advice was sound. Jo later told Jim that 'Lawrence Levi, the Jew who provided the articles & utensils I required for the voyage ... was either ignorant, or lying in the interest of his trade, in what he told you regarding the value of a hair mattress'. No one wanted to purchase the one he brought on board to sell for profit.[11]

Jo told his diary he had no lack of friends in the ship – from the captain downwards. 'Frequently I used to flatter myself with being a universal favourite.' He certainly stood out in one respect. The tallest person on the ship, his bearing meant others often gravitated to him recognising that although he was better educated and well-spoken, he would and could talk with everyone on board. Josiah also recognised one of the failings among the passengers. With two-thirds of them belonging to two families, which in some respects functioned as one, there was a lack of variety and too few fresh outlets for entertainment. Josiah was better off than most of the others. He had books to read and to re-read.

On 14 July he wrote of nearly finishing a book which he had borrowed – *John Halifax, Gentleman* by Dinah Craik (1856) – 'a finer tale it has seldom been my lot to peruse'. Jo considered that the main characters 'might well serve as models in an age when honesty, integrity, noble-heartedness and kindly humanity are not the chief characteristics. It is a book that will do the thoughtful reader good.' The 'models' included the ideal Victorian woman; that is, a wife and mother who was devoted to, and dependent upon, her husband. In 1881 Josiah married what he thought was that ideal Victorian woman.

A second feature of the 'Diary of a Voyage' was that his comments on the passengers and crew showed him to be in many ways a snob who nonetheless had an acute eye for judging character and detecting weaknesses.

He began his commentaries on his fellow travellers when the *St Vincent* was moving through the Bay of Biscay on the second Sunday at sea. Josiah noted how the crew, cleaned up and dressed in their best, spent time reading, smoking and talking to each other or telling passengers stories of their adventures. The steward brought him a bucket of salt water and he bathed and then scrubbed himself with a coarse towel. All 'aglow', he felt the beneficial effects all day. His good mood stopped short of a charitable assessment of the 'Highland people' on board, namely, the fourteen passengers of the two families. Josiah described them as 'simple' and 'honest', but 'wretchedly ignorant of the ways of the world'. They had a 'superstitious dread' of the Bay of Biscay and their membership of the Communion of the Free Church required them to cast aside secular books and volumes of poetry on the Sabbath and work their way through severe religious texts. Sitting in his cabin later in the day, Josiah listened to one of the men read aloud psalms which were subsequently sung by the families as a long and miserable dirge which 'recalled a week-day singing-class, rather than what I was accustomed to at home'. One of the fellows took to reading aloud 'some absurd, old commentary for family worship ... in a snivelling, unintelligible tone, and disgusting, repulsive to anyone of taste and good sense'.

Towards the end of the voyage, Josiah switched his critical attention to the two men who occupied the chief cabin. Parkes, a baker and confectioner from Adelaide and originally from Maidstone in Kent, 'is a stupidly vulgar talkative old fool ... and, like many others whose little money procures them a position they are not naturally fitted to occupy, he resembles the ass with the lion's hide'. Brooks, a commercial traveller in hardware who had charge of the aviary, was a little man who imagined himself 'a somebody' when he was really 'a nobody' who boasted 'outrageously' of this nobleman and that baronet as 'Men whom I have known'. Josiah's observations about a youth of 17 were kinder: 'intelligent but very sensitive and thin-skinned, caused no doubt by his sickly condition'. The lad, to whom Josiah gave some of his eggs, was 'bent with consumption'. Josiah resumed his severity in judging a young woman who was going out to be married. He said the husband-to-be was to be pitied. Jessie from Edinburgh, 'the most interfering, strife-stirring busybody' he had ever encountered had just one good quality (unidentified) to match her dozen faults.

He returned to the two families from Inverness. The father of the Douglas family of eight was a schoolmaster whose intellect was of a level requiring considerable time 'to ascertain that 2 and 2 are four'. Apparently, Mr Douglas intended to forsake scholastic activities and take to farming 'of some species or other'. His eldest son, a bank clerk, was 'a pleasant, conceited sort of fellow' whom the crew referred to as 'Dundreary'. The smaller children were everywhere but Josiah took little notice of them, nor indeed of the two wives other than to guess their age. He clearly approved of Mr Addison, father of the family of four, at least for his station in life: he judged Addison to be 'one of the better class of ploughman' who would gain similar employment in South Australia. Josiah had no time, however, for Addison's 22-year old son. He had never met 'a more nasty, inquisitive, conceited, contradictory fellow'. The young man reminded the notionally younger one (Josiah) of the saying, 'A little learning is a dangerous thing'. This one had a smattering of chemistry, enough to fill a weak mind with a sense of self-importance to which should be added 'he is an only and spoiled son'. Josiah was not finished: the brat was 'the most generally and thoroughly disliked by all on board'; he showed 'the greatest disrespect to his parents, which is always a mark of few brains and twisted morals'.

Josiah concluded with a sweeping harsh judgment of the families. 'For dirt, want of cleanliness, want of management, no sort of notion about cooking and want of manners I never met the equal of these lots.' He would soon enough cut their acquaintance and never had 'any great desire that it may be renewed'. Nevertheless, he liked talking about them, and especially when he looked back on the Sundays at sea.

In the case of the crew, Jo focused mainly on the captain. On 10 July, very early in the voyage, Jo walked the deck for an hour with Captain Louttit who 'talked in a very communicative manner'. Jo realised that the captain was a very different kind of sailor. Louttit suddenly appeared after a damaging storm had broken the jib-boom but his 'Dear bless my heart' got 'nowhere near the customary profanities of sea-faring men'. Jo was clearly fascinated by his unlikely companion:

> an extremely youthful appearance behind, looking just like a lad of eighteen; but you rapidly change your opinion when you see his face, which has an indescribable expression of firmness of resolution and determination. It is an ugly face – but massive with strong square jaws and resolute, masculine, compressed mouth. He possesses coolness to a remarkable degree and it would do no little to cause him to fear or despair. He is very intelligent and agreeable withal.

As an intelligent and very attentive listener, Jo learnt a great deal from the captain, and from the crew, giving him a fund of knowledge to share in his later, frequent travels by sea.

On Friday morning 14 September the *St Vincent* sailed close to Kangaroo Island and headed up the Gulf. The pilot came on board and told the passengers and crew who crowded around for the important news that a rival ship, the *Goolwa*, had not yet arrived. There was wild cheering as we had, Josiah wrote in his diary, 'thrashed our great antagonist': 'we gave three cheers for Captain Louttit who was happy and

'Make good friends of the cook.'

smiling like a "biled pertater".' The weather suddenly turned nasty and Josiah remained on board until Sunday, proud to have sailed on the ship which registered the fastest passage of the season. On that pleasing note, Jo finished his diary assuring those at home – should they kindly take the trouble to read his story – that while he now had a new home his heart 'beats as true and as sound and pure as ever it did in the land of his birth'.

The *South Australian Register* of 17 September published a testimonial signed by the seventeen older passengers congratulating Captain Louttit on a quick and successful passage. They thanked him for 'the courtesy, kindness, and attention you have shown to all of us' and expressed special gratitude for the magic lantern show which 'proved very attractive and interesting to our juvenile friends, and gave universal satisfaction'. The testimonial also thanked 'the Officers' for their kind and prompt attention to many wants. It concluded by wishing Captain Louttit well for his future trips and with the belief that 'the good ship *St Vincent* will, under your seamanship, carve herself a name worthy of you both'. Josiah signed what he called 'a very flattering letter' for which on another day and after achieving fame for his addresses he might have chosen the word 'banal' as a more appropriate description.[12]

3

'this momentous step in my life'

Josiah Symon arrived in South Australia six months after the Census of March 1866 recorded that the colony had a population of 163,487, 'exclusive of Aborigines'. In round figures while 74,000 people were born in South Australia, 51,500 had migrated from England and Wales, 14,300 from Ireland and 8,500 from Scotland. Some 8,000 Germans constituted the largest non-British section of the population.[1] Nearly half of the counted population – 78,072 – resided in Adelaide County. South Australia's leaders in government, business, mining, the professions and the agricultural and pastoral industry all lived in Adelaide, giving the capital city a unique concentration in the Australian colonies of both population and power.[2]

There is little evidence in the Symon Papers of Josiah preparing himself for a life in South Australia. He probably knew just the bare outline. The *South Australia Act 1834*, which created the Province of South Australia, implemented the Wakefield principle of systematic colonisation whereby land was sold rather than granted, with the proceeds being used to assist the passage of desirable immigrants, especially labourers and small farmers. The transportation of convicts was forbidden and religious freedoms were guaranteed; hence South Australia became what Douglas Pike called a 'Paradise of Dissent'. Initially the British Government and the independent Colonization Commission shared the administration but the Province's near-bankruptcy in 1842 obliged the former to take control and govern South Australia as a Crown Colony. South Australia became a self-governing colony in 1856 and in the following year adult males could elect a House of Assembly while a property franchise determined eligibility to vote in Legislative Council elections.

'this momentous step in my life'

David Sutherland still had two years left of his term as an MP in the House of Assembly when his nephew spent his first night on Australian soil at Sutherland's estate near Glenelg. For all his financial woes David Sutherland was a welcoming and cheerful host. Unfortunately, Josiah arrived at a time when the estate was offered for auction and the 'Dunrobin' home had to be available for immediate occupation. In his brief stay at 'Dunrobin' Josiah glimpsed what a good life might be like on the frontier of civilisation. Despite previous sales of small blocks, the estate still boasted 240 acres of some of the best agricultural land in the Colony, located within a mile and a half of Glenelg and seven miles of Adelaide. The freehold property consisted of a nine-roomed furnished brick house and three two-roomed brick cottages for servants and labourers. It boasted two wells, a vineyard, an orchard, shrubberies and 120 acres of wheat, barley, oats and hay. The livestock included several horses, pigs and dairy cows with calves and the various sheds were packed with the essential farm and winemaking equipment. In the 1890s in the Mount Lofty ranges Symon began to fashion his own world of a country residence and a working farm. Perhaps the 'Dunrobin' estate had been his inspiration.

Jo wrote a letter to Jim on 24 September 1866, by which time he had moved into the Criterion Hotel on King William Street, Adelaide. He had no complaints, smugly asking his brother to imagine him eating a breakfast of 'three or even four average sized mutton chops, and a large piece of shining beef steak'.[3] Jo did find it 'strange', however, that the pain of separation from home and his dearest friends hurt even more keenly despite once again mingling with a busy and active world. He was affected 'very acutely by this momentous step in my life', but did not wish 'to be constantly moping over what was a deliberate act of my own' which he hoped would ultimately have its reward.

Three days after writing this letter Jo took the first step on his journey. On 27 September Symon 'placed and bound himself' as clerk to James De La Zouche Sutherland for a term of five years in 'the profession of a Barrister, Attorney, Solicitor and Proctor of the several Courts in which ... Sutherland is authorized to practise'. Josiah would have known in advance that, unlike England and Scotland, and contemporary NSW and Victoria, the legal profession was fused in South Australia. There was no separate, independent Bar. There were 90 lawyers in South Australia in 1866, of whom 69 practised in Adelaide. All were male[4] and all had qualified to practise as barristers and solicitors. After his own admission, Josiah could expect to join a law firm which might employ him both as a pleader and a land conveyancer.

Symon promised to serve James Sutherland 'faithfully & diligently'. He would not 'cancel, obliterate, spoil, destroy, waste, embezzle, spend or make away with any of the books, papers, writings, monies, stamps, chattels or other property' of the said James Sutherland or any of his clients or employees. Further, the said JH Symon 'shall and will from time to time and at all times during the said term' of five years 'keep the secrets of the said ... Sutherland and readily and cheerfully obey and execute his lawful and reasonable commands'. He shall not leave or absent himself from the service and during the term shall 'conduct himself with all due diligence, honesty & propriety'. On receipt of the sum of five shillings, 'the said ... Sutherland ... shall & will take the said JH Symon as his Clerk' and 'shall & will by the best way or means by which he can and to the utmost of his skill and knowledge teach & instruct, or cause to be taught & instructed the said JH Symon in the said practice or profession of a Barrister, Attorney, Solicitor and Proctor'. At the end of five years, provided Symon 'faithfully and diligently served his said clerkship', Sutherland agreed to 'cause and procure' his admission to the Supreme Court of South Australia.[5]

The formalities completed, Josiah prepared for his trip to Mount Gambier. He needed plenty of writing paper because he planned to send many letters home. The most valuable letters were the long ones sent to his brother Jim. Each letter was written in time to catch the monthly mail to Britain. Jo used his letters to respond to Jim's comments sent to him, and to tell Jim of his experiences and of his contacts with 'Cousin' (James) and 'Uncle' (David), and what was happening in the firm. Jo also delivered extended and mostly unflattering appraisals of 'colonials' and the 'colony' as well as sending orders for book purchases and relaying feelings and advice on family issues. Two themes stand out. First, although Jo instinctively aligned himself with the liberalism of William Ewart Gladstone, he proposed a conservative remedy to what he saw as the coarseness of frontier society. Edmund Burke's 'great oaks' and

'this momentous step in my life'

effective class distinction were needed to maintain order and establish appropriate moral standards. Secondly, the diarist of the *St Vincent* voyage became even more critical of individuals who had succumbed to weakness or lacked good breeding, an education and a commitment to self-improvement.

In his letter of 24 October 1866 Jo said that when he and Cousin left Adelaide they travelled south-east by coach, staying overnight at Strathalbyn, 'a large straggling township with a majority of Scotch settlers'. Next day they reached Wellington Station owned by Allan McFarlane, who originally came from Wick. Symon thought Wellington 'a most repulsive place' for its arid sandhills near and far without any sign of green, a scene which took his imagination back to what he had read of Egypt. They crossed the Murray River in a punt, and then travelled along the shores of Lake Alexandrina thickly populated with wild fowl. Symon observed a couple of tiny bark canoes, each with a naked 'blackfellow' standing upright and handling his paddle with dexterity. Another he saw engaged in fishing among the tall reeds, 'but most strange of all there was a fire to all appearance in the canoe'. McFarlane was 'a fine fellow ... will keep you laughing a whole evening'. Symon thought him 'a very superior man', principally because his book collection was better than he ever expected to find in the Australian bush. The shelves carried nearly all of John Stuart Mill's writings as well as *Essays and Reviews* (1860). At the age of 20, Josiah measured a man's 'breeding' by the existence and composition of his library.

Eventually the pair reached Mount Gambier with its population of 3,396 either living in town or its surrounding district. According to the Census, Mount Gambier had two lawyers – Cousin was presumably one of them – but no clerks. Jo met 'Cousin Caroline' ('Carrie') on his arrival. Twelve years older than Jo, and rendered lame since childhood because of an accident, Carrie lived in the Sutherland house in town. She asked Josiah to pass on her love to his brother. Josiah continued: 'Everyone is very kind & I endeavour not to weary for home. Cousin Carrie is very pleasant & cheerful, & one of the most amiable young ladies I've met. We go out riding together of an afternoon. Fancy my long uncouth legs astride of a horse!'[6]

In his letter of January 1867, Jo told Jim of his progress on a horse under Carrie's guidance and of accustoming himself to heat and bushfires in the summer of this 'expansive land of scrub and gumtrees, gold, copper & kangaroos'. The extreme and consistent heat of the past four weeks had almost incapacitated him for thinking. It was 'unprecedented in this neighbourhood, & certainly during all my previous life'. People in 'the old country' could have no conception of 'the unpleasantness of the atmosphere, especially when a hot wind charged with minute sand grains and hot ash blowing over the mouth of the bottomless pit, almost chokes you'. Virtually every plant and blade of grass was parched or shrivelled. The entire surface of the country had 'a yellow dried up appearance'. Bushfires became alarmingly frequent, and Symon soon learnt to measure their severity against the horrific stories he heard about 'Black Thursday' in Victoria in 1851.

Bushfires on 12 January 1867 ruined many small farmers around Mount Gambier by annihilating their wheat crops which were ready for the sickle. At 6.30 am on that day the articled clerk set out on horseback to ride 20 miles south-west of Mount Gambier for 'Curratum', the homestead of a Scottish squatter and stockholder. Josiah was to serve a Supreme Court Writ of Summons for £1160 claimed on an overdue account. He rode fast and smart for half an hour and stopped at a homestead where the manager was another Scot. There he obtained directions for the next stage of his trip and he later posted them to Jim in London:

> ride for a mile, go straight between two fences, when the left hand one ceases then turn to the left hand & hold straight through the scrub across an open extensive plain with tea-trees and she-oaks until you come to a gate through which you pass, keeping the fence on the left till a second gate is reached, beyond which is an extensive limitless flat full of wombat holes, terminated by a brush fence, over or through you must go to find a track on the other side leading straight through the scrub to Curratum.

The young clerk explained to his brother that a reference to a gate might mean three of them, and the flat on the other side of the brush fence extends in breadth six or eight miles '& goodness knows how many in length'. Jim, he wrote, would find it hard placing entire dependence in the directions afforded you in perfect good faith by men 15 miles distant. Josiah called it 'the most solitary & scary ride or journey that ever I undertook. I saw not a living soul, nor a house nor sheep for 15 miles, & all the while I had the fierce morning sun glaring down upon me.' The saving grace was the proof that he could do it, and the hospitality thrust upon him at 'Curratum' and at another homestead on the way back.[7]

Jo apprised his brother of Cousin's plan to take a gentleman of 36 years of age as his partner. A qualified barrister and solicitor, Arthur Waterhouse was recently-appointed clerk in the firm earning £200 a year. The new arrangements did not interfere with those regarding Symon who, initially, spoke well of Waterhouse: 'he is a very good solicitor & looks well after the office, in which particular I believe he will be of most use as Cousin can then attend to all the pleading himself.' His physical aspects were a different matter. Waterhouse 'is a very little fellow with long black whiskers & moustache – no beard & constantly wears spectacles. He walks along, as Cousin Carrie says, like an old black crow.' Symon also observed that Waterhouse had lived in London until he reached 19 which explained why he would say, quite naturally, 'everythink' and 'nothink' all the while abusing his 'h's'.

Cousin completed the details for the ten-year partnership to begin on 1 February 1867 whereby Waterhouse would receive one third of the profits and the same proportion for loss and liability. There was, however, a problem. Cousin had entered the arrangement before being fully conversant with the man's character, conduct, antecedents and personal prospects. Soon after formalising the partnership, Cousin realised he despised Waterhouse and wondered how he could sever the connection without causing scandal and evil talk. Josiah had worked out that Waterhouse was 'more of an adventurer than anything else'. He had also become aware of the new partner's chronic weakness: he was an alcoholic. Jo told Jim late in February 1867 that Waterhouse was at his best around 9.00 am after which he became 'a little muddled & confused in brain' and his senses eventually became 'quite inoperative – a result of frequent application to brandy & water, & the hot weather'. Josiah acknowledged that, when sober, he was 'a very good Common Law Clerk & I daresay I shall be able to pick up a good deal from him'. Yet one image stayed in his mind. Waterhouse bore in appearance 'a very close resemblance to some of the ridiculous specimens of the legal fraternity as portrayed by Dickens'.

Later in his life Symon had to deal with alcoholics in his own family – his brother Bill and his own son Oscar – while Jim and two of Jo's sons, Charles and Carril, became hard drinkers. At one stage in the 1880s Symon had to look at his own drinking habit. Arthur Waterhouse was probably his first encounter with anyone in the grips of the disease, and Symon did not start with a sympathetic approach. By March 1868, when Waterhouse had left to practise in Naracoorte, Josiah was totally unsympathetic. He wrote of Waterhouse 'gradually burning out the miserable fragment of his little heart & soul with strong drink. His diminutive frame must be rapidly dwindling away & doubtless before many months expire we shall hear of his shovelled scarecrow of a frame being deposited in a drunkard's grave.' His spectacles or 'barnacles' have long since established their claim to be 'the brightest part of him'.[8]

The young man also expressed concern about the broader incidence of drinking he encountered in Mount Gambier. 'I don't wish to give a teetotal lecture but I wish to say how lamentable & how gross is the drunkenness in this township.' Josiah believed that in proportion to population there were more public houses in Mount Gambier than in almost any place in 'the old country'. Inside the bar, and despite the high price and 'obnoxious quality of the "grog" ... [there was a] seething mass of unwashed, unshaven, unkempt wretches, passing through all the various stages towards stupid drunkenness & rioting, quarrelling, shouting and dancing'. The practice of 'shouting' leads to the abuse of an individual who declined to throw away his money and or refused to drink. The former was stigmatised as 'a mean shabby beggar' and the latter as 'unsocial and a prig'. By staying away from public houses Symon avoided the abuse and accepted the less offensive label of 'bookworm'.

Drawing on personal observation and 'reliable information', Symon attributed much of the inebriety, low morals and sensualism 'to the free & easy, hail-fellow-well-met, untrammelled state of Colonial society'. He proposed a solution: the introduction into South Australia of 'more distinction of class, more of the dignified demeanour and gentlemanly reserve arising from noblemen and integrity of soul' would be so much the better for its lasting prosperity and elevation. Taking this view appeared to place Symon in opposition to the one he called the 'quickest and most admirable champion' of the British working man. He knew that Gladstone

'this momentous step in my life'

wanted to procure the admission of British workers to an equitable share in governing their country. (Symon had probably read or heard of Gladstone's speech in favour of the Liberal Party's 1866 proposals for electoral reform). Jo told his brother in March 1868 that 'I don't admire universal suffrage as it exists [in South Australia]. A degrading system so far as my miniature opinions go.'[9]

He was, however, more upset by behaviour he felt sure Gladstone would find equally objectionable. 'Everybody out here is very familiar with everybody else.' Jo gave his brother an example of what he detested. A 'felon', a client of theirs, was acquitted of a crime of which he was guilty, had 'actually ... wished cousin and myself to go on hobnobbing with him'. Josiah called that 'an extreme case' but there had been 'more than a single occasion [when] a filthy, foul smelling wretch, who perhaps in the way of business I had served, has accosted me and asked me to drink with him'. Josiah would decline the invitation, the 'wretch' would become abusive and violent, and Josiah would express sorrow that he should take such matters to heart and wish him good morrow.

Sometimes, Symon identified the problem as one of behaviour rather than of class. In any case he judged the intelligence of 'the labouring man in this colony' as lower than that exhibited by men 'occupying a similar station in the old country', except for the tendency of most to cheat their fellows. He had also observed how men 'from a comparatively humble sphere', having moved to South Australia and come into positions of wealth and influence, 'have largely developed overbearing, arrogant and assumptive dispositions'. Twenty and thirty years later there were men and women in Adelaide who would have numbered Josiah Symon among that list.

For all his criticisms, Symon did try to fit in. Possibly soon after he arrived in Mount Gambier, he refereed a boxing match between Cousin, who fancied himself in the ring, and Adam Lindsay Gordon, better known as a poet, who was briefly an MP in South Australia and something of a pugilist. There is no record of Symon's knowledge of boxing or of his participation in the sport, and no report of the bout or of its outcome. He also turned out at least once for the Mount Gambier Football Club which won 4–0 against the Tradesmen's Club. His diary entry after the game noted he felt 'very stiff in limbs down'.

In September 1867 he joined the Mount Gambier Cricket Club, and immediately regretted doing so. Jo told Jim that the subscription cost one guinea which he could ill afford, but he did not like to be 'ostracised & hooted'. He would pay the money, be stoic and resign before it was due next year. If he were 'less short-sighted' he 'might make a good player', though 'defects of vision make all the difference'. Josiah Symon already had the perfect excuse to explain a subsequent disaster. The Mount Gambier Cricket Club put on a match between two teams chosen from its own members. Josiah played in the side led by Mr G.A. Harris which made 54 all out in its first innings. Mr W.W. Williams' team replied with 34 all out, a stock, station and land agent taking eight wickets with the ball and the other two wickets being run outs. The Harris team batted again and made 36 all out and the Williams team scored the necessary 56 runs without loss and won by ten wickets. Jo did not make any impact on the game. He scored a duck in each innings. If he bowled, he did not take a wicket and he did not take a catch. His diary entry for 23 November 1867 said his team was 'licked': 'I begin to hate cricket.' He acted as scorer for the next and possibly the last game of cricket in which he was involved.[10]

Josiah felt more at home when he joined the Mount Gambier Amateur Dramatic Society at its formation on 12 September 1867. He appeared in the Society's first two nights of entertainment. On the second night, held on 30 January 1868, Josiah had roles in two different plays. One was a complicated comedy in which he played a minor character opposite another minor character who forgot his lines thereby obliging Josiah to prompt 'time after time until I was sickened'. The *Border Watch* had obviously failed to observe what he had to endure. 'Sir Adonis Leech was very well impersonated by Mr Symon; but there was a slight degree of stiffness in his motions which will doubtless wear off, when he has more frequently trod the boards.' Worse still, Josiah's minor character in the second play – a farce – appeared opposite one played by Cousin. Apparently, Cousin had no memory for pages of prose dialogue but did have 'an inordinate notion of his capabilities as an actor'. He was also never punctual. Twice he was due to appear on stage with Josiah and on neither occasion did he arrive on time. Josiah felt this keenly as the last person to speak before there was dead silence. He believed that the audience blamed him for forgetting what he was supposed to say next.

'this momentous step in my life'

Hence the *Border Watch*'s dismissive verdict: 'Mr Symon's Alfred Weston was respectably performed.' Josiah's resolve not to act with Cousin again was never tested. Cousin did not appear in the next two nights of entertainment in 1868. The Society did not put on any shows in 1869 and disappeared in 1870. The *Border Watch* had already delivered Symon's theatrical epitaph when reporting his role in yet another farce in 1868: 'Mr Symon exhibited a very advanced knowledge of the histrionic art.'[11]

The articled clerk and his employer were like brothers in the early days of the relationship. Over time, however, Jo feared greatly for Cousin's future. At first, he found it remarkable that Cousin was not embittered but generous, unreserved, open-hearted and kind. Yet even in the early days of their association Jo thought him overbearing and mostly dogmatic. Cousin's perceptive faculties in business and calculation were neither keen nor acute, though his powers of observation of objects in nature and men were sharp and constantly being enriched. Josiah believed that, unlike men reared and educated in the mother country, colonial males accustomed to Australian bush life could appreciate the value of sharp and true physical vision. The shortcoming in colonials was their lack of deep reading and the reliance on a small stock of literary and scientific knowledge. In Cousin's case, he perpetually applied in argument or conversation what he had read in the latest magazines.

Symon acknowledged he could not expect to meet a kinder and more hospitable fellow. If anything, Cousin was too extravagant and, despite being opinionated and self-confident, did not have a grain of selfishness in his composition. Jo realised that Jim considered his brother 'obstinate' and 'pigheaded' and visualised him contradicting and irritating Cousin in argument. Josiah could not deny being influenced by every Scotch quality of 'dourness' and was always ready to stand by his opinions to the last in spite of the feelings of others. Even so, he also had 'a store of Scotch caution & prudence & good policy'. He knew only too well he should hold back when in contention with someone who had been so generous and who was his senior by ten years. While not appearing to adopt Cousin's conclusions and opinions, Jo would not 'abusively' press his own. 'I value Cousin's friendship highly, and we are friends. Whatever my heart findeth to do for him I shall willingly strive to accomplish, & I shall ever be ready to uphold his character and name.' For Josiah, it was just a pity that

Cousin never read an instructive book and seldom read the newspapers. He preferred company. Consequently, Cousin was often hurt when his articled clerk absented himself for some quiet study on his own.

By the end of 1867 Symon had encountered more of Cousin's flaws. Cousin liked to intersperse conversation with disparaging and often unfounded remarks about absent persons. If their personal appearance did not display anything sufficiently prominent to be ridiculed, he would turn to blemishes in their speech or education to make uncharitable comments. Josiah worried that unless Cousin guarded against 'the gradual prevalence of a pernicious practice ... this habit ... will become developed to an almost deplorable extent'. The objects of Cousin's criticisms were often, as Symon would tell him, paying clients. The clerk also noticed that his employer at a young age 'exhibits such strong tendencies to obesity'. Josiah may have been disturbed by Jim's suggestion that 'I may become in physical dimensions huge as Cousin'. His answer by implication was that, whereas Cousin 'is so stout ... he is unfitted for exertion of even a moderate kind' he, Josiah, was always active. His recurring criticism, however, was that Cousin never engaged in 'heavy intellectual reading'. Specifically, he never read a law book 'unless when absolutely required, he hunts up a reference' meaning that 'Cousin's knowledge of the principles & practice of Common Law even in the Colony, is of the scantiest and meanest order'. Fortunately, little was required in Mount Gambier beyond a knowledge of the *Local Court Act*, and Cousin was 'very well acquainted with conveyancing practice but does not improve & add to it'. The clerk knew what he must do:

> I firmly believe that as for myself, should I succeed in passing and be authorised to practise, I will read more during the first year or two thereafter than during the currency of my Articles. Of course my present conviction of what I would do may be falsified by the event.[12]

Some two months after giving his brother in London further information about Cousin Josiah told him how Uncle and Cousin were conducting themselves in what was Josiah's first experience of an election in South Australia.

Mount Gambier was located within the two-member electoral district of Victoria in the House of Assembly. Three candidates nominated: John

'this momentous step in my life'

Riddoch, a Scottish-born pastoralist and an MP who had represented Victoria with Adam Lindsay Gordon; H. Kent Hughes who was Riddoch's running mate; and W. West whose claims to be an Oxford graduate Jo felt entitled to doubt. Although David Sutherland had decided not to re-contest his own seat of Encounter – he was again on the edge of bankruptcy – he joined the campaign for Victoria on the side of West. Jo informed his brother in a letter of 25 March 1868 that Uncle's appearances at the election meetings had not been a credit to himself or of comfort to his friends. 'Uncouth & clumsy as a speaker at all times', he was out of his element at 'rough & tumble meetings' where he would lose his temper, ramble incoherently and gesticulate wildly, curl his mouth like Aunt Esther used to do when out of temper. Jo saw Uncle as 'an excellent practical man', well informed on financial matters and roads but 'frenzied about politics ... a bad speaker, ungrammatical, illogical and not possessed of the temper or skill to sway an assembly of working men'. He thought Cousin was a better speaker than Uncle and altogether cooler in temper, but no less manic and no more aware of the dangers caused by careless remarks on the platform. Jo added: 'Being 21 years of age I could have a vote if I chose; but I am utterly destitute of ambition in that direction.' Riddoch and Kent Hughes were elected on 7 May.

Josiah Symon never lost sight of the reason he went to Mount Gambier. He wanted to be a lawyer and, with no legal background, had to work long and hard to achieve his goal. Cousin did not give him the necessary advice and assistance, and the library facilities in his office were very limited; hence Jo's letters to Jim included requests for legal books. The fact that Cousin himself needed assistance proved beneficial. Jo helped him prepare his cases and advised him during court hearings. Josiah happily recorded the big moments in his 1867 diary: on 21 February he drafted his first lease and on 13 March thought he made something like £8 for the firm that day. He always mentioned the days he went to the local court. At the end of May, he noted a comment by William Blackstone: 'The dread of evil is a much more forcible principle of human actions than the prospect of good.' Throughout June and July, he read large sections of Blackstone's *Commentaries on the Law of England* and was especially interested in Blackstone's observation that legislators prefer punishments to rewards for breaches of the law. 'And even where rewards are proposed as well as punishments threatened, the obligation of the law seems chiefly to consist in the penalty: for rewards, in their nature can only *persuade* and *allure*; nothing is *compulsory* but punishment.' The diligent and practical clerk was taking particular notice of the thinking and practice of the criminal law.

He was rightly proud of the fact that, after less than two years of articles, he led, albeit briefly, a case which ended up in the *South Australian Law Reports*. Jo also prepared some of the arguments which Cousin used in Court and led to the decision made in Mount Gambier being overturned on appeal to the Supreme Court. This case – *Carey v Sutherland* – arose out of a paragraph in the *Standard* newspaper relating to the 1868 election. Riled by the piece, an unsteady Cousin publicly kicked one of the proprietors in the groin and received a £20 fine from the Full Local Court of magistrates. Cousin appealed on the ground that the Local Court did not have the power to conduct criminal proceedings other than to proceed according to the rules of the Common Law. Even if local courts had the power, such jurisdiction could not be exercised until such rules and orders regulating the practice had been made. Acting Chief Justice Gwynne and Justice Wearing of the Supreme Court upheld this view and the Local Court decision was reversed.[13]

In mid-April 1868 Symon encountered Samuel Way, a leading Adelaide barrister. Way had travelled to Mount Gambier to attend the four-day session of the Circuit Court where he was to prosecute several cases.[14] Born in 1836 into a Bible Christian family in Portsmouth, Hampshire, Way had attended schools in Devon and Kent before joining his father James Way, his mother and younger siblings who had previously migrated to Adelaide. James Way had become the superintendent of his Church. Samuel arrived in 1853 and was articled to Alfred Atkinson whose fortuitous bout of insanity gave his clerk the opportunity to manage the practice before his admission in 1861. Way's good fortune continued. He could afford to buy the Atkinson practice in 1863, found a suitable partner to free him for work exclusively at the Bar, led the case for dismissing Justice Boothby from the Supreme Court and obtained briefs in cases which went through the higher courts.

Symon, notebook in hand, attended the hearings whenever he could. He did have the role of preparing one case for the prosecutor. Mary Ward

'this momentous step in my life'

pleaded guilty to the charge of wilfully and feloniously setting fire to a stack of her employer's hay. The jury found her guilty and the judge sentenced her to three years jail with hard labour for a crime he declared second only to murder. Although Symon believed the case was 'conducted with much ability on both sides' he had mixed feelings about the man who would become the bane of Symon's life for nearly half a century. He described Way as 'a rising young lawyer of unprepossessing appearance but of great knowledge energy & ability with only a moderate share of the faculty of eloquent speech. He is very little & slight, wears gold (!) rimmed spectacles & has a growth of goatlike beard ... on his chin.'[15]

From this first meeting, Symon set out to promote a closer relationship. He had taken possession of a living turtle which he shipped to Adelaide as a present for Way. Presumably, Way had expressed an interest in turtles. Addressed to 'My Dear Sir', Way wrote to Symon on 16 February 1869 after returning from a visit to Tasmania. (Few people at the time, and certainly not Symon, would have known that Way's lover, Susannah Gooding, a former serving girl of convict heritage, had moved to Tasmania. She eventually gave birth to the five children sired by Way, a devout Methodist and staunch mason, on his various visits during legal vacations.[16]) Way was not at home when Symon's 'very kind present of a living turtle came to hand'. Way had never seen it. The turtle had been placed in the bathroom but it eluded the vigilance of his servants. That, he told Symon, was how he expected them to explain the turtle's disappearance, rather than to say 'it escaped their confounded carelessness'. Way would have greatly valued it and hoped he would be 'fortunate enough to get another someday'. He offered a reward but nothing had materialised. Way expressed the hope that he might return to Mount Gambier when the Circuit Court next sits 'to plague' Symon as he did last time.[17]

Way went one step better. He spent a year in England from mid-1869 and on return invited Symon to continue his articles with Way's firm in Adelaide. On 6 June 1870 Symon ended his formal attachment to Cousin.

4

'I can address a jury as effectively as the best of them.'

Josiah Symon moved to Adelaide in June 1870, completed his articles with Way & Brook and was admitted to practice in December 1871. Brook's death in 1873 created an opening and Way took Symon into a partnership which ended when Way became Chief Justice in 1876. By June 1881, Symon was the senior partner of the very successful legal firm of Symon, Bakewell & Symon, Jo's younger brother Bill having arrived in Adelaide two years earlier. Josiah was then a leader of the Adelaide Bar, a Queen's Counsel and a member of the exclusive and prestigious Adelaide Club. He had briefly held office as South Australia's Attorney General, and looked secure in his seat of Sturt in the House of Assembly. Symon had entered the property and share market and could back his minimum of 50 guineas a day for a Court appearance with dividends from various investments. The connections he established in the law and other professions, and in business and farming, all assisted his advance in society. He might not measure up against the richest men in the Colony – like Sir Thomas Elder and Robert Barr Smith – but he could send welcome funds to family members in Scotland, London and Mount Gambier. Symon now rented part of 'Wootten Lea', a grand two-storey, 17-room bluestone home in Glen Osmond. In 1880–81 Symon could afford a twelve-month trip through the United States, the United Kingdom and parts of Western Europe, confident of his firm's capacity to function effectively in his absence.

His progress through the 1870s was neither inevitable nor untroubled. Symon had to overcome self-doubt, survive personal disappointment and make up for the misused years spent working under Cousin.

Symon left Mount Gambier on Friday 3 June 1870. Two weeks later he

'I can address a jury as effectively as the best of them.'

told Jim that, although Cousin expressed a desire to assist his departure, he was 'passively resisting' it by finding numerous matters which needed completion before his clerk could leave. Jo was so exasperated he demanded to know whether Cousin would actually allow him to go to Adelaide. After an altercation, where he spoke 'very freely' and 'very effectively', Jo left by the mail coach for Penola which he reached on Saturday at 4.00 am. After drinking hot coffee, Jo travelled all day and the following day to reach Adelaide 'almost dead with fatigue' at around 7.00 pm on the Sunday. He stayed the night at a hotel. Next morning, he forsook the opportunity of a short holiday, deciding it would hardly be a 'treat' because he knew nobody in Adelaide. He had breakfast, bought 'a respectable black felt hat' and presented himself at Way's Chambers at 61 King William Street on Monday 6 June.

Way greeted him 'very cordially' and told him that his duties consisted of meeting clients, supervising the office and managing common law, equity, insolvency and cognate business. Brook was absent on leave until early in 1871, and Symon was assigned his dingy office. It was better, Symon decided, to work rather than be idle and he started straight away.

'The first thing I learned was how very ignorant I was of innumerable things I ought to have known, & this sense of ignorance was so keen that I despaired of ever undertaking the duties assigned me.' It did not help to discover that 'Mr Way ... is a hasty impatient, noisy little animal' who must be thinking that his new articled clerk was collecting £3 a week 'under false pretences'. Way subsequently apologised for his behaviour and Symon felt they started to work better together. Nothing, however, could alter one simple fact: 'my last three years have largely been wasted.'[1]

In a later letter, Jo apologised for being so down-hearted on arrival in Adelaide. Despite now thinking that there were four and not three 'wasted years', and despite his 'procrastinating and indolent disposition', he felt confident about making up for lost time. He thought he had 'an average intellect – if a sluggish one'. Jo in fact had an above average mind and probably did not want his brother to think he was boasting. Jo saw his problem as one of being easily diverted by newspapers and good literature. He knew the solution: for the next twelve months, 'I shall have to devote myself assiduously to law in all its aspects & all my other studies must have some bearing thereon'.[2]

Jo was conscious of having no real friends outside his family with whom he could confide. Indeed, he probably never spoke with other family members as he did to Jim. He told his brother of his one great fear: if Jim did not bring him down quietly from the pinnacle on which he had placed him, 'I shall tumble down with a crash whether you like it or not'.

> It is vain for me to hope & dream of being an orator or a sufficiently finished speaker to take a prominent place in the S. A^n. Bar. Even if I possessed the necessary command of language & the power of chaste and eloquent expression, added to the faculty of logical thought my timidity & nervousness, from the sensitiveness of my nature producing confusion, would be an insuperable barrier.[3]

Jo was about to turn 24 years of age when he wrote those words. His future rivals at the Bar and in politics probably regretted he overcame these self-doubts; that is, if Symon ever disclosed their existence.

Symon in 1870 could still dream. He told his brother on 8 November of spending an afternoon and evening in Way's company where he learnt that, in the year Way formed a partnership with Brook, he collected £5000. 'What do you think of that? There is no doubt the business is a splendid one. Would that there was the faintest hope of my becoming a partner in it – even with a very small share – rather be a minor/minnow among the tutors than vice versa!'[4]

Samuel Way was probably too busy to involve himself in preparing Symon for the examination to pass his articles. His junior partner, James Brook, took on this task when he returned from leave. Brook was born in Edinburgh in 1840 where his father was a supervisor in the Inland Revenue Service. Educated principally at Bristol Grammar School, where he acquired a good classical knowledge, Brook arrived in South Australia in 1853, and worked in law offices before doing his articles with Samuel Way and being admitted to the Supreme Court in 1868. He subsequently went into partnership with Way and managed Way & Brook when the senior partner took leave in England in 1869–70. He also edited the first volume of the South Australian *Law Reports*. According to the *Express and Telegraph* of 28 August 1872, Brook 'was unquestionably a man of sterling integrity, and his geniality and many good qualities secured him a wide popularity'.

'I can address a jury as effectively as the best of them.'

After Brook returned to Adelaide, an agreement was reached on 27 May 1871 acknowledging that Symon had served his articles under James Sutherland until 6 June 1870. He was now assigned as Brook's pupil and paid a fee of ten shillings, double the sum Symon paid to Sutherland.[5] Brook was painstaking and thorough, and well-placed and motivated to provide his pupil with better and more comprehensive advice than Symon ever received from Cousin. Symon was confident when he gave notice on 23 October 1871 of his intention to apply for admission as a practitioner of the Supreme Court. He was admitted on Saturday morning 25 November 1871, the sole business of the Court on the final day of the legal term. Louis von Doussa was admitted at the same time.[6] The press had trouble with Symon's name. Many 'Symons' were mentioned in the South Australian press in 1871 so adding one more to the list seemed reasonable. The *Chronicle and Weekly Mail* of 2 December was one of the few newspapers to refer to the admission of 'J.H. Symon'.

In a letter to his brother in September 1872, Jo announced unhappy news: 'Poor Brook died very suddenly.' Way and Symon had been working together when they learnt the junior partner had fallen ill. They took a cab with two horses to Brook's home in Unley Park to find he had 'breathed his last'. Jo found it 'very hard to realise the terrible fact'. Although he had known Brook for just 18 months, Jo thought him 'very kind' and possessed of a 'cynical turn' and 'keen sense of humour' which never became 'bitter or malicious'. Jo saw in Brook something he himself lacked: 'the power of concentration & abstraction.' Furthermore, in contrast 'to our miserable cousin', Brook had 'unflinching integrity'. His one defect – Brook read very little general literature – remained hidden by 'natural shrewdness, good sense & quickness'. Symon realised he would miss Brook's advice and support, but acknowledged Way's loss would be greater. Way told him they had been close friends for 18 years, including a period where they played games of leapfrog in Adelaide's parklands. Brook gave everything of himself to Way who would miss him in the business.

Brook's demise became Symon's opportunity. He was now earning £416 a year, and if he had the mental and physical strength there was 'a very strong possibility of my being in partnership with Way next year'. Jo advised his brother not to lay much store on this. He doubted whether he could place himself in a position to grasp the chance. Jo urged his brother to believe him sincere in saying he would rather have Brook alive than for his chances of succeeding him increased. Nevertheless, he had a duty to do the best for his family, though not for himself because 'the ambition is eaten out of me' for which he was probably most to blame.[7]

The *Evening Journal* reported on 16 April 1873 that Samuel Way QC had taken J.H. Symon, the former managing clerk of Way & Brook, into partnership and the 'extensive business' of the late firm will be carried on under the style name of 'Way & Symon' – 'of course in the old and well-known chambers'. The agreement was dated to have come into effect from New Year's Day 1873.

Jo sent Jim a copy of the agreement marked 'strictly private', yet he would be happy if news of the partnership happened to reach the newspapers in Stirling. Under the agreement he was entitled to one-quarter of the firm's profits in the first year of the five-year term of the partnership, a proportion rising to one-third from the second year. Should Way die, Symon could expect to pay £5000 to purchase the senior partner's share, but hoped this was 'a very remote contingency' though the sum would be 'a mere bagatelle for such a business as ours'. Symon had told Way he wanted to go to England during the five-year term of the partnership. Way had suggested the holiday himself, but it was not mentioned in the partnership agreement. Jo assured his brother the trip would happen but not before the end of the first three years.

Symon was now the partner of the second most important barrister in Adelaide. The first, Randolph Stow, had the 'more persuasive gifts of advocacy'.[8] To be Way's partner 'in such a business is something – I confess I do feel proud'. Symon also felt humble given the limited qualifications he brought to the partnership. Symon said he now has 'a grave responsibility' but he was 'equally free of the miserable feeling of suspense & despondency' which has shown itself in some of his letters home. He must show his appreciation of what Way had done for him. Way was more than ten years his senior 'but that does not lessen our mutual sympathies'. In fact, it increased Symon's desire 'to serve him well & relieve him as much as possible of the labor & anxiety which I a younger man might bear'.[9]

One month before Symon signed the partnership agreement another of Way's favoured clerks was admitted to the Supreme Court. Charles

'I can address a jury as effectively as the best of them.'

Cameron Kingston was born in 1850. His father, Sir George Strickland Kingston, a surveyor who became a mining engineer and a politician, arrived in South Australia in 1836. Thrice married, a republican and always a fighter, the father served terms in both the Legislative Council and the House Assembly and was the Speaker of the latter when his son joined the firm of Way & Brook. Charles Cameron Kingston was outspoken. He had a brilliant mind and flourished at J.L. Young's non-denominational Premier Private School which provided an adventurous education for the children of religious dissenters. Like Symon he stood at just over six feet tall; together, they towered over the pint-sized senior partner of Way & Symon.

Way clearly liked Charles Kingston, and went out of his way to assist the elevation of someone who openly flouted conventional morality. In 1873 Way persuaded the Supreme Court to examine Kingston for admission to practice before the time for doing his articles had expired, thus saving him from waiting until the following term. More importantly, when Way proposed Kingston's admission in March 1873 he argued that an objection to the application should not be heard. The elder brother of Lucy McCarthy wanted to tell the Court that Kingston had broken his promise to marry Lucy, had been unfaithful and had tried to extort money from her. Way said the complainant had not submitted the appropriate papers in advance and therefore did not have *locus standi* to appear. Justice Gwynne said that even if the brother had observed the necessary procedures and the complaints were true, the objections should be dealt with in a civil action. In effect, the deficient moral character alleged in the complaint was not a ground for denying Kingston's admission to practice. As will be shown, Josiah Symon believed that Kingston's behaviour ruled him out of a partnership. Kingston's marriage to Lucy on 25 June 1873 did not temper Symon's disapproval.

Way and Symon worked well together in partnership, and Symon's name regularly appeared in press reports of cases in civil and criminal jurisdictions. The junior partner continued to live in lodgings, to send small sums to his family in Stirling and to order books mainly through Jim in London. In addition to his legal work and reading books and newspapers he planned his visit to the northern hemisphere. Meanwhile, Way, who did not appear so often in Court, took on a new role in February

1875 when he was elected for the seat of Sturt in the House of Assembly and in June became Attorney-General in James Boucaut's ministry.

Jo told his brother on New Year's Day, 1876, that all the difficulties had been overcome and he expected to leave Adelaide on 26 February. A managing clerk (Kingston) had been appointed to take charge of conveyancing on £400 a year. Jo reported that Way was about to take his annual trip to Tasmania and would be absent for six weeks, so there would be little time between his return and Jo's departure. The junior partner began finalising the details of his trip, telling Jim he expected to spend May and the best part of June in England and Scotland, and there would be time for the two of them to visit Europe. He wanted some more visiting cards and to pass on the advice he had received from a barrister in Adelaide that Bill would be best served by joining the Inner Temple. Way, in Melbourne, contacted Symon on 31 January to discuss unfinished cases and to express the hope that his partner was educating the clerks to take most of the work from Way's hands. Way had no intention of trying to produce a fair copy of all the correspondence.[10]

Jo knew that his visit to the United Kingdom in 1876 would be the last chance to see his father who was probably holding onto life in the hope of spending time with his second son. His mother wrote to 'Dear Josy' before his departure from Adelaide. She was replying to one of his which 'brought back the remembrance of days long past never to return'. She sometimes thought of those days when sitting of an evening and 'Father' was in bed, 'but I know I should not, as we are surrounded by so many comforts which your considerate kindness has given us and are still increasing'. Bill had been with them over the New Year, and it would have been dull without him. If they were 'spared', there is 'the prospect of seeing you which I hope and trust will be managed'.[11]

On 25 February Jo sent his final letter before boarding his ship. Josiah was still trying to decide whether to take a break in Bombay and Cairo. He told Jim it was costing him 'no little trouble & hard work to get everything in such a state that I can get off with some mental comfort to myself – & it would look as tho [sic] I wished you to regard me as a hero or martyr if I told you what sacrifices I am making to get away'. The firm's 'larger and more lucrative' business – it had made more money in the previous year – placed greater burdens on the junior partner. There was, however,

'I can address a jury as effectively as the best of them.'

time available to attend the dinner party Way gave to mark Symon's departure. The guest of honour described it as 'a brilliant success' with the other guests including Charles Mann, a former (and future) Attorney General, W.B. Rounsevell MP, George Hamilton, the Police Commissioner, J.W. Bakewell, the solicitor who would become a partner in Symon's firm, and J.H. Parr, a prominent auctioneer. The dinner was one of the last occasions for nearly 40 years when Symon sat comfortably in Way's company.

Symon boarded P&O's steamship, RMS *China*, on Sunday 27 February. He was looking forward to a faster and more comfortable voyage than the one he experienced on the *St Vincent* in 1866. On 15 March, just before reaching Galle in Ceylon (now Sri Lanka), Symon wrote another letter to Jim finalising his itinerary and giving Jim time to arrange leave from Customs. Jo planned to visit Bombay and to call at Aden and Suez. He might disembark to see Cairo and the Pyramids though this seemed unlikely. He would go onto Venice and expected to reach London on about 23 April and must leave Southampton on 29 June or Venice on 7 July. Jo wanted to travel for some time with Jim, and thought Bill might join them. He hoped that Jim had arranged for Bill to enter the Inns of Court and worried only that some travel arrangements might leave him with just a month to spend at 'home'. There was an unspoken message. Josiah wanted to see his family but the trip offered him his first opportunity to have a holiday since leaving Gravesend ten years ago and he wanted to visit historic and literary sites in England, France and Italy.

On 17 March, William Boothby, the court Sheriff from South Australia and a fellow passenger, handed Symon a telegram Boothby had received on the ship's arrival in Galle. It bore a simple message: Hanson, the Chief Justice, had died of heart disease. Way had also sent a telegram direct to Symon telling him to return home immediately: the firm would pay all his expenses. Symon recognised he had no alternative. He sent a telegraph to Jim in London: 'visit postponed Way telegraphs Hanson dead return immediately'. He subsequently wrote to Jim on 17 March. 'My inference is that Way has the Chief Justiceship within his grasp. Of course I have no alternative so at once telegraphed that I shall return at once, arriving in Adelaide about 10 April. All my plans are gone.' Turning back to Adelaide made him cry; he felt his heart had been 'taken out of me'. Typically, his head worked as fast as ever. He gave Boothby some small parcels to deliver to Jim in London and told Jim that Bill must not lose time in joining the Inns of Court.[12]

Symon found a berth on the *China* which was leaving Galle on 18 March for Australian waters. In Adelaide, on that same day, the Executive Council approved the appointment of Samuel Way QC as Chief Justice of the Supreme Court. Way, as Attorney-General, recommended himself for the post and was a party to the decision which accepted his recommendation. By the time Symon reached Glenelg on 8 April Way had already been sworn in as Chief Justice and was hearing cases.

On board the *China* again, Symon could barely contain his anger. He had been obliged to forgo seeing his family and enjoying a holiday for which he had waited so long. Compounding his distress, decisions had been taken without consultation between the partners. The root cause, as Symon saw it, was Way's vaulting ambition and selfishness.

Way greeted Symon with a note upon his arrival at Glenelg on Saturday 8 April. It could only have intensified Symon's anger. Written on 6 April, Way expressed his wish that the telegram sent to the Sheriff and his own message to Symon had prepared his former partner for the news and reconciled him to the loss of his holiday. Way said he did not intend to meet Symon at the steamer (in the circumstances, probably a wise decision) but wanted to welcome him back at the earliest moment Symon could meet him. The Chief Justice attempted humour and offered consolation. He described the telegraph as a 'beneficent Institution'. Without it, Symon would have experienced the gales of England instead of those of the Great Australian Bight and been 'quite unconscious of the rate at which we have been making History in your absence'. Way hoped that Symon had derived as much benefit to his health as if he had been all the way to England and back, and that 'the disadvantage of being so suddenly recalled may be amply counter-balanced by the substantial benefits of your new position'.[13]

Whether Symon replied to this note he certainly commented on Way's next one. On 7 April, the Chief Justice told 'My dear Symon' that he was sorry to trouble him when he was so occupied with business matters but thought Symon would agree it was desirable to reduce an arrangement to writing 'without further delay'. He wanted to clear his mind of the

'I can address a jury as effectively as the best of them.'

business before dealing with criminal matters in Court next week. Way asked Symon for a meeting of an hour or two in the evening. Alternatively, they might exchange memoranda. It would be best, Way added, that they should act with our discussion still in mind. Symon pencilled a copy of his reply onto Way's letter. He wanted Way to realise just what he had done: 'the news of my recall from Galle destroyed my father's mind.'[14]

Symon later discovered that Way had first prepared his negotiating position on 15 March; that is, eleven days after Hanson's death and three days before the Executive Council appointed Way to the Bench. He had formulated a 'Memorandum of Agreement' of which clause 1 read, 'The Partnership heretofore subsisting between the parties is hereby dissolved from this date [15 March].' Symon agreed to purchase all the deeds and title deed books, papers and vouchers belonging to the business successively carried on by Atkinson & Way, Way & Brook and Way & Symon. He also agreed to purchase together with all the rights to custody of all deeds, drafts, papers and vouchers held by the firm on account of clients and all the furniture, fittings, plant, safes and stationery of or used by the firm but excluding Way's library. There were complicated arrangements setting out the appointment of valuers to determine just what Symon would have to pay. Symon was to collect, free of any charges, all debts owing to Way & Symon. 'The agreement having been entered into in Mr Symon's absence is not to be binding upon him or his representatives (except as to clause 1) unless ratified by him or them.' Way's signature was attached and so was that of Symon's presumed Attorney, J.W. Bakewell.

It was a shock to learn in April that the partnership had been dissolved in mid-March, and in the absence of the junior partner. No doubt Way had to act once he was appointed Chief Justice but there was no compulsion to act before the Executive Council had approved his elevation. Perhaps another less ambitious or self-centred man might have waited until Symon had set foot in Adelaide. Way, however, was too astute to allow the supporters of the two sitting Justices the time or opportunity to press their case. Justice Gwynne certainly had comparable claims to the post of Chief Justice while Justice Randolph Stow clearly surpassed Samuel Way as a barrister, a lawyer and a human being.[15] Way behaved exactly as an ambitious and egotistical man should, and acted as he was fully entitled to do.

Symon soon became aware of another of what he saw as Way's least pleasing characteristics. He reported to Jim: 'I found (Way) as I told him had quite as keen a sense of his own pecuniary interest.' They had several meetings and 'some of them rather acrimonious ... (and) a good deal of plain speaking has been exchanged between us'. Way's first and last negotiating position required Symon to give him £5000 or a year's income for the goodwill of the business. Symon called Way's demand 'absurd', forgetting or simply ignoring his comment in 1873 that £5000 was 'a mere bagatelle' in view of the riches obtained. In 1876 the Way demand required the junior partner to hand over 'nearly the whole of what I had made by dint of ... hard work during the last three or four years for something I don't want because I would very much rather the firm of Way & Symon continued for ten years longer'. On a private undated note, Symon wrote that the estimate of £5000 was 'too much'; the correct figure was 'certainly not more than £2500'. He also pointed out that the 'dissolution of the partnership is not of my seeking' and all to Way's benefit and 'I lose my holiday'. Symon eventually offered £2500, payable at the end of 12 months because the money had to come out of what he would make in the future and not out of his past earnings. Way was 'very much dissatisfied but I was firm'. There were also many other points of difference but Symon told his brother he expected them all to be settled by the next mail.[16]

Way, it seems, stared him down, while making significant concessions. Symon agreed to pay Way £5000. Whereas Symon understood that the £5000 included an allowance for the 'goodwill' of the practice, Way's biographer claimed that Symon received the goodwill 'for nothing'. Instead of Symon collecting debts owed to Way free of charge he would be paid a small fixed percentage of what he collected and passed on. Way agreed to pay Symon £1500 for funds in the firm's accounts which properly belonged to him, with Way having full and free access to the Way & Symon books. The parties reached an uneasy agreement by mid-June 1876. Way's biographer felt that Symon, being 'self-centred and abnormally sensitive to any real or apparent disregard of his interests ... kept the quarrel alive for years'. Symon saw a side of Way that evidently eluded the biographer. It took two men to keep the quarrel alive until Way's approaching death. For four decades there was a certain 'atmosphere' in courtrooms where Way presided and Symon argued a case.[17]

'I can address a jury as effectively as the best of them.'

Given Jo's feelings about Way, Jim might have been surprised to learn that the reorganisation and choice of staff had caused his brother 'infinitely more worry[,] anxiety & unpleasantness than anything else'. The staff included 'a very strong willed, bad tempered & as it turned out unprincipled fellow named Kingston'. Symon acknowledged that Kingston had considerable ability and as Chief Clerk had developed a useful speciality in conveyancing. In Symon's absence, Way may have led Kingston to believe that a partnership was within sight. Soon after Symon returned, Kingston applied for a partnership and to Symon's surprise seemed to consider he had some claim to one. Kingston told him that he had 'preserved the business' in Symon's absence. Symon said Kingston was just doing his duty. If Kingston had left the firm upon Way's appointment 'he would have been acting dishonourably', though perhaps within his legal rights because the dissolution of the partnership freed him from his engagement.

Symon told Jim that a partnership with Kingston was out of the question. He could not embrace him because of his temper and manner, his slovenly business habits and personal repute involving 'all sorts of disreputable escapades'. The latter included Kingston first living with his present wife, the daughter of a notorious brothel owner, as his mistress and taking other mistresses after marrying her. Symon told Kingston he 'had not the least intention of associating his name with mine in the firm'. Kingston became so offensive in manner and language that Symon told him his continuation within the firm would not be comfortable for either of them. Symon advised him to go, 'and go he did'.[18]

At least Symon had found 'a capital partner'. J.W. Bakewell, the son of the late Crown Solicitor and a Cambridge graduate who had been called to the Bar at the Inner Temple, had been practising for six years and would bring in business worth about £1000. The terms of their partnership included a financial breakdown in which Symon's entitlement was three-quarters of the profit while guaranteeing that Bakewell's one-quarter share would not be less than £1500. After one year, the breakdown would be two-thirds to one-third. The partnership itself was dissolved after 12 years when Bakewell retired from practice.

If Way's biographer had read Way's letters to Symon in April 1876, he might have focused on the claim that any disadvantage to Symon for being recalled to Adelaide 'may be amply counter-balanced by the substantial benefits of your new position'. Symon had benefitted from Brook's death but the departure of Way to the Bench proved to be the single most important lever in Symon's legal career. It was not just a matter of taking charge of what many contemporaries regarded as the most prestigious legal firm in Adelaide. Symon now had nowhere to hide. He was the face of Symon & Bakewell. Opportunity and necessity propelled him to confront his doubts and deficient knowledge. The result was that within four years of Way's elevation the senior and junior members of the Adelaide Bar regarded Symon as one of the two or three leaders of the profession in South Australia.

Two months after taking over, Symon was telling Jim he was 'fearfully busy'. Business had not diminished in any way since Way's departure; if anything, the conveyancing load had increased. In addition to Bakewell and himself, staff numbers now stood at 12. The firm needed another partner but Symon wanted to keep a space open for Bill who was seeking admission to one of the Inns of Court in London. His own full employment proved an antidote to depression and, better still, his day-by-day court appearances and his victories helped him deal with self-doubt.

> Pitting myself against the other men here – the best of them – I have nothing to fear. I am not being egotistic – I was always diffident & shy of company & putting myself forward ... I still have the same feelings ... but ... the opinion is I can address a jury as effectively as the best of them.[19]

Between 1876 and 1879 Jo kept his brother supplied with press accounts of his triumphs, occasionally pointing out where the reports were inadequate or created the wrong impression. Jo also made repeated references to being 'overwhelmed' by work, forcing him to reduce many of his monthly letters to two or three pages of hasty scribble compared with the eight or more pages he had regularly sent from Mount Gambier.

In April 1879 Jo told Jim he did not think that any advocate who practised in South Australia 'had a larger business than I have at this moment'. He had so many cases before the Supreme Court that he had to decline briefs for the inferior courts. After telling a potential client he would charge 100 guineas a day to appear in his case in Mount Gambier

'I can address a jury as effectively as the best of them.'

Jo realised he could not take the brief at double that amount. He was 'in very good health & on the whole in capital spirits – the more Counsels [*sic*] I have in Court the better I always feel – particularly if I am winning my cases as I have been of late'. In a subsequent letter in May, Jo thought it was a rare experience for a Counsel to win 12 or 13 cases in a row.[20]

Clients often recorded their gratitude, even when Symon failed to win their case. Henry Edwards, a serial thief aged 41, had acted as a look-out for a robbery at the Adelaide house of the Rev. Charles Hall. He ran away as the police arrived and when arrested tried to swallow several Victorian bank notes. On the day before he had stolen a piece of cloth valued at 30 shillings which Symon valiantly tried to prove had an unknown ownership. Edwards received a sentence of seven years with hard labour. He wrote to Symon from the Adelaide gaol on 22 November 1878. Although convicted on two charges, he told Symon 'you did your utmost in every way'. Edwards hoped that Symon's great ability as a lawyer and a barrister 'will assist your future in the Honorable Profession to which you belong'.[21]

Symon won an important libel case in April 1879. Robert Taylor, the landlord of the City Hotel, Adelaide, sued the proprietor of the *South Australian Advertiser*, Thomas King MP, and sought £1000 in damages for an article which appeared in the *Advertiser* on 20 January 1879. The article headed 'The Haunts of the Unfortunate' stated that the 'City' had become a rendezvous for the 'willowers' who herded together at night under the willows on the banks of the Torrens. One sentence attracted the most attention: 'More men than women were hanging about the "City" but at times the scenes enacted there would not bear open description.' The case was heard in the Supreme Court before Chief Justice Way and a Special Jury. Symon led for the defence and Charles Mann QC, the State Treasurer in 1878, appeared for the plaintiff.

Symon used his interrogation of witnesses and two addresses to show how the evidence of the police was more applicable and trustworthy than the views of the landlord's respectable lodgers and friends. The hotel was indeed a meeting place for prostitutes and 'bad characters'. Symon argued that the jury was not entitled to treat any 'excess of language' as evidence of malice. The law, he said, threw a ring of protection around a writer who had honestly done his duty to himself, the press and the community.

After some 90 minutes the jury returned a verdict for the defence. A letter dated 28 April 1879 arrived from the *Advertiser* offices offering Symon the warmest of thanks.

> We feel that the favourable result is attributable to the care and attention you bestowed upon the case & the masterly & eloquent manner in which you addressed the jury on behalf of the liberty of the press & vindicated its right to comment & speak strongly upon questions of Public importance.[22]

As Symon continued to grow in self-confidence, he spoke freely to Jim about his fellow barristers in Adelaide. He wrote to his brother on 13 June 1878 just after William Bundey and John Downer had been appointed QC's.[23] 'Bundey is no lawyer – he is singularly illogical – has no facility of legal argument – but be can sometimes make an effective … speech to a Jury: & I believe him to be sincere in his friendship for me … he considers me the best lawyer … at the Bar.' Symon was not overly impressed by the personal comment. He thought Bundey had 'a tendency to talk in hyperboles', as Symon himself became prone to do. Downer, on the other hand, 'has great ability, but he is greatly wanting in Culture, refinement & manner'. Apparently, Downer told Symon he regarded him 'as quite his equal in the profession'. Jo added the opinion of the 'Junior ranks' – who were not likely to be jealous – that he and Downer 'are the foremost men in active practice at the bar'. Symon had one more compliment to pass on. One of the oldest practitioners at the Bar (W.C. Belt, admitted to practice in 1851) told him, 'I think you are quite as much entitled to be made a QC as Bundey and Downer'. Symon thought even more of the comment given that in court he had been sarcastic at Belt's expense.[24]

In a later letter, Symon referred to the elevation of James Boucaut to the Supreme Court in September 1878. Boucaut succeeded Randolph Stow who died prematurely on 17 September. Stow's contemporaries, among them Way and John Downer, regarded him as a great judge despite his short term on the Bench (1875–8). When Symon compared Stow to Boucaut he thought the one represented 'sunlight' and the other 'moonlight'. Symon did, however, acknowledge that Boucaut was a QC and considered him to be a good man. He also saw Boucaut's appointment as another opportunity. He told his brother that in a few months he would apply to the Chief Justice to appoint him to the vacancy at the senior bar.

'I can address a jury as effectively as the best of them.'

Symon appreciated that his move would involve some 'delicacy' in view of his relationship with Way but, for the moment, would say nothing more on the subject.[25]

Symon maintained his rage about Way's actions but was circumspect, even in confidential letters to his brother. He did make occasional comments to Jim about Way's lack of height and presence and liked to record the number and length of times that Way, having been appointed Lieutenant-Governor, held office as Acting Governor of South Australia. Two Governors in quick succession had suddenly left Adelaide for health or other personal reasons. On 27 June 1877, Jo observed that honours were being 'heaped on friend Way' who was now looking at a long period as Acting Governor. Jo had noticed that Way liked dressing up for ceremonies and 'will certainly be the smallest & in appearance most insignificant [personage?] who has ever been addressed as "Your Excellency" ... He is certainly destitute of personal presence & dignity.' By contrast, Stow was 'the most dignified & eloquent of our Judges'.[26] Symon had a more serious objection to Way's role at Acting Governor. He considered it unacceptable for a member of the judiciary to assume executive duties and took up the issue with vehemence during the federation debates in the late 1890s.

Jo kept up his flow – of shorter letters – to Jim in 1876–8. Among other things, they reproduced two important elements of his outlook and character. First, his attachment to family remained strong, inspired by affection and a sense of duty. He was understandably deeply moved on learning that 'Father' had died on Boxing Day 1878, having learnt from his mother that his father had drifted away after his stroke on the day 'Josy' first arrived in Adelaide in 1866. At least Jo could regularly express his feelings with monetary gifts to his mother and unmarried sisters in Stirling, including the money to buy a larger and more comfortable house in the better part of the historic city. Jo more than repaid his original debt to Jim, largely financed Bill's training in law and sent money to Caroline and Uncle who were experiencing hard times.

Secondly, Jo expanded the role he adopted at Moray House in Edinburgh early in 1860s. He became the family counsellor who proffered advice, issued thinly-veiled instructions and became accepted by the family as the embodiment of sound values and, in effect, its head. He carried authority in part because he was the family's success story. Once Jo's mentor and benefactor, Jim and Jo had reversed roles. The younger brother Bill, who may have been the brightest in the family, was about to join the Symon law firm in Adelaide. Jo had the highest hopes for Bill but had almost given up on Cousin. Apprised that he was close to a total wreck, Jo signed an order to place a drunken Cousin in hospital.

Bill reached Adelaide in May 1879. A proud older brother watched as William Bundey QC, the Attorney-General, moved for Bill's admission to the Bar, saying that the surname was pretty well known in the Court. Chief Justice Way interposed, 'We have heard the name before (Laughter)'. Bundey reported that the applicant was called to the degree of 'utter barrister' by Gray's Inn in January 1879. The Chief Justice said Symon was clearly entitled to admission and the Order was granted.[27] Two days after admission the Chancellor of the University of Adelaide formally admitted William Symon, MA, University of St Andrews, to the degree of MA *ad eundem*. Naturally, the Vice-Chancellor of the University, the ubiquitous Chief Justice Way, attended the ceremony.

Bill's name was added to the firm which from the end of July 1879 presented as Symon, Bakewell & Symon. At that stage Bill as a salaried partner earned £650 a year; from December he would be on £1000 a year. Soon after Bill arrived in Adelaide Jo began introducing him to valuable contacts and arranged for the Attorney-General to recommend him for honorary membership of the Adelaide Club. A very pleased Jo wrote in September that Bill had dropped into the practice 'as to the manner born'. Critically, Symon would not have any misgivings about going overseas in 1880, and he now had someone with whom he could talk. 'I have had a good many years of comparative isolation.'[28]

William Bundey hosted a champagne lunch at the Hotel Crown & Sceptre on Thursday 22 January 1880 to honour Josiah Symon who was about to leave South Australia on his twelve-month holiday. It was an occasion for prominent members of Adelaide society, who were members of the Bar, to farewell him. As Bundey said when proposing a toast, Symon's successful career at the Bar had been 'recognised by the profession and by the public in an unmistakable manner'. Symon replied saying that although he had not been born in the Colony all of his experience of the law had been gained in South Australia. He was proud

'I can address a jury as effectively as the best of them.'

to be a member of its Bar and, wherever he went, would carry with him 'lively feelings of gratitude for the kindness and consideration' he had received from the Attorney-General and the Bar.[29]

Symon left Adelaide a month later and arrived at San Francisco at the end of February. He visited Sacramento, the seat of government in California, where he met a number of state senators – 'a rough uncouth looking lot' – one of whom, taller than Symon, leant over a polished mahogany railing and squirted tobacco juice on the good carpet below him. Symon then travelled by train to Salt Lake City and Chicago, to Toronto and the 'glorious' Niagara Falls, and Washington and Philadelphia and New York. On 25 March he set sail for Liverpool and eventually reached Stirling on 7 April. In a letter sent to Bill on the following day he described what it all meant to him:

> Last night was I think the happiest of my life, and I really do feel as though I had been some good in the world. To see my mother and my sisters after so many years of absence – so many years too filled up on their side with trial and suffering and breavement and on mine with toil and misery also – with times of brightness no doubt but more generally seasons of gloom and depression – to see them after that interval was much; but it was more to see them happy and cheerful and comfortable.[30]

5

'your dogged determination to succeed did most of the climbing.'[1]

Josiah Symon appears to have left little record of his time in the United Kingdom between 7 April and mid July 1880. He did send a letter to Bill from Great Yarmouth on 6 May, written after travelling by train through the East Anglian countryside. The journey reminded him of how much he admired and loved the green of rural England, its quaint villages and moss-covered churches. 'No wonder she produces unequalled landscape painters, when the sweet and varied and reposeful beauty of her landscapes are themselves unequalled.' This letter also mentioned the several plays he saw in London, his plans to join Jim in returning to Scotland and to travel with him through Europe.

The two older brothers left London for Antwerp on 20 July and moved at some pace through Belgium, Germany, France and Italy. Jo later travelled through Spain with an ailing friend from Adelaide. The tourists saw a great deal without stopping anywhere for very long. Jo sounded like so many Anglo-Celts abroad when he sniffed at the absence of soap on wash basins and commented unfavourably about the location of *pissoirs* in 'conspicuous places'. He liked some cities – Dresden 'very much pleased' him – and dismissed others – Berlin was 'not much'. The Scottish Protestant also marvelled at many of the cathedrals.[2]

In his longest letter to Bill, dated 25 July 1880, Jo suspended the narrative for several pages to talk about his Will. He feared he had been too casual in formulating it when he left Adelaide and some matters remained incomplete. He wanted Bakewell and Bill to pay his executors £4000 to cover the cost of the business and 'goodwill' in taking over the firm. He noted that Way (Symon referred to him as 'our little friend the CJ – the great QC') asked for £5000 and Jo had agreed to £2500.

'your dogged determination to succeed did most of the climbing.'

> I did not think at that time, harassed as I was – only 29 years of age – no experience in Supreme Court practice – uncertain that the old clients would remain with [the] junior partner – under these circumstances I did not consider myself justified in giving more than I gave besides paying £500–100[0] for office furniture [etc] – after events showed it to be worth more to <u>me</u>. And in my judgment the business – as it would remain to me if Bakewell retired, is now well worth <u>£5000</u> to you and anyone joining you.

Symon then talked about the initial £1000 worth of business Bakewell brought to the firm and noted he had a small number of clients, most of them investors. Jo wanted Bakewell and Bill to have equal shares in the event of his death, because Bill's possession of the name 'Symon' more than equalled Bakewell's longer personal connection to the business. In the event of Jo's death and Bakewell's determination to retire, or decision not to pay his share of 'goodwill' and the costs of purchasing the materials of the firm, Bill would pay to his brother's estate the full £4000 minus the £1150 of his debt to Jo which his brother had cancelled.

The letter makes clear that, being unmarried and childless, Jo had decided to regard Bill as his principal heir and successor. He was sure the rest of the family would concur with his decision to bequeath all his books to Bill, perhaps an even more significant gesture than his arrangements for the firm. Jo talked freely to Bill about the future 'in the event of my death' because he was still experiencing unaccustomed ill-health. He had seen a doctor in Stirling and 'Alas! my grog is stopped' and 'I'm going steadily to undermine my constitution with eggs, milk and all kinds of farinaceous food'.

Jo's priorities shifted sharply within 18 months of thinking about Bill taking over the firm. Returning to Adelaide on 19 February 1881, he entered State politics, briefly became Attorney-General, joined the Adelaide Club and took silk. In December 1881, he married the young woman he had met in Paris through her relatives when she was making her own Grand Tour of Europe and the United Kingdom.

Soon after his return in February 1881 Symon attended a political meeting at Glenelg and on 1 March announced himself as a candidate for one of the two Sturt seats. Evidently, he had talked to others about a political career before he left for the United Kingdom. No doubt his friend Thomas King had encouraged him. A proprietor of the *South Australian Advertiser* and related newspapers, King was MP for the seat of Sturt (1876–1881) and from 1878 Minister for Education in the Morgan Government. There were no parties or factions for Symon to join although there were personal combinations, but none so settled and substantial to produce stable government. South Australia had 35 ministries between 1837 and 1881.[3]

Symon could enter office before winning a parliamentary seat, and did so because a ministry had to be revamped. On 10 March 1881 William Morgan, Premier since 1878, re-formed his Cabinet following the departure of Charles Mann to be Crown Solicitor and the retirements on health grounds of William Bundey and Thomas King. The process of forming a new ministry took time because Morgan wanted John Bray, the Leader of the Opposition, to join the Government. When Bray finally refused, Morgan confirmed the rumours of the previous ten days by appointing Josiah Henry Symon Attorney-General to replace Bundey in that portfolio.

Symon joined three other candidates in the contest for Sturt. William Townsend, an auctioneer from Mitcham, had been one of the two MPs for Sturt since 1870 and shared the electorate with Way in 1875–6. The other candidates were William Stock, a solicitor and former Mayor of Glenelg, and George Cotton, an agent from Glenelg. Symon opened his campaign at Glenelg on 1 March when he spoke at a meeting called to determine the 'fitness' of candidates for election. The *Evening Standard* reported that the audience greeted him with loud and prolonged cheering. Symon's opening gambit – he had always regarded Sturt as 'the queen of constituencies' – provoked an interjector: 'We don't want to be soaped.' Undeterred, the political novice responded: 'Was not the gentleman present alive to the importance of his own district?' Symon continued with his theme. The district was regarded as 'the gateway to the Colony', hence his hesitation in offering himself to represent a place and a people of such significance. Indeed, as 'an untried man in politics', he had vacillated about putting himself forward until just two hours before the meeting. Should the voters choose him to represent them they would place him under an obligation he could not repay.

'your dogged determination to succeed did most of the climbing.'

Read in cold print, the speech probably warranted interjection. There was no sign, however, of any general scepticism. The fluent lawyer evidently impressed the audience with his sincerity. In any case, it appeared that Symon merely needed to introduce himself and talk mainly in generalities. Many notables in Glenelg and the city had already declared their support. William Wigley, for example, stood aside for him. A lawyer, a local councillor and former Town Clerk and Mayor of Glenelg as well as a former MP, Wigley had previously announced his own candidature.

The new Attorney-General entered the House of Assembly after winning the second Sturt seat on 8 April. Townsend headed the poll with 663 votes, Symon came second with 494, Stock obtained 404 and Cotton 251. Of the main polling places, Symon easily topped the voting in Unley, just headed Townsend in Mitcham, came last in Brighton, third in Goodwood and second in Glenelg. The *Advertiser* on 9 April described the Symon v Stock result as 'pretty close'. Nonetheless, prolonged cheers greeted Symon at the declaration of the poll. Symon spoke of having given the electors 'a fair, honest, fearless exposition' of his opinions and expressed his gratitude for the confidence shown in a newcomer to politics.[4]

The South Australian *Gazette* of 2 June 1881 announced that the Governor in Council 'has been pleased to appoint the Honourable Josiah Henry Symon, M.P., Barrister of the Supreme Court, to be one of Her Majesty's counsel learned in law in this province'. In his Downer biography, John Bannon wrote that by 1881 Symon 'was seen as Downer's chief rival for leadership of the Bar, although he was not a QC. On becoming Attorney-General, however, he immediately took silk.' Symon was sworn in as Attorney-General on 10 March 1881; his appointment as QC was gazetted on 2 June 1881. Bannon seems to have stretched the meaning of 'immediately'. The *Evening Journal* of 1 June 1881 reported the following:

> We learn that on the recommendation of the Chief Justice, His Excellency the Governor has conferred "silk" upon the Hon. J.H. Symon, the Attorney-General. The distinction is well merited, and the action of His Honor, which, we believe, was altogether unsolicited, will meet with general

approval of the profession and the public. Indeed, to many it will be a surprise to learn that Mr. Symon has only now been appointed Queen's Counsel, as it was a common impression that he already held the dignity.

If accurate, and the report was unchallenged at the time, Symon did not solicit his appointment. As required, Chief Justice Way had recommended it.[5]

Within days of taking silk, Symon ceased to be Attorney-General. Morgan's private debt worries had forced him to retire. John Bray succeeded him and appointed John Downer as Attorney-General. Symon sat on the Opposition side of the House and tangled enthusiastically with his successor.

Marriage became Symon's next mission. Mary Eleanor ('Nell') Cowle was born in Launceston on 8 December 1858, the second daughter of Charles and Margaret ('Maggie') Cowle. Nell's grandparents had left Devon, England, in 1833 to settle in Van Diemen's Land (Tasmania since 1853) where her grandfather was a schoolmaster for many years. One of his sons, Charles Cowle, had joined the English, Scottish & Australian (ES&A) Bank and in 1879 had accepted appointment as Manager of the Adelaide branch. The Cowle family moved into a house on Pennington Terrace, North Adelaide, one of the many properties Symon had acquired in the late 1870s.

Slight in build, afflicted as she grew up with headaches – possibly migraines – Nell had learnt to speak and read French, Italian and Spanish, developed a love of theatre, novels and poetry, was proficient in needlework and could play the piano and a small harp. She grew up to be very shy, though not all the time. Meeting Jo, Nell opened up to him in conversation and in letters, while remaining so private that her children had no idea she could be knowledgeable, playful and assertive and could match their father's mind and wit. In her letters of 1880–1, she liked to intersperse French and Italian words, to quote poetry, discuss articles in newspapers and magazines, test Jo with literary references and mock the pomposities and dullness of State politics.[6] She barely tried to stay with him on legal issues, preferring to remain ignorant rather than become bored. Nevertheless, Nell knew enough to ask Jo for legal advice: if they ever married, would he constitute 'real' or 'personal' property?

'your dogged determination to succeed did most of the climbing.'

Jo was not in control of what appears to have been his first relationship. Nell frequently left him uneasy. Mostly, she avoided declarations of affection let alone of love. She began by signing off as 'Yours very sincerely Eleanor Cowle', tried 'Yours faithfully' and settled for 'Yours E.C.' She often sent him messages which must have been unsettling. In one letter, undated though evidently written in 1881, she referred to a time in the previous year when she was very miserable and wondered what he now thought of the woman 'who promised you so much & cared so little'. Judging by her letters the pair often argued, though Nell may have been having fun with her very serious suitor. After Jo dined one night at the Cowles, the family asked Nell if she and Jo had been quarrelling. As Nell later told Jo, she admitted making 'two or three nasty little speeches (but then, that is your fault as you invariably let me say what I please) but I don't remember if we declared war'. At Jo's request they did spend time talking about him. Nell was often at her sharpest on these occasions. 'As you would like to be a "Dictator" I don't think you could be a success in that role, it suits me much better, at any rate.' Jo wanted Nell to explain why he had been so successful. She replied: 'I don't quite agree with your notion of "luck", granted that there must be some allowance made for "the flood of the tides", I fancy your dogged determination to succeed did most of the climbing.'

They agreed to marry at the end of 1881 and selected a date and a place: 8 December, Nell's birthday, at St Peter's Cathedral. There were two outstanding issues. First, there was the wedding dress. Nell had taken out her 'willow-pattern' dress for the wedding – 'it will do for that important affair perfectly – I have a queer sort of dislike of the "conventional" white'. If Jo really did not like it, she had another dress but always associated it with her 'famous want of confidence'. Wisely, the bridegroom decided not to make a fuss and the 'willow pattern' dress arrived at the Cathedral.

If Jo objected on the second issue he was overruled. Nell wrote to Dr Dendy, the celebrant, on the morning of 8 December asking him to perform the ceremony on that morning instead of the grander wedding set down for the afternoon. As Nell explained, she did not want to face 'that [Adelaide Club] crowd in the Cathedral this afternoon'. Jo's prospective father-in-law sent a note to the bridegroom: 'It seems to me Eleanor wants to Euchre the gentlemen who intend witnessing the marriage ceremony.'

Charles Cowle did not know how the change would suit Jo's arrangements; any time would do 'but before noon was preferred'.[7] Nell had her way; the wedding took place at a small private ceremony in the Lady Chapel at the back of the Cathedral on the morning of 8 December. The couple had lunch with the family, Jo went to work at his office after which he collected his bride and the pair went home to 'Wootton Lea'.

An impending marriage barely interrupted the rhythm of Jo's life. On the day before the wedding Symon appeared in the morning for the defendant in a case of malicious prosecution and malicious damage. The plaintiff and the defendant owned eating houses next to each other. The plaintiff sued for £50 and was awarded eight guineas by the four magistrates.[8] In the afternoon Symon joined a number of leading citizens at the well-attended funeral of the prominent lawyer, Rupert Ingleby, QC. The Supreme Court and local courts adjourned for the afternoon. Symon had to work on his wedding day because he faced a difficult case on the day after the ceremony. He defended one Francis Reed who stood accused in the Supreme Court of setting fire to a haystack on a farm at Morphett Vale. The circumstantial evidence looked overwhelming. Symon did not call any evidence, relying instead on interrogating Crown witnesses to expose the difficulties in linking Reed to the fire. Despite his best efforts the jury found the defendant guilty and Justice Andrews sentenced him to seven years hard labour.

There were still more briefs requiring his attention. Symon was back in the Supreme Court on the Wednesday and Thursday of the following week to represent the defendant in a complicated two-day hearing in which the plaintiff sought payment of rent and interest amounting to £800. Richard Chaffey Baker, for whom Symon would develop a profound dislike, appeared for the plaintiff and Chief Justice Way presided. Symon successfully negotiated a settlement of the claims and counter-claims whereby his client paid the plaintiff £250 in addition to the £179-14-4 already paid into the Court. Symon then appeared in an insolvency case leading to the Christmas break.

The newly-married couple had a short honeymoon in Melbourne before Symon returned to court work and parliamentary affairs. They did, however, produce five children between 1883 and 1886. Elizabeth Margaret (Margaret) arrived on 9 March 1883 and the twins Eleanor

'your dogged determination to succeed did most of the climbing.'

Dorothy Jean (Lenore) and Alison Esther Dorothy on 2 February 1884. Tragically, Alison survived for only two months. Leslie Kilmeny (Kilmeny) was born on 16 April 1885 and the first son, Charles James Ballaarat, was born in the Great Australian Bight on 1 July 1886 when the Symon family was returning from England on board the *Ballaarat*. The family now lived in a large house on Fitzroy Terrace, Prospect, for which Jo paid £3000 to take over the lease of the land and ownership of 'Fitzroy House'.

Symon had gone into politics with many principles but had one immediate objective. He wanted to remove the requirement for witnesses in judicial proceedings to take an oath upon entering the stand: that is, 'to tell the truth, the whole truth and nothing but the truth, so help me God'. Symon pointed out that a law already existed to punish perjury. No witness could tell the 'whole truth' and no Judge would allow a witness to take sufficient time to attempt the exercise. To invoke the Divine Being meant placing God in the mouths of atheists and infidels while threatening continuing and after-death punishment for transgressors.[9] Significantly, Charles Kingston, elected for West Adelaide in 1881, proved to be one of Symon's strongest supporters in pressing his case. Rejected in 1876 as a partner in Symon's legal firm, Kingston was a welcome political ally in the 1880s, standing in for him on procedural matters while Symon attended to his practice.

On 6 February 1884 Symon came within one vote of winning his cause in the Legislative Council. In the same month, the Bray Government introduced a motion calling on the British Government to introduce a measure establishing a Federal Council along the lines adopted by the Inter-Colonial Convention which met in Sydney in November-December 1883. Symon's entry into the argument marked the beginning of his public involvement in the cause of federation and of his refusal to accept half-measures and what he saw as pointless arrangements.

Symon spoke against the Bray motion on 27 February, the second last meeting of the Assembly before the 1884 election.[10] He dismissed as 'self-glorification' the Attorney-General's heated response to the member who had criticised the Convention which Downer had attended. The Attorney, Symon said, had employed 'the irate and rampage method' of debate. Downer had claimed that the Convention's findings reflected a united Australia when the delegates achieved unity only by striking out issues of major importance – such as tariff barriers – which exposed the greatest divergence. Symon visualised the Council proceeding in one of two equally unacceptable directions. Either it would have the standing of a parish vestry or a limited company or it would undermine the freedoms our 'fathers' had gained in the form of representative institutions. Accused by the Government of opposing federation, Symon claimed that if the Convention proposal became law the Federal Council itself would be 'a stumbling block to federation'. He hoped one day to see 'all these great colonies ... welded together into one great and powerful and beneficent nation'. The debate on 27 February lapsed for want of a quorum, probably by a 'preconcerted arrangement'.[11]

The 1884 election for the two Sturt seats in the House of Assembly was held on 23 April. Townsend who topped the previous poll had died in 1882 while Thomas King recovered his health to contest and win a by-election. He and Symon worked together for their re-election. Symon was no longer 'an untried man' but there were residual doubts about him as a politician. William Sowden, a satirical columnist who signed himself 'A Scribbler', inserted the following in the *Adelaide Observer* on 1 March 1884:

> A polished speaker, but with voice too unsympathetic; with matter too discursive and manner somewhat cold; with all an eloquent pleader's love of repetition, and with consequent handicapping as a Parliamentary orator; with plenty of ambition and any amount of ability to match it. Who, with a little less of law and a wee bit more of politics, wants but the key of warmer sociability in the Room to open the door of quick success by a majority vote. – 'tis Mr. Symon, friend, who's (parenthetically) a leader of the Opposition.[12]

At least Symon demonstrated he did possess one of the important weapons in a politician's armoury, namely, eye-catching hyperbole. Sharing a platform with King at a meeting in Unley on 24 March, Symon called the Bray Government 'the feeblest and the weakest' in the Colony's history.[13] He did offer substantial evidence to support his claim.

King and Symon expected to be unopposed. At the last minute, a third candidate – named as 'Thomas Errington of Plympton gentleman' – secured a place on the ballot paper. This action provoked the *South Australian Advertiser* to publish a scathing editorial on 16 March. It

'your dogged determination to succeed did most of the climbing.'

said Errington owed his nomination to 'an eccentric few, or a handful of individuals who consider a mock election a lark'. His appearance supported the case for requiring a £50 deposit to be forfeited on not receiving a certain proportion of the vote. Errington in fact never graced any platform, and never published his views about politics or, indeed, about anything. If his nomination had any serious purpose the final voting figures suggest its purpose was to provide Symon's critics with an opportunity to express themselves. Errington received 99 votes against 522 for King and 464 for Symon.

The Bray Government appeared to have survived the 1884 election but was defeated by six votes in the Assembly on 13 June. John Colton had the numbers to receive a commission. Symon, regarded by many as the real Leader of the Opposition, declined Colton's request to join the new ministry as Attorney-General. He was not prepared to sacrifice anything of his private practice. Colton accepted Symon's advice to appoint Kingston to the position, much to the surprise of many who mistakenly assumed Kingston was a 'buffoon'.[14] The new government proceeded to invite Charles Mann, the Crown Solicitor and a former Attorney-General and Treasurer, to fill the vacancy on the Supreme Court caused by the death of Justice Andrews. Mann declined, and the invitation was passed onto Symon. He also declined. Symon had no desire to serve alongside Chief Justice Way; he and Nell wanted to take an extended visit 'home'; he expected to have more children to support and, as a barrister, he could earn a great deal more money while living an independent life. Symon might also have resented being the second cab on the rank. William Bundey QC was worried by the thought of a reduced income but had no qualms about being the third choice. The barrister, whom Symon had said was no lawyer, accepted the appointment and remained on the Bench until his retirement in 1903.[15]

William Symon could still one day expect to inherit the central role in Symon, Bakewell & Symon. On 4 April 1884 he married Laura Louise Stow. It appeared to be a good match. Laura's father, Jefferson Stow, was a former editor of the *South Australian Advertiser* and in 1883 had taken an appointment as a special magistrate in Naracoorte. Jefferson's brother was the late Justice Randolph Stow of the Supreme Court. On Saturday 12 April, the newly-married couple sailed on the *Ballaarat* for London.

They returned to Adelaide well before Jo's planned six-month holiday in the United Kingdom. Jo, Nell, baby Kilmeny and a nurse left Glenelg on 2 January 1886. The other daughters, Margaret and Lenore, remained with staff at home.

It was not the best of times to be overseas. Fraudulent actions by both the manager and the accountant caused the Commercial Bank of South Australia to fail in February 1886. A coincidental depression further affected a range of enterprises and several men of property. Josiah Symon was not immune, and subsequently spent some three years retrieving his financial situation by working longer hours and dispensing with under-performing shares and rental properties.

The Symons saw enough of the depression in the United Kingdom to think more positively about the stories from home. In any case, there was much to see and do. They spent a day enjoying the scenery in Virginia Water of the Borough of Runneymede, had the best seats for plays in London, visited galleries and attended the Countess of Rosebery's reception at the Foreign Office where they met the Prince and Princess of Wales. They travelled to Scotland for Nell to meet more of the family. In London, Symon attended the trial of three members of the Social Democratic Federation – Hyndman, Champion and Burns – charged with sedition following a riot in London. Symon sat on the Bench next to Justice Cave on the first day of the trial which ended in acquittals. As President of the Free Trade Association in South Australia he was delighted when the Cobden Society offered him an honorary membership.

Symon attended further memorable events, two of which he discussed with a reporter when back in Adelaide.[16] He and Nell attended the Queen's official opening of the Colonial and Indian Exhibition of 1886 in South Kensington which was designed to stimulate commerce and strengthen the bonds of Empire. Symon described it as 'a magnificent success' and he 'sincerely' thought that the South Australian 'court' was 'the best'. His assessment was not widely shared, unless he was comparing the exhibits from the settler colonies; the popular attention seemed to be focused on the Indian contribution. Symon said he was fortunate to be placed in a position where Her Majesty passed within a yard of him: the moment 'I shall ever have imprinted on my memory'.

Another event had an even greater effect on him. Symon found in

'your dogged determination to succeed did most of the climbing.'

England that 'the momentous question' of Irish Home Rule 'was the great topic of conversation', certainly among the political circles in which he moved. On the night of 8 April, Gladstone would deliver the second reading speech on his Government's Home Rule Bill. South Australia's Agent-General gave his ticket to Symon who noted how the galleries and the Chamber were soon crammed to the limit. One hundred MPs struggled to find standing room in the Chamber. When Gladstone emerged from behind the Speaker's Chair, he moved quickly to his place between two Liberal stalwarts, Sir William Harcourt and John Morley. Symon noted how 'tremendous cheering' from his own followers and from the Parnellites[17] greeted the Prime Minister's arrival. Gladstone's voice sounded 'husky' when he answered a procedural question so that 'a good many fancied that this great speech was likely, from an elocutionary point of view, to be a failure'. Yet as Gladstone went on 'he seemed physically and mentally as fresh, his voice as ever it was heard'. After three-and-a-half hours, he sat down and this time the cheers, as Symon heard and saw them, came from all sides of the House; 'a tribute of admiration to his power and transcendent greatness as a Parliamentary leader and orator'. Symon would regale others for years how the whole House and the galleries eagerly gazed at 'this old man with his dim figure and pinched-looking care-worn face' as he expounded a policy which one side thought would save the Empire and the other side believed would bring certain ruin.

At the end of February 1887, Robert Barr Smith led a delegation of prominent citizens to meet Symon at his Selborne Chambers in Pirie Street. The delegation included members of the Brighton, Glenelg and Unley Councils, two senior MPs from the House of Assembly and one from the Legislative Council as well as prominent citizens such as John Downer's brother, George. Barr Smith described the deputation as 'very influential, their enthusiasm was great, and their belief he would be returned was firm'. They wished they could guarantee him what he deserved – no-contest – and said it would be a great blunder if the district lost him. Barr Smith explained his own presence: 'It was his personal regard and admiration for his political and private character, his belief in Mr Symon's integrity – and ability, that made them so exceedingly anxious that he should be in the next Parliament.' Symon expressed his appreciation: the delegation's approach would be 'a permanent source of satisfaction throughout what might remain of his political career'.

There was nothing unusual about a delegation in colonial politics approaching a candidate to nominate or re-nominate for a parliamentary seat. It was, however, unusual for two separate delegations from very different seats miles apart from each other to approach the same individual. Symon had to tell Barr Smith he had also received 'a spontaneous invitation from the people of Victoria (District)', the seat located in the south-east of the Colony and which included Mount Gambier. The Victoria District, he told Barr Smith, was 'the birthplace of any success he had had in life' and the people there had been the sponsors for his future career. It would be hard to resist their request, just as it was hard to remain 'insensible' to the Sturt request. After all, he had represented Sturt for six years, was an elector and resident of the district where a large proportion of his property lay. Some constituents had differed with him but had always shown him great kindness 'and had recognised the purity and honesty of his motives'.[18]

Symon finally settled for Victoria District while delaying his nomination until one of the two sitting members, John Bagot a company director, decided not to re-contest the seat. Assuming he wanted to remain in Parliament, Symon seemed to go out of his way to offend large sections of the voters in the Victoria District. His name, background and connections became a good focal point for opposition. A relatively rich man, he opposed payment of members. A member of a profession which protected itself, he opposed tariff protection which offered job opportunities to the disadvantaged. With personal links to the well-positioned squattocracy in Victoria District, he opposed a land tax. Symon was an obvious target for the growing complaints about there being too many lawyers in the House of Assembly. Early in March, the Trades and Labour Council decided that Symon must be defeated in Victoria. The Council inserted a newspaper advertisement in the south-east of the State urging the working classes not to support Symon. It intended to approach the Farmers' Associations with a similar message to small-holders.[19] On 5 March a public meeting in Millicent invited Daniel Livingston, a local store-keeper, to stand for election. Strictly speaking he was not working class; but at least he was not an Adelaide lawyer. The

> 'your dogged determination to succeed did most of the climbing.'

active supporters of Livingston and Friedrich Krichauff MP formed an alliance against Symon and friends urged Symon supporters to 'plump' for him.[20]

In an editorial on 2 April, Mount Gambier's *Border Watch* advocated a vote for Symon while saying it had nothing against the other two candidates. To have Symon sitting in Parliament would constitute 'a distinct gain' for the south-east and 'a greater gain' for the Colony as a whole. The 'birthplace' of success in his career soundly rebuffed Symon on Wednesday 6 April. He received 348 votes against 800 for Livingston and 767 for Krichauff.[21] He might not have fared much better in Sturt. J.G. Jenkins, a future Premier, who was a protectionist and favoured payment of members and a progressive land tax, had a very handsome win in that seat.

When it was all over, Symon inserted a note in the *Border Watch* for 13 April: 'To the Electors of Victoria.'. He thanked those who voted for him and the many friends who actively supported him. 'Your great District, whose welfare I have hitherto endeavoured to promote, needs effective representation. This I sincerely hope you may always secure. I bid you respectfully farewell.' Approached several times in the 1890s to nominate again for the House of Assembly, he turned them all down. He saw himself primarily as a lawyer in a successful private practice. Colonial politics and a colonial ministry demanded too much of his first love and its material rewards.

Symon was, however, prepared to expand his business interests. In 1887-8 he took over the mortgage of the Auldana Vineyard Company and became sole proprietor of 116 acres of the best grape varieties developed in South Australia. The vineyard was situated near Magill, about six miles from Adelaide, on the sloping sides of the lower portion of the Mount Lofty range. Patrick Auld, a Scottish-born vigneron, had bought and developed the site from the 1860s, managing it for a group of proprietors – eventually including Symon – and gave the Auldana name a standing in the Australian colonies, England, Europe and the United States. Auld's son, Patrick, took over from his father but left the vineyard in 1888. By this time, Symon had appointed the French winemaker Edmond Mazure to manage the estate. In May 1888 Symon contemplated selling Auldana for £22,000. He soon appreciated that Mazure's reputation and Auldana's quality whites and reds provided him with status as well as substantial financial returns. Auldana, speculative mining investments and full employment as a barrister soon enabled Symon to recover from the setbacks of the mid-1880s.[22]

On 23 January 1888, the Symons acquired another daughter; sadly, Una Daphne Lois died five months later. Romilly Josiah Edward, a second son, arrived on 19 August 1889. Jo intimated to Jim some months later that Romilly was not progressing at the same rate as his siblings.[23] Within a short time, Jo and Nell had to accept Romilly's intellectual disability. They decided he must be greatly loved and sheltered. Although Romilly remained at home, his parents became personally and financially involved in 'Minda' (a Karuna word meaning 'place of shelter and protection'), the 'Home for Weak Minded Children', which was founded in 1898.

Jo spent more of his family time in the late 1880s dealing with problems presented by two of his siblings. Bob kept pressing him to agree to his migration to South Australia. Jo was not convinced Bob would succeed in the printing industry and feared his brother would become a dependent. Bob had long owed Jim £100 and, after taking over the debt, Jo gently suggested that Bob might consider repaying some or all of it. Bob did not respond so, thinking of his own financial difficulties, Jo proposed to charge five per cent interest, waived if Bob immediately repaid £50. Bob appears to have been unabashed. He sent letters to his older brothers with a hare-brained scheme he thought would make a lot of money. Bob raised their hackles by couching the proposal in what the brothers considered to be offensive language.[24]

Bill presented the more severe problem. When he returned to Adelaide in 1886, Jo became increasingly aware that his brother did not share the senior partner's work ethic. Jo also learnt that Bill had borrowed heavily from the firm and was in debt to the ES&A Bank. Confronted with his debt to the firm, Bill decided to tell Jo more about his financial woes. In a letter dated 7 March 1887 Bill admitted owing £900 to Jo, £800 to Bakewell, £300 to the ES&A Bank, £200 to another bank as well as two major loans totaling £5000. 'In these melancholy circumstances what I propose is to come to some arrangement which I am certain I can privately effect.' He set out a 'plan' to repay where he could by cutting expenditure, selling furniture and cashing insurance policies. Bill accepted he was entirely in

> 'your dogged determination to succeed did most of the climbing.'

Jo's hands and would leave the firm if required but he could stay on until Bakewell's return from leave.[25]

The 'plan' did not work, and matters came to a head in March-April 1889. Jo finally acknowledged what he should have recognised much earlier. Bill was an alcoholic. Jo wrote to him on 23 March 1889 to say he could no longer tolerate his 'total neglect of business'. Remonstrances and warnings were in vain; all he had said and written had been ignored or forgotten. As further forbearance would make no difference, Jo intended to dissolve the partnership on 30 March. If Bill wanted to talk to him, he should make an evening appointment during the following week; Jo's daytime hours were fully taken up with court work.

Jo explained in a letter to Jim on 1 April that Bill was 'never very energetic nor has he ever displayed much zeal or earnestness in his profession'. For the last three years 'his inattention to business has gone from bad to worse …[and] during the last twelve months … all his easy going self-indulgent disposition and a number of unfortunate companions have led him into wasteful habits, a want of regard of money, and drinking'. Until recently, Jo imagined that Bill's worst fault was inattention to work. He now realised that his brother's 'drinking and boozing in public houses' caused this lack of attention. It will be recalled that in 1886 a Scottish doctor advised Jo about his own drinking, and he had learnt to exercise control. Jo assumed that Bill simply needed pulling into line. He saw it as a matter of character. Waterhouse in Mount Gambier did not have it or exercise it. Bill was in the same position. Jo was not unsympathetic; he just did not recognise that warnings and financial inducements were not sufficient to combat a 'disease'.

Apparently, Jo and Bill did have a conversation, and the former explained the revised arrangements to Bill's wife Laura. Jo said he hoped they would 'relieve your mind in one or two respects'. He had placed his brother on an annual salary for the first year of £450, of which £350 was available at weekly amounts of £6/14/0 with the balance held back for debt repayments. Bill would be handed the weekly amounts in cash; he was not to open or keep a bank account. Laura was relieved; she felt as if 'risen from hell into heaven' and assured her brother-in-law she would help Bill to keep his promise and 'to try & pay off what we owe'.[26] Bill said all the right things to his brother:

> I very gladly & willingly pledge my word of honour that I will devote my whole time & attention to the business in your interests, and I will abstain from touching all intoxicating liquor for a period of twelve months. I hope this will be acceptable to you, & that I may very shortly regain your confidence, & I hope I may still remain, Your affectionate Brother.[27]

Jo told Jim on 15 April that their brother was doing 'thoroughly well'. He was 'quite sure what has happened will be a lesson & a warning of great value to him'. Jim and Jo, alone, should know of what had occurred. In the meantime, 'I have no doubt that Bill will soon establish a better future for himself'.

In July, Laura told Jo she now realised it was 'useless' to expect Bill's 'total reform'. She needed to find a job to deal with debt. Her own family could not find £5 and Laura did not want to rely on Jo to help Bill again, 'though poor fellow he'd be in a sorry way once you say good-bye to him for good'. Laura wrote again to Jo on 26 September returning £50 which appeared to be part of the £71 cheque he had handed to his brother. She said it was 'useless' trying to help them; Bill 'has been as bad as ever these last two days' and of the £1 missing from the cheques he had cashed she could only find eleven shillings in his pockets, meaning 'he calmly spent (nine shillings) on his own pleasures'. Laura and the children went to live with the Stow family, Bill decided to visit his other brother, David, in Western Australia,[28] and Jo gave up trying.

By the end of the 1880s, Symon had reached the pinnacle as the leader of the Adelaide Bar. He also had a special reputation as a criminal barrister who either won improbable victories or obliged judges and juries to be very sure of their ground. One of those victories occurred in the Supreme Court in June 1889.

Albert John Bonney, a house painter, returned home from a fishing trip at 9.00 pm on Saturday 20 April 1889. He found his wife, Johanna Gertrude Bonney, passed out, drunk, on the floor of their bedroom. He tried unsuccessfully to lift her onto their bed, and then prepared a meal for their daughter, Lillie, the eldest and sole survivor of their four children. Bonney went to bed and rose around 8.00 am to find that his wife remained prone on the floor. Accepting she was dead he went a police station and a doctor was summoned to the Bonney home. Dr Thomas

'your dogged determination to succeed did most of the climbing.'

Corbin certified that Johanna was dead and her body was taken to the mortuary where Corbin performed a post-mortem. Bonney was later charged with murdering his wife. Appearing before the City Coroner and a jury on 25 April he was committed for trial, the jury having complimented Dr Corbin for his care in preparing and delivering his evidence.

Bonney did not have the means to pay counsel and, given that a conviction for murder carried the death penalty, it was important for him to have good legal representation. His employer, D.F. Harrison & Co, Painters and Decorators of Adelaide, had asked 'Symon Bakewell & Co' on 23 April to take a watching brief for the case. William Symon had attended the inquest on Bonney's behalf. On 6 May Justice Boucaut ordered the Sheriff to pay £50 to William Symon to prepare Bonney's defence and to retain counsel and summon witnesses. Bonney's employer agreed on 22 May to contribute ten guineas to Josiah Symon's fee, as well as a doctor's fee of two guineas, but could not guarantee more. The Chief Secretary on 5 June 1889 agreed to grant 'Our Royal Licence' to Symon QC as counsel for the prisoner 'as often as there may be occasion' in the specific case.[29]

Public sympathy sided with Bonney. Details emerged of an upright young man aged 28 who had been married for eight years to an habitual drunkard who had failed in her 'duties' as a wife and mother to keep a clean and tidy house and to feed her family. Life for him had been 'hell'. If found not guilty, his mother would be his sole help in bringing up his daughter.

The trial was set down for Wednesday and Thursday, 5–6 June. The Crown Solicitor and Public Prosecutor, Charles Mann QC, appeared to have a very strong case. Dr Corbin, the key Crown witness, had deposed on oath that the cause of death was shock partly caused by haemorrhage but 'chiefly by injuries done to internal organs' as 'the result of violence'.

Some of the bruises could have been caused by falls but other injuries Corbin identified could not have been self-inflicted. Contrary to expectations, he also found no evidence of alcoholic poisoning. The deceased was 'a healthy, well-nourished woman'. So what did occur inside the house? Here the neighbours, the Websters, with no record of hostility to the Bonneys, reported hearing the following through paper-thin walls at around 3 am on the Sunday: 'I will murder you'; 'oh, don't Johnny'; 'you dirty low bitch what did you do with the money I gave you?';

Lillie crying out, 'Oh Papa, don't kill Mama'; and the sound of someone being picked up and thrown down. Well after the event a blood-stained hatchet was found inside the house and near where Corbin first saw the body.

Symon prepared at some length, judging by his notes and underlining of testimony taken at the inquest.[30] He did not call witnesses; Symon wanted to hammer the point that, apart from Lillie, there was no one who saw anything. Rather, he relied on a technique which had served him well in representing the defence in criminal cases. He took the Crown witnesses through their evidence highlighting inconsistencies, their reliance on speculation and without observation and, above all, showing where the Crown case depended on a theory about what did happen or must have happened behind closed doors. He deliberately involved Corbin in an argument about what might have happened in order to underscore the many areas of doubt. Symon was so effective in destabilising Corbin's certainties that the Chief Justice ('friend Way') in his summing up said Counsel had been unfair to him; Corbin was there to describe what happened to the body and to answer questions, not to comment on a theory. Symon dealt quickly and effectively with the hatchet, and Chief Justice Way on this occasion broadly supported him. While Corbin thought it could have been used in killing, Symon simply pointed out it did not fit the size of a key wound, that Bonney had used it to chop wood and its arrival in the bedroom after the inquest may have been a 'police dodge'.

In his final address, Symon pulled together an argument highlighting all the areas of doubt and urged the jury to treat every doubt in Bonney's favour. He contrasted this 'poor wretched woman' who had been a sad curse to herself, her husband and her family with 'a kind and affectionate father' and good son of his widowed mother. Using a formula which had worked in the past and would do so in the future, he prayed that, convinced as he was of Bonney's innocence, he had not failed to make the jury see the truth. After speaking for 90 minutes Symon sat down 'amid subdued applause'. The Chief Justice emphasised Counsel's point about the need to prove 'malice aforethought' and the jury retired. It was out for 20–25 minutes and returned with a verdict of 'Not Guilty' and,

'your dogged determination to succeed did most of the climbing.'

by implication, cleared Bonney of manslaughter. The consensus in and around the courtroom was that Bonney's barrister had saved him from the gallows.[31]

At the end of a very difficult year personally, Symon decided to take a four-week holiday by himself in New Zealand. He told Jim that Chief Justice Way was 'a travelling companion' on the boat: 'I hope we shall enjoy the trip.'[32]

6

'There is a first place and you alone occupy it.'

Josiah Symon entered the final decade of the 19th century as a happily married man and the head of an expanding family. Acknowledged as the leader of the South Australian Bar, he had acquired substantial chambers in Adelaide, a convenient house in 'town' and a successful and improving vineyard. Symon was in demand in the 1890s to head and address federal and literary bodies. The young man who never had a university education sat on the Council of Adelaide's university (1893–1901), alongside another non-graduate, Samuel Way, who had been its Vice-Chancellor and from 1883 to 1916 its Chancellor. In 1891 Symon took possession of a new estate – 'Manoah' (place of rest) in the lower Mount Lofty ranges – which would evolve into a working farm with a dairy and an orchard. After many additions it became the grand home of Upper Sturt, 'prettily situated on an eminence between two gullies',[1] extended to accommodate overseas and local visitors of importance as well as what grew into a family of twelve. 'Manoah' had a tower from which to survey beautiful surroundings, a tennis court, gardens and substantial servants' quarters. For Symon, however, the pride of 'Manoah' was his ever-expanding 'gentleman's library' which provided cerebral enrichment and the resources and the solitude for reading and writing.

The federation decade began well when a Convention in Sydney approved a draft constitution for Australia. The momentum faded during 1891–4, especially in NSW where a new politician, George Reid, emerged as a prominent opponent. Nonetheless, federation revived as a popular movement which brought the politicians back to the forefront leading to the election of delegates for the Convention of 1897–8, two referenda,

'There is a first place and you alone occupy it.'

approval by the Imperial Parliament, endorsement by Queen Victoria and the launch of a federated Australia in January 1901. Symon made it clear several times in the 1880s that he supported federation but opposed the Federal Council which he saw as an obstacle to its formation. Elected unopposed in January 1895 as President of the South Australian branch of the Australasian Federation League, he made vigorous speeches in support of federation, won election as a South Australian delegate to the 1897-8 Convention and chaired its judiciary committee, worked hard in the two referenda and demanded an unamended approval of the Constitution by the Imperial Parliament.

Despite the distractions caused by his brothers during 1890, Symon had a full working year at the Bar. He returned refreshed from his four-week break in New Zealand at the beginning of 1891. Symon was eager to learn the fate of the Sydney Convention for which Kingston, the Attorney-General, and Thomas Playford, the Premier, were two of the six South Australian representatives. Inglis Clark of Tasmania, Kingston and Samuel Griffith, the Premier of Queensland, had produced draft constitutions. Kingston's exertions earned him a reputation as a skilled legal draftsman. On 19 March 1891 he sent a telegram to Symon seeking his advice on a proposal to disallow appeals to the Privy Council from the highest court in Australia. Kingston's action began a decade of topsy-turvy relations with his longstanding friend.

Symon replied on the same day to 'My dear Charlie'. He went straight to the point: 'Don't abolish appeals.' Symon observed that the Canadians had kept the existing system while the United States had 'cut the painter'. In Australia's case, 'it would be a calamity at present to sweep away this appeal'. That time might come when Australia's population reached 20 to 30 million. For now, '(t)he tribunal of ultimate resort should be removed as far as possible from local circumstances'. Kingston voted for a resolution approving the abolition of appeals except for cases where the public interest of the Commonwealth or of any State or other part of the Queen's dominions was concerned. This decision was approved with Inglis Clark's casting vote and later ratified at the full Convention by 22 votes to 19. At the 1897-8 Convention Symon joined Kingston in supporting the total removal of appeals to the Privy Council from the High Court.

Concluding his letter with a message for Playford, Symon wrote: 'I agree with him. Federation is the task of politicians & not of the people.' In 1899, when the Constitution had been approved by the second referendum, both Kingston and Symon interpreted any amendments sought by the Imperial Parliament or by dissidents in Australia as a defiance of the 'Australian people'.

Next day, Symon sent a longer letter to Kingston telling him that the Convention had aroused no interest in Adelaide. Dull articles appeared frequently in the *Register* and occasionally in the *Advertiser*, 'read I should imagine by nobody'. Symon thought there would be more satisfaction if, instead of returning with a constitution, they came home without one. South Australians would be looking to the protection of State rights and of the weak. If Kingston wanted to do something popular he might propose Adelaide as the capital of a federated Australia; such a suggestion 'would stir up a little more interest here in the "talk" of federation'. Symon concluded by reiterating his views on appeals to the Privy Council while leaving open the means whereby the Federal Parliament could vote for their cessation.[2]

The benefits of the New Zealand trip had long disappeared by the end of 1891 when Symon was now affected by back trouble. To recover, Symon arranged a four-month trip to India, England and Scotland. Nell chose to stay at home. She had to care for a new baby – Oscar Sturt, born 28 March 1891 – as well as Romilly who required special attention. Nell had reliable domestic staff and a nurse to help her at home and never wanted an excursion where her 'big husband', as Nell called him, would have 'rushed about' – his words – and fatigued her.[3]

Symon left Largs Bay jetty, just north of Adelaide, on the SS *Orotava* on 30 December 1891. Felix Cowle, Nell's younger brother, accompanied him to Albany. Symon provided Felix with letters of introduction to four of his good legal and vigneron contacts in Perth. Jo's brother, David, met him at Albany, 'looking uncommonly well, getting bigger and more muscular than ever' and 'quite the Parliamentary member amongst the people ... and evidently popular and hail-fellow-well-met with them all'. David planned to host a public banquet in Perth for Jo but, as his older brother shrank at the thought, David, 'as he meanly puts it, has saved about £50 or £60'. As for Bill, now separated and living in the West, Jo learnt 'he got £75 from David!! He is, I fear, irredeemable ... And David naturally is furious at the upshot.'

'There is a first place and you alone occupy it.'

In the letters the 'big husband' wrote to 'My own Nell', Jo liked to tell her of the places he visited and of the individuals and 'races' he encountered. For this biographer, another principal interest lies in what he said about the place of Nell and the children in his life.

Jo decided on 1 January that in terms of 'happiness' this trip, so far, 'is a mistake'. It may be good for his health but shorter trips within South Australia would be, as Nell had pointed out to him at Largs Bay, 'more sensible'. Jo continued:

> My only desire to visit England now is with you and the children. I never felt till now the full strength of the silken threads and hooks of steel by which I am bound. It is wrong to say so, but I do not seem to care to see even my mother and sisters unless I can produce to them all my treasures, Nell, and say – these are my jewels.

In a later letter he began writing about the ship. The captain, the discipline, the attendance, the 'table' – all impressed him. He moved quickly to a more important subject: 'My health and strength are yours, my darling and all our little ones, even more than they are my own. This is a duty holiday. I cannot have any real pleasure holiday till I have you all with me.' Later, he had another thought: 'When the final parting comes we must all seek strength from God to bear it but till then we must have no more long separations.'

Most of his comments about Nell and the family were made during the long days sailing between ports. Jo hated tedium and, apart from a Colonel Campbell and his war stories, his fellow passengers offered little relief between Albany and Ceylon. Symon broke some of the monotony by holding a wine party where he served some of the two dozen bottles of St Henri claret and the mixed biscuits that Mazure, the Auldana estate manager, had put on board the *Orotava*. A guest who claimed to be a connoisseur said he would never have believed he was drinking Australian wine had he not been told. Jo's mood darkened as the ship neared Ceylon, and not because of memories of landing at Galle in 1876. He learnt that he would be staying longer in Ceylon than desired and he wrote to the agent in Adelaide asking for a rebate. Jo mentioned in this letter how much he was missing his family. Perhaps he did think of them more when he was bored or unhappy. On rare occasions Jo could and did unleash inner feelings.

The letters he wrote about Ceylon reflected attitudes common to many Anglo-Celts of the late 19th century. Jo hated Colombo, partly because the 'natives' were so noisy. He did hesitate about taking a rickshaw: 'such a brutal use to put your fellowman to.' Apparently, Colonel Campbell assured him they were not fellowmen and did not have souls. Jo was not reassured by this observation but by the experience: 'when you get into the thing an active, muscular "nigger" runs off with you at the rate of 6 or 7 miles an hour and keeps it going for miles "without turning a hair" you begin to think it is one of the nicest modes of progression ever invented.' Symon was relieved to discover splendid scenery inland from Colombo where there were no beggars and the 'natives' seemed 'well-to-do'.

He spent over a week in the company of the English, Scottish and Irish tea planters of Ceylon. They gave him the 'good advice' Symon repeated on returning to Adelaide. Of all the 'native' labour in these parts of the world, 'the Tamil is far and away the best … docile, industrious … very free from the racial prejudices and other characteristics which make other native labourers difficult of management'. The one problem was supply. As the tea planters had to seek Tamil labour in southern India, it would be hard to procure such labour for the Northern Territory which South Australia had administered since 1863.[4] Jo liked the tea planters. They showed 'a better breeding' than the Australian squatters 'and look and talk like thorough English gentlemen'. There was 'none of the Australian democratic feeling' among the Europeans in Ceylon. Better still, 'they are all monarchical and very loyal'. His new friends spoke 'with bated breath of the bereavement of the Royal Family' when they learnt of the 'terribly sad event' which occurred while Symon was in Ceylon. The Duke of Clarence, the eldest son of the Prince of Wales and the heir presumptive to the throne, died at the age of 28 of the influenza pandemic sweeping through the UK.

Leaving Ceylon, Symon cast his eye over his fellow passengers on their way to Bombay. The 5th Baron Ashburton and Lady Ashburton and Ashburton's brother, the Hon, Frederick Arthur Baring, 'are our most aristocratic travellers'. They held themselves aloof and 'are either idiots or snobs'. After travelling through the Indian Raj, Jo delivered a final judgement: 'The Ashburton party and a couple of Jews … are all equally cads.' Some 'types' he encountered could by their attitudes threaten

'There is a first place and you alone occupy it.'

the security of the Indian Empire. In Delhi he asked a Captain of the Grenadier Company of the 81st Regiment if there was any chance of another 'Indian Mutiny' (1857–9). The officer told him it would depend on their getting a leader. He also related a story about a Hindu Rajah who had been invited to dine at the Regimental Mess and overheard someone asking, 'What is that d—d nigger doing here?' The Rajah made an excuse to leave and never came back. The Captain told Symon that the English are 'too arrogant'. Later, in Delhi, Jo exercised his own form of arrogance. The 'natives' were a problem wherever he went. Jo wrote of the crowds gathered around the Great Mosque in Delhi that 'you can scarcely conceive how filthy these people can be'. The 'natives' of India, unlike the princes, did not please this tourist.

Jo felt remorseful after reading one of Nell's letters. 'I ought never to have come away and left you with all the responsibilities. You were really suffering more than you would admit … I know you bravely tried not to show it for my sake.' He made a resolution: 'we must forever share our trials and troubles, our good and bad ill health, and good and bad fortune together … you must never persuade me for health's sake or anything else to leave you like this.' Jo had never before realised 'the full height and depth and length … of my love for my wife and children'. Once again, he felt bound to lower the place of 'my dear old mother' and sisters 'in my inmost heart'. He felt like a traitor but Nell would know what he meant. 'There is a first place and you alone occupy it.'

While in Bombay, Symon met more than his match in height and weight when he encountered Tom Playford. Premier Playford was visiting India with his wife, ostensibly in search of 'coolie labour' to assist development in the Northern Territory. Jo told Nell that 'old Tom Playford' was wearing a pith helmet because 'he thinks it makes the niggers or black devils, as he calls them, look after him'. Playford reported to Kingston, the Acting Premier, that Symon looked 'very well and jolly' as he showed Mrs Playford the various Indian-made items he had bought for family members in the UK. The three of them had a very pleasant night together.[5]

Jo described what he saw in India: the birds, vegetation, natives, hotel rooms, the food and buildings. He found the Taj Mahal more wonderful 'than I had ever dreamed', rode an elephant which shook him 'to pieces', loved the peacocks but detested monkeys ('nasty creatures') and alligators ('loathsome looking reptiles'). Symon admired and liked the Maharajah of the princely estate of Jeypore, describing him as an 'enlightened prince' who had established an excellent hospital and museum – called 'Albert Hall', to commemorate the visit of the Prince of Wales – 'one of the finest and most beautiful buildings'. He felt much the same about the buildings in the European quarter of Bombay. The courts of justice were finer than those in England while the Victoria Railway Station was probably the finest he had ever seen. He also admired the work emanating from the Agra Gaol where he bought a carpet for Nell. The Queen and German Emperor had acquired their carpets there so Nell's present was 'in good company'. Jo refused to reveal the price until he knew she liked the carpet. He offered one hint: 'I felt a little extravagant in buying it.'

The sea trip from India to the UK took too long for someone who really wanted to be going home to Adelaide. Symon complained to Nell that neither the food nor his fellow passengers relieved the tedium. He told her that the next trip, which would involve all the family, must be well planned. The ship called at Aden where Jo learnt the sad news that Elizabeth's husband, Geordie Nicholson, had died. He knew that everyone connected to the family in Stirling would have been shaken by the death of such a well-liked man. In Ismailia, Symon posted an article, subsequently published in the *South Australian Register* on 1 April, commenting on a piece in the English press supporting the abolition of the judicial oath.

Writing from England on 11 March, Symon said the weather made him 'miserable & nervous'. In London 'its vileness is intensified by the dull, heavy, foggy, filthy atmosphere', and his voice became hoarse at the end of the day 'from breathing the solids of the Metropolis'. Symon called on the new South Australian Agent-General, Sir John Bray, visited the Colonial Institute and saw Jim and his new family.[6] He went 'home' to see his mother and sisters, presumably without disclosing his message to Nell that her letters constituted 'the only real pleasure this trip gives me'. The weather remained 'infamous', although the winter he experienced was not as bad as the previous one or the two which followed his time in the UK. More seriously, a doctor advised he was not fit to travel and would have to delay his departure date for Adelaide by a fortnight. Yet a visiting South Australian who met him in Cheapside in March thought

'There is a first place and you alone occupy it.'

he looked 'exceedingly well'.[7] Originally booked to leave England on 18 March, Symon departed on 10 April, reached Largs Bay on 11 May and went immediately to Upper Sturt.

In June 1892 William Holder became Premier after the Assembly carried his no-confidence motion against the Playford Government. In October, John Downer succeeded Holder following another successful no-confidence motion, and Richard Baker became the Leader of the Government in the Legislative Council. On 14 December, Baker said in the Council he had been attacked by a gentleman (Kingston) 'well known to be as big a coward as he was a big bully, who was a member of and a disgrace to the legal profession'. Next day, Kingston retaliated in the House of Assembly, claiming he had proved Baker 'to be false as a friend, treacherous as a colleague, mendacious as a man, and utterly untrustworthy in every relationship of public life'. Kingston backed his words by challenging Baker to a duel. He acquired a pair of matched pistols, sent one to Baker and informed him of the time for their duel in Victoria Square, Adelaide, on 23 December 1892. Baker informed the police about Kingston's intentions and they arrested Kingston shortly after he arrived at the Square carrying a loaded revolver.

Kingston briefed Symon to defend him. He appeared to dissociate himself from his barrister in the court room, possibly angry because Symon had forewarned him of the approach he felt obliged to take. Symon admitted all the facts laid out in the police information. He advised the defendant – as any counsel would – to submit to any orders about keeping the Queen's peace and to agree to any sureties which the magistrates might require. Counsel cited authorities supporting his position that the information might be withdrawn if the defendant gave those assurances. The Crown Solicitor (J.M. Stuart) agreed, and Baker was heard to remark, 'a farce as I expected'. The magistrates accepted the arrangements and bound Kingston over to keep the peace for 12 months. The Speaker of the Assembly and a prominent solicitor agreed to provide sureties of £250 each.[8] Kingston gave no sign of being happy with the outcome and in August 1893 was still disputing Symon's fee.[9]

By late 1892 it was known in political circles that Kingston and Symon were growing apart over politics. Lord Kintore, the Governor of South Australia since April 1889,[10] invited Symon to dine at Government House on 2 January 1893. Edward Milner, the Governor's ADC, sent letters to separate addresses to make sure that Symon knew Kingston would be a fellow guest. In one Milner wrote, 'I do not know if you meet him in society or not.' In the other he said, on the Governor's suggestion, 'I think it only right to tell you that Mr Kingston will be there but trust that political differences do not interfere with social intercourse'.[11]

The April 1893 election and its aftermath divided Symon and Kingston as never before. Kingston's more radical Liberals aligned themselves with the Holder and Playford factions and won 23 seats in the election. The newly-formed United Labor Party secured ten seats and supported the Liberal alliance. The Governor subsequently commissioned Kingston to form a government which held office under his leadership for six years, then a record term in South Australia. Downer's Conservatives constituted the 21-seat Opposition. Although more strongly placed in the Legislative Council, the Conservatives could not halt the Government's far-reaching political, social and economic reform program. Kingston enfranchised women and established a state bank, a high protective tariff, passed industrial relations and factory legislation and increased the rates of land and income taxation.

Josiah Symon had not entered the 1893 election campaign except to chair a public meeting at the Upper Sturt post office. The Labor candidates for the two Sturt seats were Tom Price, a future Premier, and Henry Adams, a future member of the Legislative Council and President of the Trades and Labour Council. They wanted to address a meeting in the district and probably asked Symon, regarded as the local squire, to preside. Symon left the chair in order to ask questions and make a speech. He declared himself 'as democratic as any man born' and spoke warmly of the intelligence and suitability of the two Labor candidates. Nonetheless, Symon moved the successful motion declining to support them on polling day.[12] Price topped the poll in Sturt by one vote. John Jenkins, the American-born sitting member, took the second seat, defeating Adams by just 21 votes. Following the poll, Symon invited Price and Adams to visit 'Manoah' on the afternoon of 6 May. Both regretted having to decline Symon's 'very kind invitation'; they had genuine prior engagements. Price appreciated Symon's letter of congratulations saying, 'your admiration of our Party, with the kind and frank manner which

'There is a first place and you alone occupy it.'

you have stated the same, is further evidence of your noble character'.[13]

The serious break with Kingston began on Symon's part with the Government's seeming determination to downgrade and humiliate the Governor. Lord Kintore thought his term of office was due to end in April 1894, and he wanted to take leave of absence toward the end of 1893 to attend to private business. The Kingston Government sought to take advantage of the Governor's early departure by saving money in the depressed economic conditions of 1893. Acting on a suggestion of the *Adelaide Advertiser* on 18 May, the Government decided to make Chief Justice Way a long-term 'temporary' replacement for Lord Kintore when the Governor took his leave of absence in December. Forsaking his judicial salary of £2500, Way would do two jobs for the price of the Governor's annual salary of £5000. Way would sit for some cases but the other two judges – Bundey and Boucaut – were expected to share the rest of the load without additional remuneration.

After initially accepting the Government's proposal, Bundey soon changed his mind and with Symon's help drafted a letter of protest. Normally a man of 'equable temper',[14] an aroused Bundey described the proposal as 'unfair' and said the 'whole burden' fell upon two of the three judges of the Supreme Court and retrenched the judiciary in a manner 'both irregular and unconstitutional'. Bundey foresaw a damaging outcome of Kingston's approach to executive and judicial powers as the loss of judicial independence at the hands of the executive. In preparing his response Kintore obtained from Symon, with Bundey's permission, copies of the judge's letters. Symon spent several hours on the night of 3 July at Government House dining with the Governor and drafting a telegram for Lord Ripon, the Secretary of State for the Colonies. Symon's major contribution consisted of preparing the memorandum which, after Kintore's minor changes, became the Governor's six-page despatch to Ripon of 19 July.[15] Symon argued that the retrenchment decision was autocratic and anti-democratic, made without consulting parliament let alone the people of South Australia. Retrenchment opened the way for the Government never to recommend a new appointment or allow it to introduce an elected governorship. Using Chief Justice Way as a long-term 'temporary' appointment also breached the principle of the separation of executive and judicial powers and functions.

Sir Josiah Symon KCMG KC

Kintore sent a message to Symon after it was all over: 'I shall always be grateful to you for much timely help.[16] Lord Ripon settled one issue. He informed Kintore that his term of office was six years. So, the Governor duly went on leave, Way acted in his place, and Kintore remained Governor until April 1895.

Whereas Symon's involvement with the Governor's difficulties never attracted public attention, Symon and Kingston engaged in a very public slanging match towards the end of 1893 over Symon's involvement in a land dispute. In 1892 Symon accepted a brief from the Government of the day, of which Kingston was the Chief Secretary, for an opinion on whether and under what circumstances the Crown could resume land leases. In June 1892 Symon advised that it could resume leases if it required the land for purposes of public utility. He changed his mind, however, after listening to Kingston's persuasive arguments during a private discussion and withdrew his original advice. Curiously in 1893, when Kingston was both Premier and Attorney-General, the Government acted on the original Symon advice and resumed leases in a particular case, the details of which are not of concern here. In these circumstances, Symon felt at liberty to accept a brief to act for the leaseholders against the Government.

In what one newspaper described as the Premier's characteristically 'uncompromising style',[17] Kingston accused Symon in parliament on 26 October 1893 of breaching professional etiquette. In the two decades they had known each other, Kingston would have been aware that nothing could hurt Symon more than to impugn his personal and professional integrity. On 27 October and 2 November, Symon responded with letters published in the *South Australian Register*. He referred to Kingston's 'violent and unscrupulous personal attack made upon me by that prince of traducers'. It evinced 'a diabolical though a cheap kind of courage to slander ... an absent man' when speaking under parliamentary privilege. In the course of explaining his words and actions, he attacked Kingston's 'gross misrepresentations and offensive insinuations', 'sheer calumny' and 'farrago of invention'. In the second letter Symon observed that before Kingston had 'ruthlessly assailed' his professional honour he had claimed to be on 'the friendliest terms'. Indeed, half an hour before Kingston's eruption he and three of his colleagues exchanged friendly

'There is a first place and you alone occupy it.'

salutations with Symon when passing him in the street. There was no hint of grievance or complaint 'or that they were on their way to breathe forth fire and slaughter against me'.

Between writing these two letters Symon wrote to the Crown Solicitor returning his retainers from the Government:

> I decline to accept any further briefs or retainers from the Government so long as Mr. C.C. Kingston is its chief law officer. No counsel of self-respect could possibly give his services to any client who could – in reckless disregard of every principle, not only of professional propriety but of fair play – publicly malign him as the Attorney-General has wantonly maligned me.[18]

Symon continued to seethe well beyond November 1893. In July 1894 Justice Bundey had invited him to dinner at the Bundey home. Bundey explained that Kingston would also be a guest. Symon asked, 'with a real sense of disappointment' if he might be excused because attendance would require 'a sacrifice of self-respect'. There were 'some injuries not to be lightly condoned, and I am unwilling even to seem to palliate Mr Kingston's conduct to me by consenting to meet him in the Society of a friend's house'.[19]

As a lawyer Symon remained more than ever in demand. He also became a popular choice as a lecturer. In July 1893 Symon addressed the Port Adelaide branch of the Caledonian Society. He described a national literature as a precious possession; it 'fed and strengthened patriotism' and became 'a large factor in a people's greatness'. Symon dated Scotland's marked progress in literary acquirements from 'the assured introduction of Protestantism'. Symon reeled off writers who had both a contemporary and lasting reputation, including John Knox, David Hume, Adam Smith and Robert Louis Stevenson. Symon placed Sir Walter Scott and his historical novels above them all. This 'most kindly, tender, and pure of writers' had given to Scotland 'a citizenship of literature'.

Shakespeare became a favourite subject for a public performance. Symon explained to his audiences, including those supplied by the University Shakespeare Society, that he did not come before them 'as a Shakespearian student of the so-called critical orders'. He was just 'a humble admirer of the great poet' who had been 'a pilgrim to the Mecca

[Stratford-upon-Avon] of his worshippers'. His perennial topic in 1894-7 was the quotable Shakespeare.[20] The Bard offered insights and tutoring with phrases and words covering such subjects as love, death, murder, anger, defiance, drunkenness and all the pleasures of life. Symon said we 'go to him for everything; the grave, the melancholy, the merry – all find aptness and sweetness in his expression'. A reporter for the *Evening Journal* in 1894 claimed that a 'large audience' was 'held in rapt attention to a masterly and most delightful discourse'. Perhaps what surprised them most was the extent to which everyday language drew upon quotations from Shakespeare. According to Symon, 'we' did not regard using quotations from Shakespeare as 'plagiarism' but 'an inheritance', even though his argument was that 'we' freely use Shakespearean words and phrases in ignorance of their origin.

In September 1894 Symon addressed the Young South Australian Patriotic Association with a call to arms in defence of democracy. He urged the young to resist the demagogues and to stand up for democracy, to cling tenaciously to law and order and respect private property. The Patriotic Association claimed that Symon's 'exceedingly able and statesmanlike address ... attracted a great deal of attention throughout Australia'.[21]

Symon took his public appearances to another level when on 19 November 1894 he addressed a meeting of the Australian Natives' Association (ANA) in Adelaide.[22] This speech marked the beginning of his sustained promotion of federation. He began by saying that the ANA was the antithesis of Disraeli's cosmopolitan who loves every country but his own.[23] 'You are devoted to your common country; you seek her welfare; and you are united to advance her interests and maintain the Australian sentiment.' Symon, however, did not hide his resentment; he was not native-born so did not qualify for membership of the ANA. Why was it necessary to divide South Australians into sections? After all, the English did not have an association for English natives in London and the French did not have organisations for the French natives of Paris.

Symon expressed some classically conservative views as he proceeded to develop a broader argument against dividing the people. First, as noted earlier, he attacked the Government, without ever mentioning Kingston's name, for its 'socialistic' and Labor policies. Symon saw himself as a democrat. 'Popular power, the power of the people, is everything', he said, 'but it is of the whole people not of a section or of a class'. Class antagonisms would ruin true democracy. There were also immediate practical consequences:

> Is there not a tendency on the part of the baffled class to constant and mischievous legislative activity? It is a transparent dodge. [Kingston] seeks to cover his failure to help his devoted followers by seeming busy in their interests. And so every industry is worried, trade is harassed, discontent is fostered, and capital is cursed. Surely a little respite from this malignant fever of legislative interference might be good for the health of the State. We are being perpetually physicked when we don't want it, and it is the physician that makes us ill.

As Symon railed against attacks on property and on those who were successful in life, members of his audience may have wondered if he was planning a comeback in State politics. The invitations to do so mounted during 1895–6. Symon could not admit one of his reasons for declining all approaches: the inadequate parliamentary salary, which in principle he opposed, would not compensate for the reduction in the number of briefs he could accept. His present and projected expenses were also rising. The Symons had produced two more sons: Carril Hector Nicholson born on 22 September 1893 and Oliver Jose Lewers on 25 May 1895. In any case, Symon had no desire to enter the local parliament. His eyes were fixed on federation. Symon told the ANA that with 'the dawn of federation ... we shall forget the local night of gloom through which we are now passing'. He made an impassioned plea for a coming together of all South Australians and of all Australians, and above and beyond all the material advances 'we shall, as a united people, show that we can be great in all that ennobles a nation and in the breadth and the permanence of our freedom'. He urged the ANA to work for this end and to 'make this your magnum opus'.

Within two months of delivering this address, the ANA sponsored Symon's election as President of the South Australian Federation League. What looked like a consolation prize or an apology was Symon's opportunity. In one of his early actions Symon contacted George Reid, ostensibly to introduce South Australia's Deputy of Taxes who wanted to talk to Reid about direct taxation. Symon pointed to his own free trade connections and his new role with the Federation League and 'respectfully' offered his congratulations for Reid's election victory of 24 July 1895.[24] From a distance Symon saw Reid continuing as an obstacle to federation, even after Reid led the State Premiers' meeting in Hobart to introduce enabling legislation to hold elections for delegates to attend a constitution convention. Besides, Symon had long been in friendly contact with Edmund Barton, Reid's principal opponent in NSW, whose federalist credentials were far more compelling.

Symon first met Reid nine months later in Adelaide. The circumstances were not propitious. Reid arrived in the city on Saturday 25 April 1896 on his way to Broken Hill. It was election day held against a background of acrimonious exchanges between Kingston and his conservative opponents. The ancient Parkes died while Reid was in Broken Hill. The two had fallen out and Reid was left to say the right things about his former leader. Returning to Adelaide on 30 April Reid attended a luncheon at the York Hotel which Symon had organised. Allowing for a couple of exceptions, the attendees were all opponents of the re-elected Kingston Government. It might have been amusing to sit at the main table. Symon was flanked by Reid on his right and by 'friend Way' on his left.

Superficially, the luncheon achieved its objectives. Reid and Symon spent time together in a convivial atmosphere. Yet reading the two principal speeches, it is easy to understand why they never managed to establish a warm relationship. After some light-hearted remarks Symon went overboard when proposing the toast to 'Mr Reid and federated Australia'. The death of Parkes meant the 'mantle of Elijah' had now fallen on Mr Reid and however much they 'missed the ripe statesmanship, the great gifts and eloquence, and the picturesque personality of Sir Henry Parkes', it was consoling to know they had someone 'worthy of the noblest aspirations of the cause'. Reid could tolerate flattery, though it would not help his standing in NSW if South Australians could represent him as someone ready and willing to give them everything they wanted in pursuit of the federal cause.[25]

George Reid probably felt more comfortable in Adelaide among travelling companions from his home state and from the Queensland and Victorian governments. He seemed either unwilling or unable to make

'There is a first place and you alone occupy it.'

many generous comments about his host although he was able to speak glowingly about two other South Australians. Reid had found 'no more ardent Federationist than the gentleman who is at present the head of the Government in this colony'. He never uttered Kingston's name but went one step further in saying he found the same gentleman 'a staunch ally in all of my efforts to frame a successful Federal Union'. Reid also expressed the greatest pleasure in meeting 'my distinguished friend the Chief Justice'. Throughout Australia, 'he is a gentleman whom we all delight to honour'. Reid continued: 'Of course, he belongs to you, and you are all proud of him, but he is one of us.' While his position precluded him from 'public demonstrations', Chief Justice Way had 'exerted great and useful influence ... in the sphere of private life'.[26] Symon must have felt relieved when Reid sat down.

Kingston and Symon resumed their hostilities just before and during the 1896 election campaign. Symon spoke at a public meeting at Noarlunga south of Adelaide at the end of February. South Australians, he said, 'had no sympathy' with the Government's 'meddlesome, mischievous and quarrelsome policy' and were 'disgusted ... with the tyranny and brutality of their administrative acts'. Kingston responded to the Noarlunga speech with some good-humoured mockery of Symon's pose as a democrat and of his managing to better the informal vote in the year he was 'kicked out of Parliament'. Derided as the 'Friend of Humanity', Kingston said he 'had more humanity in his little finger than Symon had in his whole carcase'. By now he had moved beyond humour to what another paper in the *Register* stable called Kingston's 'vitriolic Billingsgate'. Even in the courts of justice, Kingston declared, Symon 'spat venom and squirted malice on all and sundry' and people 'might as well search for the milk of human kindness in a glass eye as in Mr. Symon, or for bowels in a billiard ball'.[27] On 25 April Kingston won the election with a slightly reduced majority.

The trading of insults reached its lowest point just after 1896 election during the so-called 'Hospital row'. Once again the details are not important for this biography, except to note that Kingston had become the central figure in disputes which first arose in 1894 over government involvement in the day-by-day management of the publicly-funded Adelaide Hospital.[28] Symon became embroiled after being approached to represent two aggrieved nurses. He published a letter in the press claiming that Kingston planned 'to play the game like a cardsharper, or like a pugilist who carries a knuckle-duster in his breeches pocket'. He called Kingston 'a political gamester' and 'a social pariah', and said the Premier added 'treachery' to 'falsehood and calumny'. Yet he did not hate Kingston: 'He is not worthy of feeling. I despise him.' Kingston preferred more inventive and lurid prose. He likened Symon to a 'death's head at the wedding feast':

> A gruesome ghoul with lips reeking with mendacity and foetid with malice, prostituting public opportunity to poison with malignant spite every drop and dreg of the festive cup which he hypocritically pretended to drain to the good health of his friend and guest. Who can doubt that the wretched breast of this Bible-reader by political profession, and evil speaker and slanderer by personal practice, was then consumed by the hell fires of hate?[29]

Of the two masters of vituperation, Symon was usually milder and the more easily hurt. Kingston did not detest Symon as he most certainly detested Baker. He respected Symon as a barrister, enjoyed their jousting and probably understood that Symon had climbed a much longer pole than Kingston was required to do. Unlike Symon, he never appeared to worry about self-respect. If abuse was his weapon of attack, Kingston seemed, certainly in Symon's case, to move on once the blow was struck. Their good times together since 1873, and their joint commitment to a federated Australia, meant more to Kingston than their explosive exchanges. Symon for his part may have been shocked by some of Kingston's behaviour with women and felt undermined by some of Kingston's words and actions. Nevertheless, Symon also valued their times together and their joint commitment to federation. By the end of 1898, the immediate past would count for nothing.

It was probably just as well some of the past never became public. For example, Jo sensibly confined his thoughts of late March 1896 to his loyal and discreet older brother. In the midst of his fiery exchanges with Kingston, Jo confided to Jim he was under 'very great pressure … from all parts of the Colony to go into Parliament at these elections'. He did not want to be thought vain in telling Jim,

> there would be rejoicing from one end of S. Australia to the other if I consented – I honestly think that at this moment I am the most popular – truly popular – & influential private Citizen in this Country. But I have declined. With my large family & responsibilities of various kinds it would be madness for me to go into politics … I should be expected to take the lead. I am sure I should be Premier at once. This blackguard Government of Kingstons [sic] would crumble to pieces. But that would mean giving up my profession. I could not do both without killing myself.

He was not very enthusiastic about political life in South Australia and, in any case, Jo planned to wait a year or two before re-entering the arena.[30]

Almost 12 months after writing this letter, Symon stood for election to become one of the ten South Australians to attend the Australasian Federal Convention. It transpired that, at best, he was the most popular private citizen in a poll ignored by 70 per cent of South Australians. Five practising politicians headed by Charles Cameron Kingston were placed ahead of him. Throughout his political life, Josiah Symon had a poor record as a forecaster.

7

'it is for the people to say how they shall be governed.'

The emergence and growth of federal leagues in NSW and Victoria and of nationalist organisations (notably the ANA), the renewed efforts of individuals (notably Barton and Deakin) and the Peoples' Conventions held in Corowa in 1893 and Bathurst in 1896 underpinned the revival of the federal idea. The resolution attributed to John Quick at Corowa kick-started a critical process. The resolution proposed that each colony should pass legislation to provide for the election of representatives to consider and adopt a Bill to establish a Federal Constitution to be submitted by some form of referendum 'to the verdict of each colony'. George Reid appeared converted to the federal cause after succeeding Parkes as NSW Premier. He called for a meeting of Premiers in Hobart in January 1895 where four of them agreed to pass enabling legislation to establish the mechanism for holding a constitutional convention. Queensland stayed out and Sir John Forrest, Premier of Western Australia, remained equivocal. Kingston drafted enabling legislation which South Australia and NSW enacted at the end of 1895. Tasmania and Victoria followed suit early in 1896. Each colony agreed to send ten delegates to the Convention, elected according to the franchise applicable in the respective colonies. Western Australia passed similar enabling legislation in October 1896 except that Forrest maintained his hold by insisting Parliament should select the colony's delegates. Queensland remained outside.

At the end of January 1897, Symon announced he would be a candidate for election as a South Australian delegate to the Convention. He opened his official campaign with a major speech at the Adelaide Town Hall on

'It is for the people to say how they shall be governed.'

Monday 8 February.[1] Charles Tucker, the Mayor of Adelaide (1894–8), a future State MP and jailed felon, presided. Symon spoke for 105 minutes.

He first addressed the question of why issues 'of comparatively insignificant importance should excite so much interest' when the one 'of bringing these great colonies into one homogeneous whole excited so little popular feeling'. He explained that the prevalent 'apathy' was not due to 'supineness' but to general support for federation. South Australians agreed on the desirability of federation and now thought it would be implemented:

> It is the people who govern; it is for the people to say how they shall be governed. (Cheers.) In essence Australia is a democracy – the freest democracy under the sun. (Loud cheers.) Its institutions are democratic; the people are sovereign.

Symon had come a long way from the young man in his early twenties who had seen and heard enough of Australian democracy in Mount Gambier to doubt whether the working class should have the vote.

He also explained the meaning and justification of federation:

> the union of co-ordinate and independent commonwealths, while preserving their separate existence as self-governing States. It is defined to be a political contrivance intended to reconcile national unity and power with the maintenance of State rights.

Against that background Symon then spelt out what he saw as four 'cardinal principles' in framing the constitution: 'it must secure as indestructible and enduring personal and political liberty'; 'there must be complete autonomy for each State'; 'as between the States there must be absolute freedom of trade and commercial intercourse'; and the union 'must be permanent and indissoluble'.

For much of his speech Symon spoke of practical considerations. He favoured a Commonwealth takeover of the existing colonial railways, wanted guaranteed South Australian access to the Murray River waters, insisted that the Senate as the States' House with a membership selected by the State parliaments should have power to amend and reject money Bills and he wanted a new Federal Court to be the final court of appeal. On this latter point it will be recalled how in 1891 Symon told Kingston that, until Australia had a population of between 20 and 30 million, the court of ultimate resort 'should be removed as far as possible from local circumstances'. By February 1897, he believed that if a people of three or four million could not constitute a court of final appeal for the administration of justice 'it [Ausralia] is really unworthy of being the nation it aspires to be'.

In South Australia the hot summer accounted for some of the sparse attendances at public meetings. The large crowd which attended Symon's speech was almost the only exception. Symon's key backer had no illusions about the turnout. According to the *South Australian Register* of 9 February, 'the eloquence of the speaker would probably have attracted an equally large crowd, supposing that he had discussed the nebular hypothesis instead of nation-building'. Not everyone admired Symon's delivery. The ever-critical *Quiz and the Lantern* of 11 February described the Symon style as akin to preaching, claimed he had just two notes to his voice and called the outcome 'laboured', 'prosy' and 'monotonous' and exhibiting 'a painful lack of fire'. The *Register* worried about a broader issue: the people of South Australia regarded 'an epoch-making event' with 'apathy' and 'this is disquieting'. Its own view was that the event which had attracted just two-thirds of the colonies should be held over. Any constitution which emerged would be like the one of 1891 and treated as 'so much printed matter' which the parliaments would not endorse.

Josiah Symon entered the campaign determined to prove the *Register* wrong. Yet there were limits to his commitment. Symon had no intention of returning or not accepting briefs. He did leave Adelaide on three occasions; travelling 154 miles to speak at Petersburg, addressing a public meeting in Port Pirie and speaking on a platform at Clare. Invited to speak at Mount Gambier, four other named centres and unidentified others, Symon regretted that his caseload prevented acceptance.[2] In place of appearances, he arranged with the *Register* to print hundreds of copies of his Town Hall address which supporters distributed throughout South Australia.

Neither Symon, nor Richard Baker QC, could use work commitments to justify their absence from a special session of the Criminal Court on Monday morning, 15 February 1897. The Bar had assembled to

'it is for the people to say how they shall be governed.'

congratulate Chief Justice Way on his appointment to the Judicial Committee of the Privy Council.[3] Kingston QC – as Attorney General and the head of the local Bar – spoke on behalf of the profession. In the course of much adulation he said Way's name had for years in South Australia 'been a household word in all spheres of public usefulness'. A critic suggested that for all of Kingston's 'boot-licking', Way was not satisfied with the quantity of flattery thrust upon him. He cried out for 'more', and 'flattered himself and his high office until blue in the face'.[4]

Another newspaper offered possible explanations for Baker's and Symon's non-appearance.[5] Each had long-standing personal objections to Way. Both could also claim that Justices Boucaut and Bundey were on holiday within South Australia and would soon be returning to Adelaide. Surely they were part of the honour being bestowed on the province? Baker, still smarting from Symon's effective rescue mission to save his client from jail, had his own reasons for avoiding all non-essential contact with Kingston. Symon, who knew Kingston's true feelings about Way, probably wanted to avoid unbearable hypocrisy.

Symon never sought to add his name to a party ticket. Kingston's Liberal Union had started the party games by announcing a ten-member ticket consisting of six Liberals and four members of the Labor Party, with Kingston and three of his ministers heading the list. The Progressive League of South Australia followed with six names: Baker, Downer, Glynn, Howe, Solomon and Symon.[6] Kingston jeered at the League's choice of a 'Tory crew' which, he said, made a mockery of the name 'Progressive'.[7] He omitted to mention that the League left four positions vacant. It subsequently published a list of ten names, adding Kingston, Holder, Charleston and Gordon to its original list.

Thirty-two men and one woman, the reformer and feminist Catherine Helen Spence, nominated for election as delegates. George Ash MP, a partner in Kingston's law firm, died of typhoid fever on 27 February, his name remaining on the ballot paper. Questions were raised over Spence's eligibility to sit on the Convention if elected. In the event she came 22nd in the poll with 7470 votes, and Ash came last – though he did receive 698 votes despite being dead.[8] The ten elected delegates and their votes were as follows:

Sir Josiah Symon KCMG KC

Kingston	24,682
Holder	24,320
Cockburn	23,095
Baker	22,003
Gordon	21,958
Symon	21,281
Downer	20,426
Glynn	20,390
Howe	19,741
Solomon	18,463

It was widely assumed that the South Australians had elected six 'conservatives' – Baker, Symon, Downer, Glynn, Solomon and Howe – and four Liberals – Kingston, Gordon, Holder and Cockburn. Candidates supported by the Labor Party finished 11th–15th. All ten elected delegates had served in the Colonial Parliament, though Symon had left the Chamber ten years previously and Glynn was temporarily without a seat. It appears that South Australians had voted for the names well known to them; in Symon's case because his court appearances, public speaking engagements and news of Auldana were regularly covered in the press. Significantly, only about a third of eligible voters bothered to exercise their vote.

South Australian historians like reproducing Deakin's admiring comments about the South Australians. 'Measured by all-round ability, the South Australian delegation was undoubtedly the strongest'. Deakin's condescension could be overlooked or forgiven: 'Howe and Solomon who constituted its tail were men of business training and shrewdness who were capable of taking part in debate.' Clearly, Deakin grasped the important point: 'The varied quality of the South Australian team and distinctive qualities of its members rendered them when united the most powerful phalanx of debate.' There was just one problem. All the South Australians had a strong political passion 'but personal antipathies were violent'. Referring to the exchanges in 1896 over the Hospital dispute, Deakin wrote: 'In France or the Western States Symon's correspondence with [Kingston] would have justified half a dozen duels.'[9]

Symon had created valued contacts in the other colonies, one of which

'it is for the people to say how they shall be governed.'

dated much earlier than the approaching Conference. On 29 November 1894, he wrote to Edmund Barton in belated commiseration after Barton had lost his Randwick seat in the election which Reid had won in July of that year. Barton had sent Symon a copy of a letter he had distributed to Randwick electors, and Symon said he was 'disgusted' they had rejected him; the loss was not his but 'theirs and Australia's'. He looked forward to chatting to Barton in Sydney early in 1895, sent him a copy of his ANA speech and asked whether Reid was sincere about federation. Barton replied on 4 December that Reid's sincerity for federation was 'a riddle', though 'very few believe him sincere about anything – that is, very few public men, of any party'. Barton said he was gratified to see that Symon was 'so staunch on Federation', and especially liked the moment in his ANA address where Symon spoke of 'our people' preserving their physical vigour and moral fibre through federation. Barton thought that Symon could do 'a great deal' to attain their mutual objective.

Barton had another message. Referring to a drive they once took together, accompanied by Auldana wines, Barton remembered thinking how Downer and Symon had so many principles in common. He longed now for the day when Downer and Symon joined up 'for the destruction of a dishonest & pernicious régime – for the ascendancy of Kingston can be nothing but harmful to your colony & to the ways of political thought all over Australia'. Six years later, Barton selected Kingston to join him in the first Commonwealth ministry.[10]

Symon renewed contact with Barton on 16 March 1897 just before the Convention was due to meet in Adelaide. Names were being tossed around as delegates considered who should be President of the Conference. Gillies, the Victorian Premier, had been President of the Melbourne Convention in 1890 and Parkes, the Premier of NSW, had presided at the Sydney Convention in 1891. When, finally, Reid had accepted Adelaide as the venue for the 1897 Convention, there was a clear precedent for Premier Kingston to be President. Reid, however, said in Sydney on 12 March that a Premier had too much to do about the constitution without presiding over a meeting. Besides a Convention was very different from a Premier's Conference. It would be regulated according to parliamentary forms and therefore a Speaker was a more appropriate person to preside. He recommended Sir Joseph Abbott as a senior Speaker who presided over the NSW Legislative Assembly, the senior of the colonial parliaments. Symon sent a message to Reid supporting his proposal. He agreed that an experienced Speaker was the most suitable choice. Symon did not need to add that Kingston would be displeased.

In his letter to Barton of 16 March, Symon said that John Downer, responding to Reid's proposal of Abbott, had contacted Symon with the idea of proposing Barton for the presidency. Symon told Barton he felt 'pretty sure' the majority of South Australia's delegates would not favour Kingston if they were offered 'any reasonable alternative'. Yet the more Symon thought about it the less he liked the idea of seeing Barton 'shelved' in the presidency. Barton's 'wisdom & moderation' would be 'absolutely indispensable in the active work of the Convention'. Symon thought federation had reached 'a critical stage. It is now or never – at least not for many years.' Barton simply could not be spared to serve in an honorary office.[11] Barton later claimed he had no idea when he arrived in Adelaide on 21 March that he would be asked to take a responsible position. Geoffrey Bolton, Barton's biographer, commented: 'maybe that was true.' Bolton knew of others like Sir Philip Fysh of Tasmania and probably Alfred Deakin who were already speaking of Barton as Leader.[12] Symon's name should be added to that list.

J.H. Gordon sent Reid a telegram from South Australia registering his opposition to the Abbott proposal. Receiving no reply, Gordon wrote a letter to the editor of the *Adelaide Advertiser* and simultaneously posted Reid a letter, a copy of which he released to the same newspaper. Gordon did not doubt Abbott could discharge the duties of President. The question, as he saw it, concerned 'the honour of South Australia and its status in the Convention'. Gordon quoted Sir Samuel Griffith, 'a most eminent federationist', who seconded Parkes for the presidency of the 1891 meeting in Sydney. Griffith said the appointment of Parkes was 'in accordance with universal custom, as well as official courtesy, seeing that the Convention was held in New South Wales, of which colony he was Prime Minister'. Should custom and courtesy be recognised in Sydney and Melbourne but ignored in Adelaide?

Josiah Symon wrote to Reid on 18 March, the day when Gordon's letter appeared in the *Advertiser*, and he enclosed copies of both Gordon letters. As ever, concerned with the proprieties, Symon expressed disapproval of

'it is for the people to say how they shall be governed.'

a letter being published before Reid had received the original. He objected to Gordon's message to Reid, saying the suggestion of Abbott for the presidency would be 'most unwelcome here'. Symon thought such an assessment more properly applied to Kingston. He may have been right with reference to the majority of elected delegates, but almost certainly wrong about majority opinion in South Australia. Symon agreed with Reid's central argument about the 'inexpediency' of a Premier occupying the presidency. The position needed someone who had the qualifications of a Speaker. No doubt Symon hoped that Reid would organise the numbers for Abbott to take the post. He perhaps overlooked Reid's general approval of Kingston and, more importantly, did not appreciate the extent of Reid's other preoccupations.[13]

The Premiers met privately on the night of 22 March 1897 in anticipation of the Convention opening on the following day. They probably agreed to support Kingston for the presidency. Reid later claimed he suggested the appointment of Barton as Leader of the Convention. Deakin was not present at the Premiers' meeting but said Reid had not been consulted and did not approve of Barton's election to the position. According to Deakin's account, Turner, the Victorian Premier, proposed Barton for the position and Downer and Symon heartily endorsed the idea.[14]

Replying in 1920 to a column published in the Melbourne *Argus*, Symon told a very different story. At an informal meeting in Parliament House on the morning just before the Convention opened for business on 23 March, the delegates discussed preliminaries and procedure. Symon rose without knowledge of any previous arrangement. He moved that Barton should be Leader of the Convention. Reid seconded the motion, wondering only whether it was premature to act before the Convention was formally constituted with a chairman. Symon put the motion which was carried unanimously. So far as Symon knew, Reid never felt he had a claim to the position, and there was no preconcerted arrangement by a majority to exclude him in favour of Barton. Symon had acted upon his own initiative and not as the spokesman of an arranged majority. Barton knew this to be true and 'never forgot as he used to say, "that Symon proposed him as leader"'.[15]

In most respects the questions of who did what, when and why in the third week of March 1897 are not germane to a biography of Josiah Symon. One point, however, does matter. Symon has generally been regarded as a poor or inadequate politician. Either he was out of his depth among the wire-pullers and manipulators or, to be more generous, he just saw himself above the machinations of the power hungry and the self-promoters. It will be shown later that he backed many losing positions in federal politics and did not bother to build support for the positions he took. Nevertheless, Symon did have a sense of what could and should work in achieving what he desired. Hence he supported Barton for the leadership of the Convention and to chair the drafting committee to prepare a Bill for a constitution. It might be more accurate to see him not so much as an amateur alongside the professionals but as a half-time politician working by desire and necessity in another near full-time job.

The Convention met formally in the House of Assembly in Adelaide on Monday 23 March 1897. NSW delegates sat on the ministerial benches to the right of the Chair opposite the Victorians; the South Australians occupied the cross benches; the Tasmanian delegation sat behind NSW and the West Australians behind Victoria. Symon sat behind Baker and Downer on the Victorian side of the cross benches.[16]

Edwin Blackmore, the Clerk of the Legislative Council and Clerk of Parliaments in South Australia, inaugurated the proceedings by reading a proclamation signed by the Governor of NSW and referring to the proclamations signed by the Governors of the other colonies attending the Convention. Blackmore called the roll and the delegates signed themselves in. The Convention then moved to implement the important, albeit predetermined, decisions.

Reid moved and Abbott seconded Kingston's appointment to the presidency. On this point, Deakin may not have told an entirely accurate story. He said that 'Baker, Symon, Downer, Howe and Solomon were cut to the quick by the unexpected contingency of the election of Kingston to the Presidency of the great national gathering'.[17] Kingston's elevation was undesired but not 'unexpected', and was hardly a 'contingency'. Reid's unwillingness to lobby for Abbott or anyone else left the dissidents with a sense of resignation. There may have been, as Deakin claimed, a response of 'silence and scowls' from 'his local enemies' to Kingston's uncontested election. Perhaps the scowls multiplied when Kingston later proved not

'It is for the people to say how they shall be governed.'

to be 'shelved' by his elevation. At least the dissidents could welcome the unopposed election of Barton as Leader of the Convention as well as his later election, along with Downer and Richard O'Connor (NSW), to the drafting committee.

On the first night of the Convention, the Kingston Government hosted a banquet for the delegates in the Jubilee Exhibition Building. Baker and Symon were among the very few who did not attend. Unlike other absentees, they did not send an apology. Wives were not invited to the banquet though some may have sat with the 'ladies' who watched the proceedings from the galleries.[18] The banquet was just one of the entertainments organised for the delegates. The Governor, Sir Fowell Buxton, and Lady Buxton hosted a dinner on the following Thursday evening, and some delegates, including just one from NSW, accepted a trip to Broken Hill on the second weekend of the Convention. Symon made his own contribution when seven members of the Judiciary Committee visited the Auldana vineyard in the third week. He did not attend when a dozen pressmen from the other colonies enjoyed an earlier wine-tasting trip to Auldana. At the end of the first week, Symon appeared at insolvency sittings of the Supreme Court and in one opposed Paris Nesbit QC[19] over a projected appeal to the Privy Council.

Apart from Queensland's absence, two problems relating to attendance were known before the first meeting of the Convention. The Western Australians would arrive days after the Convention opened and would leave before the end of the fourth week. More seriously, the Premiers were due in London in June for Queen Victoria's Diamond Jubilee celebrations and a Colonial Conference. A sense of urgency overhung the Convention from the second week. Delegates wanted to approve a draft Bill before the Convention reassembled in Sydney and Melbourne. Nothing deterred them, however, in the first days from delivering often long set speeches. Josiah Symon took two hours to give his on Thursday afternoon, 25 March. La Nauze, who saw Symon as an orator, said his 'able if overelaborate speech soared to an eloquent peroration'.[20]

Symon spoke with passion about making the High Court the final court of appeal, about leaving it to the Federal Parliament to deal with the differences between the colonies over the franchise and about reconciling responsible government to a federal system – which Richard Baker considered impossible – by giving the House of Representatives the sole power to make and unmake governments and to introduce money bills. Delegates who remained attentive when Symon delivered his peroration might have wondered about its message. Symon, the self-styled leader of what he liked to call the 'States' Rights party', said that, while '[t]he spirit of Federation is undoubtedly the spirit of compromise', delegates should not assume 'we are to give up too readily the principles which we cherish'. Symon promised he would struggle long and hard for what he conceived was essential and 'to give up nothing until I am convinced it ought not to be longer fought for'. These words may have been lost as Symon rose to his concluding sentence: 'if we succeed there will arise in Australia, a new and beneficent power, great in her civilisation, great in all the arts of peace, and, above and beyond all, great in the comfort and happiness of her people.' In effect, Symon told the Convention he wanted federation more than he wanted his preferred version of it. At the Adelaide Convention this priority existed only in his rhetoric. It became reality when Symon went to the Sydney and Melbourne sessions.

The Deakin portrait of Symon is worth quoting in full:

> J.H. Symon, Q.C., the leader of the Bar of South Australia, above the medium height, blonde, well-poised and so nearly absolutely bald that what little hair he had was invisible, had passed through but a short parliamentary experience and still retained more of the traditions of the court than of legislature. He had however taken an active part in public affairs as an antagonist of the radical party and most particularly and personally of Kingston, with whom he had recently engaged in a public correspondence the most violent in vituperation that the colony had ever witnessed. Thoroughly well-informed, above the middle height, endowed with a rich and powerful voice and an impressive manner and a great command of language, he was if not the best, decidedly one of the best set speakers at the Convention. An expert lawyer and practised advocate, he had every trick of the practised pleader at his fingers' ends and employed them without stint where necessary.[21]

Deakin qualified his assessments of delegates whose merits mirrored some of his own. Hence his appraisals of Symon and Glynn had to be moderated; Symon, 'if not the best, decidedly one of the best set

'It is for the people to say how they shall be governed.'

speakers'; Glynn, 'if not the best-read man of the Convention, certainly carried more English prose and poetry in his memory than any three or four of his associates'. La Nauze added to Deakin's assessment of Symon: 'a leading barrister, eloquent in formal contexts, acute and alert in debate, vindictive and scarifying in controversy'.[22] Contrary to received opinion, while Symon argued strongly when he felt the need for firmness and clarity, and like most delegates wished that Higgins of Victoria would stop interjecting, Symon was mostly patient, constructive and polite. The lawyer in him prompted many interventions during the Adelaide Convention to assist with the wording of clauses and resolutions, but he would gracefully withdraw in the face of better arguments and formulations. He was rarely 'vindictive' or 'scarifying'.

Symon had one critical duty. On 31 March, the Convention approved the appointment and membership of the Judiciary Committee, the smallest of its three committees.

>   NSW: B.E. Wise and J.T. Walker
>   Victoria: H.B. Higgins and A.J. Peacock
>   South Australia: P.M. Glynn and J.H. Symon
>   Western Australia: G. Leake and W.H. James.
>   Tasmania: H. Dobson and M.J. Clarke.

The five Premiers were all *ex officio* members of the Committee. Kingston attended one meeting but did not vote and none of the other Premiers attended any of the meetings. Of the ten regular members La Nauze noted that only Symon, Wise and Higgins had claims to eminence in their profession. Five of the others did have legal qualifications; Peacock and Walker had none. When the Committee first met on 31 March it unanimously elected Symon as Chairman. La Nauze thought that the choice of Symon was as much a case of recognising the only QC on the panel as it was a compliment to South Australia. It is not obvious that Wise and Peacock had either consideration in mind when they proposed Symon. Perhaps they and the other members either knew Symon or had seen enough of him already to feel confident about his chairmanship.

The Committee began its substantive meetings on 1 April and on that day Symon telegraphed Samuel Griffith for advice on whether State courts could and should exercise original jurisdiction in federal matters in order to avoid a multiplication of courts. As La Nauze mischievously called him, 'the great man' delivered a 'magisterial' response. Griffith had no objections, save for exceptions relating to the extent of jurisdiction. Symon's Committee proceeded with this approach and spent four half days and one full day reviewing and amending the clauses of the 1891 document. Higgins moved 11 motions of amendment, of which the Committee passed one, and that was later reversed. There were 19 divisions and Symon used his casting vote just once, in that instance to deny cases involving admiralty or maritime law being added to those types subject to appeal to the Privy Council. The key clause passed without dissent.

> No appeal shall be allowed to the Queen in Council from any Court of any State or from the High Court or any other Federal Court, except that the Queen may, in any case in which the public interests of the Commonwealth, or of any State, or of any other part of Her Majesty's dominions are concerned grant leave to appeal to Herself in Council from the High Court.

At the final meeting, held on 6 April, Wise moved and Higgins seconded a motion, which was carried unanimously, 'that the thanks of the Committee be accorded to the Chairman, Mr Symon, for his great services to the Committee and for the ability and courtesy with which he had guided and assisted their deliberations, and that this resolution be recorded on the minutes'.[23] The Committee reported on 8 April 1897.

Invited to comment on all the proceedings, Sir Samuel Griffith did not approve of the work of the Judiciary Committee.[24] He observed that what he called 'the Catalogue style of drafting' was not 'compatible with the dignity of a great instrument of government'. Griffith objected to the words used in the clause restricting appeals to the Queen in Council. He considered them 'discourteous' and contrary to 'established usage'. It was not usual to tell the Sovereign or her Representative what they 'shall' or 'shall not' do. Griffith questioned one provision by declaring it 'remarkable'. Section 80 laid down that no judicial officer should be appointed to administer the government of the Commonwealth. This was a decision made when the Convention was sitting as a committee of the whole. In line with his commitment to the separation of powers, and his

'it is for the people to say how they shall be governed.'

experience of Chief Justice Way expanding his empire in South Australia, Symon strongly supported the addition of this section.

Griffith's assault on his draft hurt Symon. He told William McMillan of the NSW delegation, a new friend, that Griffith's criticisms appeared 'spiteful & as though he resented his own work of /91 being so much recast'. Symon was in any case unmoved: 'as a piece of draftsmanship the Bill of /97 is immeasurably superior to that of /91.' La Nauze was probably right: Griffith as Chief Justice of the High Court found when he clashed with Symon as the Commonwealth Attorney-General in 1904–5 that the Attorney had a long memory.[25]

The Constitutional and the Finance Committees also filed their reports and the drafting committee of Barton, O'Connor and Downer worked hard to produce a draft Bill on 13 April. The Committee of the whole Convention, chaired by Baker, focused immediately on the clauses dealing with the Money Bills. Forrest and the West Australians wanted to settle one very important issue before their early departure: should the Convention reinstate the 'Compromise of /91' which allowed the Senate to affirm or reject money bills but not amend them. George Reid moved an amendment on 13 April to insert four words (see them in italics below), into the first sentence of the drafting committee's clause 53 (1). If accepted, the clause would read: 'The Senate shall have equal power with the House of Representatives in respect of all proposed laws, except *laws imposing taxation and* laws appropriating the necessary supplies for ordinary annual services of the Government, which the Senate may affirm or reject, but never amend.' The Premiers of NSW and Victoria both argued that federation would be 'impossible' if the amendment were not approved.

La Nauze claimed that Isaacs and Symon made the best of the elaborate speeches with Isaacs making the best one of the day.[26] Deakin spoke just before Symon on 13 April. He claimed, as Symon would do, that the Senate would 'attract to it the intellect, the character and experience of the nation'. In this position, according to Deakin, the Senate 'will be able to press on any House of Representatives, however recalcitrant, a due and proper consideration of its will.' Symon argued that because the Senate would be 'a body of dignity and power', coupled with a strong sense of patriotism, it would not engage in small-mindedness and nit-pick over amendments. Deakin and others asked the Senate or the smaller States to trust in the good judgement and conscience of the House of Representatives; why did they not think the same about the judgment and conscience of the Senate?

Symon also addressed the Reid and Turner claims that their electorates would reject a situation where the smaller States could use the power of amendment to exercise control over the two larger States. He drew a distinction between the Convention, where delegates could vote as they thought fit, and the views of electors who, Symon believed, could be persuaded by Convention delegates committed to a draft Bill. Behind this argument lay a new Symon conviction: 'trust the people'. Behind that conviction stood a barrister who had come to believe in his own powers of persuasion. He had another, more credible argument. The smaller States did not want concessions; they were asking for their 'rights' within a federated Australia. Giving them the opportunity to make suggestions was a roundabout way of doing things. The simple fact was that the Senate would be elected by the same people exercising the same franchise by which they elected the House of Representatives. The former had, or should have, rights comparable to those possessed by the latter. Why should the people voting in different territories not have the right enjoyed by the people voting in a national electorate?[27]

Gordon of South Australia called for a division at the end of the day whereupon Barton intervened, complained of a bronchial cold, and asked if he might speak on the following day, 14 April. The division, which almost certainly would have placed Symon on the winning side, was postponed by what Quick and Garran called a 'providential catarrh'. Overnight there was considerable lobbying, of which Symon and Forrest were almost certainly ignorant. Next day, an obviously refreshed Barton delivered a fine speech and helped to convince the wavering William McMillan of NSW to change his mind about voting with the smaller States. After all, why should Western Australia, at best lukewarm about federation, be allowed to wreck it for those who really wanted it?

In the vote on the Reid amendment taken on 14 April, five delegates from the smaller colonies – Kingston and Glynn (South Australia) and Brown, Henry and Lewis (Tasmania) – voted with the solid NSW (including McMillan) and Victorian blocs. Winthrop Hackett of Western

'it is for the people to say how they shall be governed.'

Australia had returned home on undisclosed private business, and Baker in the chair required an even split to exercise his casting vote. The result was 25–23 in favour of adding the four words to Clause 53 (1).[28] Whether or not federation would have failed on the issue of the Senate's voting powers will never be known. What is known is that, despite the continued resistance of Forrest and Downer, the issue itself was effectively decided on 14 April 1897. When the issue re-emerged at the Conventions in Sydney and Melbourne, Symon lived up to the promise of his peroration.

8

'the finest instrument of government that ever was framed'

The Premiers arrived in London in mid-1897 to attend the celebrations for Queen Victoria's Diamond Jubilee and the Colonial Conference which met from 24 June to 8 July 1897. While in England, Reid and Kingston declined the offer of a knighthood but Turner accepted one. Forrest, Braddon and Hugh Nelson (Queensland) had already been knighted. All six Premiers were sworn of the Privy Council. They were absent while their parliaments in Australia debated the conclusions reached by the Adelaide session of the Convention. During this time, Chamberlain presented Reid with two memoranda designed 'to avoid the possibility of friction hereafter'. The memoranda set out amendments thought necessary for the Adelaide decisions to meet Imperial concerns. Chamberlain produced a third memorandum for Reid's 'private and independent consideration' containing the Colonial Office's 'friendly suggestions' for drafting changes. On his return to Australia Reid probably gave the first two documents to the three-member drafting committee, and possibly the third as well. He agreed in London to act as 'an honest broker' but not as Chamberlain's advocate.[1]

Meanwhile, on 21 May 1897 Josiah Symon delivered an oration in Adelaide Town Hall to mark the Diamond Jubilee. He spoke at the invitation of the South Australian Chamber of Manufactures.[2] The State Governor, Sir Fowell Buxton, presided and Lady Victoria Buxton attended the occasion as did the Governor's private secretary, Captain Edward Wallington. Symon was forming a friendship with Wallington who became a useful contact in vice-regal and royal circles for 35 years.

Symon entitled his oration 'Tis Sixty Years Since', thus borrowing the

'the finest instrument of government that ever was framed'

alternative title of Sir Walter Scott's first Waverley novel. The Town Hall was packed, the city organist played melodies for a quarter of an hour and the audience sang 'Song of Australia', whereupon Symon took centre stage. He said the tale he had to tell

> was real and vivid for weal or woe; it was an imperishable fact in the history of the age, and it transcended anything the unaided imagination of man had conceived. It told of the vast and unending expansion of the mightiest Empire on which the sun had ever shone; it told of the wondrous march of physical development; it told how the very elements and forces of nature had been subdued and disciplined to aid in civilisation and progress.

Queen Victoria was central to Symon's story. In her reign, men and women

> have been born and grown old. Their children and children's children have come and gone, knowing no other Sovereign. We can hardly realise the British Empire without Queen Victoria. Loyalty to her is personal devotion. Her sway has been illumined with all the highest attributes of a Christian monarch – the loving mother of a free people – and she has shed amongst her myriad subjects a living, pervading influence that tends to noble thoughts, and noble conduct.

Other ages were characterised by maritime, military or intellectual achievements and full of heroic adventures. The last sixty years marked an achievement of another kind: the greatest material improvement of any other period of history. Symon ranged far and wide on triumphs in science, medicine, exploration, railway expansion, manufacturing, education, social reform, banking, trade, the establishment and work of the London County Council and the decreasing national debt.

Notwithstanding the relative absence of heroic moments over the previous 60 years, Symon stressed that the 'sentiment of patriotism' was no less strong. Moreover, it was as 'vehement' on the banks of the Ganges as on the banks of the Thames, in 'the turmoil of South Africa' as in 'the unmeasured areas of Australia'. It was unclear whether he included the population of the Indian sub-continent in the 'British race' or just found room for those like the Maharaja of Jeypore whom he met in 1891. For him, the important point was that the quality of the 'British race' was the source of the supremacy of the British Empire.

Symon concluded by asking whether Australians would prove themselves 'worthy of those from whose loins they had sprung'. While it was fine to cherish historical memories and achievements of the past, other things were greater: the duties of maintaining and broadening free institutions, of preserving the physical vigour and moral fibre of the people, of holding fast to the liberty handed down to them, and holding aloft the high standard of British humanity. Symon spoke of his 'firm article of faith': 'the federal impulse ... would make for the moral grandeur, social strength, and permanent happiness of the continent.' Therefore: 'Seek ye first the just federation of these colonies, and all other things will be added unto you in full measure heaped up and running over.' He wanted it all to happen 'before another year was added to the reign of the Queen' to create a country 'great in the beauty of moral and material strength ... within whose borders no sound of oppression should be heard and truth and justice should prevail'.

Loud and prolonged cheering followed Symon's speech and the audience in full voice sang 'God Save the Queen'. One historian wrote that Symon's oration 'was long remembered in the city'.[3] It was different from most of his other prepared speeches in that it had relatively few literary allusions. In addition to Scott, Symon did find a place for a line from Milton's *Paradise Lost* and for a stanza from a lesser known Rudyard Kipling poem. He also quoted a Daniel Webster speech delivered in the United States Senate in 1834 referring to the 'morning drum beat' of the British Empire 'following the sun' and circling the earth 'with one continuous and broken strain of the martial airs of England'.

Not everyone was impressed. The *Quiz and the Lantern* never missed an opportunity to sneer:

> Symon, Q.C., as a rule is a canny Scotsman, but in his lecture, 'Tis Sixty Years Since', he betrayed himself as a thorough-going Jingo. He even infused some of his enthusiasm into the hard-headed members of the Chamber of Manufactures. If Symon had stuck to politics he would have been Sir Josiah long ago. He has the gush of which colonial Knights are made.

'the finest instrument of government that ever was framed'

The weekly paper did have a point; the speech did resonate with 'gush' and 'jingoism'. A letter sent to the editor of the *Adelaide Observer* drew attention to another feature. Identifying himself as a native of Sir Walter Scott's land of 'brown heather and shaggy wood', the writer objected to Symon's persistent use of 'England' and 'the English' in preference to 'Britain' and 'the British'.[4]

These criticisms focused on Symon's words without looking closely at what they conveyed. If the critics had been writing a biography they would have recognised that Symon was fusing his several identities. He remained a proud Scot who had become proudly Australian, and had attached himself culturally, socially and politically to England, to the Empire and to the monarchy. Symon was also conscious of 'race'. Where it suited he used words like 'white' or 'European' as prefixes but 'British' was more preferable for his purposes. It was after all the 'British race' (and, notably, its 'English' element) which at once established and incorporated the moral values Symon associated with the Empire.[5]

Another element of the fusion – Symon was also a proud South Australian – was more evident in his Convention speeches. As he prepared himself for the Sydney session Symon had to balance what he saw as the demands of the States and the federation. Joseph Carruthers, a Convention delegate from NSW who had opposed State representation in the Senate, no doubt boosted Symon's self-regard with the letter he sent him on 14 July 1897.[6] Carruthers commented on a Symon complaint about the 'local oratory' in Adelaide attacking the Convention. He felt the same way about the non-participants in Sydney who thought they could do better. Carruthers believed that the Sydney session 'will do a vast amount of good' in showing how 'a National movement can be conducted by the best men'. More importantly, while Carruthers was not prepared to modify his views on 'State Rights v People's rights', he believed that a compromise was possible, although 'our people' think NSW will have 'to carry the heavy end' for a time. Carruthers wanted Symon to 'bring his great mental powers' to bear on the problem of how much the smaller States could concede to the larger ones whose populations had been educated to believe in equal political rights for all citizens. Carruthers believed that equal rights to the States could be conceded on State questions but 'Social and Civil Right Questions' were a different matter. He told Symon 'we' need someone who could work the different perspectives into acceptable stipulations.

Carruthers concluded his letter by telling Symon that people in Sydney were keen to meet him because the NSW delegates had spoken so well of his bearing in Adelaide. In a later private opinion Carruthers was effusive. Symon was 'one of the most striking members of the Convention'. Little known in public affairs prior to the Convention, Symon took most in Adelaide by surprise and 'became a favourite speaker to whom it was a delight to listen'. Carruthers noted how Symon had 'a very easy and convincing style and was absolutely free from any rhetorical effect'.

> He spoke with an evident mastery of his case, and never faltered in his easy delivery. He had pungency and a subtle wit (tho at times rather mordant) in his way of dealing with the arguments against his view, whilst he put forward those necessary to make his case with a persuasiveness that in which no other delegate surpassed. Behind his fine manner there was a sledge-hammer force in his advocacy of the view he espoused. On matters of constitutional law he gave evidence of his great knowledge; and he was ready at a moment to answer any dissenting interruption from the other side, with facts and precedents and reasons. I regarded him, as did also many others, as one of the great forces in the Convention Debates.[7]

The Premiers returned from their feasting and talking in London and the Convention delegates began assembling in Sydney. Symon arrived on Tuesday 31 August 1897 and booked into the Union Hotel in Kent Street. The Convention first met on 2 September but adjourned on 24 September, the Sydney session being foreshortened by the departure of the Victorian delegation to prepare for an election on 14 October. Queensland did not join the proceedings and the delegations from the five colonies remained the same except for Western Australia where four members of its Legislative Council replaced four delegates who had resigned in late August. The Convention had to consider the 286 amendments proposed by the ten Houses of Parliaments. To expedite proceedings, it resolved that Sir Richard Baker as Chairman of Committees should move the amendments proposed by the colonial parliaments.

On 3 September, Barton moved for the re-appointment of the drafting committee of himself, Downer and O'Connor. Walter James of Western

'the finest instrument of government that ever was framed'

Australia proposed to add three delegates: Kingston, Symon and Isaacs. La Nauze thought the additional names 'unexceptionable': 'Kingston was a celebrated draftsman, and Symon and Isaacs had been powerfully impressive as legal critics.'[8] All three were probably aware of moves to add them to the committee. Supporters of the amendment believed that the additional names would strengthen the committee and extra eyes would reduce the chances of mistakes. Baker opposed the motion, while quick to describe the proposed additions as 'three of the most qualified men in Australia so far as draftsmanship is concerned'. He just thought that the additional membership would make the committee 'too large'. Baker was not so bothered about size when in the preceding discussion the Convention had agreed to double the membership of the committee to investigate finance. Perhaps Baker felt that a firm assertion by an august figure such as himself was sufficient to achieve his objective, namely, to block the elevation of his two greatest enemies in Kingston and Symon. Other speakers emphasised a different point. They treated the James amendment as a criticism of the work undertaken by the existing committee. Kingston and Symon pointedly said they had no criticism to make of the drafting committee. As Symon put it, he did not believe 'that in any assembly in the world, or in any body of the profession, you would be able to find three men of greater capacity for the work which they undertook than the three members of the Drafting Committee selected in Adelaide'.[9]

James' motion vote was lost 21–20. Of the ten South Australians, Kingston, Symon and Downer abstained, Cockburn, Gordon and Holder voted for the amendment and Baker, Glynn, Solomon, and Howe voted against it. Barton and O'Connor joined Downer in abstaining, Reid supported the amendment while the Victorians, including Isaacs but excluding Quick, opposed the amendment. Symon was not upset about the outcome and continued in the role of legal critic. There was, however, a noticeable change in his approach in debate. Symon became less patient in dealing with objections and less tolerant of opposition. This shift became even more pronounced when the Convention moved to Melbourne.

Quick and Garran concluded that four questions dominated the discussions in the month available for the Sydney session: finance, the basis of representation in the Senate, the power of the Senate in relation to money bills and the provision for deadlocks between the two Houses. Symon was particularly interested in the latter three but intervened briefly on the finance question.[10]

Carruthers notionally headed the opposition to equal State representation in the Senate. He proposed proportional representation as the alternative. Carruthers argued that none of the three great purposes of federation – taxation, defence and White Australia – were State questions. He worried that, while the representatives of NSW and Victoria wanted to prevent the immigration of undesirable aliens, the three smaller States might throw open the ports of Melbourne and Sydney to men 'who may degrade our manhood and our womanhood'. Carruthers would, however, accept equal representation if the procedure for resolving deadlocks between the Houses left the final decision to the popular vote.

Higgins spoke on 9 September. He claimed that more people in Australia were recognising the 'absurdity' of the arrangement reached in Adelaide whereby in all legislative subjects 'a man in New South Wales is to be treated as equal only to one-eighth of a man in Tasmania'. Such an arrangement rested on the 'fallacious principle' that in a federation legislation required 'the consent of the states as well as the consent of the people'. He defied anyone to point to any real authority who claimed this proposition to be 'an essential principle of federation'. Higgins pressed the point: the only principle in favour of equal representation was that without equal representation there would be no federation.[11]

Symon agreed with half of Higgins' argument:

> whilst it may be a matter of expediency, whilst it is indeed an absolute necessity in order to secure federation, and an early federation, it is also founded on what we believe to be right principle and just reason.

Symon replied to Higgins for 75 minutes elaborating what he meant by 'right principle and just reason'.[12] A federation represented the middle ground between unification and a confederation; that is, the States would continue to exist and required equal representation within part of the legislature for a federation to exist. His best example was the United States which created a Senate with equal representation for each of

'the finest instrument of government that ever was framed'

the thirteen original colonies and provided equal representation for each of the added States. Unlike in ancient Greece, the system of equal representation survived, thrived and became entrenched in the modern United States.

In support of his case, Symon frequently quoted Edward Augustus Freeman's *History of Federal Government* (1863).[13] Higgins and Symon quibbled over Freeman's findings, with some irritation evident on both sides. Freeman may have demonstrated that equal representation in the Senate was necessary to establish the United States and that equal representation 'worked' in America. Yet Freeman could not help Symon confront Higgins with a 'right principle' of sufficient power to match one man-one vote, let alone one vote-one value. At best, Symon provoked Higgins to interject that he did not think the States should be represented in the federation, thus enabling Symon to conclude that Higgins 'is not a federationist at all'. He was a unificationist who wanted to absorb the States and was like the celebrated Cassowary bird which

> *On the plains of Timbuctoo,*
> *Ate up the missionary,*
> *Body, bones and hymn-book, too.*

The supporters of equal representation had another easy victory. The Convention voted 41–5 in support of its retention; in Adelaide, the vote was 32–5. The five on both occasions consisted of Carruthers and Lyne of NSW and Berry, Higgins and Trenwith of Victoria. In Sydney the South Australians voted in a bloc on the representation issue, except for Baker who was in the chair and Glynn who had left for Melbourne to get married.

There was no such unity on the question of Senate powers in relation to money bills.

Forrest and Downer led the smaller colonies in their quest to reverse the Adelaide resolution to set aside the 1891 decision to give the Senate the power to amend as well as reject money bills. Symon made an uncharacteristically brief speech on 14 September. He acknowledged that the direct power of amendment 'is of great importance to the strength, and to what is, perhaps, of as much consequence, the dignity of the senate'. He also agreed with Forrest that the giving up of this power was to acknowledge the Senate's inferiority to the House of Representatives in relation to 'a certain class of bills'. Yet even without this power the Senate 'may still hold with effect a great and patriotic position in the councils of the nation'. The Senate's present control over finance 'is sufficiently large to enable it to exercise a very strong and very satisfactory power in the state'. In his view the clause accepted in Adelaide 'will not materially weaken the senate'. Symon believed that 'the irrevocable moment' in the movement to federation had arrived, and he would be guided on all questions of greater or lesser consequence 'to remove every obstacle ... so long as it is not entirely essential to this great cause'.[14]

The final vote was 28–19 for the retention of the Adelaide decision. The six who detached themselves from their blocs in Adelaide – Brown, Fysh, Henry and Lewis of Tasmania and Glynn and Kingston of South Australia – were now joined by Symon, James of Western Australia and Clarke of Tasmania. As he saw it, Symon had lived up to his Adelaide promise to vote for federation.

Quick and Garran saw the deadlocks debate as the 'longest and most important' of the Sydney session.[15] It was also inconclusive. There was general support for some device to break deadlocks, which a few delegates like John Downer were not convinced would occur. The options included the dissolution of both houses, either consecutively or simultaneously, and a national or a dual referendum. The NSW and Victorian delegates wanted to ensure that, in the end, the Senate would have to give way to a majority in the House of Representatives. Delegates from the smaller colonies were watchful of proposals which directly or indirectly undermined the benefits of equal representation.

Symon figured prominently in the deadlock debates in Sydney. He had success when the Convention voted 27–22 in support of his amendment that, should a deadlock continue after dissolution of the House of Representatives, there should be a dissolution of the Senate.[16] He did not expect his amendment to be the final solution. Symon wanted to establish a 'safety valve' whereby what he called 'the two forms of democracy' – the Commonwealth vote and the States' vote – should have an equal role.[17] He was implacably opposed to a straightforward national referendum and clashed several times with Higgins, whom he said at one stage 'is always poisoning something or other'.[18] The deadlock debate marked a turning point in Symon's manner at the Convention. He became prone to heavy sarcasm and argued in a warlike manner. Higgins spoke earlier about the debate reaching the stage where the greatest self-restraint had become necessary to achieve federation. Yet 'Mr Symon ... spoke as if he were going to lead an army with a free and flashing sword against the larger states if there were any infringement of what he considered to be the rights of the smaller states'.[19]

Bernhard Ringrose Wise (NSW) had successfully moved that Symon's dissolution of the Senate should be replaced by a double dissolution. There remained the problem of establishing finality if the two Houses stayed deadlocked after a double dissolution. Carruthers, acting as he often did on Reid's behalf, proposed that the measures in dispute should go to a joint sitting of both Houses where a three-fifths majority would be required to pass legislation. Howe tried to raise the required majority to two-thirds, while Higgins wanted a bare majority. Symon voted for the original Carruthers proposal which he decided 'would reach finality with the least possible mischief'.

Symon normally regarded Reid, Higgins or Carruthers as his principal opponents because they wanted to ensure that 'the People's House' held sway over the 'States' House'. In the deadlocks debate he also had to contend with miscreants from his own province. John Alexander Cockburn, a medical doctor, a former Premier (1889–90) and from 1893 Minister for Agriculture and for Education, was considered the most radical member of the Kingston Cabinet. He was also seen as least likely to hold onto an idea and the least down-to-earth. The *South Australian Register* dubbed him 'the Doctor of Fanciful Notions'. Cockburn did, however, have an unshakeable commitment to State rights. He believed that the Carruthers proposal would be a final blow to the existence of the Senate because it would be outnumbered two-to-one in a joint sitting and in debating talent, and would not be supported by the press. Cockburn wanted to 'take a last loving look at the senate before it disappears into the interior chamber of representatives'.[20]

Symon responded with his own 'fanciful notions'. He believed that the members and senators who met after a double dissolution would be actuated by a desire to come to a reasonable conclusion. He did not think that in a joint sitting the smaller states in the Senate and the larger numbers in the House of Representatives would combine to override each other.[21] Symon expected that the underlying constructive and non-partisan outlook he detected in the Convention would be replicated in both Houses after federation.

The Convention moved to Melbourne for a session lasting almost two months: 20 January–17 March 1898. It had to endure almost unbearable summer heat. Quick and Garran concluded that three debates proved to be of pre-eminent importance: the rivers question, finance and railway rates.[22] Symon participated with his customary vitality in the debates on all three subjects and was a principal participant in a vigorous debate on deadlocks, the judicature and appeals to the Privy Council.

On 21 January J.H. Gordon proposed a motion, which originated in South Australia's Legislative Council, calling for the federal power to regulate navigation of the River Murray and to manage the use of its waters and those of the Darling, the Murrumbidgee and the Lachlan.[23] When Sir William Zeal of Victoria objected to the inclusion of the tributary rivers Gordon delivered a sharp response: 'If the honorable member got into a canoe at the head of any of those rivers, and has not after a long political career lost the art of steering straight, he would at the end of his journey find himself at the mouth of the Murray, and in South Australia.'[24]

Glynn, rather than Gordon, is usually and rightly remembered as the authoritative and persistent advocate of the South Australian position. Few in 1898 or later noticed that Symon intervened 19 times in the debate and delivered well-researched and effective speeches and counter-points proffering many amendments and amendments to amendments.[25] He began with a crisp statement: 'We desire that the Federal Parliament shall have and shall exercise such a control over all these rivers that navigation below shall not be impeded and lessened.' Throughout the tortuous hours of debate he kept insisting on one central point: 'All I ask you [the Convention] to say is – "This is a federal matter; put your faith in the Federal Parliament".' He refused to be diverted by Reid's pleas and dishonesty:

> Reid: if you throw yourselves on charity, and come to us, we will be with you, as we have always done – treat you in the most handsome matter

'the finest instrument of government that ever was framed'

Symon: You would not give us a cup of cold water if you could help it from these waters. You not only do not give us a drink, but you put our remonstrances in your pigeon-holes.[26]

After what La Nauze called 'a marathon debate', covering 21–25 January, a private failed conference, and then 1–5 February, the Convention agreed to a new s.100 which, with a crucial word printed here in italics, became:

> The Commonwealth shall not, by any law or regulation of trade or commerce, abridge the right of a State or of the residents therein to the *reasonable* use of the waters of rivers for conservation or irrigation.

Downer had proposed the addition of the word 'reasonable', infuriating Reid and pleasing those like Symon who wanted to 'Trust the Parliament'. La Nauze concluded that the passage of time rendered the debate to be 'much ado about nothing'.[27]

Symon played a central role in an issue – appeals to the Privy Council – which he believed had been settled in Sydney (1891) and Adelaide (1897). The text of what was then cl.73 laid down that there should be no appeal to the Queen in Council from any State or Federal Court or from the High Court, except that the Queen would have the right in matters which concerned the public interests of the Commonwealth, of any State or of any other part of her dominions to grant leave to appeal from the High Court to the Queen in Council. Sir Joseph Abbott believed that the Privy Council should be the final Court of Appeal in all matters. Knowing he must compromise, Abbott moved in Melbourne on 11 March the addition of the following words: 'saving any right that Her Majesty may be pleased to exercise by virtue of her Royal prerogative.' He quoted an earlier Symon comment – 'We are creating a nation which is to be self-contained, self-sufficing in every possible respect' – to make his point that the present clause meant Australia would not remain 'an integral part of the British Empire'. Abbott believed that every subject of the Empire had the right of appeal to the Sovereign which was 'a grand right, and a grand link for the whole of the British Empire' while 'the unity of final decision preserves a unity of law over the whole empire'.

Abbott assembled several additional arguments, some of them

pertinent. Gladstone's Home Rule Bill preserved appeals from Irish Courts to the Privy Council. The Privy Council, unlike the High Court, would not be circumscribed by local factors around Australia, and it was not dilatory or overly expensive in handling appeals. In 1875 the British Government had rejected a similar Canadian attempt to cancel appeals and Chamberlain would probably do the same with the Australian proposal. Twenty-six petitions had been lodged opposing the abolition of appeals and none arrived in favour. It would be 'a great loss' to pass up the opportunity of having the Privy Council decide 'difficult and complicated points of law which from time to time may arise in the local courts'.

Abbott showed signs of irritation at the regularity of interjections and appealed to an exasperated Baker for assistance from a fellow occupant of a Chair. His irritation increased when Symon spoke in reply and appeared to misrepresent him. Abbott, perhaps rightly, considered Symon's remarks 'very impertinent' for saying that Abbott was becoming 'uncommonly touchy and sensitive'; he had been 'a little more moderate before lunch, but something at lunch must have been unpalatable to him'.

Symon's arguments were probably better organised but a quorum had to be called to bring his audience back into the Chamber. The petitions did provide him with some new material. Symon enjoyed observing that they nearly all came from the same source – the banks and other lending institutions – and contained errors which suggested an ignorance of English courts. Symon focused on the petition of the Metropolitan Board of Works in Melbourne which claimed that to take away the right of appeal to England would weaken its credit. The Board already owed the Victorian Government £2.5m and up to £2m to English bondholders. Symon added: 'if the enthusiasm of these gentlemen [the petitioners] for federation is of so Laodicean a character that it requires to be galvanized into vitality by the establishment of an additional law court, it is not of much value to the cause.' Symon was perfectly happy to reproduce his remarks which Abbott had quoted. A self-contained and self-sufficient nation which is capable of making laws ought to be capable of interpreting them. Abbott's amendment would affix 'a badge of inferiority on the National Court'. 'I call that a Little Australia policy', and 'my honorable friend is, in this matter, the leader of the little Australians'.

'the finest instrument of government that ever was framed'

For Symon, one question remained: where did he stand on the Empire?

> I am not Australian born myself, but this is my country; it is my home. For all that, I do not wish for one moment to loosen any tie which connects us with the mother country. I am proud to belong to the race ... which is first among the strong ones of the earth, the race whose footfall is heard in every clime.[28]

This declaration did not save the day. The Committee voted 20–19 to approve Abbott's amendment. Deakin, Forrest, O'Connor and Reid supported the amendment while Barton, eight of the South Australians and Isaacs and Higgins opposed it. Symon saved the day a few minutes later. He moved to add the following to the Abbott amendment: 'and until the Parliament otherwise provides.' Abbott argued that Symon's amendment negated his approved amendment and was, therefore, out of order. Barton said it was not, and Baker ruled that it qualified but did not negate it.[29] Symon's amendment was carried 21–17: Carruthers, Deakin, Lewis, O'Connor and Reid changed sides and Solomon, Berry, Quick and Glynn went the other way.

On the same day, 11 March, the Convention returned to another of Symon's causes. Clause 80 of the draft laid down that:

> No person holding any judicial office shall be appointed to or hold the office of Governor-General, Lieutenant-Governor, Chief Executive Officer, or Administrator of the Government, or any other executive office of the Commonwealth.

The clause had survived earlier assaults but there had been a lot of re-thinking in private. The eventual vote of 26–11 eliminated the clause altogether.[30] Symon was joined by Cockburn and Downer but five South Australians voted against him. Isaacs and Higgins delivered the more significant negative votes. As will be shown in Chapter 17 Isaacs proved to be a beneficiary of this decision in 1930. Higgins in 1898 stood alongside Sir Samuel Griffith: 'we have no right to dictate to her Majesty who should be her agents.' The rebel was not always radical.[31]

The Carruthers who admired the Symon he encountered in Adelaide was much more critical of the one he met in Sydney and Melbourne. He thought Symon was rather bitter in retort and in personal criticism, a failing which at times somewhat spoilt the effect of his very fine speeches. According to Carruthers, Symon was obstinate in clinging to his opinions and would restate them with impatience. Sometimes he was humorous, but his humour was often tinged with unnecessary sarcasm or irony. He ranked with Barton and Isaacs in his knowledge of his subject but, like Isaacs, he was rather partial in his opinions; in this respect he was unlike Barton, who was and strove always to be impartial.[32]

Symon was well aware of the criticisms which had been levelled against his manner during debates. In his final speech to the Convention, he tried humour to deflect some of the attention: 'Even I myself have been told that my natural sweetness of temper has shown slight signs of wear.' Symon asked his audience not to misinterpret any harsh words.

> But I hope, sir, if any word of mine or any departure from my natural equanimity has even seemed to wound any honorable member of this Convention it will be forgiven me, and that it will be understood that there was no sting in anything that I said that was intended to hurt anybody in the slightest degree.

Symon then highlighted what he would, much later in his life, recall as one of his significant achievements: his proposal, accepted unanimously, that Barton should lead the deliberations and proceedings of the Convention. Symon said Barton had 'outstripped his reputation'. Barton's efforts in the cause of federation had become a source of pride to every member of this Convention and to 'every man, woman, and child in Australia who loves his or her country, and appreciates the advantages of union'.

Like the other delegates who spoke at the final meeting of the Convention, Symon applauded their joint efforts. He referred to the proposed Constitution as the 'new Magna Charta', but wanted to pinpoint a key difference: 'The Great Charter was wrung by the barons of England from a reluctant king. This new charter is to be given by the people of Australia to themselves.' Resuming his life as 'a private citizen', Symon intended to accept the Constitution 'without reservations and without misgivings'. It was a human creation and therefore not perfect. Even so, it was 'an elastic Constitution' – many judges and legal counsel set out to prove it so – and it will be found 'saturated with those principles of free government which are inherent in the British race'. For that reason,

'the finest instrument of government that ever was framed'

Symon felt he could say 'this Constitution is the finest instrument of government that was ever framed'.[33]

He could also claim to have influenced its construction even though his contribution would be generally undervalued. Lesser figures from South Australia are better known or remembered – Paddy Glynn for the insertion of the Deity into the Constitution and Howe for persuading the Convention to add age and invalid pensions to the list of the Commonwealth's powers.[34] Symon could not expect to win rapt attention for repeatedly intervening to improve the wording of clauses. He did achieve notice at the time and later for piloting the Judiciary Committee and its findings through the Convention. With the zeal of a convert, Symon fought to make the High Court the final court of appeal and became identified with the cause in the press of the capital cities. Less obviously, he was the voice of conviction rather than of resignation in mounting the argument for retaining the 1891 decision for equal State representation in the Senate. Barely noticed, Symon sacrificed strongly held principles to secure federation, especially when he accepted the Senate's inferior status in relation to money bills. It was one of those occasions during the Convention when Symon felt that federation itself lay in the balance.

Symon's stand on money bills did not endear him to Downer and Forrest and other members of the State rights party. Nor did his frequent references to the pervasive 'federal spirit' he detected moving the Convention to accept compromise for the sake of the greater good. Later in his life Symon praised those who maintained a 'federal spirit', disparaged those whom he thought had lost sight of it and pitied those, like Prime Minister Stanley Bruce in the 1920s, who was too young to have experienced it. Post-federation, Symon looked upon the High Court to implement the 'federal spirit' by protecting State rights while, at the same time, adopting a 'progressivist' approach by bringing the Constitution into line with modern needs and exigencies.[35] As will be seen, the Colonial Office and the High Court obliged Symon to re-think several of his positions.

He never doubted that the Australian people would accept the Constitution Bill. Symon worried only about the number of 'stay-at-home' voters and, like Alfred Deakin, feared that the failure to achieve a union at this time would mean a failure for a generation or more. The delegates now had the task of helping people to understand the Bill so they would be prepared to support it in the ballot box. The prize was

> a union with strong foundations set deep in justice, a union which will endure from age to age, a bulwark against aggression and a perpetual security for the peace, freedom, and progress of the people of Australia, giving to them and to their children and to their children's children through all generations the priceless heritage of a happy and united land.

Kingston, Holder and Glynn were the first of the South Australian delegates to enter the referendum campaign. Symon followed on Monday 4 April with a two-hour speech at the Adelaide Town Hall under the auspices of the Patriotic Association of South Australia. Howe and Solomon and representatives of various Associations joined him on the platform. The *South Australian Register* reported that Symon addressed 'a large and enthusiastic audience' and delivered 'a masterly exposition' of the principal features of the Commonwealth Bill. The pro-Labor *Weekly Herald* admitted that the speech was 'clever' but, beyond that, amounted to 'a mere mass of high flown platitudes, bombastic assertions, gaudily coloured pictures of impossible conditions and vague unsatisfactory generalities'. The editorial found 'plenty of glitter but no gold, plenty of rhetoric but no reason'. Symon's 'burning patriotism' could not hide the fact that he was unable to show how 'the condition of the wealth makers of the country will be improved'. To do that 'was too great a task even for Mr Symon's genius, and so he wisely left it alone.' In effect, Symon received notice that Labor-oriented opinion was hostile.[36] The 'Personal Gossip' column of the *Critic* described the speech as 'one of the poorest, for him, the writer has heard'. It was a mistake for Symon to use notes because the practice did not suit his style of oratory. Having heard nearly all his major court speeches in criminal trials the writer observed that his best one – given when successfully defending Benjamin Watts in the Eudunda murder trial in 1891 – was delivered without using a single note.[37]

Symon made a point of praising Barton and Reid and especially the latter for his speech of 28 March delivered to an audience of nearly 5000 at the Sydney Town Hall. Reid spoke, as he himself described it, with 'the deliberate impartiality of a judge addressing a jury'. For about two hours and mostly without notes Reid reviewed the clauses of the Bill, identified

'the finest instrument of government that ever was framed'

his wins and losses for NSW and showed the audience the 'dark' and the 'light' places in the Constitution. He concluded with the hope that every man 'will judge for himself' but 'I consider my duty to Australia demands me to record a vote in favour of the bill'. Initially, the anti-federalists attacked Reid for seeming to abandon their cause. In Adelaide, a week later, Symon told his audience on 4 April how he 'tingled with pride' when he read Reid's final sentence saying he would vote for the Bill: 'no man would take a higher place' in the history of Australia at this time than George Reid. By June, Symon had joined the pro-federalists who felt let down by 'Yes-No Reid' and re-interpreted Reid's judicial assessment as equivocation bordering on treachery.[38]

While continuing with his court work, Symon campaigned for the 'Yes' vote in South Australia. On 18 April, he joined the other nine South Australian delegates in signing a one-page letter addressed *To the People of South Australia*. The argument for union was cast in the most general terms. The delegates said the duty conferred on them had been accomplished after four months of 'patient labour' assisted by 'a prevailing desire to be just and a patriotic spirit of conciliation'. The delegates agreed to a speaking plan whereby Kingston and Glynn were to stump the central areas, Baker and Gordon took the south-east and Howe the north, while Symon and Solomon should 'go where they please'. Symon went to Wallaroo on 18 April and spoke for two-and-a-half hours and was cheered 'to the echo' after a giving lucid and instructive 'lecture'.[39] Accompanied by Holder, he spoke in Burra on 29 April. He used the 19th anniversary of the Young Men's Christian Association and his role as 'Governor' at the Literary Societies' Union Parliament to advocate a vote for federation. By arrangement, Symon and Gordon undertook a letter-writing campaign in the press replying to the Bill's leading independent and Labor opponents.[40]

The result of the referendum in South Australia, held on a public holiday on 4 June, was a foregone conclusion. The 'Yes' vote of 35,800 represented 67.39 per cent of those voting. There were 17,239 'No' votes. The worrying fact was that the voter turnout stood at just 30.9 per cent. Unabashed, Symon said South Australia 'has done her part nobly'. The poll had shown that provincialism was 'surely dying' while 'the cause of union has had a glorious victory'. Of the other colonies, Victoria and

Tasmania each recorded 'Yes' votes of over 80 per cent although the turnout in the latter was only 25 per cent. NSW registered a 'Yes' vote of just under 52 per cent but fell more than 9,000 votes short of the statutory minimum of 80,000 affirmative votes imposed by the NSW Parliament in 1898. Symon refused to believe that 'the people of the mother colony will allow the stain of having broken faith with Australia – for I consider the 80,000 clause a gross breach of faith – to rest upon the colony'.[41]

In the wake of the NSW result George Reid telegraphed the other Premiers suggesting further negotiations to make the Bill more acceptable to NSW voters. He intended making a successful revised arrangement 'a vital part' of his Government's policy for the NSW State election of 27 July.[42]

Others discussed the forthcoming State election. Bernhard Wise told Symon on 5 June that 'we intend to mete out justice to George Reid – the most faithless imposter that ever wore the cap and bells in Australian political life'.[43] Deakin wrote to Symon on the following day: 'I felicitate your province not only upon the result but upon the harmony which has prevailed among all her representatives.' The position in NSW is 'very critical' and he trusted that every effort would be made from South Australia to influence both Barton and Reid 'though I fear the latter will prove impervious'. If they failed with Reid, 'we must trust to Barton to fight the election'. Deakin wrote a further letter to Symon on 9 June. His information relating to Western Australia was 'rather discouraging'. Deakin had written to Forrest and hoped that Symon would do the same because 'your' relations with Western Australia were 'more intimate than ours'. As for NSW, 'if Reid merely desires an excuse for taking up the Bill ... we should do well to afford him that or any other means of escape that we can without sacrifice of principle'. Deakin thought the longer they could keep Reid from declaring against the Bill the better it would be; if 'we can secure him' the more votes would come from NSW where they were needed. While he described Kingston's response to Reid as 'manly' Deakin hoped that Kingston 'would lend a hand to his weaker brother Premier for the sake of the cause'. In yet another letter Deakin passed on to Symon a verbal request he had received from 'Sydney' for financial support for candidates in the Broken Hill seats.[44]

For all their hopes, and for all that Reid's Free Trade Ministerialists now depended on the Labor Party to stay in office, 'Yes-No' Reid remained

'the finest instrument of government that ever was framed'

Premier. The other Premiers accepted his proposal for a conference which eventually met in Melbourne between 29 January and 3 February 1899.

Symon, the self-proclaimed 'private citizen', remained on the sidelines in the second half of 1898. Looking ahead to 1899 he planned to take a six-month holiday with most of his family in the United Kingdom, France and Italy. In the meantime, he worked long hours on his legal practice. Judging by his own papers and press reports of his cases Symon never had to worry about unemployment. He was in demand in the second half of 1898 for long-running lucrative cases in estate management and took many briefs in divorce proceedings and in cases where Symon defended the respectable and the disreputable who frequented illegal betting establishments.

Two trials featuring George Newman, a former headmaster of a private school in North Adelaide, attracted considerable public attention. Newman was charged with 'unlawfully and indecently assaulting' a boy of 15 on or about 19 November 1897 and a boy of 14 on 27 May 1898. At the trial on the first charge, Symon ridiculed a Baptist minister who had acted as a moral policeman of the Free Church variety and had informed the accused, the Police and the Court that Newman was guilty. Symon declared it would have been 'better for the boys, better for the institution, better for the interests of social morality, better in the interests of social justice, that this case should never have come before the court'. The jury took just 15 minutes to find Newman 'not guilty'. In the second instance, Justice Bundey ordered the jury to find Newman 'not guilty' after Symon demonstrated that the Crown had no case at all. It was difficult to proceed when the boy could not recollect anything of the alleged incident relevant to the trial. A sterner judge might have spoken strongly to the Crown Solicitor about taking such a weak case to court.[45]

While dealing with the Newman case Symon had to think again about the make-up of his firm. The partnership of Symon, Bakewell, Stow and Piper, formed in 1892, collapsed overnight when Symon's three partners walked away to establish their own legal firm. No details were released but the gossip in legal circles suggested that Symon did not foresee or want the break-up. On the other hand, his reputation, and the record of rapid success of former partners and clerks he had trained, meant he could launch a new partnership – Symon, Rounsevell and Cleland – within a few weeks. Rounsevell had served articles under Symon, practised on his own for three years, taken a partnership with a very successful firm with offices in Perth, Coolgardie and Kalgoorlie before returning to Selborne Chambers. E. Erskine Cleland had, like Rounsevell, served as an associate to Justice Bundey, and worked in another Adelaide firm before joining Symon as a well-regarded and bright young lawyer who was expected one day to join the Bench.

Symon continued to live a full life outside of his legal career and federation activities. He was President of the Literary Societies' Union, of the South Australian Law Society and of the Home for Weak-minded Children. Symon attended meetings as a member of the University of Adelaide Council and addressed a meeting of the Adelaide Jewish Literary Society on William Shakespeare and presided at meetings of the University's Shakespeare Society of which he was Vice-President. There were family moments when he could feel optimistic. His wayward brother William had been admitted to the Bar in Perth.

The year 1898 ended well for Symon, though he was not then aware of the mostly high regard in which he was held in one unlikely circle. Sidney and Beatrice Webb, two London Fabians, visited New Zealand and Australia in the second half of 1898. They kept a diary which reflected their well-developed superiority complexes. Beatrice wrote that all the ministers they met in Melbourne were 'mediocre in capacity except the Attorney General – [Isaac] Isaacs – a clever pushing young Jew of whom I think, more will be heard'. Sidney was first inclined to dismiss Samuel Way as 'a fussy little methodist [sic] deacon; presently you discover he is good and wise'. Beatrice thought Kingston was 'a burly ruffian ... an unsavoury combination of the demagogue and a London vestryman of the old type ... [and] somewhat disreputable in his private life'. The Webbs delivered three assessments of Josiah Symon: he was 'the only man we met in Australia who can lay claim to the indescribable quality of "distinction" as understood by fastidious society'; he was the 'most considerable person in Adelaide, from an intellectual standpoint'; he was 'a man of fifty, tall, grey and grave, with a gentle well-bred manner, he has a keen, cold, unimaginative intellect'.[46]

James Symon Snr: Josiah's father
[Elizabeth Dyer Papers]

Elizabeth Symon (née Sutherland): Josiah's mother
[Elizabeth Dyer Papers]

Margaret and Esther: two of Josiah's older sisters
[Elizabeth Dyer Papers]

Josiah Symon, articled clerk: c. 1865
[Elizabeth Dyer Papers]

James Sutherland ('Cousin'): c. 1865
[Elizabeth Dyer Papers]

Josiah's four brothers, from left:
Robert, David, James, William, c. 1870
[Elizabeth Dyer Papers]

Josiah Symon, senior partner,
Symon & Bakewell, c. 1878
[Elizabeth Dyer Papers]

William Symon of
Symon, Bakewell and Symon, c. 1879
[SLSA B63465]

Samuel Way, 1870
[SLSA B25119]

Josiah in Scotland, c. 1880

The Symons lived in 'Fitzroy House', re-named 'Selma',
in the inner city suburb of Prospect from about 1883.

'Manoah': the residence [SLSA B62720]

'Manoah': part of the working farm [SLSA B62721]

Christmas at 'Manoah', 1895: from left, Romilly on the horse, Kilmeny, Josiah, unknown servant, Oliver, Oscar, Charles, Nell, Lenore, Carril, unknown visitor, Margaret [SLSA B62726]

The five sons: clockwise, Charles, Carril, Romilly, Oscar and Oliver [SLSA]

Convention delegates, Adelaide, 1897
Top right: Symon standing between Higgins on his left and Walker on his right; Kingston is seated in the centre of the front row with Reid and Fysh to his right and Turner and Forrest to his left. Carruthers is standing between Kingston and Turner, Deakin is standing behind Carruthers, and Barton is on Deakin's left. [SLSA B12752]

Symon family at 'Manoah', 1903.
rear from left: Margaret, Kilmeny; middle from left: Lenore, Charles, Nell, Carril, Romilly, Josiah; front from left: Oliver, Angel, Mary, Oscar
[SLSA B62727]

A corner of the 'gentleman's library' at 'Manoah' [SLSA B62728]

The first High Court: from the left, Justice Barton, Chief Justice Griffith, Justice O'Connor, two of the first three Associates stand behind them. [NLA]

The short-lived Reid-McLean ministry
Back row: Sydney Smith, Dugald Thomson, James McCay, James Drake
Front Row: Sir George Turner, George Reid,
Baron Northcote (Governor-General), Allan McLean, Sir Josiah Symon [NLA]

Sir Josiah Symon in his KCMG attire [SLSA B7506]

Josiah, Commonwealth Attorney-General
[SLSA B63465]

Lady Symon: presentation at Court, 1907
[PRG 249_13_34]

Auldana vineyards
[PRG 280_1_43_159]

Auldana cellars: Edmond Mazure on the right, c. 1910
[SLSA B62610]

Angel, Josiah, Mary and 'Scamp': c. 1910 [PRG 249_13_97]

Josiah's sisters, Margaret and Esther, and his three eldest daughters –
clockwise from the top – Lenore, Kilmeny and Margaret, c. 1914
[Elizabeth Dyer Papers]

Supreme Court Bench, c. 1914: Sir John Gordon, Sir Samuel Way, Sir George Murray [SLSA B10458]

A twentieth-century man
[Elizabeth Dyer Papers]

9
'a great paean of triumph in the closely knit union of the race.'

George Reid's proposed Premiers' meeting took place in Melbourne between 29 January and 3 February 1899. The sessions were held *in camera* but their eight formal decisions were made public.[1] Critically, the Premiers agreed to reduce the requirement of a three-fifths majority to an absolute majority to pass measures at a joint sitting, thereby confirming Lower House supremacy in the settlement of a deadlock. The Premiers resolved to amend the 'Braddon clause' as proposed by the Tasmanian Premier – requiring that one quarter of customs and excise revenue go to the Commonwealth and three quarters to the States – by limiting its operation to ten years. The meeting also agreed to maintain the decisions on inland rivers and money bills, and to locate the seat of the Commonwealth government within NSW, albeit not closer than 100 miles from Sydney. Reid believed that the other Premiers wanted to meet the wishes of NSW and his biographer concluded that they made 'very significant concessions'.[2] 'Yes-No Reid' had won enough to secure his unequivocal commitment to the Commonwealth Bill.

In Adelaide, Sir John Downer believed that the Commonwealth Bill as it now stood did not provide for a true federation which depended on 'making the States' and the People's Houses co-ordinate in authority as in the United States'. NSW, 'as usual', proposed the three-fifths majority as a final settlement when in fact it was 'a means for asking for something more'. It had now obtained the resolution that destroyed the co-ordinate powers of the two Houses. Gordon telegraphed Kingston: 'Hearty congratulations on great success. Well done, good and faithful servant.' Josiah Symon's message to Kingston read: 'I do sincerely congratulate you upon the outcome of the Premiers' Conference, and your share in it.' The Premiers had 'worthily served the great cause and every one of us should acknowledge it'. Symon admitted that some of the decisions did not commend themselves to him, 'but in the general result I unaffectedly rejoice'.[3] He felt certain that the mooted changes would secure a resounding 'Yes' vote in the proposed second referendum.

The Symons left South Australia on 25 March 1899 on the French steamship *Polynesien* for a holiday in the United Kingdom. Josiah and Nell were accompanied by their three eldest daughters and two eldest sons. Nell's youngest and unmarried sister, Olive, joined them; at age 30 she could help with managing the family. Stopping off at Albany in Western Australia, Symon travelled to Kalgoorlie where he addressed 'a phenomenally large' gathering. Three days later he delivered 'a long speech' at the 4th annual conference and banquet of the ANA in Fremantle. He used his time in the West to tell the population they had to decide whether Australia would be a lopsided nation or one magnificent whole.[4] In Fremantle the Symon party boarded the German steamer *Prinz-Regent Luitpold* which took them to Naples. From there they began a leisurely trip through the cultural sites of Italy and France before reaching Dover in mid-May. They established their base at 72 Porchester Terrace, Bayswater, W2.

According to a 'Special Correspondent' in London on 18 June 1899, 'Mr. J.H. Symon QC is rushing about sight-seeing with the vehemence which so often appears to afflict colonists who come home rather late in life'. They do, however, make 'better tourists' than the younger generation 'and are models of Australasian deportment'.[5] Symon was more than a tourist. He wanted to catch up with his family in London and Stirling, probably sensing he would never see his mother again. There was also business to occupy his attention. One important engagement involved a luncheon with the Directors of the Great Boulder Proprietary Gold Mines Limited. Symon was one of the two local directors of the company in which he had invested heavily. Symon also visited the Colonial Office where he made a contact he sought to use during the following year. He met Lord Selborne, the son-in-law of the 3rd Marquis of Salisbury, then in office for the third time as the Conservative Prime Minister (1895–1902). Salisbury had appointed Selborne Under-Secretary of State for the Colonies, junior

'a great paean of triumph in the closely knit union of the race.'

to Joseph Chamberlain. Symon took an early opportunity to press upon Selborne both his, and what he believed was Australia's, view that the Commonwealth Bill should have a straightforward passage through the Imperial Parliament.

Symon learnt some welcome news while in England. He already knew that South Australia's 'Yes' vote had climbed to 79.46 per cent in the second referendum held on 29 April. The turnout had also risen to a more respectable 54.4 per cent. The referendum results in 1899 produced victories of landslide proportions for the 'Yes' vote in Tasmania and Victoria and clear-cut majorities in NSW and Queensland.

	Yes	No	Turnout
NSW – 29 June	107 420 (56.49)	82 741 (43.51)	63.4
Tas. – 27 July	13 437 (94.49)	791 (5.60)	41.8
Vic. – 27 July	152 653 (93.96)	9 805 (6.04)	56.3
Qld –28 September	38 488 (55.39)	30 996 (44.61)	54.4

Symon sent congratulatory cables to his friends in those colonies.

The outbreak of the Second Anglo-Boer War on 11 October 1899 gave Symon something more to cheer. He never doubted that the Empire would come together against President Kruger and the disloyal Boers of the Transvaal in South Africa. The jingoism of the late 19th century affected all classes and Symon was delighted to witness the response to Australian involvement:

> The general feeling is one of affection and pride, and that was never more splendidly exemplified than in the send-off given to the New South Wales Lancers. It was the most wonderful spectacle I ever saw. In the historic centre of the city, there was a seething mass of English men and women in simply an hysterical state of enthusiasm. The shouts and songs of the people were, [sic] really a great paean of triumph in the closely knit union of the race.[6]

Sailing on the German steamer *Bremen*, the Symon party reached Adelaide on 26 November. Two days later, the Kingston Government was defeated 26–25 in the House of Assembly. The Governor, Lord Tennyson, rejected Kingston's advice to dissolve or prorogue the Parliament and Vaiben Solomon, the former Convention delegate, formed a conservative government which lasted a week in office. Frederick Holder, Kingston's long-serving Treasurer, replaced Solomon and Holder remained Premier until he resigned in May 1901 to enter the Federal Parliament. A closer Symon-Kingston relationship was one outcome of these changes.

Symon heard on his return that O'Connor and some friends in Sydney had decided to raise money for Barton's wife and family. They wanted to thank Barton in this way for the financial sacrifices he had made in pursuing the federal cause. 'Toby Tosspot', as the *Bulletin* nicknamed him, had spent extravagantly and lived well. Acting without authority, a partner in Symon's firm had donated 50 guineas in the senior partner's name. On 15 December, an angry Symon expounded his views to James Walker, a treasurer of the fund-raising group. He was appalled to learn about the hat going around for Barton, all the more so because federation was not yet 'an accomplished fact'. Symon would gladly give to a 'publicly got-up & publicly-given' testimonial but taking the hat around 'in apparently surreptitious fashion is simply the solicitation of alms'. Sir Richard Baker may also have disapproved of the method, but changed his mind under pressure from Walker. Taking charge of the South Australian campaign, Baker assembled lists of possible donors and selected 25 individuals, including Symon, who were to contact prospective subscribers. Baker also imposed rules which Symon thought compounded the original impropriety. Subscribers, for instance, were not to know who else had subscribed. Symon informed Walker he was 'exceedingly disgusted with the whole affair'.

Walker replied on 20 December, telling Symon he was 'scarcely right' about the fund-raising. The money was being collected for Mrs Barton and the children's education. When the fund collected reached £1500-£2000 an appeal might be made to the general public. Walker intended to ask the Committee in Sydney to give Symon and others access to subscriber lists. So far the fund had collected £1400: South Australia had contributed £414 and Tasmania a little over £200. Nothing had yet arrived from Victoria and nothing much was expected from Queensland. Symon's gift was the largest single donation. Walker concluded by asking if Symon wanted his cheque returned. Before Symon could respond, the Sydney Committee sent him a replacement cheque which Symon forwarded to the Bushmen's Contingent Fund for the Boer War.

'a great paean of triumph in the closely knit union of the race.'

After seeing copies of the Baker-Symon correspondence Walker told Symon on 22 January 1900 'you do not come out as well as I thought you might have done'. Walker saw himself as a friend of both men and regretted that 'any coolness should have arisen between you, as apparently it has'. Determined as ever to clarify his position and have the final word, Symon replied three days later: 'I know that particular gentleman [Baker] a good deal better & much longer than you; I have had experience before this of his ways. However, *finis coronat opus* (the end crowns the work).' The war with Baker was resumed a few months later.

Symon had nothing against Barton, and just hoped he would not demean himself by accepting alms. He told Walker that if Barton approached him privately and in confidence about his financial situation Symon would be happy to help as far as he could. Nevertheless, Symon could not resist referring to his own sacrifices for the federal cause, for which he had never asked for a shilling in compensation. Although the two sets of circumstances were hardly comparable – unlike Barton, Symon was a wealthy barrister and investor – Symon made a fair point: Barton was responsible for the choices he had made.[7]

From Symon's viewpoint, Barton would play a crucial role in the coming months. Symon had spoken to Premier Holder on 21 December 1899 on the question of possible amendments to the Commonwealth Bill. Next day he wrote to Barton to say Holder 'is quite in agreement with my own views'. Both men believed that other than dotting an 'i' or crossing a 't', nothing should be amended. Symon assured Barton that his contacts earlier in the year with the Colonial Office and members of the House of Commons satisfied him 'that nothing of the kind will be attempted unless by some private member'. Symon did have a member in mind. Leonard Courtney, a West Country MP and former Gladstone minister might insist the Bill provide for the 'Hare-Spence system of minority representation!!' As he soon learnt, Joseph Chamberlain and the Crown Law officers constituted the real threat to an easy passage of the Commonwealth Bill.

As far as Symon was concerned there was no surer way of killing federation than by allowing amendments which, if accepted, would have to be taken back to the people. Once the idea of amendments was admitted there would be a succession of proposals from interested parties thus causing delays. In that situation, there would be a choice between re-opening 'the whole business' or standing aside while the Imperial Parliament decided what the Australian people would have to 'live with'. The most Symon would admit was that the Imperial Parliament had 'the *legal* power' to amend or reject the Bill but he insisted that it did not have the '*constitutional right* to do either'. Symon assured Barton he 'will find that they recognise this'.[8]

These thoughts acquired greater significance when Symon learnt of Joseph Chamberlain's telegraphic despatch of Christmas Eve 1899. Chamberlain expressed the hope that delegates would be sent to England 'to assist and explain when Parliament is considering the Federation Bill'. The delegates could confer with Her Majesty's Government and Crown Law officers and such a conference 'might avoid any protracted debates and any opposition, on technical grounds' before approaching the Parliament. Chamberlain asked, 'when may I expect them?'[9]

In response to this despatch, Allan McLean, the new Premier of Victoria, approached Deakin at the beginning of January 1900 to accept nomination as Victoria's delegate for the meeting with Chamberlain. He later assured Deakin that his appointment was 'universally applauded' by the other colonies.[10] Holder spoke out against McLean's actions and contacted the other Premiers to say he saw no need for a delegation. If there were to be one, the delegates should be appointed by the federating colonies.[11] He had no objection to Deakin representing Victoria but he did object to the Victorian Government making the appointment.

Chamberlain's despatch and McLean's action inspired Symon to assume a role as 'Defender of the Bill'. He strongly endorsed Holder's position in a letter sent to the Premier on 15 January. Symon called the Deakin appointment 'a hasty blunder'. McLean had been 'an uncompromising opponent of the Commonwealth Bill' and was not much guided by the federal spirit. If, as Holder said, there was to be a delegation it should be federally appointed and represent the federating colonies. Those colonies were as one in their acceptance of the Bill and in their desire to see it become an Imperial enactment without delay. If each colony sent a delegate it could keep alive the appearance if not the fact of disunion. Above all, as Symon saw it, there should be no room for the notion that any amendment or alteration of the Bill was permissible at the

'a great paean of triumph in the closely knit union of the race.'

hands of the Imperial Parliament. The very fact of sending a delegation 'may tempt or encourage efforts to amend'. The sole function of any delegation 'would be to remind the Imperial authorities that they are not asked to frame a Constitution for us and that they will wisely refrain from amending or interfering with what we have framed for ourselves'. A joint cable message should be sent to Chamberlain intimating that no alterations would be acceptable. The Australian people will accept 'the Bill, the whole Bill and nothing but the Bill'.

Symon did not express a thought which probably occurred to him at the mention of Deakin's name. He would certainly have remembered that Deakin was one of those in the Melbourne session who voted for the Abbott amendment on appeals to the Privy Council. Could Deakin be trusted to stand firm?

On 17 January Symon sent an eight-page memo to Lord Selborne. He referred to the 'consternation' of Australian federalists caused by Chamberlain's cablegram which was 'almost universally disapproved as unfortunate in itself and inopportune in time'. He wanted the Colonial Office to understand that the people voted to elect delegates to the Convention and then twice voted for the Bill proposed by the Convention. There could be no amendment without the direct approval of the Australian people. Rejection or amendment by the Imperial Parliament was 'unthinkable'. Any delay or rejection or amendment would reopen closed controversies, especially now that an anti-federationist (William Lyne) had taken office as Premier of NSW.[12] Symon claimed that the Chamberlain cable had caused friction between the colonies and imported delay, and asked why, if consultation were necessary, it was not sent much earlier. The only safe course now was to let it be clearly understood 'that Australia requires the Bill, the whole Bill and nothing but the Bill, and that no amendment affecting or altering in any particular the details of the federal scheme embodied in the Bill can be entertained'.

Symon wrote again to Selborne on 24 January against the background of the Premiers' meeting in Sydney that day to choose the delegates, and when Victoria's chosen delegate – Deakin ('no better choice could be made') – was leaving for England on 25 January. Symon's main objective in this memorandum was to remind Selborne of the arguments he put to him at their meeting last year in the Colonial Office, namely, that the

Australian Constitution, unlike the Canadian one, is a truly federal one based on that of the United States; the withdrawal of appeals to the Judicial Committee is a withdrawal from one of the Queen's courts and not an interference with the Royal Prerogative; Australia could establish a High Court of unquestioned authority.[13]

Looking further at the question of delegates, Symon was now less worried about McLean's 'hasty blunder'. Symon told Deakin in a letter he wrote on 19 January that he had read Deakin's comments made at a farewell party in Melbourne, at which Deakin said the delegates to London would 'in unison' explain, interpret, justify and defend the Bill that had come from the people. Symon wrote that Chamberlain's cable had created 'much uneasiness' about possible attempts at amendment. 'Your emphatic declaration has reassured us.'

Symon sent Deakin a further handwritten 'Private' note on 25 January 1900 to wish him 'bon voyage'. By now, Symon's 'only apprehension' about the delegation was that it was 'so late'. It should have gone to London a month ago because the wording of Chamberlain's message would, without any contribution from the Sydney anti-federalists, seem 'to suggest & has been taken as suggesting … the possibility of amendment. Like you, I am an ultra-Federalist, & I dread anything that will re-open closed controversies.' Symon assured Deakin that there 'is not a true Federalist in Australia [who] does not completely rest his hopes upon you'. He hoped for many reasons that Barton would accompany Deakin and would be glad if Kingston could be with you both 'but I hear that is impossible'. Symon sent his compliments to Lord Selborne and wished Deakin 'an early & triumphant return'.[14]

The Premiers' meeting of 24–27 January 1900 approved the appointment of five delegates to go to England. As La Nauze observed, four of the chosen ones – Barton, Deakin, Kingston and Fysh – had all been involved in the federation movement and constitution-making since 1891. None of them in 1900 held political office. James Dickson of Queensland, a current minister and a former Premier, was a latecomer who did not have the emotional attachment to the Commonwealth Bill held by the other four delegates. Western Australia appointed S.H. Parker, a barrister, as its representative. New Zealand selected Pember Reeves, its Agent-General in London. Both men were supposed to ensure that

'a great paean of triumph in the closely knit union of the race.'

the final version might allow their governments to join the federation on reasonable terms.[15]

Symon believed that Kingston was hesitating about making the trip to London. He was horrified on 27 January when the *South Australian Register* supported Baker for appointment should Kingston declare himself unavailable. Symon told William Sowden, the acting editor, that Baker would be a 'mischievous element'. He wrote again to Sowden on 2 February after learning that, if Kingston declined the appointment, the position would be offered to John Hannah Gordon. Symon thought both men were acceptable although Gordon would be 'inadequate' because he was 'by no means a strong man'. Should both men decline appointment Symon believed he ought to receive the next offer. 'I don't consider any one in this colony entitled to rank in front of me ... or that anyone is better qualified.' For one thing, he had been to the Colonial Office where he had exchanged views on the Commonwealth Bill. For another, 'as Chairman of the Judiciary Committee of the Convention, it would be fair & proper that I should be chosen to defend the Judiciary clauses & those dealing with appeals to the Privy Council which, it is an open secret, are those most likely to be attacked'. Sowden had told Symon that such a mission would involve him in a great sacrifice (presumably Sowden was thinking of lost legal business), but Symon was 'prepared to make almost any sacrifice to see our great work accomplished without any further avoidable delay'.[16]

Symon was miffed at not being considered. He told Charles Kaufman (his London stockbroker), much later, he was 'greatly disappointed' not to have come to England as a delegate. 'There are always wheels within wheels and solely for local political reasons another choice was made instead of myself.' He could have gone to London 'unofficially' but 'on reflection' realised his presence might have caused 'friction' and been 'undesirable' for the cause.[17] Putting his hurt to one side, Symon provided an impecunious Kingston with an undisclosed, non-refundable sum to help him with accommodation and expenses. Kingston returned the favour by keeping his supposed 'enemy' informed of what was happening in London. Their long association meant that Symon had learnt how to decipher Kingston's execrable handwriting.

Symon also went to war on a second front. He had been subscribing to the *Spectator* for some 30 years when he received his copy of the weekly edition published on 2 December 1899. It contained a short notice of a book by W.J. Galloway MP entitled *Advanced Australia*. Describing the author as 'an intelligent British tourist', the reviewer focused on his 'brief but pointed condemnation' of s. 74 of the Commonwealth Bill. Galloway had warned the Imperial Parliament that by not amending this clause it would loosen 'one of the essential bonds of empire – the judicial prerogative of the Crown'. The reviewer said that when Mr Chamberlain came to deal with the clause he would discover it was 'mainly the work of one or two prominent colonial lawyers – such as Mr Symon, Q.C., of Adelaide – who naturally wish to divide the fees of the Final Appeal Court'.

An outraged Symon dashed off a rejoinder of more than 4,000 words to the *Spectator* on 24 January. The anger showed: half or even a third of the number of words would have been sufficient to establish his argument. Sarcastic references to 'an intelligent British tourist', and repetition and over-statement, turned Symon's remarks into a speech at the Bar. Nonetheless, the article captured the essence of his stand against any amendment of the Commonwealth Bill which he expounded in public speeches, letters to the editor, messages to the like-minded and rejoinders and assaults in other written exercises throughout the year. His central points were that the Commonwealth Bill was drawn up by delegates elected by the people, the people twice endorsed the Bill and Australians were perfectly capable of interpreting their own work.

John St Loe Strachey, the *Spectator*'s long-serving editor, apologised to Symon for not striking out the offending personal reference in the review and for not having the space to accommodate his response.[18] Symon maintained his subscription; after all, Strachey opposed Home Rule and supported imperial expansion in Africa despite thoroughly despising Cecil Rhodes. Besides, Symon had a second objective; he reproduced his article as a pamphlet and distributed it free within Australia and in England.

Symon entered another controversy early in February 1900. Sir Samuel Griffith sent two letters to Sir John Forrest prior to the Premiers' meeting in Sydney. Griffith provided the Sydney *Daily Telegraph* with a copy of the second one which the paper published on 24 January. Griffith argued that if the other colonies really wanted to complete federation it was not too late for Western Australia to join; the proposed constitution was not

'a great paean of triumph in the closely knit union of the race.'

'sacred writ'. It was a means to an end and that end was not approval without alteration but 'the establishment of the Commonwealth on a satisfactory and workable basis'. On 30 January Symon wrote to his friend Henry ('Harry') Gullett, the former acting-editor of the *Sydney Morning Herald* (*SMH*). He attacked Griffith's 'very shocking and misleading letter' as not only 'a disingenuous and Jesuitical production' but 'calculated ... to do mischief.'

> Sir Samuel Griffith always speaks as 'Sir Oracle' and he had got into the habit in connection with federation of presuming upon his position and either patronising the members of the recent Convention or sneering at their labours.[19]

Symon hoped Gullett might arrange publication of his reply, preferably in the *SMH*.

The *SMH* published Symon's reply on 5 February. It began by dealing with Griffith's 'unwarranted assumption' that the other colonies had denied Western Australia's inclusion as an original State. Forrest had been given every opportunity to join, including concessions and inducements denied to the other colonies. Forrest had made pledges and then withdrawn them and then asked for still more concessions. Symon found many 'curiosities' (that is, 'pompous truisms') in Griffith's letter. He seized on Griffith's reference to his own 'tolerably long and varied experience' when declaring that all legislation could benefit from verbal amendment. No one, Symon observed, would disagree with that. No one would query Griffith's 'portentous announcement' that he regarded the Commonwealth Bill 'as merely human work, and therefore as possibly containing errors'. No one, so far as Symon was aware, had pronounced the Bill 'perfect'. Griffith had found 'grave difficulties' in the Bill's construction which might lead to litigation. Symon thought this piece of profundity amounted to stating the obvious about what might apply to all Acts of Parliament.

At this point Symon moved from the 'curiosities' to what he saw as the truly damaging and reprehensible aspects of Griffith's intervention. Griffith had written of the Imperial Parliament's duty 'to remove the ambiguities by explanatory and declaratory provisions or in some other way'. Here, in Symon's judgement, Griffith had moved beyond 'verbal' amendment'. How, Symon asked, would Griffith feel if the Imperial

Parliament found that the words Griffith saw as plain were 'ambiguities' and then explained or declared them 'out of existence'? How would the Australian people feel if the Imperial Parliament told them that the words they had approved did not mean what they wanted them to mean and were to be excised by a Parliament in which they were not represented? Symon did not want the Imperial Parliament to alter a word of the Bill. In any case, the body best suited to interpret and explain the Bill was a home-grown court of law.

After appearing to revise his earlier emphasis on simply improving and clarifying wording, Griffith returned to 'modifications of language' being the sole requirement when discussing the inclusion of Western Australia. Symon asked some more questions. What did the Queensland Chief Justice know of Forrest's current and future demands? If he did know what Forrest wanted, how could they possibly be 'formal amendments'? If he did not know what they were, his letter written 'by someone in his station, is worse than vain'. Sir Samuel Griffith may well have brought with him the memory of that sentence and of many others when joining the High Court in 1903.

On 15 March 1900, the delegates met Joseph Chamberlain and the Crown Law Officers in London. There followed three months of exchanges between the Colonial Office and the delegates.[20] In Adelaide, Symon briefed himself as counsel for the defence of the unamended Commonwealth Bill and of the Australian delegates in England. He wrote letters to the editor, took part in interviews and made speeches while keeping an eye on negotiations as reported in the Australian press and, later, in the British press and journals, Kingston's telegraphic messages and the official cables from London. He gave no indication of being troubled because Paris Nesbit and another 61 barristers and solicitors in Adelaide had informed Chamberlain that they 'strongly' supported retaining appeals to the Privy Council.[21] Symon was, however, incensed upon learning that Chief Justices Griffith and Way and Sir Richard Baker had sent secret messages to London supporting the retention of appeals. Symon admired the solidarity of four of the five delegates – Barton, Deakin, Kingston and Fysh – in the face of imperial pressure and a campaign for amendments in Australia. (Deakin said Dickson 'went boldly over to the enemy' and Symon dismissed him as a 'backslider'.[22])

'a great paean of triumph in the closely knit union of the race.'

Symon worried that the Premiers were not wholeheartedly behind the delegates when they met in Melbourne on 19–21 April. He worried even more when Chamberlain removed clause 74 from the bill he presented to the House of Commons on 14 May. He was perplexed by Chamberlain's complicated replacement but supported the delegates in accepting it. Symon was simply disbelieving on reading much later Deakin's claim that the delegates were so delighted by Chamberlain's compromise clause that on 17 May he, Barton and Kingston, when alone in the room together, seized hands and danced in a circle expressing their jubilation. Symon knew the men well, and dismissed the 'fandango' story as 'apocryphal'.[23] After more changes the final version of the clause was telegraphed to the Premiers on 19 May.[24]

Two overlapping episodes in May-June 1900 compelled Symon to focus more on developments in Adelaide. First, Chief Justice Way had published two 'Observations' in favour of retaining and increasing appeals to the Privy Council. Secondly, Kingston had nominated for election to the South Australian Legislative Council having resigned his West Adelaide seat upon accepting appointment as a delegate to London.

Symon was shocked to read in the *Advertiser* on 2 May that an English journal had referred to a pamphlet then in 'private circulation' in London, purportedly written by Sir Samuel Way on the subject of appeals to the Privy Council. According to the *Advertiser*'s 'Special Correspondent' the pamphlet had made 'a considerable impression'. Symon wrote immediately to Way saying he would be 'glad' to receive a copy. Way replied that he had not authorised the reference to his pamphlet. Symon would receive a copy, should he publish it. More letters flowed as Symon, who had sent Way a copy of his *Spectator* article, expected reciprocity. Way replied that Symon should not expect to receive a confidential pamphlet in exchange for a published document. On 15 May, the *Advertiser* and the *South Australian Register* printed Way's covering letter and his lengthy 'Observations' on Privy Council appeals originally sent in confidence to 'English and American friends'. On the same day, an *Advertiser* editorial said that the Chief Justice acted 'wisely' in handing his pamphlet to the press. Symon subsequently handed the Symon-Way letters to the *Advertiser*, claiming they might shed light on what Kingston in London had denounced as Sir Samuel Way's 'extraordinary extra-judicial and secret intrigues'.

Way's covering letter made three points: there was an absence of precise information about the appellate provisions of the Bill; his opinions had no representative or official authority and 'must stand or fall on their merits'; and clause 74 should be amended 'to make it consistent with the permanent union of the mother country and Australia and in the best interests of the Commonwealth'. Way related the history of appellate proposals from 1891 to the 1897–8 Convention showing that opinion was almost evenly divided on whether appeals should continue. Abbott's successful amendment would have left the prerogative intact to grant appeals from State Courts and the High Court but Symon 'at once' (in fact, another debate took place first) 'adroitly' moved an amendment which 'almost completely destroyed' the effect of the Abbott amendment. Way believed that the 'far reaching consequences' of both amendments had not been brought to the Convention's notice. Way continued his 'Observations' by suggesting that the meaning of clause 74 was unclear and its application to specific functions uncertain. He claimed it 'can hardly be disputed' that the stability of government and confidence in the judicature would be enhanced by having the authority of the Judicial Committee behind High Court decisions. There would be cases, as in the rivers issue, where decisions by a distant court would have more authority than a local one which appeared to favour one State over another. Further, the abolition of appeals did not have widespread and expressed support in Australia. The referendums approved the Bill as a whole but not the specific proposals, and amendments may be necessary because the British Government had not participated in the Convention.

Symon intended to respond immediately but was diverted by the controversy arising out of the speech he made on 15 May at a meeting in Stirling, nine miles south-east of Adelaide.[25] His advertised subject was 'Federation and the Commonwealth Bill' but Symon focused instead on what he saw as the Colonial Secretary's attempt to subdue 'the self-governing vitality' of the Australian people. Chamberlain wanted to amend the provisions curtailing access to the Privy Council. He also wanted 'to feel the Australian pulse'. As Symon put it, Chamberlain listened to the Governors, and notably Lord Lamington, the Governor of Queensland; to Chief Justices Griffith and Way and Sir Richard Baker who worked secretly to countermand the people's vote; and to 'the banks,

'a great paean of triumph in the closely knit union of the race.'

capitalists and moneyed institutions'. Symon had a second objective. He wanted to support Kingston for the Legislative Council election due on 19 May. The *Southern Cross* of 11 May had called Symon's plan a 'political sensation' and re-worked a Rudyard Kipling quotation: 'while Kingston saved the Empire, Josh Symon saved his place.'

Symon devoted the first part of his Stirling speech to those who 'interposed' in this public and national conflict 'to the detriment of the will of the people'. Griffith had done great service to federation 'but never seemed to have got over the fact that the Convention of 1897–8 did its work pretty well without him'. He was jealous, partisan and prejudiced, but at least had openly advised Forrest and the Colonial Secretary. Sir Samuel Way had no excuse. Nor did Sir Richard Baker, the President of the Legislative Council. He was another secret accomplice, 'a smaller man but one with a considerable capacity for mischief'. Symon claimed that Baker's letter to the Imperial authorities implied that an amendment was expected and, in effect, Baker invited an amendment to clause 74. As Chairman of Committees he had a 'solemn duty' to support the decisions of the Convention. Instead, he said an amendment would probably be moved and accepted. His actions amounted to 'treachery' and Baker 'had covered his name with shame'.

It could have been worse. The *Register* had said that if Kingston did not go to London then Sir Richard Baker might take his place. Symon asked the audience if anyone still queried why he supported Kingston. Acknowledging that he had opposed him in the past and would probably do so in the future, 'our country's welfare is our first concern'. The differences between Kingston and himself 'were all as dust ... compared with the vast national issue upon which Mr. Kingston now served his country'. Symon said it would '[be] cowardice' to stand back and not do justice to a man who 'had stood firm for the rights of the people'. There was no other way for him to show his disapproval of those striving to circumvent Kingston from doing his public duty and against whom Kingston was contending.

Symon knew he was taking a risk. The Stirling crowd kept cheering him, and one voice was heard to say, 'you are a better man than I thought you were'. Symon realised that his more natural constituency outside the hall, the conservatives who had come to loathe Kingston and all his works, would be at best puzzled and at worst appalled. Symon felt bound to state his position on conservatism:.

> The best Conservatism was that which answered the expressed will of the people. (Loud cheers.) Whether he was a Conservative or not, he would be no party to a Conservatism which preferred crooked by-ways and back door methods of resisting the people's will. (Hear, hear.) He wished to preserve Conservatism from that taint, and to make its political creed worthy of honorable men.

Many times in later years Labor supporters were suspicious when Symon deferred to the 'expressed will of the people', just as they scoffed when he called himself a democrat. Symon's version of what he understood to be Gladstonian liberalism seemed incongruous to them.

On 26 June 1900 Vaiben Solomon, who was now Leader of the Opposition in the South Australian House of Assembly, called Symon 'a traitor and a renegade'. This remark triggered an exchange of letters in which, starting with 'I never suspected you of the necessary truth or manliness', Symon employed sustained vituperation.[26] One conservative told Symon by letter that until she heard it from Symon's lips she would not believe it. Sowden was clear where he stood, informing Symon that Kingston was 'an utterly self-seeking ingrate' and 'a great – such a colossal – Humbug!'. Langdon Bonython, an *Advertiser* proprietor, saw things differently. He was glad that Symon and Kingston 'have fixed up matters' between them. Although the *Advertiser* disagreed with both men over appeals to the Privy Council, he hoped the reconciliation would be 'permanent' and that Symon would 'come over to our side of politics'. Bonython saw him 'at heart with us'.[27]

Baker reacted angrily to Symon's speech, calling it 'a tissue of misrepresentation'. In submitting memoranda to England he had refrained from expressing an opinion on clauses 73 and 74. He sent the documents at the time when there was no idea of sending delegates to England. It was understood in the press that amendments might be suggested for these clauses and he sent information on these matters. Baker recounted the progress of the appellate provisions through the 1891 and 1897–8 Conventions, recording the closeness of some votes while highlighting Abbott's attempts at Melbourne to restore the Queen's right to entertain

'a great paean of triumph in the closely knit union of the race.'

appeals and Symon's adroit action of excluding subjects relating to constitutional matters. Like Way, Baker did not feel inhibited by the limitations placed upon him by the positions he held. On 19 May he made a prediction about the first election to the Federal Parliament: 'I will be elected; Mr. Symon will be rejected – neither side believes in "apostates".' Baker was right only about his own election.[28]

John Lancelot Stirling (Conservative) topped the poll in Southern District with 4507 votes, Gordon, the Attorney-General, came second with 3844 and Kingston last with 3291. Kingston was not unduly distressed. He cabled Symon on 21 June after hearing the news of the Stirling speech: 'Kindly accept assurances deep gratitude and warm good will would that all in Australia were equally loyal to Australia.'[29] Kingston later won a seat in the House of Assembly which he retained until he joined the federal parliament.

Chamberlain's proposed new clause of 19 May caused a minor furore in Australia. The poor drafting was bad enough but the idea of disallowing an appeal from a High Court decision unless by the consent of the Executive government concerned was widely vilified. Chief Justices Griffith and Way criticised it, the latter more publicly with his second 'Observations' published in the same two papers on 11 June. Symon weighed into both of them while directing most of his fire at his former senior partner. Symon's first two 'Observations' were published in the *Advertiser* and the *South Australian Register* on 15 June 1900 and the third in the latter on 16 June.[30] Each one numbered over 2,000 words and in total just over 6,300. Symon attacked both Griffith and Way for being secretive, accused them of sabotaging the four official delegates and of causing a delay in the legislative process in England. Symon exposed Way's major absurdity: the Chief Justice, acting without authority, proposed an amendment to replace Clause 74 and now accused the delegates of acting without authority in approving Chamberlain's amendment which Way now opposed. Symon's fundamental objection to Way was unassailable. He invoked Blackstone: 'nothing is to be more avoided in a free constitution than uniting the provinces of a judge and a Minister of State.'

Either Way had become insensible to the distinction or, like his laudatory biographer years later, believed he was not contravening the strict convention about a judge taking no part in politics; the issue was one of constitutional law not one of politics and was not a party matter. Way was merely giving guidance on 'so difficult and so technical a matter ... of constitutional law'.[31] Symon believed that Way had clearly over-stepped the mark, but not until 1930 did he learn from Sir William Sowden the full extent of his lobbying. In the winter of 1900 Sowden, as Acting Editor of the *South Australian Register*, was summoned to 'Montefiore' where the Chief Justice made 'vigorous efforts' over 'a long time' to persuade the editor to support his case for extending appeals to the Privy Council. Way intimated that he had the Governor, Lord Tennyson, on his side. The Chief Justice was not merely offering technical enlightenment and, according to Sowden, never forgot the episode.[32]

In June 1900 Symon modified his inflexible approach to support whatever the trusted four delegates felt they could achieve. He even wrote in favour of the role of the executive in deciding what cases might go to appeal in London. Symon was relieved when he learnt of the final version of clause 74. While the new clause left open the possibility of the Queen granting special leave to appeal from the High Court, the Parliament could make laws limiting the matters in which leave could be sought – provided the laws proposing limitations were reserved by the Governor-General for the Queen's pleasure. The High Court might also grant leave to appeal to Her Majesty in Council. When interviewed in Adelaide, Symon agreed that he and Downer had cabled Kingston – through Premier Holder – an amendment identical to the one finally (and already) adopted. Connor and Wise in NSW had done the same. Symon believed that the federalists had, in substance, achieved what they wanted.[33]

Symon saw that good things had happened in 1900, so many of them in July. On 9 July Queen Victoria gave her assent to an *Act to Constitute the Commonwealth of Australia*. The tenth and last surviving child of Jo and Nell was born on 19 July. Her two given names – Mary Arden – commemorated Shakespeare's mother. On 31 July Western Australia decided by 44,800 votes to 19,691 to join the federation. The goldfield electorates, where Symon always felt more comfortable when visiting the West, voted 26,330 to 1813 in support of the Bill. Symon sent telegrams of congratulations to his leading friends, who now included Forrest.

In September Symon added to his reputation both as an orator and as an admirer of the Bard. While in England in 1899 he and Nell had

'a great paean of triumph in the closely knit union of the race.'

made another pilgrimage to Stratford and he assembled his findings in a lecture entitled 'Shakespeare at Home'. He delivered it a meeting of the University Shakespeare Society, with Patrick McGlynn occupying the chair. For someone Beatrice and Sidney Webb decided had a 'cold, unimaginative intellect', a central feature of Symon's lecture was his imaginative re-creation of Shakespeare's life from school-age to his death in 1616. He drew on his knowledge of Shakespeare's texts and on what Symon had learnt of Stratford and London in Elizabethan times and of the national vitality which followed the victory over the Spanish Armada.[34]

There was one sad Symon story in 1900. Jo's brother, Bill, died in December. He had been residing in Boulder, then a suburb of Kalgoorlie and the base of Jo's principal investment, the Great Boulder Pty Gold Mines Ltd. Throughout 1900 Richard Hamilton, the General Manager of Great Boulder, became Jo's point of contact for Bill who was notionally working as a lawyer but was sometimes in hospital or 'drying out'. Jo kept changing his mind about the source of his brother's problems and about how to deal with them. Early in the year he described Bill as 'a hopeless wastrel' who was his own worst enemy and is 'now reaping the bitter fruits'. After 'a great many years of constantly helping him' Jo was becoming 'really rather tired of doing so'. He could not, however, let his brother suffer, and authorised the payment of £1 a week for the necessities of life, with the proviso that Bill should not be allowed 'to finger any money whatever, and no liquor is to be allowed to him, or paid for'. By March Jo was prepared to assist Bill's return to Adelaide, provided his wife, Laura, requested it. He correctly assumed she would not. Jo now decided that Laura was largely to blame for Bill's 'fall', hardly an accurate explanation of his brother's alcoholism. Jo felt 'little or no sympathy' for Laura, despite very occasionally handing her a cheque long after Bill's death. In late November, Hamilton informed Jo he had secured Bill's admission to a government hospital. Symon gave Hamilton authority to pay for the now-imminent funeral and other costs but he should avoid unnecessary expenses while doing the necessary 'simply and respectably'. On 11 December Hamilton telegraphed the news of Bill's death. Jo closed his office on the afternoon of 12 December to coincide with the funeral. He later asked Hamilton to thank those who showed kindness to William and sought photos of the grave to pass on to his mother and sisters. In a further letter Jo sought a list of the outlays and attached a 'not very accurate' account of his brother's life published in the *Advertiser* on 12 December.[35]

The second youngest of Jo's seven siblings, probably the brightest of them all, had died in his 46th year. Bill and Jo had stood out as the most likely of the five brothers to succeed in life but Jo had known for ten years that his brother was heading for the grave. Jo was appalled by the waste, but never in the final year did he seem to feel anything more than a brotherly obligation.

10

'I am jealous of the rights of the Commonwealth'

Lord Hopetoun, a former Governor of Victoria, returned to Australia in mid-December 1900. His first principal task was to appoint a ministry in advance of the inauguration ceremony of 1 January 1901 where he would be sworn in as Governor-General. On 19 December he invited William Lyne to form a government. Hopetoun's action, labelled a 'blunder' by many historians, was to an extent understandable. Lyne was the Premier of NSW, the largest State. He did, however, have two major strikes against him: Lyne was not Edmund Barton and he had vigorously opposed a federation he thought would disadvantage NSW.[1]

Lyne failed to muster support for his appointment as Prime Minister. Important and self-important figures – especially Barton and Deakin – refused to participate. Others, such as Turner and Holder, vacillated. Kingston was another who stood out. As Bannon wrote, Charles Kingston 'had been adamant that Barton should be chosen and declared he would not serve under Lyne'.[2] Yet Kingston was not always 'adamant'. According to Josiah Symon's account, probably written 30 years after the event but with his records at hand, Kingston consulted Symon on Friday 16 November. Anticipating an approach or responding to one, Kingston sent Symon a copy of Lyne's 'Platform' and the two men talked further on 17 November. Symon did not regard the NSW Premier as 'a true federalist' and saw no reason for appointing him Prime Minister of a federated Australia. Kingston sent a 'Very Confidential' note to 'My dear Josser' on 28 November. He had been approached to join a Lyne ministry. Kingston told Symon he faced 'a terrible temptation and I want to think it over and let me have a talk with you tomorrow'. Kingston and Symon met on the following morning, and both concluded 'it would be a fatal mistake for (Kingston) to assist Lyne and he decided to decline his overtures'.[3]

Symon understood why Lyne's offer was 'a terrible temptation'. Kingston would be the sole South Australian in a Lyne ministry, and did not yet know whether Barton or anyone else would offer him a position. Symon knew that Kingston 'was a strong protectionist' and with Lyne as Prime Minister he would be part of a strong protectionist ministry. Symon's free trade convictions took second place in 1900 to his commitment to a federation governed by 'true federalists'. The recovered Symon-Kingston friendship also mattered: 'Josser' did not want his friend to damage his reputation by aligning himself to a politician who had no moral right to head the government of the new Commonwealth. Kingston was now 'adamant': he would not join a Lyne ministry. The NSW Premier had to return his commission. Barton became the first Prime Minister of Australia, and Deakin, Lyne, Forrest, Turner, Kingston, Dickson, Lewis and O'Connor joined his ministry which was to take office on 1 January 1901.

The Symons left Adelaide for Sydney on 22 December 1900. They were official guests for the celebrations to launch the Australian Commonwealth. Nell had been ill for some time and her husband made special arrangements with the authorities for them to travel by sea rather than by train to Melbourne. They boarded a German-built and -owned passenger and cargo liner making its maiden voyage to Australia. From Melbourne they travelled on a special train to Sydney.

Symon's appointment as KCMG became public on New Year's Day. Embarrassingly, the official warrant had gone 'missing' in the post. The envelope was eventually 'found', unopened, in 1907. Symon joined some illustrious federal company on the day. Barton and Griffith were appointed to the Privy Council, Forrest was promoted to GCMG, McMillan and Dickson (Symon considered him an aberration) were each appointed KCMG, Quick was made a Knight Bachelor and Blackmore and Garran were each appointed CMG. HRH the Duke of Cornwall and York (the future King George V) would invest Symon with the second insignia of the Order on the opening day of the First Parliament.

Symon had a second reason for wanting to be in Melbourne on that day. He aimed to be one of the six South Australians elected to the Senate. Sir Richard Baker gave him an additional incentive by predicting Symon

'I am jealous of the rights of the Commonwealth'

would not be elected to either House. Symon nominated as one of eleven South Australian candidates for the Senate. There were 17 nominations for the seven South Australian seats in the House of Representatives for which, in 1901 only, there would be a State-wide poll.

The deaths of two women took away some of the joy Symon experienced in January 1901. His mother, Elizabeth, died on 14 January in her 86th year. Jo resolved to continue looking after his sisters' financial needs. He had to apologise occasionally for temporary reductions in the size of regular payments sent to Stirling. School fees for the boys and governesses for two daughters were among the increasing calls on his funds. Queen Victoria's death on 22 January at aged 81 distressed Symon differently, perhaps even more so. The Queen embodied the Empire for which he had developed a profound attachment. The war in South Africa brought the fortunes of the Empire into sharper focus.

Symon launched his Senate campaign in the Adelaide Town Hall on 25 February. He spoke for more than two hours in a speech punctuated by 'laughter' and 'cheers' and ended with 'Loud and long-continued cheering'.[4] 'My policy', Symon said, 'if a phrase be necessary, is "Revenue without injustice" – without injustice to the producers, to the consumers, to the rich or the poor, without injustice to the mass of the people of this country.' Symon devoted 85 per cent of his speech to the fiscal issue, divided almost equally between highlighting the destructiveness of protection policies, the benefits of free trade as exemplified in Britain and the 'slipperiness' of Barton's approach to the tariff.

The candidate spent the remainder of his speech giving the audience his views on a few current issues. Symon wanted Australia to adopt the adult franchise which applied in South Australia and Western Australia. He wanted to see an end to talk about amending the Constitution. While he approved of J.H. Howe's success in giving the Commonwealth the power to introduce old age pensions, Symon said the country could not presently afford them. The Barton policy on pensions was 'merely an electioneering placard. (Laughter)'. Symon criticised the absence of a policy towards the Northern Territory which had become a serious financial burden on South Australia. He pointed out that two-thirds of the Territory's population of nearly 5000 'are Asiatics, chiefly Chinese'. He could see no point talking about the kanakas in Queensland, who constituted a small proportion of Queensland's population, when 'we have this larger and more difficult problem at our doors. (Cheers.)'. Symon left no one in doubt where he stood on racial purity.

> No man has ever more strongly insisted than myself upon keeping the white race pure, on keeping Australia a white man's country – free from the menace of that perpetual black problem which is the despair of our kinsmen in America. (Loud cheers.)

Symon focused on a different message in the flyer he distributed. The *Sydney Morning Herald* of 1 March 1901 provided a reference: 'one of the ablest members of the Convention' and 'a tower of strength to any State'. Symon pointed to his record in the Convention where he was 'the champion of the small States' and 'the foremost fighter for equal representation and a strong Senate'. He highlighted the key difference for South Australians. Whereas they had just seven members in the House of Representatives against 23 for Victoria and 26 for NSW, they had six senators like each of Victoria and NSW. The implication was clear: Symon was largely responsible for the power South Australians had in the Senate and he was the man to ensure they received the benefits. His other message was one his generation would have expected and understood. At a time when voting was not compulsory, Symon spoke of 'a sacred duty' to vote for the sake of 'the Commonwealth and State, for home and children', and reminded eligible voters that the 'welfare of South Australia and the harmony and success of the Commonwealth' depended on their choice.[5]

The *Register* of 3 April reported one unusual feature of the first Federal election in South Australia: 'the absence ... of a fiery party spirit was abundantly manifest.' Candidates, notionally competing with each other, travelled together to provincial centres and small towns to appear on the same platform. Symon accompanied the Free Traders Holder and Glynn and Labor's Protectionist Senate candidate O'Loghlin to Naracoorte and Mount Gambier. He joined Holder and O'Loghlin in Kapunda and Port Augusta. Kingston and Symon, on opposite sides on the tariff issue, appeared together before a 'crowded house' in the Petersburg Town Hall on 15 March.

Kingston and Symon took time out to discuss another issue during the campaign. There had been talk of a new Imperial Court of Appeal, and of

'I am jealous of the rights of the Commonwealth'

Griffith or Way serving on it. Symon sent a long handwritten letter to 'My dear K' on 12 March weighing into both justices. If one must go, it should be Griffith – he was 'the least disqualified'. Griffith had rendered 'yeoman service' in 1891; without him, Queensland would not be in the union. On the other hand, Griffith never subsequently lifted a finger to help the movement. When Griffith saw something was inevitable he looked for the means to make something out of it. 'He hits upon the method of sycophancy to the Imperial authorities and treachery to his own country – Australia – both in combination.' Griffith worked secretly in ways which might lead to his personal advancement, and in 1899–1900 worked with Way against the approved Constitution. Symon wondered whether these 'self-seeking men' should occupy the Bench.[6] Nothing came of the proposed court.

The Free Traders in 1901 were reluctant to direct serious fire at Barton. They campaigned for a revenue tariff as the sole available source of income for the Commonwealth government. In South Australia, the principal conservative organisation – the National Defence League – decided against supporting the seemingly avowed conservative Sir Josiah Symon. Some 300 delegates attended a meeting of the League early in March where they voted to exclude Symon from their list of preferred candidates. Symon's friend, Theodore Bruce, spoke warmly in support of his inclusion. Henry Short, whom Symon had supported in 1877 for the Adelaide mayoralty, spoke so well against Symon for championing Kingston in the Legislative Council poll that the delegates overwhelmingly rejected him.[7]

The election of 29–30 March resulted in the Protectionists taking 31 of the 75 seats in the House of Representatives. Free Traders won 28 seats, Labor 14 and Independents two. The Barton Government could govern with Labor's support. Kingston topped the poll in South Australia for the House of Representatives, and Bonython and Poynton were also elected as Protectionists. Glynn, Holder and Solomon won seats as Free Traders; and E.L. Batchelor took a seat for Labor. The Free Traders with 17 seats formed the largest single grouping in the Senate. The Protectionists won 11 seats and Labor 8. In South Australia there were three surprise results for the Senate: Symon topped the poll; Baker came two places behind Symon; and Downer finished fourth which meant he must face the voters at the next Senate election.

Sir Josiah Symon	FT	37,642
Thomas Playford	Prot	36,892
Sir Richard Baker	FT	35,235
Sir John Downer	Prot	30,493
David Charleston	FT	29,153
Gregor McGregor	Prot/Lab	26,264

Symon topped the poll in nine of the then 27 electoral districts in South Australia, came second in another six and never finished lower than sixth in the remainder. Bannon claimed that 'Symon's success was largely attributable to Kingston'.[8] Kingston certainly advocated a vote for Symon among Labor voters, and Baker and Downer complained to Barton and Deakin that their ministerial colleague, Kingston, had reduced their numbers by supporting a vote for Symon. Yet in a low poll of 40 per cent, a man who was a fine public speaker and a fierce campaigner for federation and South Australia, whose name appeared constantly and favourably in the Adelaide and country newspapers on so many different counts had much to recommend him alongside Kingston's glowing reference.

Symon received many letters and telegrams of congratulation from within South Australia and from most other States.[9] Paris Nesbit said Symon's federal political career 'will add new lustre to an already brilliant reputation'. Mindful of Symon's Scottish heritage, the journalist and entrepreneur, R.S. Smythe, sent a telegram from Melbourne: 'All hail Macbeth that shalt be chief hereafter'. The Shakespearean scholar of 'Manoah' might have found this message worrying. The Loyal Orange Lodge Institution of South Australia told Symon it was praying he might be spared to carry out his responsibilities. Their prayers might have included one for Symon to stop numbering the Catholic Archbishop John O'Reily among his good friends.[10] Some well-wishers wanted to lobby as well as congratulate him. Lt-Col Neild, a senator-elect for NSW, hoped that his long career in State politics would persuade Symon to support his case for election as Chairman of Committees. L.S. Spiller wrote a long letter principally to recommend himself for a senior appointment in either Treasury or Trade and Customs. Sir William Zeal, a Protectionist who came second in the Victorian Senate poll, did not bother with

'I am jealous of the rights of the Commonwealth'

congratulations. He merely wanted to inform Symon of his intention to stand for the presidency of the Senate.

Kingston wrote to 'Josser' on 13 April with reference to the copy of the Judiciary Bill which Deakin, as Attorney-General, was sending to Symon. Kingston wanted him to 'give us the benefit of your most careful criticism and further suggestion' and to give Kingston a copy of his views at the same time Symon sent them to Deakin. Griffith had been 'allowed' to draft the Bill but Kingston wanted the opinion of the Chairmen of the Judiciary Committee – Clark in 1891 and Symon in 1897 – 'with a view to its final settlement & perfection'. Symon replied on 17 May, after he had been sworn in as a senator, saying he had 'spent some hours over that miracle of bad draftsmanship – the Judiciary Bill'. Clauses, he said, seem to have been shovelled in 'without any pre-designed scheme or plan'. Symon had done what he could to rectify the situation.

He was particularly concerned that 'Rules' should not be a schedule to the Act but detached and applied after the Act came into force and judges had been appointed. They could then work on them and improve them as Rules of Court. Their omission from the Bill would help it through parliament. Some comments stand out in a faded document. Symon urged that the references to judicial expenses be struck out. Such allowances were undesirable unless for circuit purposes and 'should be provided for in the clauses (if any) dealing with circuits'. He objected to clause 11 of the Bill which

> proceeds on a misconception of what the High Court is. It is not meant to be migratory or peripatetic although the individual judges may make circuit arrangements. The High Court must have a permanent seat just as the High Court of Justice in England and the Supreme Court of the United States has.[11]

Symon had marked out the territory he would defend as Attorney-General.

The Duke of Cornwall and York opened the Federal Parliament on 9 May 1901 in a grand spectacle at the Exhibition Building in Melbourne.[12] After a swearing-in ceremony, the senators assembled in the Legislative Council Chamber of the Victorian Parliament. Whereas members of the House of Representatives occupied the frugal accommodation of the Legislative Assembly, the senators luxuriated in cushioned seating. They sat under an ornate ceiling with sculptural reliefs of female figures along its sides symbolising concepts such as 'Justice', 'Peace', 'Mercy', 'Victory', 'Wisdom', 'History' and 'Plenty'.

Imported enmities could operate just as well in this environment and, when it came to Sir Richard Baker, Sir Josiah Symon had no intention of forgiving or forgetting. The Senate had to elect a President and, quick on his feet, Symon nominated a fellow Free Trader, Sir Frederick Sargood of Victoria. He rejected Zeal's overtures, remembering him from the Convention as a 'diehard conservative'. Symon also ignored a letter warning him of losing prestige by backing Sargood, 'a wily old rogue' with a record of fraud, misrepresentation and cheating in business.[13] Symon wanted to thwart Baker's ambitions, even to the extent of his backing Labor's defeated motion for an open ballot. Baker won the subsequent election by an absolute majority, receiving 21 votes against Sargood 12 and Zeal 3. Symon stayed resolute. He declined the invitation when the President and the Speaker (Holder) invited the Symons to lunch on 26 May in the Queen's Hall, Parliament House. Symon replied to Holder: 'I refuse to accept any invitation from Sir Rich [sic] Baker, or with which he is associated either personally or officially'.[14]

In the Senate, Symon did not sit with the main body of Free Traders on the left of the President's Chair. Instead, he sat on the cross benches next to Gregor McGregor and in front of the other Labor senators. It was a bizarre situation because nearly all the Free Trade senators looked upon Symon as their leader. J.T. Walker, who called himself the Convenor *pro tem.*, wrote to Symon on 21 May 1901 telling him that the senators elected to support a Revenue Tariff would be meeting to choose a leader of the Party in the Senate. The date was eventually fixed for 6 June. Symon probably attended it as he was in Melbourne at the time. Walker formally reported that the meeting voted unanimously to ask Symon to accept the leadership of the Revenue Tariff Party in the Senate, allowing him time to consider whether to accept or decline. Symon replied on or soon after 19 June. He called the proposal 'a high compliment' but his professional business engagements in Adelaide made it impossible to accept the responsibility and 'my clear course in the interests of the party is not to accept it'. He was in 'complete accord' with the meeting,

'I am jealous of the rights of the Commonwealth'

that the Revenue Tariff Party cannot be regarded as a general party of opposition in the ordinary sense, or its leader of opposition as ordinarily understood. The party is united on one issue only. That issue is not yet before the Senate – when it is I hope to be found in the forefront of the fight for fiscal freedom, and prepared to make every effort to secure the adoption of a revenue tariff.[15]

In mid-August 1901 Symon was appointed leader of the Revenue Tariff Party in the Senate.[16] His friend and follower, Senator Clemons of Tasmania, was chosen as secretary and, in effect, the party whip.[17] Symon was absent in Adelaide in the week following his election when the Free Traders in the Senate sought to block legislation concerned with the collection of customs duties. Symon had a prior commitment. He had been briefed to defend the Adelaide and Hindmarsh Tramways Company against a plaintiff who sought £450 in damages after falling over a piece of timber outside his shop. Chief Justice Way dismissed the jury and declared a 'nonsuit', upholding Symon's point of law disallowing a plaintiff's claim to damages where there was clear evidence of contributary negligence.[18] Symon's absence from the Senate was noted but he was prepared for a leadership role when the full tariff measure reached the Chamber from the House of Representatives

Senator O'Connor representing the Government in the Senate regarded Symon as the unofficial Leader of the Opposition. Symon added substance to O'Connor's approach by his regular interventions in debates. In appearance at least, Symon often led for the Free Traders in arguing for minimum interference with what the Convention and the referenda had delivered. On Thursday 27 February 1902, he attacked the Government's Electoral Bill which introduced a system of proportional representation for the Senate. Claiming that no one seemed able to explain how the system would work, he moved an amendment to the Second Reading stating it was not expedient to proceed. Symon returned to Adelaide at the weekend. On the Monday 3 March he was sitting in a train around 6.30 pm waiting to leave for Upper Sturt. He was there handed a brief to represent Maria Auguste (Mary) Schippan, aged 24, charged with murdering her 13 year-old sister, Joanne Elizabeth (Bertha) Schippan on 1 January 1902.

The Schippans were a Wendish family who lived on a small farm near Towitta at the foot of the eastern side of the Mount Lofty ranges. The Wends were of Slavic origin and lived mainly in East Prussia. Some 2000 of them had migrated to South Australia and most settled in areas already occupied by German immigrants.[19] On 30 December, the Schippan parents, Matthes and Johanne, had left their daughters and two younger brothers at their farm to visit relatives at Eden Valley. Two other siblings were away working on distant farms. Mary's boyfriend, Gustave Nitschke, who had persuaded her strict father of his honourable intentions, had sex with Mary on a sofa in the lounge early in the evening and then left the house. Mary joined her sister in the bed they shared while the two brothers slept in the barn some 80 yards away. Mary claimed that around 10.00 pm she woke to find a bearded man straddled across her chest. She struggled with him for ten minutes before escaping from the house and arousing her brothers who eventually contacted a local constable. Next day, Bertha was found dead, having been slashed and stabbed about 40 times. After a coronial inquest Mary was committed to stand trial in Adelaide.

Chief Justice Way presided at the trial which began on Tuesday 4 March. Symon sought an adjournment to 2.00 pm to allow him more time to prepare a defence. Way said it would not be wise to take on a case of such importance without giving it the fullest consideration, and adjourned proceedings for 24 hours.

The arrival of an eminent counsel added even more interest to a trial which had drawn a large crowd and attracted interstate attention.[20] Peter Donovan considered that Alfred Foster, Mary's solicitor who had been at her side during and after the inquest, had 'prepared the case in detail and outlined the strategy to be followed'. Foster's involvement is borne out in the material and the notations he handed to Symon, a copy of which is held in the Symon Papers. Symon's own comments on those files show that, as ever, he prepared his own trial strategy. He was, after all, in a familiar situation of showing a jury that the Crown did not have a case amounting to proof beyond reasonable doubt.[21]

Symon made extensive notes on witness statements heard at the inquest, all the time steadily accumulating evidence which collectively turned minor disagreements into serious holes in the Crown case. Trivial

'I am jealous of the rights of the Commonwealth'

inconsistencies could be linked to other minor discrepancies to raise questions about the reliability of witnesses. Police incompetence and a lack of leadership at and around the scene of the crime gave Symon several openings. He found that no record of evidence had been kept. Items of hair and bloodstained clothing had been mixed up with other evidence and just dumped in a room. It took the police a week before they found the murder knife located in a readily observable place.

Symon used every device to arouse sympathy for Mary. At the trial he portrayed the lover of this lonely girl as a despicable rake who used her for sex. Even Chief Justice Way spoke of Nitschke 'debauching' Mary earlier on the day of the murder. It seemed immaterial that Nitschke was probably long gone from the Schippan house at the time of Bertha's death. He was a villain for the crowd inside and outside the courtroom to despise. Symon succeeded with another ploy. He persuaded Way to prohibit the publication of the trial proceedings. There was so much blood everywhere, so many signs of extreme violence, and Symon did not want thousands of newspaper readers associating Mary with such horror.

The Crown's case rested squarely on circumstantial evidence.[22] It could not find a plausible motive for a vicious slaying. Symon remarked a few times that the Crown prosecutors, led by J.M. Stuart KC, had gone out of their way to be fair and understated. He, on the other hand, was characteristically overstated. He wanted drama and began his final address accordingly. 'I am here to ask you in the name of British justice and fair play to acquit Mary Schippan of the terrible and unnatural crime with which she stands charged.' Symon confronted the jury with the seemingly incredible and preposterous: how could this 'loving sister' commit such a horrible crime? He wanted jurors to look to their individual consciences: could they convince themselves, eliminate every doubt, and send Mary to the gallows? He kept returning to a simple point: if there was any doubt the jury had no option but to acquit. Symon went through each critical piece of evidence and testimony to show where doubt was present. In cross-examination he turned on the key Crown witness, Dr Ramsey Smith, a forensic expert, and was so dismissive of him in his final address that Chief Justice Way in his summation felt the need to rehabilitate the witness. Symon concluded:

Sir Josiah Symon KCMG KC

> I commit the life of Mary Schippan to your hands, believing that you will turn an eye of pity upon her unhappy condition, and that you will solve every doubt in her favour, and that by pronouncing her Not Guilty of this atrocious and abominable crime you will do right by her and carry home ... the unspeakable satisfaction of an approving conscience. May the Great Father of us all direct you aright.

The Chief Justice left some in the courtroom with the impression that Way believed Mary was guilty. The jury returned within two hours with a verdict of 'Not Guilty' and the courtroom and crowd outside erupted in cheers. The foreman of the jury told journalists that the great majority of the jurors regarded the Crown's evidence 'as by no means conclusive', and had made up their minds before counsels' addresses and the judge's summing up. Given that the jurors at the inquest had unanimously agreed Mary should stand trial perhaps the foreman might have noted one key difference between the inquest and the trial; Symon KC exposed the Crown case by his cross-examination of its witnesses.[23] Importantly, he did not have to offer an alternative explanation for a murder which has remained unsolved.

Symon's political life resumed in earnest in May 1902 when the House of Representatives, having completed eight months of debate, delivered its Customs Tariff to the Senate. Anticipating its arrival, Reid sent a handwritten note to Symon on 14 April from the Melbourne Club where he was staying prior to attending the Bathurst Circuit Court. He had spoken to a few senators and now Reid wanted Symon to know his views on the passage of the tariff through the Senate. Reid did not think members of the House of Representatives would be seen during the Senate's deliberations. Nor did he intend to make suggestions on any particular item. 'The broad ground that keeps us all together is the principle of a Revenue tariff; and its corollary, that the tariff shd [sic] not be contracted so as to destroy or cripple its producing power.' If the Free Trade senators 'could hit upon a maximum for ad valorem duties it might be well.' Aware of the issue about the Senate trying to impose new taxes, Reid was worried about a suggested tea duty. He wanted to talk to a few senators and would give Symon all the information he could in a subsequent letter.[24]

'I am jealous of the rights of the Commonwealth'

Reid wrote again on 20 April, this time from Sydney. He imagined O'Connor playing 'all sorts of tricks' behind the scenes if 'our party' splits as it could if the Senate suggested imposing a tea duty. Reid knew that Symon opposed such a course. What Reid wanted was for the Party to wait until after the tariff work of reduction was accomplished before taking up the bone of contention. The supposed Free Trade leader had little to offer in the way of leadership.

In the meantime, Symon had a problem which he probably never raised with Reid. He had to deal with an unmanageable member of 'our party' over the tariff issue.[25] Lt Col. Neild wrote to Symon on 8 May 1902 referring to the resolution John Clemons, the Party whip, had shown him. Adopted by what Neild described as 'several Free Trade members' in the previous week, it stated that no amendment shall be moved unless the Party or Symon decided it was appropriate. Proposed amendments would be moved only by those whom Symon selected. Neild understood that the resolutions were 'stoutly opposed'. His objections were those the independent-minded Symon would have supported were he in Neild's position, though Symon would have constructed a more coherent and intelligible argument to support them. Neild denied that the Free Trade Party in the Senate, 'a somewhat undefined and varying quantity', had the right 'to shackle any representative of the people with conditions far transcending even the "cast iron pledge" of the Labour Party'. The resolution was at variance with 'the initial principles of Constitutional rule, and with the best parliamentary tradition' and 'opposed the constitutional provision for equal State representation in the Senate'. Neild would be unworthy of the trust reposed on him by the electors of NSW if he should abandon his 'rights and obligations'. None of the great Free Trade leaders ever suggested 'such an abnormal course of procedure'. He would loyally support every 'rational amendment' but claimed 'unrestricted liberty to move any amendments my sense of duty may dictate.' If this 'obnoxious resolution' were not rescinded he reserved the right to publicise his letter.

Symon replied on 13 May. He charged the Lt Colonel with cowardice. Neild had placed his letter in Symon's box after the recipient had left for Adelaide. Symon then reminded Neild that as a member of the Revenue Tariff Party in the Senate he owed it 'allegiance' and your leader 'courtesy'.

While Neild remained in the Party 'its general interests are the first consideration, and are not to be subordinated even to the idiosyncrasies of any individual members'. To do otherwise would be an 'unflattering comment' on Neild's claim of his Free Trade zeal and would hardly further the representation to which he declared himself 'entrusted'.

Symon moved to his misrepresentation and ill-discipline. The resolutions were approved by the entire party membership in the Senate; Neild alone was absent. If Neild had faulted or misunderstood them it would have been 'common courtesy' to talk to Clemons or Symon. In fact, Neild had 'read them inattentively, or quite misunderstood or imperfectly remembered' what he read. As a result, his letter 'rudely built on your disordered imagination', produced 'high sounding but empty platitudes' which no schoolboy would write 'without exposing himself to grave risk of ridicule or caning'. The Party is not 'somewhat undefined'. Neild was 'the only vague and undefined element in it'. The Party is 'absolutely united and harmonious'. Symon thought a soldier would have respect for discipline. As for Neild publishing his letter, Symon had no objection 'if you can reconcile that with your duty to the Freetrade cause and the State interests to which you allude'.

Neild called Symon's letter 'insulting and abusive' and made use of language 'gentlemen do not descend to employ'. Symon had offered time for an interview but Neild insisted he first withdraw his 'insolent letter'. Symon responded by pointing out that Neild had initiated this 'regrettable episode' so he should be the first to make an 'unqualified withdrawal'. As Symon had not withdrawn his letter Neild ended their correspondence.[26]

The other Free Traders in the Senate generally fell in behind Symon. O'Connor, the Leader of the Government in the Senate until his departure for the High Court, continued to regard him as the unofficial Leader of the Opposition. The two men had a warm personal friendship and Symon readily paired himself with O'Connor. He knew that his fellow barrister was struggling financially but may not have known that members of the Barton and Deakin cabinets contributed £200 a year to a fund for honorary ministers.[27] O'Connor contacted Symon on 2 May 1903 from his Phillip Street Chambers to say he would be sacrificing 'a good deal of money' to be in the Senate in the coming weeks. He asked Symon to continue their pairing arrangement. Symon replied on 8 May. He was

'I am jealous of the rights of the Commonwealth'

'happy ... to consider ourselves paired'. Symon had 'fairly good & plentiful' business since Parliament was prorogued but there was always the question of his availability for a case and of being able to 'see it out'. He said there was no doubt that public duties involve a heavy personal tax, and he was 'very glad' O'Connor's professional load was coming up to normal. 'Good luck to you.' O'Connor was very happy to receive Symon's kindly letter.[28]

It was apparent in the First Parliament that Sir Josiah Symon was engaged in two delicate balancing acts. First, he had to reconcile the demands of two jobs. He wanted the one in politics and wanted and needed – financially – the one in the law. The other balancing act did not require the same level of attention but remained a preoccupation and an interest for the rest of his life. Symon was a State Rights man who wanted the Commonwealth to prosper and to grow in strength.

Alert as always to symbolism and to seemingly minor insults, Symon objected when officials, from the highest to the middling, acted either beyond their station or not according to the rules or conventions of their station. He particularly disliked the pretensions of the Private Secretary of the Governor of South Australia, Lord Richard Plantagenet Nevill, the fifth son of the 1st Marquess of Abergavenny. Lord Nevill haughtily delivered one message which Symon saw as insulting to 'those who did most to accomplish Australian Federal Union'.[29] Symon was even more concerned about the circular letter he received in February 1903 from the Governor's Private Secretary on the direction of the Lieutenant-Governor of South Australia (Sir Samuel Way).[30] The letter informed him that the Governor-General would be holding an Investiture of Decorations in Sydney on 18 April. It was hoped that a large number of ministers, Privy Councillors, Knights, Companions and Members of Orders could be present. The Secretary asked Symon to inform him if he would be able to attend so that the Governor-General (Lord Tennyson) could send a formal invitation.

An outraged Symon sent a 'Confidential' letter to Barton on 19 March and another on the same day, marked 'Private', to Kingston. He asked Barton for guidance. Explaining he was concerned for the dignity of the Commonwealth in small matters as well as great ones, Symon asked if the Governor-General cannot write to a Privy Councillor or a knight without going through a State Governor. He wanted to know whether the adopted course applied to other States and whether he should ignore the circular or answer it. As he told Kingston, 'I am jealous of the rights of the Commonwealth, even in matters of etiquette & I do resent this circular'.

Barton replied with a long hand-written letter which meandered incoherently through or around several subjects. He did not care for the form of approach and it struck him as peculiar in his own case that the Governor-General should authorise a State Governor to send an invitation to his chief advisor to attend a Commonwealth function. Barton said it was unthinkable that any slight was intended or that Symon was being treated differently. Lord Tennyson 'is a good and kind man, with much common sense' but he seemed to have had little political training before coming to Australia. In the circumstances Barton found it difficult to know how to advise Symon, except to say that the circular letter was not itself an invitation. Perhaps if the Governor-General had spoken first to Barton, his chief adviser might have suggested that the wise course would have been an approach by Sir Samuel Way rather than use a Private Secretary as an intermediary (Barton seemed to have missed Symon's point altogether; a letter from Way would have annoyed the recipient even more). Barton concluded by saying he was writing 'frankly' to Symon yet felt safe 'under the seal of confidence'. He was in fact being less than frank, although understandably so. The Prime Minister was having his own problems with the Governor-General's inability or unwillingness to understand his proper role.[31]

Symon replied to Barton on 30 March. Barton's confidence would not be broken; any action Symon took would be his own. Like Barton he thought the Governor-General was 'unacquainted with things' while his common sense was 'of indifferent quality'. The course taken 'is farcical' and involved 'placating or soothing down these high & mighty State Governors at the expense of a constitutional principle'. As the Prime Minister knew, 'I am a State Rights man but always subject to the rightful paramountcy of the National Government'. The Governor-General had a duty 'to maintain the National Constitutional Status in matters of etiquette, which after all is the chief domain in which he can be effective'. Symon wrote again on the following day, explaining his outburst as a result of professional pressure. He did not, however, resile from the main point: the adopted course was 'hopelessly indefensible on every ground, constitutional or otherwise', and the Governor-General should be 'set right'.[32]

'I am jealous of the rights of the Commonwealth'

Of all the legislation introduced into the First Parliament the Judiciary Bill mattered most to both Deakin and Symon. The former moved the Second Reading of the Bill on 18 March 1902. Symon sat in the Gallery and told Deakin his speech was 'worthy' of 'the subject and the orator'.[33] The vote in the House of Representatives on the Second Reading took place 15 months later, by which time the arguments for economy and for avoiding excess federal machinery had cut the level of support. The Bill passed the Second Reading by just nine votes and was mauled in Committee. The result was a court of appeal but not one of wide original jurisdiction, the judges would not receive pensions and were reduced in number from five to three.

The Bill arrived in the Senate in late July 1903 and encountered hostility from Senators Dobson and Fraser, both Free Traders, who thought that there was no immediate need for an expensive High Court. Some senators wanted State judges appointed to the Court. Symon devoted much of his three-hour speech[34] to answering the many interjections from the Bill's opponents. He believed that Parliament had a duty to complete the federal system by establishing a High Court. Moreover, 'if it is to be a Court of Appellate Jurisdiction, and to interpret the Constitution, you cannot be penny-wise and pound-foolish'. Symon did not want senators to think he supported extravagance. 'Let us first establish our judicature, and then consider how far we can go in the regions of economy.' Symon wanted 'a strong and capable Bench' which he believed would have greater dignity if it consisted of five rather than three Justices. Once established, senators could 'take away from the court all unnecessary paraphernalia' and let them cut down as much as they like. The Bill easily passed the Second Reading by 20–6 with three pairs.

In Committee, Symon strongly supported clause 8 which provided that a Justice of the High Court could not accept or hold any other place of profit within the Commonwealth. Symon had consistently pressed this view, probably originating in observing Way's secondary career as a Lieutenant-Governor. He also wanted to amend clause 8 by removing words which might be used to allow a High Court Judge to sit on the Judicial Committee of the Privy Council. No doubt thinking again of Sir Samuel Way, Symon said, 'we have all had experience of such appointments'. Senator O'Connor supported the amendment which was accepted without a division.[35]

Sir Josiah Symon KCMG KC

The *Judiciary Act* received the Royal Assent at the end of August 1903, and attention switched to the appointments of the three justices. Symon, Isaacs, Way, Higgins, and Inglis Clark were repeatedly mentioned as possibilities in the press.[36] The *Express and Telegraph* of 29 August was so confident the Bench would comprise O'Connor, Symon and Isaacs that it considered who might take Symon's seat in the Senate. The *Advertiser* of the same date was a little more cautious; it was accepted everywhere O'Connor would be Chief Justice and 'pretty certain' Symon and Isaacs would be his colleagues.

Deakin intended all along to appoint Griffith as Chief Justice, who had sought and was given assurances he could reside in Brisbane and receive appropriate travelling expenses. Deakin also wanted a dithering Barton to meet his financial and personal needs by trading in the prime ministership for a seat on the Bench. Everything was settled by 24 September: Griffith would be Chief Justice and Barton and O'Connor were appointed puisne judges. The Government formally announced these and other consequential appointments on 24 September: Deakin succeeded Barton as Prime Minister, Drake replaced O'Connor as Leader of the Government in the Senate and Deakin as Attorney-General, and Playford replaced Drake as Vice-President of the Executive Council.

Referring first to O'Connor, Symon said we shall all regret the departure of 'our friend' from this Chamber. He had given great service to the country and to the Senate and 'no sting has been left behind'. Symon believed that O'Connor's 'great abilities', 'integrity' and 'broad-mindedness' would 'enable him to render even greater service to the Commonwealth'. He wished his friend a long life and success in a position 'for which he is admirably fitted and which, in my belief, he will adorn'. Symon congratulated Playford and Drake on joining what he called 'the Ministry of rehabilitated fragments'. He concluded: 'Of the other arrangements I prefer to say nothing. The less said the better. I say no more.' Commentators at the time, and later, correctly assumed he was speaking about the appointments of Griffith and Barton to the High Court. Few noticed that Symon was also referring to Deakin's elevation to Prime Minister.

The conventional wisdom is that Symon's disappointment on missing out on an appointment to the High Court explained his attempts when Commonwealth Attorney-General to persecute and humiliate the judges

'I am jealous of the rights of the Commonwealth'

of the High Court over travel and expenses. Symon's motivations and actions will be examined in the next chapter. The immediate question here is whether, or how far, he felt disappointed.

It will be recalled that nearly two decades earlier he had turned down an appointment to the South Australian Supreme Court. At least, he was offered a position. In 1903 he wanted to be asked to join the High Court, and it might have been hard to decline. No doubt he had already talked it over with Nell. The arguments against acceptance were similar but in material and lifestyle terms were more substantial than those operating in 1885. He now had a large family to support and a lifestyle which included frequent trips to the 'Old Country', investments in Auldana, weekends spent at 'Manoah' and expanding and enjoying his library. What he liked about the law was being a multi-skilled barrister sitting at the top of his profession. Arguably, therefore, Deakin's judicial preferences saved him from choosing a course he might well have regretted. There was nothing to regret about what he already had.

Symon immersed himself in cases in the last months of 1903. He represented Ramsey Smith, the man he had berated during the Schippan case, and successfully cleared him of interfering with dead bodies while conducting scientific and medical research. There were always disputes over deceased estates and Symon also took briefs to defend the alleged owner or operator of a gambling den in Adelaide and to appear in a libel case and in a breach of promise action. He took great pleasure in successfully defending William Ball, an honorable man who collected funds from members of the South Australian Government Railway and Tramways Mutual Association. Two sums handed to him, one of 3/6 and the other of 2/6, were not recorded as received by the Association. After an eight-hour day in Court on 16 October before Chief Justice Way, who plainly took the defendant's side, Symon persuaded the jury that the Association's books were shambolic while Ball's own chaotic records were not much better. No one quite knew where the money went except there was no evidence of it ending up in Ball's pocket.[37]

On 24 November Sir Josiah Symon KC and Sir John Downer KC[38] joined other members of the Adelaide legal fraternity in attending the first formal meeting of the new High Court to be held in Adelaide. The three robed Judges sat alongside Sir Samuel Way KC to hear the State Attorney-General congratulate them on their appointment. The Judges each made a short statement in response and, in the absence of any actual business, the Court adjourned. Symon attended a dinner at Government House in honour of the visit but was not included in the dinner Way hosted for the Judges at the Adelaide Club. The caravan moved onto Perth where it did have minor business to conduct in addition to receiving due homage from the profession at many social engagements. Chief Justice Griffith later claimed that by travelling around Australia the High Court could promote federal unity and secure public approval. In Adelaide, the future Commonwealth Attorney-General had glimpsed the Court engaging in its self-appointed extra-curricular activities.[39]

11
'he is not fit to be Prime Minister.'

Sir Josiah Symon is now best remembered as the Commonwealth Attorney-General who provoked the three justices of the High Court to take strike action in May 1905.[1] He fares badly in almost all written accounts, censured for being on the wrong side of history and his actions variously described as 'petty', 'spiteful', 'venomously spiteful', 'vindictive', 'obsessive', 'sadistic' and 'insulting'. Some commentators concede that Symon was in part motivated by high principle. A few concede that Chief Justice Griffith did not always behave well during the controversy. Nevertheless, it was Symon who suffered 'ignominious defeat' and 'humiliation'. Former Chief Justice Sir Anthony Mason administered the *coup de grace*. The legislation of 1979, which enabled the justices to administer the Court with funds appropriated to it by Parliament, 'reinforced the Court's independence from the executive government and exorcised the ghost of Sir Josiah Symon'.[2]

If it were thought necessary to explain as well as describe and condemn Symon's actions it was usually sufficient to mention one indisputable fact; he was overlooked in 1903 for appointment to the High Court. Linking this fact to the unprovable assumption that Symon would have accepted an appointment made it easy to align cause and effect. Mason did it by implication and with enviable simplicity: 'Symon had been an aspirant for appointment to the Court and wished to reduce the Court's expenses.'[3] There were other indisputable facts: Griffith criticised, even mocked, Symon's drafting of the judiciary clauses of the Constitution in 1897 and had intrigued to retain appeals to the Judicial Committee of the Privy Council. It was not difficult to add personal pique to disappointment and few commentators have been troubled by the lack of hard evidence in attributing Symon's actions to hurt and animus. After all, they knew why he was 'spiteful' and 'vindictive' and, because he was 'spiteful' and 'vindictive', he pursued the justices in a 'spiteful' and 'vindictive manner'.

Winston McMinn's biography of Symon's Prime Minister, George Reid, and his article on the 'High Court imbroglio', focused on the other side of Symon's failure and misbehaviour. McMinn showed how Symon became 'a disastrous colleague' and a 'political embarrassment' over the High Court 'imbroglio', thereby contributing to the defeat of the Reid–McLean Government in July 1905. McMinn did, however, point out that Symon was engaged in two disputes of which the one with Reid became as important for him as the one with the judges. In both disputes a fair reading of the available texts, and an examination of the disputes from Symon's perspective, explains why he acted as he did. It also reminds us that what might look like the inevitable and rightful emergence of the modern Commonwealth from its early years was not so straightforward in the first decade of the 20th century.

It is important to recognise that the Reid–McLean Government had very little chance of being a long-term administration and that Symon was a reluctant, albeit initially successful, recruit to its ranks.

The Reid–McLean Government was the third government to hold office in 1904. In February Deakin had spoken of the need for the three parties in the field to be reduced to two for the sake of political stability. Both his own administration and its replacement, Watson's Labor Government, were brought down during the year by shifting allegiances. Declaring their support for a 'fiscal truce', Reid and Deakin formed a coalition of Free Traders and moderate Protectionists in August 1904 to replace the Watson Government. Deakin probably ensured its early demise by declining to join the ministry.

Josiah Symon was not involved in the machinations which led to the downfall of the Deakin and Watson ministries. From May to September 1904 he was preoccupied as leading counsel for the plaintiffs in the long-running 'Corset case'. The Weingarten brothers of New York manufactured W.B. Erect Form Corsets, and 'W.B.' was their American trademark. Weingarten sued G. and R. Wills & Co., wholesale drapers of Adelaide, for 'passing off' their less expensive W.B. Erect Form Corsets as Weingarten

'he is not fit to be Prime Minister.'

products. Chief Justice Way presided as a single judge without a jury. Two formidable teams of lawyers appeared before him: Symon led Nesbit KC and Erskine Cleland; Sir John Downer KC, now unencumbered by politics, led for the defence with George Murray, a future Chief Justice of the South Australian Supreme Court, and James Henderson, Downer's brother-in-law. The court room looked like the inside of a draper's warehouse and neither side spared expense in assembling evidence from England and the United States and employing women as decoy buyers in Adelaide's draper shops. Symon's 'take' is unknown but what is known is that the case cost in the region of £20,000 (c. $3.2 m in 2020).

Downer took five days to deliver his final address and Symon was due to follow when he received two telegrams on 15 August from George Reid who was in the process of forming a government. Chief Justice Way agreed to postpone the hearings in the 'Corset case' while Symon met Reid in Melbourne. Reid's first telegram said he wanted to consult Symon on the subject of 'public affairs'. In the second Reid said he particularly wanted Symon to come to Melbourne the next day to assist him in forming a government.[4] Symon replied that he would arrive on 16 August but was 'uncertain' he could render the assistance Reid desired. According to McMinn, Reid and Symon were longstanding personal friends, citing their shared taste for Auldana wines and Symon's habit of sending consignments to Reid 'from time to time' ('very, very occasionally' would have been more accurate). Symon and Reid had never warmed to each other, and like all sides of politics, Symon never trusted 'Yes-No' Reid and Nell disliked him altogether.

Reid needed Symon in his ministry. He might have preferred Glynn as Attorney-General but a non-Labor Prime Minister in 1904 would risk a backlash if he dared select two Catholics – Glynn and Allan McLean – with the latter, in Deakin's absence, being the leading Protectionist he must have. Besides, the new Prime Minister needed someone of stature, someone feared as much as respected, to represent the Government in the Senate where Reid lacked a majority. Glynn sat in the House of Representatives and, though the little Irishman was bright, amusing and likeable, opponents would have relished a situation where Reid had judged him to be ahead of Symon.[5]

Jo and Nell exchanged telegrams while Symon was in Melbourne on

16–17 August, possibly the first time in Melbourne the two men conversed on consecutive days. Jo sent a telegram to Nell reporting Reid's wish for Symon to join the ministry while leaving him free to retire when he liked. Reid and Clemons were pressing him 'very hard' and Jo asked Nell what she thought. He followed up with another telegram: 'My standing aloof will prejudice new ministry but will not join unless you approve.' His wife's telegram sent on 17 August said there may be matters of which she was ignorant. Clemons had wired her to say he deliberately risked her displeasure yet was sure she would approve 'when you know the full circumstances' because 'not to join now would be fatal to the rest of us and your side'. Clemons urged her to wire 'yes'. This advice 'astonished' her; she did not know the 'circumstances' which may compel Jo to join 'against our judgment'. She had wired the words, 'Do not approve'. Nell then countermanded herself: 'Everything the old man does is always right.' Jo replied to Nell on 18 August saying he had agreed to be Attorney-General and the Government Leader in the Senate. He was returning to Adelaide on that day.[6]

The Symons never spelt out the reasons for Jo's hesitation and Nell's initial rejection. Perhaps they did not believe there was, or could be, a genuine 'fiscal truce'. Perhaps they just distrusted George Reid or queried his worth as a Prime Minister. Perhaps they had the foresight to recognise that Deakin's absence undermined the ministry from the start.

At least the ministry was evenly balanced, with four Protectionists (McLean, Turner and John McCay from Victoria and George Drake from Queensland) and four Free Traders (Reid, Dugald Thomson and Sydney Smith of NSW and Symon of South Australia). It was unbalanced in terms of State representation but not short of talent and experience. Reid, Turner and McLean had all been Premiers; Turner and Drake had been ministers under Deakin; Symon had been a State Attorney-General and McCay and Symon had served in colonial parliaments.

Many letters and wires of congratulations arrived at Upper Sturt, some addressed to Lady Symon. Rev. Anthony West of St Augustine's Church of England, Unley, thought Symon was on the way to becoming the Chief Justice of the High Court, which was his proper place. John Quick congratulated him. So did John Hannah Gordon who had been a South Australian delegate to the Convention of 1897–8 and was appointed to the

'he is not fit to be Prime Minister.'

Supreme Court in December 1903. The President of the South Australian Free Trade Association sent a warm letter and so did Fred Johns who was compiling his *Notable Australians*. Many urged Symon to have a long time in office. Sir William McMillan said the country sorely needed men of his stamp.[7] Higgins, who had been Watson's Attorney General, sent him a note on 17 August asking him to dine the following Saturday by which time Symon had returned to Adelaide.[8]

Symon's first major task on returning to Adelaide was to deliver his final address in the 'Corset case'. Nesbit KC could have filled in for the Commonwealth Attorney-General but Symon was the leading counsel for the plaintiff. Moreover, he did not regard an appointment to Reid's Cabinet as any kind of barrier to participation in a private lawsuit. Symon spoke on five days, after which Downer responded to new points made in Symon's response. Way followed with a brief statement and reserved his decision – and delayed delivering it for 20 months.

Switching his roles in the Senate, Symon proved to be an asset in the early days of the new government. David Maling, one of the original members of the Parliamentary Press Gallery, wrote warmly of Symon's early record as Leader of the Government in the Senate.

Maling had a regular column in the Melbourne *Argus* as 'Ithuriel', the angel who 'with his spear touched lightly'. According to 'Ithuriel', Senator Sir Josiah Symon had proved 'a marked success' as leader of the House: 'patient, courteous, conciliatory, imperturbable.' He had suppressed his 'combative' instincts and 'bids fair' to rival former Senator O'Connor who had a majority in most matters except the tariff. 'Ithuriel' thought practice before a jury must be good preparation for a Leader of the House. The Attorney-General had treated the Senate as if it were a mainly hostile jury 'and is determined that if he cannot win he will as far as possible reduce the damages'.[9]

Symon successfully piloted the Conciliation and Arbitration Bill through the Senate, overcoming the Labor Party on some occasions and the conservatives on others. On 8 December 1904, when moving the adoption of the Committee Report, Symon admitted the Bill did not meet with his entire approval. He nonetheless welcomed the coming division as a means of seeing who wanted to establish the system of compulsory conciliation and arbitration, and who wanted a measure entirely of their own making and 'have no spirit of compromise or conciliation'. As he pointed out, the Bill had been before the Parliament for two years and had nearly 'wrecked' one ministry (Barton's), led to the resignation 'of a most valuable member of that Ministry' (Kingston) and 'wrecked' two other ministries (Deakin's and Watson's). The final vote in favour of the Report was 14–4 with six pairs; two Labor senators voted with Symon, four Labor senators voted against it and six were paired in opposition.

The Senate rose at the end of 1904 and Parliament did not meet again until late June 1905. The Government was 'safe' from a no-confidence motion for six months. Symon could now concentrate on his job as Attorney-General alongside his calm and well-organised departmental secretary Robert Garran.

Early in 1905 Symon prepared a long memorandum for his Cabinet colleagues describing what he encountered when examining the organisation and financing of the High Court.[10] He noted how the Court's travelling expenses up to 31 December 1904 amounted to £3294/11/11 (equivalent to $528,072.05 in 2020) and would have been far higher if the States had not made facilities and officials available for free or at minimal cost. 'Other expenditure seems to be on a scale of similar liberality.' Symon described the position of the High Court in relation to Parliament and the Executive as 'ill-defined and unsatisfactory'. Some 'looseness' might be acceptable for a new court in a new situation but he found an organisation based on 'a complete misconception of the nature and functions of the Court and of its place in the Constitution'. Symon did not expect to find an essentially appellate tribunal acting like the Court of Kings Bench exercising civil and criminal jurisdiction, with each justice employing an associate and a tipstaff, a practice 'unknown and out of place in a great Court of Appeal'. Even more disturbing, he found that at 'oppressive cost' the Full Court went on circuit accompanied by an entourage of officials to hold sittings as a court of appeal in State capitals. The judges did so 'whenever they please – business or no business – unfettered and unquestioned by the Executive Government ... whose sole duty it is according to the justices to invite Parliament to foot the bill'.

> It was a novel discovery to find Judges claiming the right at their own will to travel on Circuits of their own fixing as and when and where amongst

'he is not fit to be Prime Minister.'

the State capitals they chose, and that neither Executive nor Parliament could refuse to provide the money.

It is important to observe two things about Symon's approach after making his 'novel discovery'. First, he acted upon what he found; he did not set out to 'punish' or 'humiliate' or seek evidence to justify punishment and humiliation. He may have appeared 'petty' but to assume that personal animus alone was driving him is not to understand Josiah Symon. He disliked taking on a job and not doing it thoroughly. Symon was, in La Nauze's words, 'scarifying in controversy' because he was relentless in pursuing a quarry. An historian conversant with his court work, with his speeches in parliament, arguments with railway officials about timetables, complaints to manufacturers about defects in their motor cars, protests to district councils, disputes with neighbours and farm suppliers and out-of-court rows with other lawyers might reckon that his comments were on the mild side when directed at the three retired politicians sitting on the High Court. The 'shock, horror' response of some later commentators to what was his everyday approach to pretty well everything amounts to an over-reaction. He was not 'becoming unhinged',[11] just doing what he saw as his job and doing it in his way.

Secondly, Symon combined a Scottish approach to thrift with an expectation that governments would and should be careful about spending public money. He collected a parliamentary and ministerial salary having previously opposed the payment of MPs. His major sources of income and wealth, however, were private: legal fees, Auldana, investments in mining, residential and commercial property and farm sales. The very successful barrister and investor could, and did, pay his own way. He saw no reason why members of the High Court, having chosen to live in Sydney, should expect the taxpayer to pay their fares to travel to their place of work in Melbourne. He was aware of, and sympathetic to, parliamentary concerns about costs and was familiar with parliamentary reservations about the Court's function and value. Symon knew of claims that existing State justices could fill the positions on the High Court as required. He was not over-awed by three newly-arrived High Court judges seeking respect and entitlement, especially when two of them (Barton and Connor) had not been very successful in private practice and two of them (Griffith and Barton) added their sons to the payroll as associates.[12]

Underlining his approach, Symon had a perception of the nature and function of the High Court which differed markedly from the one adopted by the three judges and most modern commentators. He had always seen the High Court as a stationary body like the Judicial Committee of the Privy Council and the Supreme Court of the United States. It should not be travelling around Australia accompanied by a full complement of associates and tipstaffs, with the associates accommodated in the expensive hotels preferred by the justices. Symon believed that the Court did not need to experience local conditions in Perth or Hobart to interpret or apply the law while sitting in Melbourne or Sydney.

Holding this view, Symon faced two obstacles. The *Judiciary Act* of 1903 presented one in the form of its s. 12: 'Sittings of the High Court shall be held from time to time as may be required at the principal seat of the Court and at each place at which there is a District Registry.' Symon might have wanted the High Court to remain stationary but it *could*, lawfully, travel, and the incumbent judges believed they *should* do so. The other obstacle was fundamental. The Griffith Court wanted to establish its stature and standing, and judicial independence was crucial to accomplishment. Symon may have wanted the High Court to be a great court but could not accept in 1905 that the judges themselves were other than what he would describe as 'high public servants of the Commonwealth', subject to rules established by the executive and the legislature. Symon may have been 'wrong' in terms of history and of what the legal profession now views as axiomatic for judicial independence but in 1905 taxpayers were not accustomed to subsidising the preferred lifestyle of those dependent on the public purse.

Prior to Symon's appointment as Attorney-General, Griffith and Deakin had made their private arrangements whereby the former would continue to live in Brisbane and receive expenses when sitting elsewhere. After a year's trial, Griffith decided to move permanently to Sydney where Barton and O'Connor resided. The justices had one matter of concern. Higgins, as Watson's Attorney-General, had informed them by letter on 29 July 1904 that their associates would receive a *per diem* allowance of fifteen shillings in addition to their fares when on circuit. Justice Barton replied

'he is not fit to be Prime Minister.'

that the sum would not meet the costs of an associate staying in the same hotels as his judge. For an associate to stay in an 'inferior' hotel 'would be not only unseemly, but so inconvenient as to be out of the question'.[13]

George Reid wrote to his Attorney-General on 16 November. He enclosed a copy of Griffith's note to the Prime Minister, dated 12 November, telling him of Griffith's decision to move to Sydney. Griffith had since added some requests to his letter of 12 November. He suggested Reid should 'seriously consider making Sydney the Principal Seat of the Court'. Sydney would be the source of the largest amount of business and offered a better chance of acquiring suitable accommodation. Griffith wanted the Commonwealth Government to provide him with chambers of sufficient size to take in his library, and suggested that a more suitable building be found in a place more central than Darlinghurst.[14]

Griffith wrote to the Attorney on 2 December 1904. He said Symon would be aware of the arrangement at the time of establishing the High Court whereby justices were not expected to change their places of residence and their travelling expenses would be computed from their homes (Symon wrote in the margin 'I was not aware'). Griffith said he had decided, after twelve month's experience of inconvenience and increasing travelling expenses, that he should move his headquarters to Sydney. He now asked for assistance to provide 300 feet of shelving for his chambers in the Darlinghurst Court House. Griffith sent a telegram on 13 December asking for a reply to his letter, as well as sending a further one seeking the provision of facilities for a Full Court hearing in Hobart on 27 February 1905.[15]

Symon replied on 23 December 1904 with what McMinn described as 'a long, argumentative, though politely enough worded letter'.[16] If it is argumentative to expound an argument, then so be it. Symon began by acknowledging Griffith's requests and said he was acquainted with the Higgins correspondence over travelling expenses. He noted the 'magnitude' of these expenses, and observed that some of them were 'avoidable' because the cases in 'remote' States hardly merited a visit from the Full Court. The Attorney proceeded to a lengthy disquisition on the functions and desired location of the High Court. His starting point was that the High Court was 'chiefly and before all else a Great Court of Appeal. Its principal seat is at Melbourne. The principal Registry is there.' There was never any notion of the High Court, Australia's 'supreme appellate tribunal', being an ambulatory Court of Appeal. It was inconceivable that the equivalent bodies – the Judicial Committee of the Privy Council and the Supreme Court of the United States – would undertake equivalent circuits. In any case, if the High Court did travel, expenses should be computed from its principal seat in Melbourne and not from the justices' places of residence.

Holding these views, Symon regretted the Rule of Court decision to arrange a sitting of the Full Court in Hobart but, as the arrangement had already been determined, he would ask the Tasmanian Government to provide a court room. With regard to the Higgins correspondence, he agreed with his predecessor that the legislation did not provide for expenses covering associates and other officers of the court. He was prepared, however, to allow the travelling expenses of a judge to include those of his associate to the extent of three guineas a day in the discharge of judicial duty, a provision to take effect from 1 January 1905. Before he obtained the necessary Order-in-Council to implement the proposal the Attorney would be pleased to consider any further observations or suggestions tendered by the Chief Justice or the other justices. Symon had also decided to defer the question of bookshelves, pending suggestions from the Chief Justice or justices for obviating appellate circuits and annulling or modifying Rules of Court providing for appeals to be heard in the State where the appealed judgments had originated.

Infuriated by the Attorney's letter, Sir Samuel Griffith replied on 27 December in a manner which ensured confrontation. He would consult his colleagues on the issue of sittings in the States as provided by the present Rules of Court. In the meantime, he observed that 'the policy of holding sittings of the High Court as a Court of Appeal in all the State Capitals was adopted after full consideration, and with the warm concurrence of the Federal Government'. Although the travelling 'entailed some inconvenience', the judges were willing to bear it 'in the interests of federal unity', and their actions had received public approval throughout Australia. Given that any change to the Rule of Court or the *Judiciary Act* could not immediately come into operation, Griffith asked for the existing arrangements, made in accordance with 'policy', should remain in place. He observed in conclusion that his chambers in Melbourne were too small to accommodate his

'he is not fit to be Prime Minister.'

library and asked again for bookshelves in Sydney by early February.

Griffith had again contacted Reid who then broke his holiday in Sorrento, Victoria, to send Symon a brief note on 1 January 1905. Wishing Symon and Lady Symon well for the coming year, Reid continued:

> I hope there is no truth in a suggestion made to me that you are going to centralise the High Ct in Melbourne. The true seat of Govt is NSW ... Sydney is the place where most work is. Don't add to the soreness of NSW! & the trouble of, ... G H Reid.[17]

Symon replied on 7 January 1905 to 'My dear Mr. Reid', explaining that he had been out of the way at Nelson on the River Glenelg 'boating, fishing and lazing' with his small boys.[18] Symon began with an obvious sideswipe at Griffith.

> I am sorry anyone shd. have been so meddling or ill-natured as, at this restful season, to make you uneasy with apprehensions of 'soreness in N.S. Wales' on my account. – Immediately before Xmas I wrote to the learned Chief Justice at some length upon various matters to which I invited consideration, chiefly affecting the heavy and as I think unnecessary travelling expenses, and I am certainly surprised to observe how the contents of my letters appear to have reached or filtered to you in the concentrated form that I am 'going to centralise the High Court in Melbourne'.

The High Court was already centralised there '<u>by law</u> – and I think rightly so'. While he was not responsible for this decision, Symon thought there was 'a clear duty to recognise it and to take care the position shall be a reality and not a sham'. Surely, he argued, no one in Australia could approve of the High Court as an appellate tribunal being 'an itinerant tribunal', sending it out with three judges, three associates and three tipstaffs &c. &c. to distant States to hear one or two appeals 'which nothing but distance or a thick haze would induce any one to classify as important'. The reason for vesting federal jurisdiction in State courts was to make any kind of circuit 'practically if not altogether unnecessary'. As for the seat of Government – that depended first on securing a capital site – he would do all he could to avoid giving 'soreness' but Sydney had no claim to be the principal seat of the Court. Nor would or could he interfere with the judges' desires to live in Sydney but they could not claim expenses while staying at the principal seat in Melbourne.

In the meantime, Garran sent a handwritten note to Symon after receiving a telegram from Griffith's associate who wanted to know how soon or whether the shelves would be provided. Garran said he supported the provision of shelving. The Chief Justice needed his library to be in Sydney where he will now live and a judge is entitled to shelving for his books. Although the issue of Court sittings had not been decided, Garran could not see any objection.[19]

On 13 January 1905 Symon replied to Griffith's letter of 27 December 1904. Symon had a definite sense of who should be responsible for what, and seized on Griffith's references to 'policy', 'federal unity' and 'public opinion'. It was 'unfortunate' that the justices had allowed these considerations to influence their actions. Questions of that kind were for the Executive and the Parliament. Symon would do what he could in Melbourne about shelving and, if the chambers were inadequate, he would seek to enlarge them. McMinn saw this letter as doing 'nothing to blunt the sharp tone of what was, in effect, a thinly disguised reprimand'.[20]

Conscious of an increasing volume of correspondence with the Chief Justice and aware that Reid was in contact with Griffith, Symon decided that he must see the Prime Minister in his room, thereby denying Reid the opportunity to send for him. Reid asked Symon at the beginning of their conversation on 28 February 'in perfect good humour & a little shyly: "Are you going to bring about Civil War[?]".' He was with Symon on the subject of the rules but wanted the Attorney to consider the position of Sydney. Symon asked if the Chief Justice had been seeing the Prime Minister. Reid said 'no'; Griffith had been sending him letters, 'a very long one sometime ago & others since'. Symon said it was 'very wrong of him to do so – no right to go behind me, but I forgive all that – What does he really want?' Reid said he could not make it out because Griffith's letters 'are quite hysterical – he seems to be going off his head'. Symon insisted that it was up to the judges to ask for concessions. Reid said it was 'all hysterical on their part' when the judges started making threats. Symon made a firm point: he was ready to hear their suggestions.

Reid told Cabinet he would write to the Chief Justice in response to his letters. That intention occupied Symon's mind and, before returning

'he is not fit to be Prime Minister.'

to Adelaide, he wrote to the Prime Minister. 'I must ask you not to commit me or indeed yourself to any concession whatsoever. The Judges are aware that I intend to apply the undisputed rule of computation from the principal seat of the Court.' If they want to be allowed expenses in Melbourne as equivalent to expenses in Sydney, as Reid invited him to consider, the request for concessions must come from them. 'I will not even consider an exception without first a recognition of the rule, and the discontinuance of the present circuit system, except as to Sydney.' He saw it as 'absurd' to think of an exception as between Melbourne and Sydney if the other avenues from travelling expenses are kept open. 'At present they simply claim as of right that travelling allowances for Judges shall count from their respective homes.'

> I decline to make any proposal for exceptional treatment to them for the reasons I mentioned to you yesterday, and also because of the Chief Justice seeking to influence you behind my back, and to intrigue with Members of Parliament as mentioned by Mr McLean to-day – but I shall give favorable consideration to any reasonable proposal which may emanate from them.[21]

Symon imposed strict rules. He informed Turner, the Treasurer, on 2 March that all vouchers or certificates for travelling expenses were to be submitted to the Attorney-General personally and none should be paid without his approval.[22] Symon had sent an earlier memo to Garran stating that the starting place for computation for travelling expenses was Melbourne. No travel expenses were to be allowed for travel to Melbourne from a judge's place of residence unless that residence was in a place where a justice held sittings and such travel involved returning from a discharge of judicial duty. No expenses were allowed while discharging judicial duties in Melbourne. On 13 April, Symon refused to approve vouchers for seven telephones for the High Court in Sydney – one for each judge, two for associates and one each for the O'Connor and Barton private residences – at a total cost of £35/10/0 for January–July 1905.[23] Symon sought information of the work undertaken by associates, tipstaffs, marshals and ushers, and eventually widened his inquiries to England, Canada and the United States. When he learnt that tipstaffs received 10/- a day when travelling by rail and 2/- a day on sea Symon wrote in the margin, 'Why anything?'. Garran tried to persuade him to accept the rail payment. Tipstaffs travelled second class or steerage by sea but went first class by rail in order to maintain contact with judges. This, Garran ventured, was 'proper'.[24]

The judges decided to make a stand over the issue of travel expenses. Justice O'Connor was due to hear a case in Melbourne on Tuesday 2 May relating to the importation of fish. The three judges met in Sydney on the previous Saturday morning, 29 April, and made a Rule of Court whereby O'Connor would not travel to Melbourne and the case would be postponed for a week. The Registrar in Melbourne was told that a telegram would arrive at noon on the Saturday. He waited until 12.30 pm and then left the office. He first learnt of the postponement when he arrived for work on Monday. Everyone connected with the case, except Justice O'Connor, was seriously inconvenienced. The Chief Justice wanted action taken against the Registrar for leaving his post 30 minutes after the time he had been told the instructions would arrive.[25] Griffith's demand was silly enough without also refusing to give the parties involved in the case and the general public an explanation for the 'strike'.

Although Symon's dispute with Griffith and his colleagues continued until early July, with neither side moving from their entrenched positions, the deteriorating relationship between the Prime Minister and his Attorney-General generated new issues.

Reid sent Symon telegrams on consecutive days in 1–3 May 1905.[26] He wanted his Attorney-General to implement what Reid called 'our arrangement' or 'our understanding', whereby judges living in Sydney could claim expenses of three guineas a day for themselves and associates for travel to High Court sittings in Melbourne. Had Symon departed from this understanding and refused expenses from Sydney to Melbourne? Reid was 'extremely anxious' that difficulties 'should not arise owing to any departure from our mutual understanding'. Reid believed that an 'absurd' situation had arisen 'since you & I agreed to allow expenses from Sydney'. Symon, he acknowledged, had made it a condition that the Judges should ask for expenses as a concession. Technically, according to Reid, the Judges had done so by submitting vouchers for Melbourne expenses, even though they claimed these expenses as of right. 'We ask them to do something which no man of self-respect whether Judge or not

'he is not fit to be Prime Minister.'

would do. Would like to see [anyone] try to put you or I in such a position.' Cabinet, Reid insisted, agreed only that expenses should be computed from Melbourne subject to 'our arrangement', and on that understanding Reid had allowed Cabinet discussion to proceed. He 'so heartily' agreed with Symon's 'fearless & patriotic efforts to place High Court expenditure on a proper basis of Economy', that he thought Symon would agree with him on giving the judges no excuse for their contemplated course. Carrying out the agreement should prevent a 'calamity'; if it does not 'we will remain united & on sound ground'. If we do nothing to implement 'our arrangement' Reid would be unfairly blamed for any 'deadlock'. Symon could regard it as a 'concession' but we must stop short of seeking to compel the judges to regard it as one.

Symon was unmoved. He told Reid there was no 'arrangement' or 'understanding' and there was no exception included in the Cabinet decision for expenses to be computed from Melbourne. The Prime Minister had created the problem. Convinced that Symon had made a concession Reid had written to Griffith on 11 March telling him that expenses for travel to Melbourne would be allowed. Symon suggested a solution. As he, not Reid, was the responsible minister, the judges should state their grievances officially to the Attorney-General. Cabinet would then remain united and Reid's fears of calamity and deadlock would prove 'groundless'.[27] In response, Reid expressed his regret for not impressing upon Symon that they had conflicting recollections. They must meet in Cabinet to thrash the matter out either tomorrow (Friday) at 2.30pm or Saturday 6 May at eleven. He was leaving for Grafton the following Tuesday.[28]

In Symon's next telegram he said he would be glad to meet on Saturday to deal with the urgent matter of the judges refusing to do their duty for 'sordid personal reasons' and causing inconvenience. It was against his conscience to give into their demands; no 'self-respecting man' or 'self-respecting Executive' would do otherwise. He had received no official communication from the justices. All he had were Reid's wires and press hints like the report in the *Advertiser* of 3 May of the Judges appealing to the Prime Minister to protect them.

The Cabinet did meet on 6 May 1905. Fifty years later the Cabinet notebooks would have provided an official record of the meeting. Symon's notes composed at the time may be the sole contemporary account of this meeting.[29] What emerges from these notes is that Symon conducted a sustained assault on the Prime Minister. He accused Reid of treating him 'most unfairly' in communicating with Griffith behind his back and thus assisting the judges 'to compromise my ministerial action' and thereby embarrassing his Attorney-General. Symon told Cabinet he first became suspicious when Reid told him of a proposal to centralise the Court in Melbourne. He suspected that Griffith had been informing the Prime Minister. Around mid-April, Reid had travelled to Western Australia to pursue his anti-socialist crusade and stayed with the Symons at 'Manoah' for five days at the end of the month while on his way home. Mail from Griffith had arrived for Reid while he was in Upper Sturt. Symon said in Cabinet: 'You should have shown me the letters you received in Adelaide.' In response, Reid explained he had a long private friendship with Griffith.

Reid and Symon lunched together after what must have been an awkward cabinet meeting. Reid wrote to Symon on the following day, 7 May, saying he had referred the Chief Justice to paragraph 6 of an earlier Symon letter and had advised him to request a reconsideration of the Sydney-Melbourne fares issue.[30] Reid also told him there would be no objection to the fixing of a daily rate.

> I am very sensible of your desire to meet my views in these matters. I explained to the C.J that I had unwittingly done you a serious injustice in writing to him that you had arranged with me that the Melbourne expenses wd be allowed – that was in my letter of 11 March. You and I have great battles in front of us and I earnestly hope that our relations of unbroken pleasantness will ever continue [sic].

Reid concluded: the case of wine arrived safely and if Symon could fix the three guineas a day arrangement it 'will give them a reasonable rate & simplify everything'.

Symon wrote the first of two letters to Reid on 9 May following a report in the *Argus* of 8 May.[31] The *Argus* reported that 'as the result of Mr Reid's tactful intervention and the mutual concessions made by the Chief Justice ... and Sir Josiah Symon the strained relations which existed between the High Court and the Attorney-General exist no longer'. Symon felt he needed to restate his position 'in the hope of relief from an intolerable sense of your influence behind the Judges, and of a firmer

'he is not fit to be Prime Minister.'

re-establishment of my confidence in you'. He accused Reid of being 'from the very outset in more than friendly communication with the Justices, and during the latter phase when they were mad enough to … refuse Judicial duty – you were literally in league with them against me'. The 'serious blunder' Reid owned he had committed on 11 March was 'mainly responsible' for the latest phase of refusing their judicial duty. Reid should not have made his statement without Symon's knowledge. In the face of the prohibition outlined in Symon's letter of 1 March it was 'unpardonable'. Symon was doubly indignant. Reid had kept his relationship with the judges secret from the colleague most concerned and then entreated that same colleague to believe the Prime Minister was not acting between the judges and Symon but acting between two colleagues. But for Symon's firmness in resisting Reid's telegrams and appeals, the Prime Minister's intercourse with the judges 'would have ruined the Government and yourself'. It would have covered the Government in shame to act as Reid implored the Attorney to do while the judges were 'on strike'. It would also have exposed Reid and the Government for allowing 'high public servants of the Commonwealth' to profit by actions not allowed for 'humbler public servants' like the railway servants of Victoria.

The Attorney detected the influence of a member of the High Court or of Cabinet in the *Argus* article. The piece was inaccurate and meant to mislead; 'tactful intervention' was not an appropriate description of Reid's 'interference'. While it was pleasant to learn that the strained relations between the judges and the Attorney-General no longer existed it was untrue to say there have been mutual concessions. Symon did not desire a concession and the Chief Justice had not asked for one. Symon did not want three guineas a day bruited abroad because at present the Attorney was dealing with actual expenses. Once again, he asked Reid to adhere to his promise to tell the Chief Justice that he should no longer communicate with him behind the Attorney's back on matters with which the Attorney was dealing. Griffith's 'influence with you' has not worked well as between Reid and Symon. It will be difficult if not impossible for the Attorney to be responsible if it continues. More sense and reasonableness and less of the sordid struggling for travelling allowances on the part of the judges will do more to facilitate progress 'than intriguing with you or members of Parliament'.

Symon wrote again to Reid on 11 May.[32] After what happened in Cabinet on Saturday, Symon failed to understand how the Prime Minister came to ask the Chief Justice to request that the Sydney–Melbourne fares be reconsidered and to tell him that there would be no objection to a daily rate. Symon did not suggest this approach which was not in accord with the hint the Prime Minister proposed to give, namely, that the Chief Justice should reply to the sixth paragraph of his letter of 26 April relating to a claim for expenses in Melbourne. Instead Symon received a 'curt' letter from Griffith returning the Attorney-General's letter unanswered for re-consideration and making no request either for an exception to the rule of computation or for a daily rate. Symon regarded this letter as 'a studied affront'. So there was presently nothing to reconsider.

The Attorney told Reid he intended to do what was right by the intention of the Constitution and between the justices and the taxpayer. Otherwise, 'it will be my greatest pleasure as always to meet your views as far as I can'. Symon was pleased that the Prime Minister had set the Chief Justice right about Reid's letter of 11 March but saw no reference to fulfilling his promise to request the Chief Justice to abstain from communicating with him on the subject. Like Reid, Symon saw

> great battles in front of us, but there is none greater or of more vital moment to the future of this Commonwealth than to establish the true Constitutional station and maintain the well ordered dignity of the High Court: and with the fine example of the Supreme Court of the United States before us both these are in my judgment compatible with – may indeed be promoted by a just regard for simplicity and the interests of the taxpayer.

On 11 May Symon also replied to a Clemons letter which he described as 'a veritable gleam of sunshine'. Symon said he had a heavy case load beginning on 16 May but hoped to get away to join him in Sydney two days later.[33] Symon said he trusted Clemons ('Behold, how I trust you. The love of David to Jonathon was not greater than that I bear you.') and sent him as 'Strictly Confidential' the correspondence he had seen as well as other Executive Council material which might make some of it more intelligible. There was also some correspondence affecting both the judges and the Prime Minister which he would bring with him.[34] 'Of course you are aware that hot-headed C.J. & his colleagues including your staid friend O'Connor are mad enough to refuse to discharge their judicial duty & suddenly adjourned the Melbourne Jury case by <u>a Rule of Court</u>.' Symon did not at the moment propose to 'proclaim the facts from the house tops, but they will be available when needed.'

> And your Prime Minister!! When you know all you will wonder why I remain with him for a day – I dare not trust myself to put into writing even to you my opinion of him. He has really behaved basely – except for his great gift of declamatory speech, he is not fit to be Prime Minister.

Symon was especially angry because when Reid was his house guest at the end of April 1905 he had corresponded with the Chief Justice 'allowing that gentleman to intrigue with him against me!' He felt that Clemons might think he had written 'too strongly' and asked only that he held his judgement in suspense.[35] Clemons later told Reid it would be 'disastrous for everybody and himself' if he did not work with Symon. Clemons also dared to advise Symon. 'Try to get the whole thing squared up even if you have to cede just a little. By just a little yielding you may win much more.'[36]

On 19 May Reid replied to Symon's letters of 9 and 11 May which had just reached him in Tenterfield.[37] The first letter, Reid said, contained statements which 'raise questions between us which suspend all friendly, and even official intercourse, whilst they remain unsettled':

> I can submit, with more or less patience, to the most caustic criticism of my capacity, or judgement, or blunders, whether deserved or undeserved; and whether it come from enemy, or friend and colleague; but charges of bad faith, of treachery, of disloyalty to, or intrigue against a colleague, touch personal honour, and the man who is willing to submit to them without protest, or resentment, probably deserves what he gets.

Reid assured Symon he had not had any communication from Barton or O'Connor on the matters of controversy, or concerning him or his department or any department. His contacts with the Chief Justice 'were few and far between', and especially since differences became serious until the threatened deadlock in the administration of justice caused him to take what he admitted was 'an unusual course' of preventing a 'grave scandal' to see if it could be averted by the head of the Government. He assured Symon that everything he had done, 'from first to last', stemmed from 'a single and pure motive', namely, that of avoiding a collision between the Executive and the Judiciary.

Given these 'full and frank assurances', the Prime Minister asked Symon to withdraw the apparent imputations against his good faith, loyalty and motives. If Symon thought Reid was guilty of treachery, intrigue or disloyalty, he would 'act rightly in heading off any further personal intercourse' with him. Reid then referred to their previous 'long friendship and harmonious official relations' and said he could not believe that Symon wanted to make those allegations against him, yet he could not help regarding the letter as making several reflections on his character. He would be 'quite satisfied' should Symon tell him that he had no desire 'to impute unworthy conduct' on his part. No one would be quicker than Symon 'to maintain a clear distinction between errors or judgement, and acts of moral turpitude'.

Symon refused to withdraw anything and, clearly in a state, Reid left a six-page handwritten letter in the Australian Club on 31 May.[38] He regretted Symon's failure to withdraw his letter of 9 May. Reid considered he was in a new situation. 'Controversy between colleagues is always a painful thing, and I have seldom had any such experience; in fact, never.' Reid said that in all the long time they had known each other down to their lunch after Cabinet of 6 May there had never been 'one single harsh word'. Reid had either not been listening, had an idiosyncratic understanding of 'harsh' or was engaging in deliberate misrepresentation for which he had 'form'. Reid repudiated the attack on him as unfair and unfounded and denied he had done anything to undermine Symon.

One paragraph of Reid's letter prompted Symon to offer an unconvincing resignation. He quoted it when writing to Reid on Thursday 1 June:

> Such was the state of things till the 27th of last month [April]. When however a disgraceful deadlock was then imminent on points … on which in my opinion they were right and you wrong I did at once enter into special communication with the Chief Justice to prevent such a calamity, such a burning disgrace to Ministers.

'he is not fit to be Prime Minister.'

Symon reminded Reid he had never at that stage heard of the judges' three points.[39] Nevertheless, if the Prime Minister felt his Attorney was responsible for the 'disgraceful deadlock', the threat of which he was kept ignorant, and for the 'burning disgrace to Ministers', then the dictates of duty and self-respect obliged him to 'place in your hands my resignation of the office I have been proud to hold, and which I shall yield up with unfeigned regret'. It was the sort of resignation offer which a weakened or weak Prime Minister was bound to refuse. Symon knew that but, in case he was wrong, gave Reid an excuse for inaction. He would withdraw his offer if the Prime Minister agreed that the whole of his letter of 31 May should not be placed before the Cabinet which was due to meet next week when Reid was in Queensland on another stage of his anti-socialist crusade.[40]

Symon was fully entitled to expect his Prime Minister's backing, and equally entitled to criticise him for not providing it. Reid was entitled and indeed required to intervene in Symon's dispute with the judges. By not taking Symon into his confidence, however, by proceeding often in secret, wanting to please and placate the Chief Justice and worst of all – deliberately or not – misrepresenting Symon's position and inventing an 'arrangement' which never existed except in his own mind, Reid was as much a 'disastrous colleague' as his Attorney-General. Reid was in an inconvenient situation, some of it not of his own making. Symon might compromise to secure the *Conciliation and Arbitration Act* but believed he was on stronger ground in defending his conception of the High Court and taking a firm line on expenses. He could not see how his approach amounted to an attack on judicial independence.

Nothing was resolved between the two men. Reid may or may not have felt reassured by the final paragraph of Symon's letter of 1 June. After recounting more examples of Reid's failure to support his Attorney, Symon declared, 'you need never apologise to me about plain and candid speech which I always welcome and of which I make no complaint'. It is worth bearing this confession in mind when reading Symon's confronting letters.

Symon became aware during June that the Government was in trouble. The more radical Protectionists were calling on Deakin to oppose the Reid Coalition. Deakin did seem to many in politics to mirror John Bunyan's 'Mr Facing Both Ways' and he provided more grounds for this view in the speech he delivered in Ballarat on 24 June 1905. David Syme's *Age* believed that the catalogue of criticisms he aimed at the Reid–McLean Coalition amounted to a 'Notice to Quit'. Deakin said that was not his intention but many did not believe him. Reid and Symon both saw the Ballarat speech as an ultimatum, and Reid requested the Governor-General to dissolve the Parliament. McMinn raised the possibility of Reid being prepared to risk electoral defeat because even that would be preferable to continuing in government with an Attorney-General whose obsession was a personal burden as well as a political embarrassment.[41] Reid could, of course, have sacked Symon but the Prime Minister was not made of 'sterner stuff'. Lord Northcote very properly turned down the proposal which Symon had helped to prepare. Deakin had Labor's support and could form a government. No one was surprised when, after a week of speculation about 'will he, or won't he', Deakin launched a no-confidence motion. Alfred was not so 'Affable' when he dumped on his friends – McLean and Turner – whom he persuaded to join the ministry for which they voted on the losing side of 42–25.

Deakin returned for his second term as Prime Minister and appointed Isaac Isaacs Attorney-General. Symon offered advice. The Attorney thanked his predecessor, and ignored him. Isaacs revoked all of Symon's orders and innovations. The bruised and indignant justices could recover their equilibrium, Deakin could feel that Providence had 'saved the virtuous maiden from the heavy villain bent on ravishing her' and, years later, Justice Michael Kirby could endorse the self-serving mantra that the maintenance of circuits provides 'an essential link between serving Justices and the legal profession and litigants in the outlying States'.[42]

Justice Gageler of the current High Court adjudged Griffith 'victorious' and his victory 'permanent'; the practice of circuits remains 'an institutional characteristic of the High Court'. Gageler was more balanced than many of the commentators, echoing Don Wright with his observation that 'Griffith's triumph and Symon's ignominy cannot gainsay the mixture of pettiness and principle which fuelled the actions of each'. It is not clear, however, what Gageler meant by his further comment that Symon was 'anything but gracious in defeat'.[43] Symon tried through a Private Member's Bill to make the High Court 'a stationary and not a

'he is not fit to be Prime Minister.'

perambulating, Court'. Using due process, he tried and failed to reduce the salaries of associates and to abolish tipstaffs and to ensure that the Court in its administrative position was subject to executive control like any department of the Public Service. What was he expected to do? Admit he was wrong in the first place because an eager-to-please incoming minister (who later benefited from his own reforms) and a recycled government had overturned Symon's approach? Griffith's victory did become 'permanent', but not in 1905.

A more complete picture of Symon's reactions to defeat would look at how on 5 July 1905 he vacated his job as Leader of the Government in the Senate. (On the same day he wrote his final letter to the Chief Justice saying that approved travelling expenses for the Full Court applied only to one associate and one tipstaff.[44]) In the Senate Symon thanked Senator McGregor, Labor's Leader of the Opposition, for his 'unremitting courtesy' and for 'faithfully observing' the compacts they together had made, even when his Labor colleagues disapproved. Symon concluded by saying, 'I had the greatest assistance from all my honorable friends opposite. Notwithstanding that we differed, and differed strongly, I do not believe that there is one rift in our friendly personal relations.'[45] Shouts of 'Hear, hear' from around the Chamber greeted Symon's final words.

As for Symon's relationship with George Reid, which was never close, it became more distant in the months after the fall of the Reid–McLean Government. Symon never expected Reid to regain the prime ministership and never had cause to revise his judgement about Reid's fitness for the role. Yet, later in his life, Symon would compare Reid favourably as an orator and platform performer to other political contemporaries. He was happy to use their connection after Reid became Australia's High Commissioner in London. In the short term, Deakin remained their common enemy but Reid's anti-socialist campaign of 1905–6 – designed in part to undermine Deakin for his reliance on Labor support – never appealed to Symon. He was focused on maintaining the Senate as the guardian of State rights, unaware or unaccepting that this cause was almost lost. At a personal level, Symon claimed in 1917 to know Reid better than anyone and felt confident to judge him: 'He is and has been all his life a selfish humbug.'[46]

12

'this combination has set me free from party'

On 1 June 1906, a year and eight months after the hearings concluded, Chief Justice Way delivered his reserved decision in the 'Corset case'. The *Herald* described the delay as 'A Grave Legal Scandal' and explained it by publishing a list of Way's extra-judicial activities and obligations.[1] Other newspapers were kinder, focusing on what Way's biographer saw as 'a model of exposition of the law and the facts'.[2] The outcome was a triumph for Downer. Way rejected every one of Symon's claims made on behalf of the plaintiffs. In a private letter Way wrote of being angrier 'than ever at having had so much time wasted over a case which was bluff from beginning to end'.[3]

Symon fared better at Way's hands in a drawn-out case extending from March to August 1906. He represented local victuallers fearful of losing their licences following local option polls on 17 February 1906 where voters supported a reduction by one-third of licences currently held in five districts around the City of Adelaide. The Temperance Party thought it had won a stunning victory with just 20 per cent of electors supporting its preferred program. A weekly newspaper edited by a Methodist minister paid Symon a compliment: 'The ablest barrister in Australia has been engaged to assist the drink sellers in an attempt to upset the local option polls.'[4] Appearing before the Adelaide Licensing Bench in March 1906 Symon questioned the validity of local option laws and the jurisdiction of the Bench. He took his case to the Supreme Court where he obtained a rule *nisi* prohibiting the Licensing Bench from removing five licensees before the court settled a 'difficult point of law'. Symon appeared against George Murray, a future Chief Justice who represented the Government.

'this combination has set me free from party'

Compared to Symon, the *Quiz* thought Murray was 'more modest than aggressive'.[5] At the end of June the Full Court reserved its decision. On 27 August 1906 the Court ruled that the polls in five districts of Adelaide were invalid and upheld one taken in the Port Adelaide district.[6] The liquor interest was delighted with Symon's achievement.

Symon had resumed senatorial duties while awaiting the decision in the local option case. He strongly supported Deakin's successful amendment of the *Judiciary Act* by restoring the original plan for the Bench to consist of four justices and a Chief Justice. The South Australian press and the commercial, legal and political community believed that Symon should be one of the two new appointments, claiming he was the most qualified next to Chief Justice Griffith. The *Advertiser* placed Symon ahead of all the 'probables' on grounds of 'sheer ability and eminence in the profession'. There was scepticism in Adelaide when Deakin invited Sir Samuel Way to take one of the two seats. The approach was not considered genuine because Deakin knew that Way would never give up all the extra-legal posts he held in South Australia. Clemons told Symon on 9 October that 'the alleged or arranged offer to Way was a studied affront on the part of the Ministry to add insult to injustice'.[7]

It is unlikely Deakin ever thought of appointing Symon. He did make a gesture by consulting Glynn about Symon, but Glynn was not overly enthusiastic. Deakin knew that Symon would not be welcomed by the three incumbent judges and he probably told Griffith he had no need to worry. Upon learning the good news, Barton wrote to Deakin on 20 September: 'I am glad for the sake of a great institution to hear we are not to have Symon.'[8]

The appointments of Isaacs and Higgins were announced on 11 October. The *Register* on 13 October stood loyally by its man, insisting that Symon was more qualified than Isaacs and Higgins to sit on the Bench and could now render greater service to his State by not joining the High Court.[9] Although Senator Dobson congratulated the Senate and himself because Symon 'can still remain our Leader', he thought Deakin had made 'an error of judgment' to appoint '2 Victorians, 2 zealous supporters, 2 Victorian ultra[-]protectionists, 2 Radicals & 2 supporters, more or less, of all the fads of the Labour Party'. He hoped Symon would head the poll and 'be in good form to lead the Senate next Parliament'.[10]

Did Symon mind a second rejection? Years later, he appeared to admit that he did. He told Joseph Cook in 1920 that Isaacs 'occupies a seat on the High Court I should have had', and then added, 'I have no regrets in that respect'.[11] As in 1903 Symon wanted to be asked, and in 1906 might have been even more tempted to accept a seat. Yet the factors which played upon his mind in 1903 (and in 1886) were still present. Perhaps Symon also sensed that he and the incumbent justices were better off without each other.

George Reid, notionally Symons' leader, wrote to him on 10 November 1906. Reid deeply resented Deakin's actions which ended his prime ministership and he sought revenge in the 1906 elections.[12] As the Deakin Government depended on a Labor Party committed to a socialist objective, Reid thought an Australia-wide campaign would expose Labor's gathering strength under Alfred Deakin's prime ministership. He hoped his former Attorney-General 'will be able to strengthen our cause in S.A.'. The prospects elsewhere were 'bright'. 'Deakin and his remnant are *in extremis*. I hope it is not a fact that you ridicule the seriousness of the Socialistic objective.' If only Symon had seen what Reid had found in Victoria, NSW and Queensland he would recognise that 'the "tiger cub" means to grow if it can'.[13] Evidently, friends and supporters had alerted Reid to what they saw as Symon's shortcomings as an election campaigner. Unlike his co-operative efforts in 1901 Symon preferred to canvass on his own and to present himself mainly as a strong senator in defence of State Rights. He opposed the Labor Party in South Australia principally to prevent it taking all three Senate seats as it had done in 1903. Symon wanted South Australians to reject any notion of one class or one party representing them in Parliament.

Although Symon rarely referred to himself as an anti-socialist, the press identified him as one of three Anti-Socialist candidates (later, 'Oppositionists') for the Senate election in South Australia. The two principal non-Labor organisations – the Australasian National League and the Farmers' and Producers' Association – endorsed him along with Joseph Vardon[14] and David Charleston. Yet apart from a meeting in Burra, where he sat on the same platform with Vardon and Charleston, Symon's campaign was an unaccompanied performance.

He launched it on 14 November in the Adelaide Town Hall, the stage of his many oratorical triumphs. The Mayor, his friend Theodore Bruce, presided and the audience probably numbered around 300. The *Register* reported that Symon gave 'an intellectual and inspiring address'; the pro-Labor *Herald* described his speech as 'one long smoodge for votes at almost any cost'.[15] Symon talked in general terms, by-passing or downplaying anything divisive. He called for a fiscal truce; a man 'would be a wrong doer who would plunge Australia into another tariff struggle extending over two or three years'. If the tariff were thrown open, he would ensure that the workers benefited. He was not frightened by the word 'socialist'; he just did not like using land taxes to break up the big estates and 'did not march one step under the banner of the nationalization of all means of production, distribution, and exchange (Hear, hear)'. Yet Symon was more interested in attacking Deakin for his untrustworthiness, calling him the 'Jonah' of the Labor Party because the much larger party had been seduced by being close to office to serve under the smaller one.

Few commentators took notice of Symon's principal argument on 14 November, namely, that he should be returned to the Senate because he had lived up to the Senate's reason for existence. He had always defended State rights and now wanted South Australians to recognise the dangers of electing another three Labor senators to join the three elected in 1903.

> it would not be good for State or Senate that men pledged to one section, one class or one particular party should have all the seats (Hear, hear) or should be in the position on questions affecting State rights and interests of viewing them through the distorting haze, it might be, of any caucus, he did not care what ... For all seats to be occupied by one class would mean as much despotism and tyranny as if the whole of the seats were in the hands of one man.

The Senate should look after the interests of the States and not advance the ideology and policies of party, let alone of one party.

Symon expanded on these views in the literature he distributed during the campaign. He began by reminding the electors they must vote for three candidates, otherwise their vote would be declared invalid. There was no mention, however, of any other candidate, no reference to his presumed allies Vardon and Charleston. The handout read: 'Give

SYMON one vote.' Symon then referred to the Convention where he was known as 'the Champion of the Small States', 'the foremost fighter for equal representation, and a strong Senate to guard and defend the rights of the States'. He repeated his line of 1901. South Australia had seven members in the House of Representative against the 47 representing NSW and Victoria. South Australians, therefore, had to rely on the Senate, and their constitutional rights were 'in peril' unless they subordinated 'mere party considerations' and chose 'strong, able and experienced men as Senators'. 'It would be fatal to have them all from one class or party.' He reminded voters that the Labor Party already had three Senators from South Australia, half the State's six seats. 'Is that fair?' Symon quoted favourable references to himself in the Sydney's *Daily Telegraph* and the *Bulletin* and the handout concluded: For six years Symon 'has been by common consent of both friends and opponents, the leading member of the Senate and a credit to this State'.[16]

Symon's election campaign was almost perfunctory. He traded on being well-known and well-regarded, made very few speeches and rarely travelled outside Adelaide. His day job as a barrister absorbed most of his attention in the fortnight preceding the poll on Wednesday 12 December. In this period, Symon prepared for, and then appeared in, what would become one of the longest criminal trials in the history of South Australia. Two customs agents – Charles Tucker, the former Mayor of Adelaide, and Frederick Forwood, an agent – faced ten counts of criminal conspiracy relating to the non-payment of duties between 1896 and 1906. Their takings amounted to some £33,000 of which Tucker collected around £2000 a year for ten years. The accused were separately represented. Symon, with Cleland, appeared for Tucker. Paris Nesbit led for the prosecution. Chief Justice Way presided over a trial by jury which extended for 31 days and introduced 97 witnesses and 8,000 exhibits. In February 1907 Tucker was found guilty as charged and sentenced to prison for two years with hard labour.[17]

The time Symon spent in court would in a later era have hurt him electorally. He already had the worst attendance record in the Senate. His vociferous supporters in the Loyal Orange Lodges might also have rendered him even more vulnerable. Sectarianism mattered more in Victoria and NSW but the Catholic *Southern Cross* of 23 November reminded voters that Symon had voted against a Higgins' motion supporting Irish Home Rule. It also reported that Symon and his wife had Orange Lodges named after them. Although the *Southern Cross* of 7 December stated that Catholics had no need to 'mark' any candidate on grounds of sectarianism, 'we are bound to point out (to "Irishmen") that Sir Josiah Symon spoke and voted against Home Rule resolutions in the Senate'. The Rev Henry Gainford, a Congregational Pastor and President of the Australian Protestant Defence Association, told Symon after the election that 'our people did not forget your Anti-Home Rule attitude in the Senate'. Symon's re-election in 1906 prompted many congratulatory letters from Protestant organisations in South Australia.[18]

Whereas just under 56 per cent of eligible voters turned out for the 1906 State elections, only 36 per cent of registered South Australian voters cast ballots in the Senate election held one month later on 12 December.[19] Symon probably benefited from another low turnout. Once again he topped the poll, and this time Kingston was not active on his behalf. After an extensive recount, the final figures declared on 8 January 1907 were:

Sir Josiah Symon (Oppositionist)	33,597
W. Russell (Labor)	31,796
J. Vardon (Oppositionist)	31,489
D.A. Crosby (Labor)	31,455
M.P. Blundell (Labor)	31,366
D.M. Charleston (Oppositionist)	30,608
T. Playford (Independent)	13,035

Playford's rejection sounded a warning to Independents: they had little chance of election to the Senate under the existing electoral system.

Reid's Anti-Socialists received a setback in 1906. Their 32 seats in the House of Representatives placed them ahead of the Labor Party's 26, but five Anti-Socialists, supporters of Sir John Forrest and sometimes labelled the 'Corner party', could be expected to vote with Deakin on most issues. The Deakinite Protectionists took 16 seats and, with Labor's continued support and the usually reliable votes of the 'Corner', the Deakin Government remained comfortably in office. Lack of effort combined with voter apathy hurt the cause. Edward Millen, a re-elected NSW senator, told Symon, 'we simply played at electioneering while the joint enemy – Caucus and the R.C. Church – worked'. After losing his supposedly safe seat of Gippsland, Allan McLean replied to Symon's heartfelt letter of commiseration. He gave several reasons for his defeat: the Public Service and the railway workers, the misrepresentation designed to prove he was in alliance with Reid on the fiscal truce, the *Age*, the Government and the socialists were 'most active and unscrupulous'. The greatest problem was that his supporters did not take the opposition seriously; nearly 15,000 of them did not bother to vote.[20]

The final composition of the Senate remained in doubt for 13 months after the 1906 election. For three weeks, Vardon, Dugald Crosby (Labor) and Reginald Blundell (Labor) were locked in a close contest for the third Senate seat in South Australia. At one stage the *Herald* announced that 'Senator Crosby' had triumphed. Vardon's application for a recount across the State led to the discovery that some 9,000 votes in the seat of Angas had allegedly been cremated (the votes were 'found' intact in September 1907). The declared result on 8 January 1907 gave Vardon a majority of 34 votes over Crosby, and he was sworn in with the other senators on 20 February 1907. By that time, the ailing Crosby had died but Blundell had lodged a petition with the High Court. Justice Barton sat as the Court of Disputed Returns and conducted hearings throughout May 1907. He declared Vardon's election void. By then Symon was back in the 'old country' though he would play a crucial role in settling the matter after returning to Adelaide in June.

Senator Symon was pleased enough to be out of Australia after he failed to win the presidency of the Senate. The first business of the new Senate was to elect a replacement for the retired Sir Richard Baker. Clemons wrote to Symon on 20 December 1906 declaring his preference for Symon; if Symon did not stand, he proposed Albert Gould (NSW) whom Symon had nominated after the 1903 election. Walker wrote to Symon on 9 January 1907. He expected Symon to nominate Gould and, if he did, the NSW senator had 'a very good chance'. Walker hoped that Robert Best, a Victorian Protectionist, would come onside but the Deakin Government might propose him while supporting a Labor nomination for Chairman of Committees. Walker thought the Anti-Socialists should have an urgent private meeting before confronting combinations on the other side.

'this combination has set me free from party'

Symon might have been happier if Walker had focused on Symon's chances. As he told Clemons by letter on 14 January, Symon felt he 'could be of service to the Senate and the Commonwealth'. It would mean a loss of personal liberty and an end of his practice while in the job; such a sacrifice was never considered when he and others were merely ministers of the Crown. Provided, however, the Senate expressed a general wish for Symon to take the presidency, 'I think I should be inclined to take it'. There was, however, an important pre-condition. 'I should not care to enter upon a contest for it, with any risk of defeat.' So, he asked Clemons, 'What is the feeling?' Symon added that if the Senate did not have the general wish he, like Clemons, would prefer Gould.

In the meantime, Symon told Clemons he remained 'up to my neck' with the Tucker defence in this 'cursed Customs prosecution'. The details were so 'wearisome' and the daylight 'so dim' that he was becoming 'disgusted' with everything. 'I am seldom at home.'

As well as replying to Walker, Symon contacted Simon Fraser, the sole Free Trader from Victoria. He wanted advice from both senators on whether he could win the presidency without a contest. Clemons assured Symon on 16 January that if he nominated for the post no one else would stand and, if Symon went ahead, he could resign later. Walker came back with some disturbing information. Until receiving Symon's letter of 17 January, where Symon did not think Gould's chances were 'good', Walker had no intimation linking Symon's name to the presidency which he thought would be a contest between Gould and Best. Walker was more concerned about Symon's proposed resignation as the unofficial Leader of the Anti-Socialist Opposition. The Government would hail his departure and there would be 'considerable ructions' over who should succeed him because there would be several contenders in the field. If Symon did not nominate, then Walker would vote for Gould.

The Senate was due to meet on Wednesday 20 February 1907. In the week preceding the meeting Best, Gould and Symon were named in the press as the likely candidates for the presidency. Symon arrived in Melbourne on 19 February, very troubled because he had swallowed a peach stone; on that matter, he told Nell, he 'must just wait events'. His focus turned to the presidency. Symon reported to Nell that 'little Walker' had been in Melbourne for days 'buttonholing & intriguing for Gould' who had been in Melbourne since Monday. Once again Symon found fault with the manners of politicians. '[I] would have thought that as they profess to look upon me as their leader they would first have had the courtesy to ascertain whether I was likely to be a candidate.' If no meeting were called he wanted the *Argus* to publish a story saying Symon would not allow his name to go forward. He was booked on the Thursday train to reach home on Friday morning.

Jo told Nell on 20 February he had decided it would be 'a little *infra dig*' to use an interview to set out his position on the presidency. Besides, he thought it would be well understood around Parliament that 'the revelations I have had of the duplicity & dishonourable behaviour of little Walker and Macfarlane [Tas.] ... are truly lamentable'. There was no way now for him to belong to the same party as those two. His attitude would become apparent when the Senate next meets after the long adjournment. Symon resolved that for the present he must try not to give anyone occasion to say, 'I am visiting upon them displeasure because of not being chosen President'.[21]

All the senators met on the morning of 20 February and endorsed a ticket which was guaranteed to succeed: Gould for President and Pearce of the Labor Party for Chairman of Committees. Senator Best, the Leader of the Government in the Senate, moved that Senator Gould be elected President. Senator McGregor, the Leader of the Labor Party in the Senate, seconded the motion. Best warned that 'it was the duty of other aspirants to this honorable position to recognise at once that the will of the Senate must be accepted without demur and without complaint'; that is, to endorse 'the will and desire' of the morning assembly. Senator Symon accepted that Senator Gould had been granted the unanimity he wanted. He warmly congratulated the man he would have supported in a vote and, in listing all the important responsibilities and duties of a President of the Senate, he singled out one for special comment. He wanted the new President 'to strive at all times to secure those great rights which [the Senate] possesses under the Constitution, that they may in no respect be transgressed or whittled away ... to secure the strength of the Senate and its efficiency for the high purposes that were designed for it under the Constitution'.

Symon as 'Leader of the Opposition' was expected to participate in the

'This combination has set me free from party'

debate on the Address-in-Reply. His colleagues learnt to their surprise he had already caught the train back to Adelaide on 21 February. The Senate would not meet again until July. Labor had agreed with the Deakinites to prorogue the Parliament to allow the Prime Minister a trouble-free break when attending the 1907 Colonial Conference in London in the company of Sir William Lyne.

Senator Symon decided he needed a holiday and booked himself to sail for London on 9 March. Nell had already sailed accompanied by their eldest daughter Margaret and their youngest son, Oliver, who was about to turn 12, and was applying for acceptance as a cadet midshipman in the Royal Navy.

Jo was delighted that Oliver got into naval college and arranged with Vice-Admiral and Lady Pearson that his boy would spend part of his first mid-summer break with them. Pearson had been the Commander in Chief of the Australia Station (1898–1900). At this stage (1907) Jo was thinking of keeping Oscar at St Peters and then sending him to Oxford for a couple of years followed by time in France to learn about the wine industry. He was not yet sure about Carril's future or about schools for the two youngest girls. Charles, the eldest son, was no problem. He was in residence at Magdalen College Oxford, and the family could celebrate his coming of age.

Symon's standing as a former minister of the Crown, as a prominent parliamentarian and a very successful barrister ensured invitations to mix with the titled and the influential. The Mayor of London invited Sir Josiah Symon and Margaret (Nell was ill) to the presentation of the freedom of the City to the visiting 'Colonial Premiers'. The two Symons sat next to the rising star of British politics, Winston Churchill. Symon attended a luncheon at the Australasian Club, and major functions at Westminster Hall and Claridge's. He listened to Alfred Deakin make speeches to large gatherings of admiring and enraptured listeners and observed how the Tory press and politicians welcomed Deakin's criticisms of the Liberal Government.

Symon did have business of his own to pursue. It all began with a letter to the *Register* published on 15 August 1906 and signed by 'Eleanor Symon, Manoah, Upper Sturt'. The letter explained that the Royal Navy had named one of the finest and largest of its new battleships HMS

Commonwealth as a compliment to Australia. It was customary in such circumstances for citizens of the place so honoured to commemorate the occasion with a gift of a shield and plate. Nell hoped South Australia might take the initiative to be 'the first in this, and as in many other desirable things', perhaps opening a one shilling subscription list. She noted how the current Mayor of Adelaide, Theodore Bruce, planned to form a fundraising committee. It is fair to assume that Nell's 'big husband' was behind the proposal, and Symon used his 1907 visit to take the matter further. He spoke to the First Lord of the Admiralty on 18 April, and received confirmation of Admiralty approval before the end of the month. Nothing of further significance happened before the matter was taken up under Symon's leadership in 1910.

Symon left London for Canada on 31 May. Nell and Margaret had remained behind for their presentation at Court, and to visit Ireland and France and to stay in touch with Charles and Oliver.[22] Nell received a letter from her 'big husband' not dissimilar to, but on a different theme from those sent during his 1891 overseas trip. 'I don't know that I ever felt so badly as when I left you at Euston and found myself in the Atlantic next morning.' He wanted to go back to London on the next train:

> The truth is, Nell, you are all in all to me, and in connection with my duties of public life – which never were congenial whatever my success in them may have been – I must have you to talk with and confer with. It's different with my professional work – it is different with Auldana and all my other affairs – but I shrink from public life without you. And quite irrespective of all these things – just because it is you and I. I cannot bear to have you away from my side.[23]

Allowing, again, for monotonous and lonely shipboard life there were two underlying truths in this confession. First, while Symon remained fully engaged as a barrister, a vigneron, an investor, a bibliophile and a farmer it was not quite the same with politics. Politics never gave him a sustained sense of purpose. Secondly, Nell assumed the role of confidante for Jo's political life before they married, and he continued to consult her and to rely upon her judgment. It was a role which she felt at times required gentle mockery.

On his arrival in Sydney on 16 July, Symon did not hold back on

'this combination has set me free from party'

the subject of Alfred Deakin.[24] Asked whether he thought the Colonial Conference was a success, he replied, 'Mr Deakin pronounced it a success before it began, and afterwards said the opposite'. Any success occurred in spite of Deakin and Lyne, 'unless by success you mean the stirring-up of political party strife'. Both men were 'inoculated with the virus of protectionist Toryism' and like the Tories did not want the masses to have untaxed food. He contrasted 'Mr Deakin's volubility' with the 'impressive silence', as some of the press called it, of Sir Wilfrid Laurier, the Canadian Prime Minister. Symon saw Laurier as 'the chief figure and the statesmanlike steadying influence on the Conference'.

Symon's return to politics coincided with the Senate's need for a good constitutional lawyer. It will be recalled that Justice Barton had declared Senator Vardon's election void. The learned judge left open one critical question: was the void to be filled as a casual vacancy or should there be a fresh election? Littleton Groom, the Commonwealth Attorney-General, delivered an opinion on 8 June that Vardon's election being declared void it should be filled as a casual vacancy under s. 15 of the Australian Constitution. Acting on this finding, the South Australian Parliament voted 32–26 to elect James O'Loghlin (Labor) to the seat. Vardon took the matter to the High Court which ruled that the Senate should decide which section of the Constitution applied. Although the High Court did not have the power to determine the issue, Parliament could legislate to allow it to do so. The Senate then referred the matter to its Committee of Disputed Returns and Elections which consisted of Symon, four Anti-Socialists – Dobson, Macfarlane, Neild and Walker – and de Largie and Turley from the Labor Party.

The Committee first met on 29 August and elected Symon to the Chair. O'Loghlin appeared before the Committee on 4 September and later submitted additional arguments. Although accused of being unpleasant to O'Loghlin, Symon provided him with a fair amount of leeway and pulled him up mainly for making statements for which he had no evidence. As Symon saw it, the election had been voided so there was no casual vacancy and, because it was 'a cardinal and fundamental principle of the Constitution' that the Senate should be elected by 'popular choice', he rejected outright the notion of State Parliaments choosing or electing senators.[25] Symon wrote the Committee's final Report recommending a fresh election which the Committee approved on 9 October. Symon sent a proof copy to Chief Justice Way; his associate passed on Way's thanks. Symon also gave a copy to his partner Rounsevell who replied with enthusiasm: he had 'read it very carefully and have enjoyed doing so. It is beautifully clear – in exposition & deduction ... What a great judge you will make – and I hope, become, as such more famous, than as a great Q. & K.C.'.[26]

On 16 October Symon moved in the Senate that the Report be adopted. He said there was little if anything essential to be added, and then spoke for nearly two hours.[27] William Russell, elected with Symon in 1906 and a recent addition to the Labor Party, attacked Symon for his treatment of O'Loghlin and made it clear he would never have signed the report. He amused himself and other Labor senators by mocking Symon for taking notice of 'the man in the street' when conservatives usually refer to the 'mob' or the 'masses'. If some words were added and few others taken out, Symon's speech 'would make a good democratic address'. How 'strange' it was 'to hear such sentiments coming from the High Priest of Conservatism'.[28] Having approved the Report, the two Labor members submitted a memorandum saying that because the Senate could not settle a difficult question of constitutional law 'we consider the question a proper one to refer to the High Court'. The Senate agreed with what became Turley's amendment to the adoption of the Report and the issue went to the High Court. The Court in December 1907 ruled in favour of Symon's view that the 'dominant' s 7 of the Constitution provided that senators 'should be directly chosen by the people of the State'.

Vardon subsequently won the fresh election held on 15 February 1908 collecting 47,130 votes against O'Loghlin's 40,982, with a majority of 7048. He collected 13,533 votes more than Symon had secured in 1906.

Symon had long talked about resigning as the 'Leader of the Opposition'. In mid-November 1907, speaking to his colleagues as Free Traders not Anti-Socialists, Symon said that as he could not be in place during the next tariff fight to meet his own standards, he could not be a candidate for the leadership. Asked to reconsider he intimated – possibly through Walker as Clemons was also absent – that his view was unchanged. Ten Anti-Socialists met in Melbourne on Thursday 21 November, Fraser and Neild also being absent, and accepted Symon's

'this combination has set me free from party'

resignation with regret. They unanimously elected Millen to replace him and Dobson to replace Clemons. Millen wrote to Symon on the following day expressing regret Symon could not be present. He would like to have heard Symon's views and been given advice. Millen now looked forward to receiving his 'advice and assistance' in dealing with the 'difficulties' of the position.

Symon was in no mood for co-operation. First, Walker's letter telling him of the party room decision had arrived after he had read the news in the Adelaide press. Secondly, Symon thought 'it was due to the Senate as well as myself that I should personally inform the Senate of my retirement. I might at least have been given the opportunity of doing so.' It was made to appear he had vacated a job held for six years 'without one word of leave-taking on my part, and without even acknowledging the kindness and goodwill for which I had reason to be most grateful. It might well seem disrespectful to the Senate. It was derogatory to me.' If Walker had wired him on the Thursday he could have been in Melbourne on Friday morning. Thirdly, Symon noted that he was not invited to participate in the choice of his successor, though he accepted it may have been desired that he should not.

There was also a parting shot: 'although I shall continue in general opposition to the Government I prefer to act independently.' He would be happy to co-operate with Senator Millen 'but I am not to be regarded as a member of your party or at the call of your whip Senator Dobson'. As for Millen's hopes and expectations, Symon told him that having got rid of the 'difficulties' he was not prepared 'to take them on again or to share them indirectly'. He preferred to be 'untrammelled'. As an independent senator he felt certain his opportunities of serving the State and the Commonwealth had not been diminished – 'at any rate I shall do the best I can'.[29]

One year after these events, Andrew Fisher, the new Labor leader, informed Deakin of Labor's decision to withdraw support from the Government. On 6 November 1908, the Government lost a vote 49–13 and a week later Fisher formed a Labor Government with the Deakinite Protectionists in support. Within another fortnight George Reid retired from the leadership of the main Opposition party following an ultimatum issued by some of his followers who wanted their party to unite with Forrest's Corner and acceptable Deakinites. Reid's departure removed a major obstacle to such a realignment. A meeting of the main Opposition party, held in Melbourne on 26 November, unanimously approved a motion placing on record 'its great regret that [George Reid] should be unable owing to the pressure of professional duties to continue in the leadership, and its high appreciation of the splendid services he has rendered the party in Parliament and on the public platform of Australia'. The motion also received 'with the greatest satisfaction the assurance that his signal ability will still be at the disposal of the party and of Australia'. Sir Josiah Symon, the non-member of any party, was present and exhibited no hesitation in seconding this motion. Reid's 'transgressions' in 1905 no longer mattered; Alfred Deakin's actions did, and they remained unforgiveable. Symon seemed unsure of where he belonged but he remained in the room when on Glynn's motion the Opposition elected Joseph Cook to succeed Reid.[30]

Parliament rose on 28 November. Symon returned to his legal practice in Adelaide and prepared to make another family trip to the United Kingdom. Symon left for 'the old country' on 4 March 1909, accompanied by Nell and a maid, as well as Lenore, Angel and Mary and the fourth son, Carril. Symon attended a civic reception held for him in Perth and, despite saying he was on holidays, spoke briefly to a reporter about federal politics. He said Australia needed 'a reorganisation of parties' where the Commonwealth 'was in the hands of a Government that is not dependent on the uncertain support of those who do not believe in their policy, but is the outcome of a strong and certain majority'.[31]

Reaching Port Said, Symon had many conversations on military strategy, imperial defence and cadet training with the much-feted Field Marshal Earl ('Bobs') Roberts, VC. Symon's arrival in London coincided with the 'navy scare'. In an atmosphere of increasing tension, the European Powers were expanding their armed forces and Germany was undertaking a shipbuilding program of large battleships known as 'Dreadnoughts'. Symon attended a meeting of the Royal Colonial Institute on Wednesday 20 April where a resolution had been submitted expressing grave concern at the Liberal Government's disclosures about the Royal Navy losing some of its lead over national fleets. The resolution asked for the present year's shipbuilding program to be augmented forthwith, thanked the colonies concerned for their gallant and spontaneous offers of battleships to the motherland and welcomed Mr Asquith's proposal for an Imperial Conference on naval matters. Symon strongly deprecated the condemnation of the British Government's policy implied in the resolution. He said the Imperial Navy must be the floating bulwark of the Empire in the Pacific as in the North Sea, and Australia was ready to pour out her treasure and blood to ensure its maintenance. Asquith's suggestion regarding the necessity for a contiguous naval policy by the oversea dominions was likely to appeal to Australians. The resolution was carried, but there were about a dozen dissentients.

This visit to the 'old country' was marked by another round of social engagements. Among them, Symon attended a dinner given by the NSW Agent-General to meet Sir Charles Dilke, the baronet who might have been Prime Minister except for being cited as a co-respondent in a divorce case. Symon dined at the House of Commons with Colonel Seeley, the Under-Secretary of State for the Colonies. Two days later he had lunch at the United Services Club in the company, among other notables, of Reginald McKenna, the First Lord of the Admiralty, and Alfred Lyttleton, the former Colonial Secretary. On 29 April, Symon sat in the Distinguished Strangers' Gallery to hear Lloyd George deliver the famed 'People's Budget' of 1909, an occasion to match his good fortune in 1886 to hear Gladstone speak on the Home Rule Bill. Just before Symon left London for Marseille and Adelaide the Symons visited the Isle of Wight to see their son Oliver now in training at the Royal Naval College at East Cowes.

His family remained behind after Jo left for home. Nell wanted to be there for Lenore's presentation at Court, to keep an eye on Oliver's progress and to re-establish her relationship with Charles. There was also the prospect of touring and visiting friends, sometimes with Lenore and with one or both of the youngest daughters.[32]

Back home, Deakin and Cook had successfully negotiated the 'fusion' of the majority of Deakinites, Cook's followers and Forrest's Corner. Before Deakin could speak at the resumption of parliament Lyne shouted 'Judas'. Symon learnt of Lyne's intervention when he reached Colombo on 27 May. Jo wrote to Nell: 'Mr Lyne [appointed KCMG in 1900] seems to have issued some vigorous – & in my judgement – appropriate language in denouncing

Deakin as Judas.' Symon had no knowledge of the combination or of who was to lead, though he assumed it would be Deakin.

> If so they will not find me supporting any Deakin cum Forrest cum Cook Ministry in the Senate. Having been strongly opposed to them for last eight years, I have no intention of being their humble follower & supporter now. They betrayed our Ministry 4 years ago & they have now betrayed their friends [in] the Labor Party. I for one will have nothing to do with them. At any rate this combination has set me free from party: & I shall take the attitude of a perfectly independent Senator for South Australia – What else can I do?

Symon acknowledged he would have to reach Fremantle before learning anything definite about the new Ministry when he supposed he would be interviewed and 'have to say something'.[33]

Arriving in Fremantle, Symon first spoke about what he knew: the story of the 'navy scare'. He blamed the Tory Opposition and the Tory newspapers for spreading alarm. No responsible person he met doubted the supremacy of the Royal Navy, just as no one doubted the necessity of its absolute supremacy or the maintenance of its strength. British ministers, he said, were unwise in the line they adopted. By talking of the immediate construction of eight instead of four Dreadnoughts they played into the hands of the Tories. In Symon's opinion, Australia's contribution should consist of establishing and developing its own resources and assisting imperial defence in some other way, perhaps by increasing its annual contribution to the cost of that portion of the navy immediately concerned in the defence of these shores. Inevitably, Symon brought Deakin into the matter. A little while back 'Mr. Deakin was all for a Dreadnought or nothing'. Now it seems 'he is for a Dreadnought or something else'.

Regarding the present state of federal politics, Symon said he was in the dark about the fusion of parties. He had hardly recovered from his surprise at the latest developments. He understood that 'Mr. Deakin' has taken the lead in ousting the Labor Government, and that the Opposition majority which until now had been bitterly opposed to him had accepted his leadership of the new party. 'There may be reasons for all this which are not at present apparent to me.' What he did see was the dissolution of

'this combination has set me free from party'

the old parties, but it was hard to know what will emerge in their place. 'The situation, too, is not without its humorous aspects.'[34]

John Clemons, Symon's political friend in the Senate, set a course for his mentor. Writing to Symon on 15 June, he supposed that neither of them doubted the other's attitude in relation to the 'Deakin ménage'. His own chief political objective at present is 'to hamper, embarrass, and oppose them in every way possible, and, as the Senate is now constituted, I am looking forward with some cheerfulness to occasional opportunities'. He intended to test 'my political elasticity to the furthest it will stretch'.[35]

Symon seized an early opportunity to let Deakin know where he stood. The new Leader issued a circular letter on 18 June 1909 referring to Labor's refusal to provide pairs and its determination to obstruct business. Deakin asked his team to make special arrangements to ensure that the Government secured the transaction of ordinary business. This was to be the last session of the present Parliament, and we could rely on 'earnest and well informed' public criticism of what we do. Deakin wanted members to arrange their affairs to ensure constant attendance in Parliament. As soon as possible they should give him a list of the occasions when they wished to be absent. 'Only by this unity of action can we achieve a fruitful session and fitting conclusion to our labours.'

Deakin's letter to Symon was marked 'Personal' and began 'Dear Sir Josiah Symon'. It concluded: 'With regards, Yours very truly Alfred Deakin.' Symon replied on 22 June:

> Dear Mr Deakin,
> Your circular letter of the 18th marked 'personal' which reached me yesterday, was quite unexpected, as you know I am not and never have been a political supporter of yours. Apart from public affairs our personal relations have been most friendly and I hope they will remain so, but in politics, as you know, I have always been frankly in direct opposition to you, and I have not been suddenly converted, as you appear to assume, from an opponent into a follower.
> With kind regards, Very truly yours,
> J.H. Symon[36]

Parliament was about to resume, and Symon wrote to Nell at the end of June to comment on what his wife called 'this unholy alliance'. He now felt confident about the way things were going. Symon also mentioned the current gossip about who should get the high commissionership in London. He did not think Deakin would take it because the high commissionership was 'the "price" to be paid to Mr George Reid for holding his tongue'.[37]

Symon and Clemons delivered their first blow on 1 July when the new Government sought Supply for two months. Labor moved an amendment to reduce the time period to one month. The amendment was defeated 15–14 in the Senate where Symon and Clemons were paired in support of Labor's amendment. Symon argued that no Supply other than what was an absolute necessity has ever been asked in this or any other parliament while a no-confidence motion was under consideration. He pointed out how in 1904 he had sought and obtained a month of Supply for the new Reid–McLean Government.[38]

The *Argus* of 5 July was perplexed by Symon's action:

> No member of the Federal Parliament had, since the foundation of the Commonwealth, offered more able or consistent resistance to socialism and all its champions than he had, and no name could have seemed more grotesquely out of place than his when it appeared amongst those of the men whose policy and methods are so directly opposed to all that he stands for.

The *Argus* could not say for certain whether Symon was acting out of personal pique – it would be 'invidious' to think he acted out of personal dislike or jealousy – or had failed to inform himself sufficiently on movements in federal politics. Nevertheless, the editorial warned Symon, and Clemons, against giving satisfaction to their enemies and embarrassing their friends: 'The former will feel no gratitude, and the latter have not deserved their hostility.'

On 7 July, Symon delivered what he told Nell was 'the best speech of my life – at any rate I felt in good form – in denunciation of Deakin & his political faithlessness'.[39] He spoke for just under four hours of which two-and-a-half were directed principally at Deakin. Fisher and other members of the House of Representatives flocked into the galleries to listen; among them, Lyne, whose smile never left his face.[40] Symon's message was simple enough. Deakin had proved himself, again, to be

'this combination has set me free from party'

'untrustworthy'. He let down parties and he let down people. 'Yesterday he was Leader of the Socialist party ... To-day he is the Leader of the anti-Socialists.' He sacrificed Turner and McLean and George Reid on the way back to the top. When referring to Deakin, Symon liked to qualify the unqualified: 'I distrust Mr. Deakin utterly as a politician, though I have a great regard for him personally.' The *Age* of 8 July noted how Deakin's 'lifelong enemy' kept insisting he liked Deakin as a person.

The same paper claimed Parliament had seldom heard such a bitter speech. The press in Melbourne and Sydney devoted many, often critical, columns to it. Understandably, Deakin's principal biographers have ignored the speech entirely. The *Age* editorial of 8 July looked on the bright side for the Liberal Protectionists, claiming it was 'not so often that an astute man makes a tactical blunder'. Symon had deprived the Labor Party of its best weapon by arguing that, far from abandoning his principles, Deakin had made the anti-socialists captive under his Liberal banner. The editorial also questioned Symon's motives. Overlooked in the distribution of portfolios, he was still in a fit of pique because he had failed to win a seat on the High Court and was still miffed by Deakin's 'Notice to Quit'. Not surprisingly, the *Labor Call* in Victoria and the *Daily Herald* in South Australia gave Symon favourable treatment.

Jo wrote again to 'My Nell' on 11 July: 'You will scarcely realise how cheering it is to know you agree with me about Deakin, & the "fusion" – Your epithet "profligate coalition" is good.' Jo thought 'the most stimulating' thing she said about him was that she hoped that her 'big husband' was 'denouncing them for all I am worth – they are false friends and false foes'. Jo sent her a copy of Hansard as well as clippings from the *Age* and the *Argus* referring to his speech 'with the usual disjointed report, leading articles upon it, & of course attacking & abusing me'. Everyone, he told Nell, seemed to take pleasure in trying to damage him. And they could not tell the story accurately. The *Argus* editorial of 5 July, for example, was 'a piece of lying impertinence'. It failed to publish the reason he gave for his stand and failed to report that he did not vote but was paired with Walker. As for Labor's warm reception for his speech, Symon wrote: 'I made it for my own satisfaction not for theirs.'

'I am afraid, my dear, there is not much chance of my being offered the High Commissionership.' Deakin and his colleagues were unlikely to forgive him. Symon knew he had no chance anyhow, for the 'simple reason' he had mentioned previously; 'the High Commissionership is I am told the reward for G.H. Reid for his acquiescence in this monstrous coalition under Deakin', the man who had betrayed Reid and his Government in 1905, and with whom Reid had not been on speaking terms since. 'Great is the corruption of that kind in Australian politics!' He longed to be out of it, and while still there would do what he could 'but it is all very sad'; he did not want 'their' high commissionership or any other office they could give.

Symon added: 'Barton is dying', and 'they' say he will not sit on the High Court again ('they' were wrong; Barton sat on the High Court until his death on 7 January 1920). If Barton's seat should be offered, he doubted even considering it. He would have thought about it six years earlier, or even when the last appointments were made in 1906 but, 'honestly and truly', he would have turned it down and it was unlikely he would even look at an offer now.

On 18 August Jo told Nell about 'a feeling growing in Parliament in favour of nominating me for High Commissioner'. He advised Nell not to attach importance to this: 'if the nomination is left to the Government there is not the slightest chance' of it happening. Jo had been asked 'confidentially', he did not say by whom, whether he would be interested, if offered. He replied he could not say anything definitely without consulting Nell and he promised to keep her informed of any movement in the matter. In his letter of 24 August, he referred again to 'a growing feeling in Parliament – certainly in the Senate in my favour for the High Commissionership'. He thought it would not come to anything 'because the Government would never allow the appointment to be the subject of ballot: but we shall see'.[41] Sir Josiah Symon would have loved an appointment to London but was right the first time about the position being set up for Reid. He was, however, probably the last person capable of measuring or knowing 'a growing feeling in Parliament' and the fact he thought a ballot was even conceivable showed how out of touch he had become.

Jo concluded a letter to Nell written over 11–14 July with a commitment and a declaration: 'Now that I have embarked on this Anti-Deakin campaign, I shall seize every opportunity of pressing it home & doing

'this combination has set me free from party'

what I can to get him out of the Prime Ministership – without of course over exerting [sic] myself.'[42] His plan did not amount to very much. He made one speech in opposition to the referendum in 1910 to approve Deakin's Financial Agreement with the States but, otherwise, was never sighted on platforms or in the press. The Fusion had set him free, not just of party but of politics as well – except for one last hurrah in 1913.

13

'I am really sick of politics & want rest'

The Third Parliament rose for what proved to be the final time on 8 December 1909. On 13 April 1910 the Labor Party led by Andrew Fisher won an absolute majority in both Houses, the first federal party to do so. Labor secured 41 seats in the House of Representatives, the Fusion held 31 and three former Protectionists were returned as Independents, two of whom generally sided with Labor. Labor took all 18 seats up for election in the Senate which, added to the four it collected in 1906, gave the Party a clear 22–14 majority over the Fusion and Symon. Sir Josiah Symon and Joseph Vardon were the sole non-Labor senators from South Australia. Two referenda were held on the same day as the election: the Constitution Alteration (State Debts) Bill passed easily enough but the Constitution Alteration (Finance) Bill – implementing the Financial Agreement – failed.

In keeping with his decision to detach himself from party politics Senator Symon did not participate in the election. He had no meaningful contact with the three Fusion candidates for the Senate, even though one was his former colleague David Charleston. Symon did, however, address one public meeting to advocate a 'No' vote for the Financial Agreement. On 8 April, just five days before the election, Symon told the meeting in the Adelaide Town Hall that the Financial Agreement was the foremost national question before the community at the present time. 'All else was a mere conflict between the Labor Party on the one side and the curious mixture, the fusion, on the other. (Laughter and cheers.)' He belonged to neither side, but asked the audience 'on that great question' of the Agreement 'not to subordinate principle to party'. He certainly would not.[1]

Symon had no problem about the Commonwealth agreeing to

'I am really sick of politics & want rest'

pay the States 25/- per head of population. He objected to the Deakin Government's proposal to insert the agreement with the Premiers into the Constitution thereby limiting the Commonwealth's freedom of movement in financial matters. The politician who was avowedly a defender of the States presented the other half of himself: the Australian nationalist and Commonwealth man. The people were being asked to strip their national parliament of an important portion of its financial control. Such a proposition, Symon said, was unheard of in any civilised country. South Australia, siding with NSW and Victoria, narrowly voted 'No' on the proposal.

Taking office, the Fisher Government moved swiftly to break up underdeveloped large estates and to reduce or eliminate absentee landlords, especially those based abroad. Taxing land became the chosen means of assault because there appeared to be no constitutional barriers to the Commonwealth acquiring or extending the tax yield. Two Land Tax Bills were introduced in the House of Representatives in August 1910. Significantly, there was no direct reference in any explanatory notes to the need or desirability of raising revenue. The Land Tax Assessment legislation, for example, bore the following descriptor: 'An Act relating to the Imposition, Assessment, and Collection of a Land Tax upon Unimproved Values.' Deakin, as Leader of the Opposition, said on 30 August that 'taxation is only a secondary and subordinate feature' of the legislation. When Gregor McGregor introduced the legislation into the Senate, he barely talked about the revenue implications. The bulk of his Second Reading speech was devoted to the objective of breaking up the large estates.

Senator Symon spoke in the Second Reading debate on 21 October 1910. Formally, he had the floor for 140 minutes. Allowing for the flow of recorded interjections his speech, in real time, took approximately 95 minutes. The President, Labor's Harry Turley, intervened on just one occasion. There was no need for firmer action. Symon could make his case effectively while conducting a well-mannered conversation with Labor senators he repeatedly called 'my honourable friends'. Nevertheless, at one moment in his speech he threatened to wage ideological warfare. He said the Government was 'bringing in confessedly a class tax' by singling out the owner of a particular kind of property which to his mind was 'wholly indefensible'. Tax the rich, by all means. Make those best able to pay, to pay according to their means. But a class tax, singling out a particular kind of property, which may in fact earn very little, was unacceptable.[2]

On 26 April 1911, the Labor Government sought through a referendum to extend Commonwealth power in respect of trade and commerce, the control of corporations, labour and employment and combinations and monopolies. For weeks, Symon neither made a public statement nor appeared on a public platform. Richard Butler, a former Premier and a prominent non-Labor figure, sent a letter to the press. Butler's acerbity was latent but discernible to anyone who remembered how Symon was hardly in evidence during the 1910 election campaign. Butler wondered when the State's senior senator planned to enter the campaign for the proposed constitutional changes. Sir Josiah 'is one of the greatest legal and constitutional authorities in Australia, in addition to being "honored" by the electors of South Australia as one of their representatives in the Senate'. Every other senator has spoken for one side or the other and 'the electors have the right to expect Senator Symon to do likewise'.[3]

Symon did not emerge from seclusion until 21 April, five days before the referendum. Speaking to 'a large audience' at the Institute Hall in North Adelaide, he began with the approach of 'Yes-No' Reid.[4] Symon did not at first advocate a 'No' vote so much as say that the defeat of the referendum vote would not hurt anyone. Nor did he speak strongly against a 'Yes' vote. In fact he liked some elements of the proposals; for example, there should be greater federal power to deal with combines. He described Deakin's proposal in 1910 as 'less defensible' and 'more complex' than the current crop of proposals. Symon claimed his standpoint 'was not a Party one', and 'not influenced by any tinge of unfriendliness to the party in power'. When, however, he reached the stage of saying that the Senate had failed to protect the States, Symon was ready to demand a 'No' vote. 'Did people want the smaller States to be absorbed by the larger ones? Did they want South Australia to become a suburb of Melbourne or a sort of ante-chamber of New South Wales?' Once he asked questions of this nature Symon knew he was on safe ground and the interjectors had no response. The Chairman, Alderman Isaac Isaacs, deftly closed the meeting before anyone could ask a question.

'I am really sick of politics & want rest'

The Curramulka branch of the recently-formed Liberal Union liked Symon's brief public appearance. The branch secretary seized the opportunity at a social and dance on the night before the ballot to read out the *Advertiser*'s report of Symon's speech in North Adelaide.[5] Many new members joined the Union on the night, perhaps inspired by Symon's words and certainly approving of them. The Union itself had been formed in the wake of the 1910 Federal defeat, achieved by a merger of the existing non-Labor organisations: the Liberal and Democratic Union (formed in 1906), the Australian National League (which underwent name changes but was first formed in 1891) and the Farmers' and Producers' Political Union (1904). The first-named was the most reluctant to join. Urged forward by the former and future Premier Archibald Peake it eventually agreed to participate by a majority of one at a conference. The secretary of the Curramulka branch thought it reasonable to include Senator Symon in the fold.

The Government proposals were roundly rebuffed on 26 April. They did receive an overall 'Yes' vote in Western Australia but the other five States returned a clear 'No'. In South Australia the 'No' vote of 61.93 per cent was the second highest negative result after NSW.

Symon had little time for politics in the immediate aftermath of the referendum. Parliament itself had been prorogued on 29 November 1910 until 7 February 1911 and was further prorogued six times to 5 September 1911. The Coronation of King George V on 22 June 1911 and the subsequent Imperial Conference kept Fisher and two senior ministers – Lee Batchelor and George Pearce – occupied in London. In the early part of 1911 Symon had several court appearances in Adelaide. Starting on 31 March, he appeared in 18 hearing days for the respondents in a case involving a claim for the payment of £975 for supplies of superphosphate and a counterclaim for £1300. Symon and Paris Nesbit, who was one of two KCs representing the plaintiff, bantered with each other throughout hearings before Chief Justice Way and two other judges. The respondents won the case and were awarded costs. Symon immediately immersed himself in two other civil cases before sailing to London on 11 May. Accompanied by Nell, Kilmeny and a manservant, Symon had official and unofficial duties. He was due to attend the Coronation as one of the 18-member Australian contingent and to attend the presentation of a shield and plate to HMS *Commonwealth* on 26 June. Jo also wanted to catch up with family members in Stirling and London and with Oscar who was now at Oxford.

The Symons arrived in London a month after leaving Adelaide. Jo and Nell took their assigned seats in Westminster Abbey for the Coronation. On the following day they were supposed to have tickets to view the Royal Progress through London. The tickets never arrived. Four days after the Coronation Symon attended the presentation of the plate and shield to the officers and men of HMS *Commonwealth*. He regarded himself as 'privileged to take home' the gift of the Australian people at the great naval review at Spithead. He participated in the formalities and along with Lady Northcote made the presentation. Symon addressed the ship's company and explained what prompted the Australian people to make the gift to the *Commonwealth*. He thought the function 'formed one of the greatest advertisements ... Australia had received for a long time'. Prince Louis of Battenberg, the commander of the Home Fleet to which the *Commonwealth* was attached, declared this to be 'a red-letter day in the annals of the Fleet'.

There were other proud moments. Symon saw the crowds gathered outside Goldsmith's Company in Regent Street where the shield and plate were displayed before the ceremony. A number of police were needed to keep the pavement clear. The excellence of the workmanship 'came as a surprise to English experts and the people in general'. Two West Australians, one of them Sir John Winthrop Hackett, the editor of the *West Australian*, joined Symon in donating £400 for investment in Australian stocks to endow prizes for the ship's company.[6]

Next day, 27 June, Symon attended a farewell lunch given by George Reid, the Australian High Commissioner, at the Empire Club in London for Lord Denman who was about to leave for Australia to take up his appointment as Governor-General. Symon joined other important Australians at Victoria Station on the following day to farewell the Denmans. While in London, Symon conferred with an Admiralty official and Samuel Pethebridge, the Secretary of Australia's Department of Defence, who had accompanied his minister Senator Pearce to the Imperial Conference. Together they worked on drafting legislation for applying Britain's *Navy Discipline Act* to Australian ships. Symon believed the Admiralty substantially adopted his few suggestions.

'I am really sick of politics & want rest'

The Symons arrived at Fremantle on 24 October. In an interview Symon expressed sadness at the death of Lord Northcote on 29 September 1911. He described Northcote as 'the best loved of the Governor-Generals' and said Australia was now 'deprived of a strong and constant friend'. Symon also commented on the death of Lee Batchelor who collapsed and died on 9 October while climbing Mount Donna Buang in Victoria. He described his fellow South Australian as 'a man of moderate and reasonable views, and of a most pleasant and attractive personality'. Symon dismissed the Imperial Conference, which he had followed closely, 'as not of very much importance'.[7] Andrew Fisher had a very different view. The Dominion leaders had been invited to a meeting of the Committee of Imperial Defence where Sir Edward Grey, the Foreign Secretary, lectured them mainly on the renewal of Britain's alliance with Japan. Grey assured them that the Japanese could not use the alliance to interfere with Dominion immigration policies. Fisher believed that the Dominions were 'no longer negotiating ... at the portals of the household'; they had been taken into 'the inner counsels of the nation'.[8] Like many members of the British Cabinet, the Australians remained ignorant of the Anglo-American military conversations of 1906 which would ensure Dominion involvement in the coming European war.

Symon spoke in Fremantle about the pride he felt by the presentation of the shield and plate. He was less proud of the Australian exhibits for the Coronation. He thought it was a 'bad advertisement' for the Government not to send troops for the celebrations in London. It was also unfortunate that people had to draw their impressions of Australia from a representation of the exploits of the Kelly Gang and a wild horse and buck-jumping show at the Crystal Palace. Neither display, he thought, would attract immigrants. The Wattle League, in which Nell was prominent, did a good job and Symon was pleased to see so many posters in England and Scotland referring to Australia as the 'land of the Golden Wattle' and displaying 'that most beautiful of our native flora'. He hoped one day the wattle would be adopted 'as our national emblem'.

Symon was further shocked on his way home when he learnt at Colombo that King O'Malley, Labor's Minister for Home Affairs, had issued a circular endorsing preference for unionists and the black-listing of non-unionists. He thought the proposal was 'a national scandal'. He believed the people would reject government-by-circular and not approve of any government, acting without legislative authority, interfering with the non-unionists' means of livelihood and personal liberty.[9]

It was altogether more pleasant when arriving at Fremantle to visit Perth and having breakfast with the Governor and his wife, Sir Gerald and Lady Strickland. Symon may have belonged to a Loyal Orange Lodge but he happily breakfasted with Strickland, a descendant of an old English Catholic family with strong Maltese connections and Lady Edeline, a daughter of the 7th Earl De La Warr.

Family matters were becoming more important for Jo. The three elder daughters were in their late twenties – Margaret turned 30 in 1913 – while Charles, having graduated from Oxford and been called to the Bar at the Inner Temple, had returned to Australia and was admitted to practice in South Australia on 22 July 1911. Jo regularly wrote to all of them when they were travelling or residing in the UK.[10] He rarely discussed work except to say he was always busy with court work and attending the Senate. Jo made sure his adult children had sufficient funds for their needs, which included attendance at concerts, galleries and the theatre, long holidays on the Continent and a comfortable lifestyle. He advised them on where to visit and where to stay. Jo was especially keen they should contact his important 'friends', a useful means of reminding his 'friends' of their association. He encouraged his children to become more proficient in French and German. Jo took every opportunity to involve Margaret, Kilmeny and Charles in family decisions about the careers of the younger boys and girls and never disguised his hopes and admiration for Charles. As he told Carril in 1912, 'Chas is always very busy & doing very well in the law. He takes great interest in his work & will certainly be a very good sound lawyer.'[11]

In 1911 Oscar was completing two years at Oxford but was heading for rustication or being 'sent down'. Jo had had enough trouble getting him into Magdalen College. Oscar was possibly the ablest of the Symon children, certainly in his own mind. In April 1909 Thomas Herbert Warren, half-way through his 45-year term as President of Magdalen, had told Symon he wanted 'to facilitate a second son of yours coming here ... I have been really pleased with your eldest son [Charles] while here'.[12] Warren

'I am really sick of politics & want rest'

had already told the Rev. T.M. Bromley to send 'your boy' forward. Oscar was studying under Bromley for his 'Responsions', colloquially 'Little Go' or 'smalls', an examination whereby Oxford verified the quality of students the Colleges wanted to accept. It was not a major test, consisting of relatively simple questions in mathematics, Latin and Greek. Thanking Symon for his cheque, Bromley said, 'Oscar is quite resolute about his work, and I feel no doubt about his Responsions'.[13]

Oscar failed Responsions, principally because of Latin Grammar. Jo could not bring himself to blame Oscar. That 'ass' Bromley should have realised he was not physically ready (Oscar was always complaining of illness and his siblings long believed he usually faked them). Jo told Nell: 'we must not be beaten or let Oscar permit himself to be beaten – the family must keep up its reputation for never giving in.' After Symon received 'a sensible letter' from Bromley, he decided that the 'ass' had actually diagnosed Oscar 'fairly well'; Oscar thought he knew something when he did not. Oscar took Responsions for a second time in 1909 and passed. Jo was relieved having paid £202 in tutoring fees, and he rested awhile from organising Oscar's life and career.[14]

After two years at Oxford, Oscar was becoming a ne'er-do-well, convinced that his innate talent and conversational gifts would see him through. He attracted friends who were replicas of himself – self-indulgent and pleasure-seeking spendthrifts. Jo had a serious talk with him in 1911 when Oscar's behaviour '& utter want of seriousness, indulgence & habits of inconsequence made me uneasy'. Oscar made promises and, feeling reassured, his father increased his allowance from £75 to £100 a quarter with payments to cease in October 1912 when Oscar was supposed to graduate.[15]

In January 1912 Margaret, Carril and Angel left Adelaide for the United Kingdom. Carril was applying for a place at Magdalen and needed to prepare himself for Responsions. Angel was to attend the Manor House school at Brondesbury. The headmistress, Lucy Soulsby, opposed women's suffrage, wanted to train women to be good wives and mothers and, though she sat on the council of Oxford's Lady Margaret Hall, did not believe that Oxford should award degrees to women. Angel soon settled in well and Carril pleased his father by passing Responsions. Charles and his father had a long conversation in Adelaide about Carril's future, after which Jo in April 1912 advised his fourth son to visit France and Germany for six weeks in mid-summer, warning him not to get arrested in the latter as a spy. Jo urged Carril to learn as much of the French language as he could and then spend four weeks preparing himself for going into residence at Magdalen in October. Aware that Carril was not especially clever, Jo suggested he try Honors Moderations but, should it prove too much for him 'please give up the idea at once. I shall not be least disappointed. I had rather you kept strong & well and got your cricket blue and had a good record in lawn tennis than passed Hon. Mods twenty times.'[16] A Pass in 'Greats' from Oxford would carry the necessary 'distinction'.[17]

Jo was 'a little disappointed' – mainly, he said, for his son – when Carril wrote that Magdalen had more or less closed the door on him. He had not done well in the matriculation exam where only 22 out of the 59 who sat the papers were accepted by the College. Carril thought that the prior acceptance of Edward, the Prince of Wales, and his Equerry 'might make a difference' in choosing 'whom they took next'. The President, according to Carril, 'only wants freshers with titles' and ten of the 22 were 'Honourables' and another two were 'Lords'. Some had not even passed 'smalls'. Normally, Symon was deferential toward President Warren. Now he was angry: 'Warren dearly loves a lord & the advent of the Prince has made him more so.' Jo, however, felt he could apply pressure on Warren through several useful contacts, 'all of whom I know'. He listed them: Lord Jersey (a former Governor of NSW), Lord Loreburn (the Lord Chancellor), Lady Northcote and Hugh Cecil, the MP for Oxford University and a younger son of the late former Prime Minister, the Third Marquess of Salisbury. Jo thought he would hold off making a move until Carril decided what he wanted to do. His father was now thinking of Oriel College, Cecil Rhodes' *alma mater*.[18] In the meantime, Jo tried to console his son; 'one college is just as good as another'. As for degrees, 'Oxford' matters not the college.[19]

While Jo was attending to Carril's misfortunes, he had to deal with Kilmeny's 'very distressing report' about Oscar. Jo realised he should have taken Oscar out of Oxford because his promises had 'turned out to be lies'. He told Kilmeny on 12 June 1912 that:

'I am really sick of politics & want rest'

> I hoped much from Oscar, not in scholarship but in manliness, good sense, energy & gentlemanliness, & these are the things that seem gone, but it is no use dwelling on what is past. One can only try to remedy the mischief, to repair the – I hope only temporarily – broken career.

It was fortunate for the family that Margaret and Kilmeny were in England to give Jo the true story about Oscar. At least Dr Warren in this instance had been 'very good & a gentleman', and could now be forgiven. Jo told Kilmeny that Oscar must return home at once: 'It would be fatal to allow him to idle about in England.' Kilmeny should not honour her brother's debts and should book him a second-class saloon passage to avoid the temptation of first class 'where he would only be tempted to show off & to indulge his unfortunate inclinations'. There was a saving grace: Oscar making a 'shipwreck' of his Oxford career should teach Carril what to avoid: 'we must look to you now to rehabilitate the Symon name at Oxford.'

Oscar did return home and made more promises which, at first, he observed. He worked for a time on a farm at Victor Harbor and at 'Manoah' before enrolling at the Roseworthy Agricultural College in 1913. When Oscar began the course, his father contacted Professor Perkins, the Principal of Roseworthy, to explain that he regarded discipline and example as of the greatest importance. The Principal had nothing to worry about in Oscar's case. He would find Oscar observing in every way the discipline of the institution and 'will exercise a beneficial influence over those about him'. Oscar was good-hearted and generous, and possessed charming and gentlemanly manners, though was perhaps too readily influenced by others. Despite his time at Oxford, Oscar had shown he could 'rough it' while working on a farm at Victor Harbor, sharing one room with two others in a galvanised iron hut and living on the 'roughest fare'. He had also worked with men on the farm at 'Manoah'. Jo described his son as fit and healthy but he wanted the Principal and his staff to keep him in order; as a young man he might be disposed to slack at times.[20] Jo did not tell the Principal anything about the other side of Oscar, even as unpaid English bills – evidence of a dissolute life – kept arriving in Adelaide.[21]

Carril's story had a happy outcome in 1912. He looked at several colleges until Margaret reported by cable to their father in October that he had been admitted to Brasenose College (BNC). Jo wrote to him: 'I heartily congratulate you'. Notwithstanding his earlier comment, Jo would have been aware that the colleges varied in reputation and that BNC lacked Magdalen's prestige. In the circumstances, Jo decided he could do more to assist Carril by sending him pages of advice.[22] He urged his fourth son to take life 'seriously' and to be 'earnest' in all he undertook. Carril should do the best he could in study and sport but not to overdo either. 'Your studies, of course, have one main direction – being called to the bar – & the best preparation for that, in addition to law itself, is a liberal education.' Carril should avoid smoking until he reached 21 years of age, and drink only in moderation and preferably the less harmful beer or stout. 'Avoid "fast" men as associates – make friends – as many as possible – with kindred spirits to yourself – & who have the instincts & behaviour of gentlemen.' Keep away from the 'bounders' who boasted of their companionship of 'loose or fast girls'; there were 'plenty of nice girls to know, without wasting time in the company of degenerates'. Jo finished with a suggestion. Carril should look to his father as his 'best & most trusted friend'. He would give him 'the best counsel' and assistance out of any difficulties. Jo urged Carril to be 'open & candid' with him and 'depend upon it I will try to help and not reproach you'. And 'look upon me, too, as your banker – borrow from nobody before first trying me'.

Jo's advice reflected the many sides of himself: the largely self-motivated and partly self-educated Scot, the young man who once wanted to go to university, the father who saw how Oxford and the 'bounders' had contributed to Oscar's destruction, the member of a university council who saw how much the young benefited in terms of a career and in life from a higher education.

Jo's fifth son, Oliver, presented a different kind of problem for his father. Jo had signed papers giving the Royal Navy authority over his son's movements once Oliver entered the service at the age of 13. Apart from their visits to England in 1909 and 1911 the parents had not seen Oliver since he went to naval college. On completing his training at Dartmouth College, Oliver was due to pass out as a midshipman in the second half of 1912 and join a training cruiser for six months. In April of

'I am really sick of politics & want rest'

that year his father wrote to Sir Graham Greene, Permanent Secretary of the Admiralty, to make two requests. First, he wanted Oliver to serve part of his training with the Imperial Squadron on the Australian Station so that he might visit and see his family. Secondly, Jo wanted Oliver to be assigned to gunnery or navigation or as an executive officer so that when the time came to join the Australian Navy he would be qualified to give the best service to Australia's defence. Symon apologised if he had not gone through the right channels, and assured Greene he had no intention of reneging on his undertaking in 1908 that his son would serve in any branch if required. Nor did he want 'to interfere with or militate against the training, efficiency, promotion and advancement of my son in His Majesty's Service which I entirely recognize to be paramount'.[23]

The Admiralty replied on 1 June to say there was no difficulty about assigning Oliver to the Imperial Squadron. Symon may not have received the Admiralty's letter when he suggested his son might serve on the recently-commissioned HMS *New Zealand*. He had to withdraw the suggestion: Oliver told his father he did not want to join the *New Zealand*. In fact he eventually sailed on the *New Zealand*, whereupon Symon contacted the ship's captain, Lionel Halsey, to suggest a timetable for Oliver's shore leave in Australia when the *New Zealand* undertook a round-the-world tour in 1913. The important point is that Symon believed he was entitled to act without consulting his son. It will be shown in the next chapter just how far he would go when exercising his parental duty and authority.

In March 1913 Symon was still thinking about whether to nominate for the federal election set down for 31 May. The new Liberal Union entered the field with every intention of becoming what it understood to be a modern political party. It might abjure Labor's policies but respected the discipline of Labor's organisation. Hence rule 39 of the Liberal Union's constitution:

> 39. To secure selection of a candidate, a member desirous of contesting an electorate must submit his name to the President of the District Committee, and state his willingness to support the principles of the Union and its platform, and not to contest the election if not selected.[24]

Symon's refusal to comply ended his political career.

Walter Hutley, the General Secretary of the Union, issued a circular letter on 24 October 1911 which, among other things, noted that Symon was not a member. When Symon sent a £5 cheque to the Prospect branch early in February 1912 the branch secretary wrongly recorded his membership of the Prospect branch of the Liberal Union.[25] In the same month, the Union resolved that nominations for selection as a Liberal candidate for the next Federal election should reach the central Liberal Union office by the end of February. Symon had not submitted a nomination and had no intention of doing so if obliged to observe Rule 39. On 18 April he made his position clear in a letter sent to the Union office. He would consider it an honour for the Union to nominate him, but would not give any pledge to retire from public life (Rule 39 made no reference to leaving 'public life') were he not selected. Twice he had been placed at the top of the poll by the electors of South Australia; it was 'for them or myself alone to say whether the hour of my retirement has come'.[26] Symon liked to point out that the Union claimed to stand for 'freedom' yet adopted some of the 'fetters' imposed by Labor and its caucus.[27]

Symon offered the Union – and himself – an ingenious escape route.[28] He asked whether Rule 39 was meant to apply to a sitting member who wanted to stand again and whom the Union did not want to oust. He further asked whether the rule 'in spirit contemplates only "selection" of new candidates and that no selection is needed where you have a sitting Member willing to continue to sit if the Electors return him?' At the same time, it would seem 'oppressive' to oblige a sitting member, who enjoyed the Union's confidence, to submit his name for re-selection at every election. There was only a need for a nomination process to fill a vacancy. Symon concluded by saying he put this view to assist the Union and hoped his action would not be considered an intrusion. It is unclear whether Symon passed on his representation of rule 39 as farce: 'they asked him to ask them to ask me to become a candidate for the Senate, but said if you comply with our request and ask us to ask you, you must first pledge not to contest the election if we don't ask you.'[29]

Was Symon simply seeking an automatic endorsement to avoid a possible – and embarrassing – defeat in the nomination process? Was this a repetition of his attempt in 1907 to win the Senate presidency without a contest?

'I am really sick of politics & want rest'

Hutley sent out a letter on 1 May 1912 reciting the rule and announcing nominations had been received from branches and district committees for nine individuals. Senator Vardon, the Union President, headed the list with 24 branch nominations and 5 district committee nominations (representing 138 branches). Symon came third with ten branch nominations and 2 district committee nominations (35 branches).[30] Unlike the other nominees Symon had not declared his candidature, let alone his readiness to abide by rule 39. Opinions expressed within the Union were virtually all in favour of his selection for the Union ticket. If a few members thought that his anti-Fusion stand and his non-participation in the 1910 election disqualified him, or merited a rebuke, there is no evidence of any movement against him. It is possible though not verifiable that Symon privately thought the Union ticket was doomed and preferred not to be associated with it. His proposals limiting the application of rule 39, however, suggest a preparedness to accept nomination; the pledge was a step too far. Vardon had told him on 2 May 1912 that his selection would be 'practically unanimous'.[31]

The Union was obviously keen to have Symon on board. Hutley sent him another letter on 13 May to say the Union expected a solid Liberal vote in the Senate of 74–75,000 and a candidate would need 81–82,000 votes to be elected.[32] There was a hidden warning: you will not win election as an independent. William Sowden, the editor of the *Register*, made this point explicit when writing to Symon on 9 June urging him to stand in the election.[33] Snowden said he was writing as 'an admiring friend', 'as a 'patriotic Australian' and 'as one who could fairly claim to be the founder of the Liberal Union'. He did not always agree with the Union's actions and opposed its methods of choosing candidates. Nevertheless, if Symon nominated there is not the slightest doubt he would be pre-selected, and if Symon stood as a Union candidate he would be elected and the Union could expect a triple victory. If Symon stood as an independent no one on 'our side' will get a seat.

In June–July 1912, several branches and deputations begged Symon to reconsider his position on rule 39.[34] Most were unaware that his non-observance of the rule was not the only obstacle to Symon's nomination; he was not actually a member of the Liberal Union. The Secretary of the Prospect branch apologised to Hutley.[35] He had mistakenly interpreted Symon's £5 cheque as a subscription to accompany a membership application. It was in fact a donation to the Union's State election campaign. Symon said he did not mention the error at the time because he wanted to save the branch secretary from embarrassment.

On Tuesday 4 June 1912, the Council of the Liberal Union selected six candidates to contest the plebiscite to choose the three men whose names would be placed on the Senate ballot paper.[36] The Liberal Union distributed 30,000 ballot papers in mid-June and some 20,000 marked ballots were returned. The results were announced on 15 August. Senator Vardon, John Shannon (auctioneer)[37] and Peter Allen (farmer) were selected.

In the wake of the Liberal Union's plebiscite, the press asked Symon whether he intended to contest the next Senate election. Symon said he had never intimated anything to the contrary, but there was a long time until the election and one could never tell what might happen: 'I have not at all altered my plan.'[38] The friends who tried to persuade him to comply with rule 39 now turned their attention to the question of his standing as an independent, some alerting him to the damage he might cause himself and the Liberal cause. A family friend, the President of a women's branch of the Liberal Union, explained in July 1912 that she would have to decline Symon's hospitality for a time. If Sir Josiah was a Labor man they could agree to differ over politics but with her being a member of the Liberal Union and Symon running against the Union 'puts me in an unhappy position of antagonism'.[39] Other friends took Fred Johns' view. Johns had no sympathy with the Liberal Union's position and the vote could split as far as he was concerned, 'so long as the Knight of "Manoah" gets in'.[40] The Loyal Orange Lodge asked other lodges to vote for Symon.[41]

Some Union supporters turned on Symon during the campaign complaining he neglected his duties as evidenced by his poor attendance record. Hermann Homburg, the State Attorney-General, published a letter in the *Advertiser* on 28 April 1913 claiming that of the 389 sitting days of the Senate of 1907–1912 Symon was absent without leave for 190 of them. Richard Butler, the Acting Premier, told the *Advertiser* on 10 May that whereas Vardon had voted in 271 divisions between 1908 and 1911, Symon voted in just 58 in the same period. Symon came back with two arguments which were difficult to refute: so much of the Senate's sittings were devoted to pointless debates such as those on the Address-in-Reply;

'I am really sick of politics & want rest'

and if he was so derelict in his duties why did Vardon say in 1912 that the Liberal Union would love him as a candidate?[42] Symon's friends chipped in with damaging attendance figures for three of the Liberals from South Australia who sat in the House of Representatives.[43]

Symon was also accused of not being 'in harmony' with Joseph Cook. He responded quickly in a letter published in the *Register* on 17 May. Symon emphasised that he and Cook had been members of the party led by Sir George Reid, and when the Fusion was formed Cook, not Deakin, should have been appointed Leader. The selection of Deakin was one of his objections to the Fusion Government. Symon made no reference to Cook's election by one vote over Forrest on Monday 20 January 1913 to succeed Deakin as Leader of the Opposition. Symon had a case in court which had concluded on the previous Friday. He had not joined his South Australian colleagues on the overnight express to Melbourne. Perhaps he was still holding out as an independent. When a representative of the *Daily Herald* had conveyed the news of Cook's election, Symon said he would like to consider the situation before making a statement.[44]

Symon did make one major speech in the 1913 election campaign. On 24 April he spoke to 'a large audience' at the Victoria Hall in Adelaide. As in earlier years, Symon had the speech printed and distributed. He now tried something new; the *Advertiser* and the *Register* each published the speech as an advertisement.[45] The speech itself was remarkable for being almost apolitical. Symon began by winning his Victoria Hall audience with the comment of appearing before them as 'a political orphan', albeit 'a very cheerful' one. He shared a version of what became his standard joke about his experience with the Liberal Union. It was like a man asking you to ask him to ask you to dinner and then asking you to promise if he did not ask you, you do not have any dinner at all. Symon then spoke calmly about current issues, more in the manner of a wise commentator than of an aroused participant. He found favourable things to say about all sides of politics and, when mildly critical, he was not heavy-handed. Of Labor, for example, Symon spoke of Fisher leading 'a Ministry of action' which achieved so much and acted with a sense of purpose. He then quoted Lord Melbourne: 'Why not let the damned thing alone? (Laughter).' There was just one subject on which Symon spoke as a committed partisan. He did not like Labor's revived attempts to amend the Constitution.

Even here, he appeared ambivalent. Instead of eroding State powers in a piecemeal and disordered fashion, it would be better to call another convention to consider unification. Symon knew he could say this because nothing of the sort was going to happen.

As befits any candidate standing for election, Symon was outwardly confident, especially at the start of the campaign. He told one supporter on 7 May 1913 that 'electoral things look quite bright and so far as one can judge so long before polling day I do not think there is much doubt that I shall be returned again to the Senate', though it 'would be more profitable and more to the liking of my family if I stood out of it'. In a letter written next day Symon was confident of receiving 'a very large vote and will almost certainly be re-elected'. He may be mistaken 'but the assurances I receive from all quarters are most enthusiastic and they are all spontaneous'. With ten days to go before the poll on 31 May he was confident of re-election and uncertain only of the order of Newland (Labor), Vardon and himself being elected.[46]

Symon was more circumspect in correspondence with his daughter Kilmeny. On 2 April Symon admitted that he had 'practically decided to offer myself again for the Senate … I think it is my duty to stand & give the people the benefit of my view on some important public questions'. At the same time, people expect him to lose and 'I should not be sorry to be defeated … I am really sick of politics & want rest'. By 8 May he was almost resigned to defeat and was looking for a consolation prize: 'I don't think there is much chance of my being re-elected, but I fancy the Liberal Union will be taught a lesson.' Sinking a little further in despair, he declared himself to be 'very sick of it all' and felt he had 'sacrificed too much for little or no advantage to the Country or myself'. He was thinking that if he wanted to take more trips to England it might be best to give it all up. Four days before the election he told Kilmeny the result would settle the issue of whether he had a political future. 'Either way I shall be content.' If he won, he would cable her; if no cable arrived, she would know he had been defeated.[47]

The election results were perplexing and inconclusive, but plain enough in South Australia for Symon to retire from politics. Andrew Fisher's Labor Government lost the 1913 Federal election by one seat. Labor did take eleven seats in the Senate against the seven won by the

'I am really sick of politics & want rest'

Liberal Party, giving it 29 seats in total to seven. In South Australia Labor regained Boothby from the Liberals and, as in 1910, won all three Senate seats. Sir Josiah Symon barely retained his deposit; at least he had not been extravagant with his election expenses.[48]

Labor	
O'Loghlin, James	96,750
Newland, John	96,179
Senior, William	94,222
Liberal	
Vardon, Joseph	82,829
Shannon, John	82,436
Allen, Peter	81,805
Independent	
Symon, Sir Josiah	18,556

Labor not only lost government in 1913; its revised referendum proposals of 1911 formulated as six questions were again rejected. Yet on this occasion three States – Queensland, South Australia and Western Australia – voted 'Yes' and the total 'Yes' vote on each of the six questions reached 49 per cent.

Unabashed, Symon turned up to the declaration of the poll at the Town Hall.[49] Greeted with 'a warm-hearted cheer' (*Daily Herald*) or 'an ovation' (*Register*), he expressed gratitude. Symon described his position as one where the Scripture applied: 'The first shall be last.' He thought it was worth making the attempt, 'even if it were a small and feeble one', to advance some way towards 'emancipating the Senate from a little, at least, of the party feeling and, necessarily, the party spirit' which had diverted members' attention from 'their supreme duty of protecting the Constitution and upholding the interests of the States'. He favoured a change in the electoral system, to produce a Senate balanced 19–17 to avoid party dominance which he saw as detrimental to State interests.

A *Bulletin* column of 12 June declared that '[o]ne of the tragedies of the election was the utter annihilation of Josiah Symon'. Symon 'was the ablest man in the Senate, yet because he despised the Fusion and its methods, and refused to swallow the opinions he had expressed when the Liberal Party was barracking for the very things it subsequently "pilloried", he was dropped'. He received fewer than one-fifth of the votes 'polled by the poorest hack of the party machines'. Australia, therefore, 'loses not only one of the greatest Constitutional lawyers in the Commonwealth but also one of its massive intellects'. Three 'decent fellows' replaced him by what was 'seemingly regarded' in South Australia 'as a sort of Consolation Stakes' whereby 'good party hacks' who had been 'poured out of their Assembly seats within the last year or two' earned a place in the Senate (all six Party nominations had recently lost Assembly seats). The *Bulletin* recorded that Labor put up one man who had previously made up the bunks on the Broken Hill express, one was a Methodist preacher and the third was a former journalist with the sectarian *Southern Cross*.

Labor's Senator Givens sent Symon a handwritten note on 17 July thanking Symon for his congratulations on Givens becoming President; 'we' hope to have the opportunity to welcome you 'to the scene of your former political labours and triumphs'.[50] Bruce Smith, the member for Parkes in NSW, was a classical liberal of the Manchester School and even more independent-minded than Symon.[51] Smith said he was sympathetic to Symon's independent stand against local organisations but had a 'counter-thought'. They were 'fighting a body of men who exercise so much thraldom in order to keep their party compact'. We Liberals must do some of the same and must accept a temporary sacrifice of principle to achieve political success. 'The good, thereby done to the country, gives the individual sacrifice a touch of heroism which it would not otherwise have enjoyed.' Smith hoped that his friend will not feel embittered by the event and would hold his valuable services in readiness for a future occasion.[52] Jo wrote again to Kilmeny on 9 August telling her he had one last observation to make: the most disappointed people were the Liberal Union folk and their three defeated candidates; 'their defeat was a perfect consolation to me'. Besides, Carril had told him that the English *Morning Post* saw his defeat as 'a truly great loss'.[53]

Seen in a longer perspective, the Senate result in South Australia was probably a good outcome for Sir Josiah Symon. He had ceased to be a force in the Senate where Labor's numbers rendered him irrelevant. The Senate was even more obviously not a States House. His principled rejection of the Fusion left him marooned in isolation, and his principled rejection of the Liberal Union's dictate consigned him to the bottom of the poll.

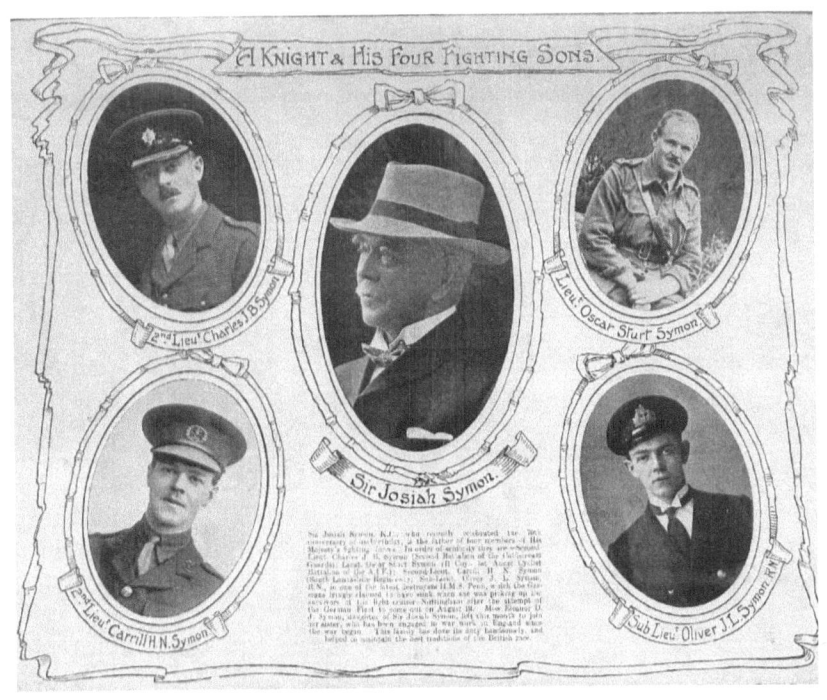

A Knight and his four fighting sons [SLSA B2264650]

Sir Josiah Symon presents and donates two flags and three bugles to the 9th reinforcements of the 47th Battalion of the AIF, 5 February 1916.
[PRG 733/279]

Charles Symon, c. 1916
[SLSA 63466]

Oliver Symon, c. 1916
[SLSA PRG249_13_122]

TO HAVE THE HONOUR OF MEETING
HIS ROYAL HIGHNESS THE PRINCE OF WALES, K.G.

THE LORD MAYOR AND THE LADY MAYORESS
request the honour of the company of
Hon. Sir Josiah and Lady Symon
at the Town Hall, Adelaide,
on Wednesday, 14th July, 1920, at 8 o'clock.

Symon: 'All ranks and classes found him an English thoroughbred.'
[Elizabeth Dyer Papers]

Sir Josiah Symon, c. 1920
[SLSA B44232]

Caricature of Sir Josiah, by John Henry Chinner, 1923
[PRG249_15]

Lady Symon Building, University of Adelaide, c. 1930
[SLSA B5168]

A short man stands tall: Sir Samuel Way, North Terrace. Adelaide
[Photo Michael Deves]

The Squire walking in his estate, c. 1930
[PRG 249_13_17]

Josiah's monument in Adelaide's North Road cemetery
[Photo Michael Deves]

Ivor Hele's 1961 portrait of Kilmeny, held by St Ann's College Adelaide

14
'My boys & girls are all in all to me.'

Sir Josiah Symon left politics in 1913 believing he had regained greater freedom of action. If anything, however, his world became more demanding, complicated and uncertain in the following five years. By 1916 his four fit sons had joined the colours and were fighting Germans in the Great War. Their father was alternately very anxious and very proud, and always desperate for news. Two of his daughters had volunteered for war work in England, and their father secured comfortable accommodation in Buckinghamshire for them and their brothers, should the latter have leave from the Front.

Symon had battles of his own to fight. In addition to his caseload, Symon took over more of the firm's workload in 1913. E. Erskine Cleland had succeeded Symon in handling South Australia's case in the long-running border dispute with Victoria. He spent eight months overseas in 1913–14 representing South Australia before the Judicial Committee of the Privy Council and enjoying a holiday. He returned to Adelaide at the end of May 1914 but not to the partnership. Cleland believed that Symon had not rewarded him sufficiently, and branched out on his own. The second partner, Rounsevell, struggled through illness until his death in 1919. He loyally accepted and implemented Symon's decisions, including the addition in May 1913 of Charles Symon to a partnership in the firm which became Symon, Rounsevell & Symon. Charles left for England in September 1915 to enlist in the British Army and the partnership agreed he should be paid the full entitlement in his absence. Work aside, Symon applied himself and his cheque book to many war-related philanthropic causes, involved himself in the conscription arguments of 1916–17, fought off complaints of professional misbehaviour issued by Cleland and another advocate and unequivocally praised or denounced with equal ferocity peoples, races, nationalities, countries and leaders depending on which side they took in the Great War.

For all that troubled him, Symon had 'a good war'. All four of his enlisted boys came home. Two were wounded but not badly, and Charles was awarded the Military Cross. In 1916 Jo established a trust for each of the four to receive £20,000 (worth $2,080,070 in 2020) if they survived the War. His daughters would later query the equity and sense of this arrangement. Jo did make provision for them, and added substantially to it later, while recognising his mistake in giving so much to young men with limited work experience. Jo, however, never regretted one of his actions. Starting in 1911 he regularly wrote to his third daughter, Kilmeny, who from this time began to supersede Nell as his favoured confidante. These letters form an invaluable source in recording how the family's 'tribal elder' who, having let his children slip into third place behind business and politics, assigned them primacy during the Great War.

Jo had organised a short holiday for 1914 in the UK. He wished to see his children already residing in England – Kilmeny, Carril, Oliver and Angel – as well as his own siblings in Stirling and London. He also intended to renew countless friendships and contacts. As Nell no longer cared to travel overseas Jo could move about England and Scotland as time and circumstances suited. He booked to leave for England on 7 May 1914, though his departure remained uncertain because of the workload in Adelaide. Symon did leave on that day but received a 'disconcerting' telegram from Rounsevell in Fremantle and expected a message in Colombo leaving him no alternative but to come home. 'My duty is the first consideration & I must not neglect that.'[1] No message awaited him, so Kilmeny could perform her assigned task. On the day Jo reached London she should insert a notice in *The Times* and the *Morning Post*: 'The Hon. Sir Josiah Symon KCMG KC late Attorney General of the Commonwealth has arrived from Australia via Marseilles.'

Jo and Kilmeny travelled together to Stirling and around the southern counties and Jo spent time with James and David and their families as well as his own adult 'children'. Symon attended the annual Australasian dinner held at the Trocadero on 11 June. Sir George Reid presided, and

'My boys & girls are all in all to me.'

the 250 guests included Prince Alexander of Teck, the Governor-General designate of Canada.[2] On 17 June Jo and Kilmeny had tea in the House of Commons as guests of the Empire Parliamentary Association. Symon was one of 600 guests who attended a reception at the Savoy in honour of Chief Justice Madden of the Victorian Supreme Court. On 7 July he went to the unveiling in The Mall, London, of Sir Thomas Brock's statue of Captain Cook. Prince Louis of Battenberg,[3] the First Sea Lord, performed the ceremony. Winston Churchill, the First Lord of the Admiralty, was also present and Sir George Reid spoke of Australia's great debt to the navigator.

Throughout July 1914 Symon's holiday was overshadowed by the rising tension in Europe and the threat of war, accelerated after a Bosnian Serb mortally wounded Archduke Franz Ferdinand of Austria and his wife in Sarajevo on 28 June. War seemed either probable or inevitable when Jo left London on 24 July, agonising about whether he should have stayed in England. Kilmeny sent him a telegram which he received on the morning of 3 August when the SS *Maloja* berthed at Brindisi on the coast of the Adriatic. 'It did me good', he wrote on 4 August, not knowing that Britain would declare war on Germany later that day.

> No news seemed good news, & even to be in touch again with you cheered me up a little. Neither yesterday nor today have there been any more telegrams to the ship. In my present state of mind this absence of news is a kind of torture.

Jo was still reproaching himself for leaving his children so far from home. 'I do hope you will not have any trouble, & be back with us in Adelaide soon.'

At the beginning of August Jo was wondering what to do about Sub-Lieutenant Oliver Symon. He wrote to Carril on 1 August asking if he had 'gathered' from Oliver whether he really liked the Navy or would rather go to Oxford like his brothers. Jo pressed Carril not to mention his enquiry to Oliver. Next day he sent another note to Carril: should anything happen to 'my dear boy Oliver' you and Kilmeny and Angel must nurse and care for him and keep him 'for his mother & father, if you can'. Jo had another question on his mind: should Oliver stay with the Royal Navy or return to Australia if needed there? At Brindisi on 3 August Jo posted a letter to Kilmeny asking her to deliver a message to Sir Graham Greene at the Admiralty requesting Oliver's withdrawal from the Royal Navy. Symon felt he could take this action without consulting Oliver himself. After all, England was not formally at war or engaging in hostilities and Oliver had previously given his father an indication that he wished to leave the Royal Navy. In his letter of 4 August Jo reiterated his request for Kilmeny to send his earlier letter to Sir Graham Greene 'if England is not actually at war & engaging in hostilities'. Jo felt he must take all the responsibility for withdrawing him, 'as it was I, without his consent, who put him there, & I have never, now that he is older, seriously asked him whether he wished to stay or retire'. In attempting to withdraw him, Jo was offering Oliver the freedom of choice he did not have at the age of 13, and to leave him 'free from any notion that I wish him to remain, or that a sense of mere obedience to me should keep him there'.

Wireless telegrams arrived at the *Maloja* before it reached Port Said reporting that Germany had declared war on France and Russia. Symon still knew nothing official about England joining in. He sent a cable to Kilmeny telling her not to consult Oliver if she contacted the Admiralty nor show him Jo's letter from Brindisi: 'it might only upset & distress him.' Kilmeny responded with a cable which Jo collected in Aden: 'Do not return all well love.' Jo was happy enough but as the *Maloja* neared Colombo on 14 August he wrote, 'I so longed to hear of dear Oliver'.

> The truth is I should not have left when war seemed so threatening. I know quite well you & Angel & Carril are safe, and of course I could do nothing for Oliver, but I should be nearer him & news of him.
>
> This trip out has been altogether terrible for me. Not a word of news since Sunday at Aden, and every day & hour the ship is in fear of capture by a German cruiser or armed merchantman. Each night all lights are put out, & we travel like a dark phantom ship. What would happen to us if captured God knows.
>
> I am getting old, & with no-one, none of my family with me, my nerves seem to be breaking down. I dread a collapse at sea. But I must bear up with all the courage I can till I see you all again.[4]

Symon's fears and distress in his situation were hardly uncommon but talking in this manner to and about his 'children' was rare for him

'My boys & girls are all in all to me.'

before 1914. Admittedly, there remained an underlying assumption: as head of the family Jo determined, or at least had to approve, the career and personal choices of his children. He was now stepping aside from this role; he did not want Oliver to stay in the Navy out of obedience to his father.

There were more instructions for Kilmeny. He now wanted her to destroy his letter sent from Brindisi about withdrawing Oliver. 'It was all too late, & I was literally distracted.' Kilmeny should also destroy Jo's letters to her and the enclosures for Sir Graham Greene where they concerned Oliver. Kilmeny must tell Oliver, if he survives the War,

> I wish him to choose himself whether he will remain in the navy or whether he would like to retire & go to Oxford while Carril is there & then come out to Australia, where I will provide a suitable career for him. He cannot like the navy if he hates gunnery & hates engineering. And I shall quite approve of whatever he does. He must not continue in the navy with any notion of obedience to me that I wish him to do so against his own desire. If he doesn't like that profession, just as any other, he should give it up.

Jo urged his daughter to use the cable freely to send news of Oliver. 'Suspense is horrible, even unfavourable news is better.'[5]

Jo's worst fears were not realised. The voyage from Colombo to Fremantle was uneventful. He wrote a long letter to Kilmeny on this part of the trip, much of it devoted to Oliver. Jo hoped he had not 'wearied or distressed' her and promised never to allude to this matter again. He did, however, try 'more calmly than before, to repair why I wrote as I did from Brindisi & Port Said'. He asked Kilmeny to forgive him for seeming 'rather hysterical' or if he had made her unhappy. She knew that 'my dear boy Oliver' was precious to all of them: 'if I have made a mistake & Oliver suffers, life will have little happiness left for me.' Jo explained himself once again but this time more clearly: he had put Oliver into the Navy; Oliver had previously mentioned that he did not like gunnery and engineering; Jo assumed, therefore, that Oliver wanted to leave the Navy; Jo wanted his son to have freedom of choice. Jo realised that he may have misinterpreted Oliver's comments about 'Gunnery and Engineering' which, with the first letters in upper case, referred to two dreaded exam papers Oliver had to face. Fortunately, a Kilmeny cable settled everything when Jo arrived in Fremantle on 25 August: 'Oliver Saturday good spirits enjoying himself Carril & I certain has never wished change in his profession.'

There was more joy for Jo. He had suggested Lenore might take a sea trip to restore her health. Although she was wretchedly seasick crossing the Bight, a few days in the West and the trip home with Jo rejuvenated her.

In one of his early actions on reaching Adelaide, Symon went to Montefiore to see Sir Samuel Way. Symon knew that surgeons had amputated the Chief Justice's left arm in the hope of eliminating his cancer. Later on the same day, 3 September, Jo reported to Kilmeny about the meeting:

> This forenoon I spent an hour with Way CJ. He is wonderful really, with his empty left coat sleeve. But certainly he has made an astonishing recovery.
> He was greatly interested in my London gossip & when I went thanked me very much & said he hoped I would regard this as only a first instalment.

Symon left no record of any later sessions but Jo wrote to Kilmeny after attending Way's funeral following his death on 10 January 1916. Symon thought much of the Eulogy was 'extravagant' and the event was 'a tedious & ill-arranged affair'. He sent her three days of press reports, highlighting the *Register*'s article entitled 'The Vacant Chief Justiceship'. Jo saw it as bad taste appearing on the day of the funeral, though he did not object to his own name being freely mentioned. If offered the job, he did not feel inclined to accept, given his age, all the boys being away, his desire to maintain his freedom of action and perhaps have a few years of rest. 'However we shall see.'[6] Justice George Murray of the Supreme Court, 17 years younger than Symon, succeeded Way as Chief Justice.

Jo was especially keen for his sons to be commissioned. He believed that their capacity for leadership would be wasted in the ranks. When Charles went to England to join the British Army, his father contacted 'My Dear Sir George [Reid]' on 9 September 1915 asking him to use 'your great influence' to help Charles get into training and a commission as quickly as possible. He told Reid he was writing to other friends as well and to Bonar Law, the Conservative Leader whom he had never met. He also

'My boys & girls are all in all to me.'

approached the new Governor-General, Sir Ronald Munro Ferguson, who subsequently wrote to the War Office on Charles' behalf.[7]

At the outbreak of the War, Carril was still an undergraduate at Brasenose College, and keeping his terms at the Inner Temple. During his trip home Symon sent his son letters similar to those which went to Kilmeny expressing frustration about the absence of news, castigating himself for leaving England and worrying about Oliver. Reaching Australia he urged Carril to look after Angel and Kilmeny. 'You must take my place & be a father to them.' On 22 September he confessed to Carril: 'My boys & girls are all in all to me. When my time comes to depart this life, I shall have no regrets if you are all well & happy. May God grant it be so!' By that time Carril had told him of his joining the Public School Boys Corps but had not volunteered to go abroad. Carril and his father were concerned about his weak eyesight which Jo believed was sufficient reason not to be involved in any fighting.

> I hope therefore you will obey my wish & not volunteer to go abroad to the front and be ready to give what service you can and your eyesight permits in the event of invasion – in defence of the homeland. I trust you will write me giving your assurance to that effect.

On 7 October Jo had learnt from a Kilmeny cable that Carril had joined the Royal Fusiliers and would go abroad in three to four months. Jo sent his love and blessing anyway, and Carril did apologise for his disobedience. He was also grateful that Jo gave permission for his son of 21 years to take up smoking. Whether Carril had started before permission was granted is unknown.

Symon now turned to the question of a commission. He wrote to Colonel Seely MP on 5 November 1914 saying that, while Carril would do his duty in the ranks, his father should like him to secure a commission 'and have the opportunity to do some leading. He has ability, plenty of mother wit, and is physically very fit.'[8] Carril was good at cricket, tennis and swimming and was a good shot before he went to Oxford. Symon asked Seeley to 'use your justly powerful influence in the right quarters' to secure his son a commission. Symon had also written personally to Kitchener, whom he knew, 'and a word from you [Seely] would I am sure be of great value'. Jo wanted Carril to give his best for King and Country and believed that, with a commission, 'he can give better service than in [the] Ranks'. He wrote on similar lines to Robert Munro MP, a Scottish Liberal MP, who became Lord Advocate for Scotland under Asquith in 1913. Symon also contacted Sir George Reid, W.H. Dickinson (then a Liberal MP) and Lewis Harcourt, the Colonial Secretary.[9]

There was a slight problem. His father discovered in January 1915 that Carril 'seems just as well satisfied to remain a Private in the ranks'.[10] Even when Carril showed an interest in promotion, army colonels were allegedly worried about depleting the ranks. Symon told Hamar Greenwood, a Canadian-born British lawyer and Liberal MP, that this reasoning was absurd; Oxford Blues with 6–7 months of training constituted the best material for filling depleted commissioned ranks.[11] In May 1915, Carril Symon was gazetted as a Second Lieutenant, 11th (Service) Battalion, South Lancashire Regiment.

The Admiralty never had to respond in August 1914 to Symon's request to withdraw his 19 year-old son from the Royal Navy. As instructed, Kilmeny had not delivered Symon's letter and enclosures to Sir Graham Greene. In November 1914, however, the Admiralty did have to reply to Symon's cabled request to transfer Oliver to the Light Cruiser Squadron, Home Waters. This request stemmed In part from Symon's fuller understanding of Oliver's first action. Oliver sailed on board the light cruiser, HMS *New Zealand*, when on 28 August it participated in the Battle of Heligoland Bight in the North Sea. The first naval engagement of the Great War ended in a victory for the Royal Navy. The Germans lost three light cruisers and a destroyer, three light cruisers were damaged and 712 sailors were killed. Thirty-five British sailors were killed and four ships were damaged.[12] Symon had two reasons for wanting Oliver's transfer: there would be more opportunities to see him should Symon return to England, and his son was unlikely to see further action in home waters. Symon also contacted Sir Francis Hopwood, the Additional Civil Lord of the Admiralty, Bonar Law, the Colonial Secretary, and Sir George Reid. Greene cabled back on 4 December to say that service arrangements prevented moving Oliver from his present appointment. Symon wrote to Greene on 30 December expressing his disappointment while accepting the decision and acknowledging Oliver's preference to be 'in the thick of things'.[13] There is no evidence he consulted Oliver before making his cabled request.

'My boys & girls are all in all to me.'

So many of the letters Symon wrote to friends during the War referred to his four sons serving King and Country. Occasionally he explained Romilly's absence; he had been 'an invalid since birth'. Jo sometimes mentioned that three of his sons were Oxford men. Oscar was one of them, albeit the one who never graduated. Despite some misbehaviour, Oscar had redeemed himself at Roseworthy, coming top in almost every subject he took and being awarded first class honours and the Gold Cup as the best student of his year. At 24 years of age he enlisted on 30 June 1915 in the Australian Imperial Force (AIF). He described his occupation as 'farmer', his postal address as 'Manoah' Upper Sturt and his religion as 'C of E'. It is not known why Oscar registered Nell as his 'next of kin' though she was apt to take his side in the family.[14]

Two weeks before Oscar joined up his father had told Kilmeny of his 'shaken confidence' in someone 'so unstable'. Jo decided he could not trust him. Within a week of Oscar entering camp Jo found it 'astonishing how readily & uncomplainingly he accommodates himself to roughing it, when he has to'. He now believed Oscar would be a good soldier and was later thrilled when he came near to top in officer training, and was soon commissioned and training in England with his battalion. His father discovered something else to like, telling Carril that 'Oscar has a great writing faculty. He should be a war correspondent – without the control of a censor!!' Jo quickly corrected a public report which referred to Oscar as 'Serjeant Infantry'; he was a first Lieutenant B Company of the 1st Anzac Cyclist Battalion. Jo proudly told Reid on 9 March 1917 that Oscar is 'very popular among his men'. A relative of a man in Oscar's battalion had recently told Symon his son 'is worshipped by them all'. Jo was worried only by an injury to Oscar's wrist; it might give way 'just when it is required for dealing justice to the Hun'.[15]

Jo reserved his greatest praise for his eldest son. On 5 December 1916 he wrote to the editors of the *Advertiser* and the *Register* asking them to publish a letter from Charles describing the operations of the Guards Brigade on the Somme. He mentioned, confidentially, that he had shown the letter to the Governor who thought it was well worth publishing. 'If you concur, good: if not, still good.'[16] The *Register* partly published the letter on 7 December and the *Advertiser* on 12 December allocated three times the space provided by the *Register*. Money for Charles was no problem. In September 1917 Symon wrote to the Manager of the Bank of Adelaide in London authorising the Bank to permit Charles to withdraw what he required up to £1000. As 'I have absolute confidence in him' there was no use in these times when communication is risky or uncertain 'to put a small limit'. Charles wanted to make provision for his next leave in England and his father thought this was the best way to have funds available.[17] On 25 January 1918 Jo told Kilmeny that the family was thrilled and proud to learn Charles had been awarded the Military Cross.[18] The *Advertiser* published the official announcement on 16 September 1918 of the award given to 'Lieutenant C.J.B. Symon, Coldstream Guards, Special Reserve' as reproduced in the London *Times*:

> He went forward on his own initiative before an attack to locate the position of the enemy's machine guns. He exposed himself fearlessly on two occasions in order to draw their fire, and was thus enabled to locate their positions and bring back most valuable information. He set a magnificent example of courage and devotion to duty to all ranks.

The Symons did much more for the war effort than send four fit boys to the Front. Lenore and Kilmeny worked long hours as volunteers in care organisations in England.[19] Kilmeny spent three years managing the Camps Library where she collected books and magazines which were delivered to prisoners of war in the hands of the enemy. She had been helping Belgian refugees in London for which Jo sent her £20, inspired by his loathing of German methods of warfare. Jo told her in December 1914 he was 'really glad you have taken on the Belgians'. By the following February, he thought the fit and able among the Belgians should be fighting and not lying idle and in October 1915 was pleased she was no longer working for them. Jo had decided that some Belgians 'have behaved most treacherously', a view his son Charles shared.[20]

While Nell wanted to be involved with the Red Cross, she was often bothered by ill-health. Jo threw himself into many organisations and gave generously to war-related projects. Some donations were small. He was moved by the story of Boy (1st Class) John Travers Cornwell, Royal Navy. Aged just under 16 ½, Cornwell was the sight-setter of a naval gun on board HMS *Chester* during the Battle of Jutland on 31 May 1916. Mortally wounded at the beginning of the action, and surrounded by the dead and wounded of the gun crew, he stood for 15 minutes at his post fully exposed to the enemy quietly awaiting further orders. Cornwell died two days later and was posthumously awarded the Victoria Cross. A sum of £21,849 was raised for a picture of him standing by his gun. The picture was placed in more than 12,000 British schools. Symon donated £25 for the private use of Cornwell's mother whose working-class husband had joined the British Army and was killed soon after his son's death.[21]

Symon also donated much larger sums to provide ambulances (he paid £500 for the cost of one) as well as aircraft for the European War. He worked closely with Sir Henry Galway, the Governor of South Australia, and went frequently to Government House. Both men were open and emphatic supporters of compulsory military service. Unlike Galway, who was often mentioned in despatches during military campaigns to enforce British rule in Benin, West Africa, Symon had never been present when shots were fired in anger. He was very conscious of this 'deficiency' when asking younger men to join the colours. Donations of time and money helped to ease his conscience.

Money was not so freely given when fringe or less deserving members of the family were involved. William Symon's son, Keith, wrote from the United States on 3 October 1914 seeking £200, 'which I know is not a large sum to you'. His investments had been hit hard, his house had burnt down before the insurance was fixed, he must look after his mother and brother and may lose his girlfriend. Keith felt he could 'only turn to my father's brother as the one man in the world who could help me'.[22] Symon replied on 14 November. He was sorry to learn that his nephew was in financial difficulty. As a result of the War and an unprecedented drought over the whole of Australia this year, financial calls on him had been very heavy and were likely to become more so. 'I regret to say that I am not in a position to comply with your request. Your difficulties seem to have been due to what you describe as "unfortunate investments"; perhaps with patience they may recover.'[23]

David Symon, Jo's youngest brother, had a habit of forgetting some of his debts when seeking financial assistance. Responding on 21 March 1917, Jo said David had 'strangely forgotten a good many things'. In one instance David's recollection 'would be amusing were it not [so?] painfully incorrect a representation of the position'. David claimed he had not authorised a payment of £165 to be debited to his brother. An examination of the statements and accounts Jo had itemised 'will suffice to refresh your memory'. Further reminders included a release from a £500 promissory note and owed interest and that David had grossly understated his debt.[24]

In his letters to Kilmeny of August-December 1914 Jo appeared to lavish money on his children. Kilmeny was given a free hand to help Carril and Oliver, and to send Angel, aged 18, on a first-class passage home. 'Everything', Jo wrote on 1 October, 'must be done for the comfort & well-being & happiness of you all'. Jo set up a trust whereby his five daughters would receive as an allowance the annual interest on sums set aside for them. In the case of the three elder daughters each would have a capital sum of £7000 while Angel and Mary would each draw the interest on £5000.[25] Jo's plans for his daughters did not yet match what he did for the boys in 1916; he still believed that Margaret, Lenore and Kilmeny might marry.

On 24 January 1916 Jo told Kilmeny he liked the idea of her taking a cottage in the country within reasonable distance of 'town'. She should make sure it was a comfortable house in 'a nice, pretty locality'. 'Don't consider cheapness so much as suitability & comfort'. It should be big enough for Kilmeny and the boys, and for himself should he come over in the Spring or Autumn. A sum of '£100 a year more or less is nothing compared to getting a suitable place'. When Kilmeny acquired 'Marlins', a cottage in the village of Penn in Buckinghamshire, Jo said he would meet all the expenses. The one problem he foresaw was the unavailability of servants.

The generous head of the family, however, kept everything under his control. On 24 January 1916, he advised the London manager of the Bank of Adelaide that he did not think Carril and Oliver needed all the money he was making available to them. Symon wanted to be told the state of their balances by return post so he could decide whether to withhold further payments or replenish their accounts. Symon was an investor as well as a father and the former saw no point in sending money which would remain idle. Until the matter was sorted, Jo did not want more money to be paid into their accounts.[26]

It will be recalled that when he travelled overseas by himself in 1891 Jo

'My boys & girls are all in all to me.'

spoke of wanting to show his family in Stirling 'all my treasures, Nell, and say – these are my jewels'. In August 1914 he said to Kilmeny,

> Sometimes I wonder if I allow myself to be too fond of my children – all of them. They are my greatest source of happiness. My greatest delight is to see them well & happy & to do everything I can for them.

Where did Nell now fit in? There are just five one-sentence references to 'your mother' in Jo's letters to Kilmeny in 1914 that took up more than 20,000 words. Nell's recurring headaches, which may have been migraines, and her increasingly lax approach to domesticity, pushed her elder daughters and the servants into the forefront at 'Manoah'. Margaret and Lenore took charge of the household and of Romilly and Mary. No doubt many fathers in their late 60s described their children as their 'greatest source of happiness'. A striking message of these letters to Kilmeny and the volumes of them thereafter is that the three elder daughters, and Kilmeny in particular, had taken over the management of their father's non-professional life. Whereas Jo had previously regarded Nell as his sole confidante, the presence of Kilmeny in England when the War began placed her in a position where, without effort or conniving, she advanced her role to one of principal confidante.

Josiah Symon had never shied away from wholehearted denunciation of people and actions. When he learnt of the outbreak of hostilities, he told Kilmeny: 'The Germans are at the bottom of all this war ... Their arrogance & bounce have been criminal. Look at their behaviour to Belgium and their threats to Italy ... Surely God will punish them.'[27] Symon appreciated that about one in ten South Australians were German-born or of German descent and they were generally accepted into the community. In writing to another correspondent he kept himself in check while discussing 'the indiscreet Germans amongst us'. He added: 'we cannot be too watchful, but it would be a pity to prematurely excite any racial antagonisms that can be avoided, especially as I am quite sure there are many Germans and Australians of German descent who are quite loyal to the flag.'[28]

Around the same time Symon continued to unleash feelings towards the external enemy. Following the outbreak of hostilities the German light cruiser, SMS *Emden*, had disrupted British commerce by attacking and sinking over 20 unarmed merchant ships in the Indian Ocean as well as a Russian cruiser and a French destroyer. On 9 November 1914, the Australian light cruiser HMAS *Sydney* fired on the German raider in the Cocos Islands forcing the *Emden*'s captain, Karl von Müller, to run his ship aground. Müller and his surviving crew were then taken into custody. The Sydney correspondent for the London *Daily Mail* reported that the captured officers and men were 'likely to be the recipients of much hospitality in Australia'. An outraged Symon responded with a long article in the *Register* on 17 November 1914. There would be no such treatment. Captain Müller of the 'notorious German cruiser' was 'nothing more nor less than a pirate'. He may have spared the lives of the crew and passengers, but he sank unarmed ships which he was duty bound to bring to port where they could be condemned as lawful prizes by a Prize Court. Symon acknowledged that Müller did not practise 'the atrocity and savagery with which German "high culture" wages war'. Müller may not have supplemented his piracy by acts of murder but there was no case for canonisation and welcoming hospitality. If the captain and officers of the *Emden* were so welcomed, 'there is some ground for our enemies looking upon the British as freaks'.

By 1916, the father of four enlisted sons was fired up, all the more so after reading of the atrocities committed at the Wittenberg 'prisoner-of-war' camp against Russian, French and British prisoners. Quoted in the Adelaide *Mail* of 3 June 1916, Symon said that South Australians will not want to retain memorials 'to such a people and country' in the form of place names. 'The retention of these German names is a blot on the map of South Australia. They ought to be obliterated.' During the War, many South Australians of German extraction were interned or placed under house arrest, some changed or anglicised their names and 69 German place names were altered.[29]

On 2 April 1916, Symon delivered a passionate speech at the Methodist Church, Upper Sturt, after Lady Symon had unveiled a Roll of Honour listing the names of men from the district who had enlisted.[30] One had already lost his life. Symon did not spare himself in denouncing anything and everything German. In a war, 'such as the world has never seen before', the Germans had employed 'all the resources of civilisation for the purposes of human savagery and murder'. Symon spoke of the Germans

'My boys & girls are all in all to me.'

waging 'a war without pity', of 'the vast difference between the mad cruelty and lust which dominates the Germans and the lofty purposes and noble aims of the British'. Germany was a 'military despotism' and the Kaiser 'a Prussian despot'. When Germany 'broke her word and let her armies loose upon Belgium to destroy, to murder, to rob, and to ravish', and sought to create 'a desolate waste and a hell of suffering', England stood by the weak and declared war on behalf of 'righteousness'. Symon pronounced himself 'proud to have lived to see it, and to have been born of the race'.

Symon wanted the easy-going and the 'shirkers' to understand that the War was about the survival of the British Empire and of Australia. If Germany won the war – he still thought it inconceivable – 'we may yet be the hewers of wood and drawers of water to a German occupying force'. All fit young men should do their duty and enlist. Symon pitied any young man 'who shelters himself behind his mother's apron'. He quoted from a letter a soldier had written during the Gallipoli campaign: 'The boys are growing very bitter against those who could go, but won't … they shall not be forgotten.' Symon pitied the mothers who held their sons back and left them marked for not doing their duty.

A few days after his speech at the Methodist Church Jo suffered a personal loss when his sisters, Esther and then Margaret, died in Stirling within a fortnight of each other. Esther was perennially ill but Jo thought 'Meg' deserved some more years for looking after her.

On 6 May Symon returned to the platform as part of the tercentenary commemoration of Shakespeare's death. His lecture – 'Shakespeare the Englishman' – joined those he gave on quotations and on 'Shakespeare at Home' which he published as a book in 1929. Symon began: 'We have come together tonight to celebrate the tercentenary of the greatest poet and dramatist of all time.' In addition to his own customary panegyric, Symon cited Sir Forbes Robertson ('scholar, actor and artist') and Sir Sidney Lee ('the greatest Shakespearean of the age')[31] as two men who also bowed before the Bard. Symon used the occasion to quote passages from Shakespeare's plays to arouse patriotic fervour and to guide recruiters. He concluded with his version of the well-known lines from Shakespeare's Henry IV: 'I care not – a man can die but once. If it can be my destiny, so; if it be not, so; no man is too good to serve his prince.'[32]

Sir Josiah Symon KCMG KC

In January 1916 Symon had told an enlisted State Labor MP that he had too many responsibilities to lead a movement in support the introduction of 'universal service'.[33] Calls for conscription became more insistent with the Australian losses on the Somme in July–August 1916. Billy Hughes, who had succeeded Fisher as Prime Minister in 1915, became convinced of the necessity for conscription during his long spell in London in the first half of 1916. Symon remained sceptical about the Prime Minister's stance. He told 'My most dear Crouch Batchelor' on 14 June 1916 that Hughes' strong speeches in London in support of compulsory service 'would be sheer, if not blatant, hypocrisy' unless he returned quickly and showed his sincerity 'by immediately establishing and enforcing compulsory service'.[34] In August 1916 the British War Office strengthened Hughes' hand: it asked Australia for an immediate recruitment of 32,500 men and called for an additional 16,500 men each month. Voluntary recruiting had yielded just 6,170 men in June 1916. Hughes subsequently led the 'Yes' campaign leading up to the plebiscite of 28 October 1916.

Symon wrote to the Irish-born Senator Patrick Lynch (Labor) on 6 October reminding him of their mutual esteem: 'I am now proud of you, with a genuine and admiring pride.' Symon had read his speeches in the Senate and it had made him happy to know 'there is one man with whose sentiments and whose expression of them I am thoroughly in accord'. In his own attack on these 'irresponsible traitors' who opposed conscription he claimed that in place of Australian conscripts in Australian battalions there will be 'conscripts from Russia or elsewhere, or India!' 'An Australian battalion will no longer be Australian but "ring streaked and spotted".'[35] Symon held nothing back in his public attacks on the anti-conscriptionists: 'Every No vote would be a vote for Germany'; those who voted 'No' 'would proclaim themselves unworthy of the men who fought and bled at Anzac'.[36]

Symon spoke at a rally in the Adelaide Town Hall on 17 October for families whose relatives had enlisted. Senator John Newland joined him on the platform, a harbinger of the coming split in the Labor Party. Symon addressed meetings in Millicent, Naracoorte and Mount Gambier. He also spoke at a particularly noisy meeting in the Adelaide Exhibition Building on 22 October where some 500 anti-conscriptionists in the audience walked out in a prearranged demonstration.[37] The Managing Editor of the Sydney *Sun* asked him for about 1000 words to publish in his paper in mid-October. Symon could hardly refuse after the editor described him as 'one of the outstanding figures of our national life' and said his arguments 'would have a great effect in this State where we are hard pressed to defeat the forces which have combined to oppose the Referendum'. Moreover, the *Sun* printed 154,000 copies which were sold in every State. Symon sent an article in two halves. The second half arrived too late but the first one 'suited us most admirably'.[38] The editor omitted one paragraph because it would have constituted contempt of court in NSW. 'It is quaint to think that a journalist has to protect such a great jurist as yourself from such a pitfall.'[39]

Whereas Symon manufactured confidence in the lead-up to his election contest in 1913, he really did believe that the 'Yes' campaign would win in 1916. He expected the electorate to do its 'duty'. Symon told William Denny on 4 October he had no doubt the affirmative will win the vote by 'an ample majority'. Nevertheless, 'a lot of extremists are causing considerable agitation, and telling no end of lies, and making no end of misrepresentations to induce people to vote "No"'.[40] He referred in another letter to 'that irresponsible bounder' Dr Maloney, and the 'wicked and ignorant malignity of his remarks'. Maloney, the left-wing and anti-conscriptionist Labor MP for Melbourne, was quoted saying that a man with an Irish name had no chance of rising in the British Army.[41]

The initial results of the poll on 28 October stunned Symon. The 'No' vote was narrowly ahead. He consoled himself with the belief that 'the vote of the Australian soldiers will wipe the "No" majority out ... and will retrieve the honour of Australia as they did at Gallipoli and Pozières'. If not (and the size of the soldiers' 'No' vote stunned Symon even more), 'the glorious sun of Anzac will have suffered an eclipse'. Symon claimed that any 'temporary triumph' will be one for 'the ignorant and the misguided, but a permanent stain on Australia'.[42] He returned to the issue when the P & O liner RMS *Arabia* was torpedoed and sunk late in the morning of 6 November, some 300 miles from Malta in the Mediterranean. Lenore Symon was one of the 437 passengers on board. Two engineers lost their lives, but the passengers and the rest of the crew were picked up by minesweepers. Lenore cabled her father: 'Landed safe and well. Proceeding to England by first ship.' Symon drew his own lesson from the episode. 'It is a sad reflection that by the "No" referendum vote it appears there are people in Australia who refuse to allow their country to do her utmost to prevent or avenge these Hun attempts to murder Australian women and children.'[43]

Throughout 1917 Symon had seen little to give him confidence: the stalemate in Western Europe, the Bolshevik Revolution, the collapse in Australia of the consensus of 1914, the rail strike and the rise of class antagonism and sectarianism. It pleased him that half the Federal Labor Party had walked out of caucus with Billy Hughes and joined with the Opposition to form the Hughes-led Nationalist Party which won a resounding election victory in May 1917. Yet Symon was sceptical, even as he considered the likelihood of such a triumph. Hughes' 'win the war policy' was 'simply a cover for the cowardly abandonment of conscription'. Unless the policy was accompanied by a definite commitment to universal service it was meaningless.[44] Meanwhile, Symon had identified another enemy: Daniel Mannix, the Catholic Archbishop of Melbourne, a 'pestilent priest' who had succeeded 'a highly respected prelate, Archbishop Carr' and was saying things which were 'seditious and disloyal'. Except for 'this poisonous product of a disloyal hierarchy' and a few others who are under his malign influence, 'most Australians are like Galileo of old, and care for none of these things'.[45]

On 20 December 1917 Hughes tried a second time to win popular support for conscription. Symon had previously written in late November to a serving sergeant in the Australian Army and spoke of hoping rather than expecting the 'degradation' of last time to be 'wiped out'. He did not think that the 'Yes' campaign 'has been quite as well arranged as it might have been'.[46] Jo told Carril on 23 December that the 'No' vote had a stronger victory, leaving him 'ashamed of Australia' and 'wanting to leave the country never to return'. In a letter he hoped that the people of England will not make a fuss of Hughes 'who made a mess of the whole thing & is utterly discredited here'. A 'German peace' would make Australia 'wake up' if Germany insisted on taking New Guinea.[47] He later told Kilmeny it had become 'a daily pain to me to live in this miserable country, which has gone back on Britain, as well as its own men at the front in refusing Conscription'.[48]

Symon fought many substantial legal cases during the War. One,

'My boys & girls are all in all to me.'

beginning for Symon in December 1914 in the Police Court was finally settled in September 1919. Francis Hugh Snow was accused of trading with the enemy. He was alleged to have sold or tried to sell 6,000 tons of copper to Aron Hirsch & Sohn, then conducting its business at Halberstadt in Germany. After leaving the Police Court in Adelaide the case went to the Supreme Court where Justice Gordon presided. It moved to the High Court, back to the Supreme Court and returned to the High Court. The case had a substantive importance but is also of interest to a biography because it pitted three very able barristers against each other, two of whom probably no longer socialised together. Cleland KC with Villeneuve Smith prosecuted and Symon KC led for the defence, and lost.

During a hotly contested libel action beginning on 28 March 1916, Symon and Cleland disagreed over whether a witness had spoken 'certain words'. When Symon insisted that he had not heard the words Cleland sought to move on: 'I must treat my learned friend like the sleeping dog, and let him lie.' Symon objected to being called a 'sleeping dog'. The remark not only hurt his feelings; it injured the dignity of the profession. A mere withdrawal was insufficient. The Bench should have something to say about it. Justice Buchanan clearly thought that enough had already been said. No one, it seems, thought that the use of the word 'lie', in the context though not in the familiar saying, was at best ambiguous.

Cleland soon found his own grounds for complaint. He wrote to the secretary of the South Australian Law Society relating to Symon's failure to meet an undertaking given on Friday 2 April to deliver a definitive answer on Monday on whether he intended to call evidence on behalf of the defendant. Symon gave his answer at 10.00 on Tuesday morning. Cleland regarded Symon's actions as 'a grave breach of professional duty and professional honour … Such conduct, if allowed to pass, will bring an honourable profession into contempt'. He wanted the secretary to arrange a hearing before the Council of the Law Society. Symon advised the secretary that the Council could not deal with a complaint but must, under its own rules, refer the matter to the Statutory Committee for investigation. Cleland was not entitled at this stage to see a copy of Symon's reply to the complaint.

Whether Symon forwarded his draft reply is unclear. It was characteristically vigorous. Cleland's 'so-called complaint is inspired by personal malignity'. Cleland had excluded Symon's junior, Francis Villeneuve Smith, from his charges, and should not have done so, and was not 'manly enough' to reveal the grounds for his belief that Symon controlled the situation within the defence; anyone with 'the most elementary acquaintance with professional propriety' would know that counsel, in consultation, are collectively responsible for their decisions. As for the central issue, Symon did not attach the 'slightest weight' to a supposed breach of an undertaking. The Court would decide if there was a breach and determine what was most likely to bring the profession into contempt and dishonour. The matter was still dragging on in December 1916 when it seemed to disappear.[49]

In 1918 Symon exchanged sharper words outside the Court with Villeneuve Smith who told the Law Society on 26 April that Symon had accepted a brief for £100 and a seven guineas consultation fee on 12 February 1918 for a murder trial. Villeneuve Smith was to be his junior. Symon returned the brief and the cash on 2 March saying that he thought it would be more agreeable to Smith and himself, and in the best interests of the defence, if he withdrew. Eventually, Richard Ingleby was appointed junior and Smith's partner, H.G. Alderman, became third counsel. Miller, the defendant, had originally wanted Symon, and friends had raised the money but a solicitor with Symon's firm stopped them from meeting its senior partner.

Smith claimed that Symon had committed 'a very flagrant and infamous breach of professional duty' by his 'cynical and dishonourable repudiation of his contractual obligations to his client'. Symon had boycotted Smith 'to gratify feelings of personal spite and ill will engendered by me publicly denouncing his nefarious practices in cases recently before the Court'. Symon wrote a 13-page response dated 8 May. He added a one-page appendix, being a copy of a letter from Villeneuve Smith marking Symon's 69th birthday and dated 25 September 1915: 'No bar can be prouder of its leader than the South Australian bar is of you; and very few bars can point to a leader who has won for it the high honors [sic] that distinguish you and therefore us.' He also thanked Symon for the many kindnesses to him, especially early in his career – all 'beyond requital'. On the back of his response Symon described the complaint as 'a piece of impertinence' which 'came to nothing'.[50]

'My boys & girls are all in all to me.'

The case itself did have a sensational conclusion. Miller, a railways employee, admitted killing Charles Mills, a tramway employee, after finding him committing an act of adultery at Henley Beach with Miller's wife. Justice Buchanan and the prosecution argued there was sufficient evidence of provocation for the charge of murder to be amended to one of manslaughter. Symon built a case around a loving husband and father, with a son serving in the AIF, who had been hurt and humiliated. In what was described as a 'delicate and judicious address', Symon claimed the provocation was so great that the accused should be acquitted. 'The measure of his love was the measure of his violence.' The jury agreed with him and returned a verdict of 'Not Guilty'. The spectators in the court cheered. Justice Buchanan ordered the jury to reconsider, Symon cited authorities to argue that the jury's decision was final, the jury retired again and returned with another verdict of 'Not Guilty'.[51]

Throughout 1918 Sir Josiah Symon seemed to oscillate between despair about the direction and conduct of the war and the joy he felt as its end came into sight. Friends who made a mark in life became welcome intrusions. Symon clearly enjoyed his contact with Charles Bulpett whom he had met before the war and whose life experiences were vastly removed from his own. Six years younger than Symon, Bulpett was educated at Rugby and Trinity College, Oxford, and played first class cricket for Middlesex where, in Wisden's judgement, he was a sound bat and a useful fast bowler. For a wager he once swam the Thames wearing a top hat and evening dress and carrying a cane. He was one of the first to climb the Matterhorn and like Byron had swum the Hellespont.[52] In 1904 Bulpett abandoned his law career and migrated to the British colony of Kenya where he became a big game hunter and established friendships with even larger-than-life characters Frederick Selous and John Boyes.[53] Symon, probably through Bulpett, also established a warm friendship with the American-born adventurer and millionaire Northrup McMillan and his wife Lucy. McMillan became one of the leaders of Kenya's white settler community.

In between jousting with Paris Nesbit at the Bar, Symon regarded his main legal rival as a good friend. Nesbit's letter sent to Symon after the war must have touched him. Nesbit said how much he sympathised with

Sir Josiah Symon KCMG KC

him 'living in the hope of seeing your boys again'. With their duty done, 'your hope will in all probability soon be realised. You must feel proud in the consciousness that your children have so splendidly upheld the honour of your family.'[54]

15

'Not a sign or whisper of discontent anywhere'

Sir Josiah Symon appeared content with what had become his world in the first years after the Great War. His law firm had all the work it could handle, Charles had returned from the War and Symon had taken on two new partners. Dr Thomas Browne was born in NSW where he became a teacher and later transferred to Western Australia before obtaining his degree of Doctor of Laws at the University of Adelaide. He practised with Mellis (later Chief Justice Sir Mellis) Napier and Senator A.J. McLachlan before replacing Rounsevell during the War. Edward Povey had arrived in South Australia at the age of 24 having worked in a law firm in Chester, England. He rose to be the managing clerk of Symon's firm where he obtained his articles and acquired a law degree at the University of Adelaide. Admitted to practice in 1916, he became a partner in Symon, Browne, Symon & Povey, but branched out in May 1920 to head the partnership of Povey, Blackburn & Waterhouse.[1]

Family relationships now affected Jo as never before and their good and rewarding aspects multiplied early in the 1920s. Initially, he could share his earnings with some of his extended family. Eric, the youngest son of brother Jim, was badly gassed in France in 1918 and Jo sent him an undisclosed sum to sustain him in recovery. In April 1919 Jo presented Eric, through Kilmeny, a further £200 and promised an additional £300 'in recognition of your long and good service with the Colours'. His promise had to be reduced to £200 because financing Oscar proved 'much more costly and a larger drain on my resources that I originally anticipated'. Jo had already given his self-styled 'affectionate nephew' the equivalent of more than $32,000 in 2020 monetary terms. Plans to give the two sons of his sister Elizabeth 'a substantial present' for joining the Colours were similarly reduced because of Oscar's demands upon his father's purse.[2]

Margaret was appointed a Justice of the Peace in 1919 and she left almost immediately for the United Kingdom. Kilmeny had already been mentioned in Despatches for her work with 'Carry-On' and Carril informed the family early in 1920 that she had been offered an MBE. Jo advised her to accept the offer – which she did – explaining that the distinction was significant as 'a recognition from the King & that you did your "bit" in the war. That & your Mention in Despatches you will always have.'[3] The father would have been proud when shown the tributes Kilmeny received from the 'top brass' of Carry-On. Kilmeny brought them home when she and Carril returned to Australia at the end of 1920.

Oscar emerged seemingly unchanged from the War and his father gave him 'a severe talking to' in April 1919. Jo reminded Oscar that at aged 28 he must earn a living, and felt sure that Oscar understood that 'he need not look for any more cash from me, or that I will ever again pay his debts'. Although his second fit son was about to inherit a sizable income from the capital grant of 1916, Jo told Kilmeny he would help Oscar 'to get a suitable farm or something of that kind, and he is now looking about for a place'.[4] Oscar subsequently acquired Edgehill Farm, some four miles from Riverton in the State's mid-north, and financed substantial improvements by borrowing money on the security of the 1916 Deed Trust. He did not first obtain the Trust's authority. Oscar made what Jo considered were extravagant improvements on an overdraft which was likely to reach £4–5000 'before long'.[5] Those improvements included the purchase of a Berkshire boar with a bloodline suggesting 'it had the makings of a great sire'. It was considered 'a distinct acquisition to the Berkshire blood already in the State'.[6] On 29 October 1921 Oscar revealed intentions to lead a new life: he married Melva Iris McBride of Toorak Gardens at St Peter's College Chapel. In December 1922 he became the father of a son.

Three deaths in the space of ten months – Deakin, 7 October 1919; Barton, 7 January 1920; Griffith, 9 August 1920 – removed the last of the giants of the federation era. Approached by the South Australian press, Symon spoke at length in praising each of them.[7] While he observed the convention of saying only good things about the dead, he adopted his barrister's practice of moving on from concluded cases. Symon

'Not a sign or whisper of discontent anywhere'

considered his battles with each of Deakin, Barton and Griffith had long gone. He acknowledged his differences with Deakin but referred only to those occurring during the Convention where there was never 'the slightest semblance of bitterness or hostility'. There was plenty of 'bitterness' and 'hostility' in their time together in Federal politics, though mainly from Symon's side. In 1920 Symon re-iterated and expanded his customary refrain of liking Deakin as a person: 'I lament his death as that of an old and much-loved friend.' Anyone who remembered Symon's reactions to the Fusion would have found this comment unconvincing.

Symon liked to assess fellow speakers, often comparing them to George Reid. Deakin, he said, had 'rare excellencies as an orator'. Although he did not have 'the solid force or broadly humorous flashes' of George Reid, he stood almost alone 'for lucidity, choiceness, and precision of language, and the persuasiveness of a well-modulated voice'. Barton 'was a fine speaker, but not an orator' and 'certainly not an orator on the same plane' as Reid. Nevertheless, Barton 'was a lucid and a most logical speaker'.

Like other contemporaries, Symon looked sadly upon Deakin's mental decline in his final years. He proffered a layman's explanation:

> His nervous sensibilities, which were always apparent, took too much out of him, and finally, I suspect, wore him out ... Mr. Deakin had a turn for delicate raillery, but never that I remember showed what is usually called wit, still less humor [sic]. He took things, I always used to think, too seriously. He was a literary man first and a politician afterwards. Politics was too wearing a life for a man of his temperament.

Symon believed that Barton eventually took the right job but at the wrong time.

> He had many of the qualities of a statesman, but possessed more of the attributes of a Judge. The work of his life was done when he retired from politics and [went] on to the Bench. His judicial career was, for him, really a time of rest. He was not a man of constitutional or unresting energies. He loved to take things easily, except on a great occasion, or when working in some special cause.[8]

Evidently, Symon's refusal in 1903 to comment on Barton's translation to the High Court was not a denial of his judicial attributes. In any case, no

Symon comment on Edmund Barton would have been complete without mentioning his role in securing Barton's election to the leadership of the 1897–8 Convention. He elaborated it in 1920 by pointing out that he had moved the appointment even though George Reid, Symon's Free Trade Leader, was a potential candidate. Symon saw his successful promotion of Barton as evidence of 'the absolute non-party spirit of that great convention'.

Perhaps surprisingly, Symon was almost unstinting in praise of Griffith. 'He was a great figure in Federal affairs, and a very powerful influence ... He was really the Father of Federation.' Although the Bill he drafted in 1891 'differed fundamentally from the Constitution as adopted by the National Convention in 1898, which proceeded more on the lines of the American Constitution', it was of much service to later federalists. 'In addition to having been a great lawyer and Judge, and an eminent statesman, he was an accomplished scholar, and had conspicuous literary gifts.' Symon acknowledged that on some public questions 'we held different views – as most public men do – but my esteem for him as a great Australian never failed, and during the years our relations of mutual and cordial friendship were very pleasant'. Symon finished by describing Griffith's death as a 'personal loss', a further example of his propensity for elevating professional contacts into personal relationships.

The deaths of three such pre-eminent figures had one long-term effect on Symon. He had become increasingly conscious of being one of a few survivors of the momentous event in his life: the 1897–8 Constitutional Convention. He made this point in most of the commentaries and letters he wrote about federation. At the same time, Symon wanted to tell his own federal story and began assembling material from his papers for a book he tentatively entitled 'The Dawn of Federation'. He saw himself as more than a survivor with a tale to tell. Pride and a sense of responsibility compelled him to defend what the constitution-makers had created. He had to speak for them as well as for himself. Symon, therefore, briefed himself as counsel for the defence of the Constitution of 1900, and of what he called the 'federal spirit' which he believed guided those who framed it.

Griffith's death had an immediate resonance. It occurred in the same month that the enlarged High Court overturned two central canons of

'Not a sign or whisper of discontent anywhere'

the Griffith Court. The Court resolved by 5–1 to repudiate the doctrines of implied prohibitions and State reserved powers in what became known as the *Engineers Case*.[9] In effect the High Court opened the way for the Commonwealth to encroach on what had been the exclusive territory of the States. The Court also asserted the paramountcy of Commonwealth laws over inconsistent State laws and introduced a new era when the words of the Constitution were to be interpreted in their literal meaning.

Symon was appalled by the decision but kept silent as he continued to savour the visit of the Prince of Wales to Australia between May and August 1920. Officially, King George V regarded the tour by the future Edward VIII as a means of thanking Australians for their contributions during the Great War. As South Australian President of the Royal Empire Society, Symon saw the Prince's tour as a means of uniting a society fractured by war. The immediate post-war visits by Admiral Viscount Jellicoe and by General Sir William Birdwood ('Birdie'), who commanded the ANZAC Corps during the War, and the Prince's tour of Canada in 1919 had shown what could be achieved.

Symon wanted to play a role similar to his part in the Birdwood visit. 'Birdie' had stayed a night at 'Manoah' and next day accompanied Symon on a visit to the Auldana vineyard. Symon approached Rear Admiral Lionel Halsey, the Prince's chief of staff, who it will be recalled had commanded Oliver's light cruiser *New Zealand* in the battle of Heligoland Bight. Symon wanted to invite the Prince to stop for afternoon tea at 'Manoah' when his party was driving through the Mount Lofty Ranges on the way to Adelaide from Port Augusta. Halsey explained that the Prince had little time available. Being young, when he did have free time, he preferred riding, squash or golf; it was not relaxing for him to sit in a car.[10] Symon did achieve three encounters with the future King. The Commonwealth Government invited him as 'one of the Founders of Federation' and as one of the first senators and early ministers, to attend a State Dinner in Melbourne to mark the Prince's arrival in Australia. Accompanied by Lady Symon, he met the Prince at a dinner in Government House on the night of his arrival in Adelaide and subsequently attended another State Dinner in his honour.

On 20 August 1920 Symon wrote a letter to his 'dear friend' Sir Edward Wallington to report on the Prince's visit to Australia. Wallington was now Private Secretary and Treasurer to Queen Mary. Symon knew that this letter, like those he and Kilmeny sent to Admiral Sir Wilmot Fawkes, the former Commander of the Australian Station, would reach the Royal Household. Symon told Wallington that the Prince 'won the hearts of the multitude; he came, he was seen and he conquered'. Symon rarely practised understatement: 'All ranks and classes found him an English thoroughbred'; 'the greatest embassy in history ... has made the Empire safe for democracy and the monarchy'; 'Not a sign or whisper of discontent anywhere'; 'Anyone who showed him rudeness or offence would, I verily believe, have been lynched on the spot.' Wallington replied on 26 September thanking him for his 'exceedingly interesting letter' which he showed to the Queen.

Jo and Kilmeny left Adelaide on Monday 2 May 1921 on board the RMS *Morea* for a long-planned, five-month visit to the battlefields of France and to spend time in England and Scotland. Within a month of their arrival in England on 15 June, Jo was telling Nell of his 'very strenuous time with lunches, drinks, receptions & so forth'. He had met 'a good many very interesting people ... & everybody says how well I look & that I should be ashamed to show so much vigour & vitality' for a man of over 70.[11]

The social round was certainly heavy. Symon sat on the platform at a mass meeting of the Victoria League at the Guildhall where the Prince of Wales presided. Lady Northcote, the widow of the former Governor-General, invited Symon to a dinner where the guests included former Governors and Lieutenant Governors of the Australian colonies or States and from other parts of the Empire. Later, Symon stayed with Admiral Sir Wilmot Fawkes and often saw Sir George and Lady Le Hunte. Sir George was the Governor of South Australia in 1903–08 and the Le Huntes were Fawkes' neighbours in Crowborough, Sussex. Symon also spent a weekend with Viscount and Viscountess Novar in Raith, Scotland. Symon first met them when Novar, as Sir Ronald Munro Ferguson, was Governor-General of Australia in 1914–20.

Symon spent an evening in London with Sir Charles Lucas, Sir Sidney Lee and George Buckle, the editor of *The Times* (1884–1912), who was writing the final four volumes of the six-volume life of Lord Beaconsfield (Benjamin Disraeli) begun by the late W.F. Moneypenny. Educated at Winchester, Lucas won a scholarship to Balliol College, Oxford, graduated

'Not a sign or whisper of discontent anywhere'

with firsts in Classical Moderations and *Literae Humaniores* and was called to the Bar at Lincoln's Inn. He joined the Colonial Service and headed the Dominions Department but retired in 1911 after being passed over for the position of Secretary. Lucas was then appointed Principal of the Working Man's College and President of the Geographical Association and regularly attended events at the Royal Colonial Institute (renamed the Royal Empire Society in 1928). Lucas published several well-regarded books on the Empire. He was a diffident, gentle man, who had a host of friends and admirers. Symon used the word 'friend' liberally; describing Lucas as one understated the extent of his appreciation and affection. Lucas and Symon regularly exchanged views on imperial, political, economic and social issues and Lucas was always urging Symon to write a history of federation. Kilmeny and Lenore had visited Lucas several times during the War and Kilmeny maintained contact with him throughout the 1920s.

While in London, Symon met Prime Minister Lloyd George and J.H. Whitley, the Speaker of the House of Commons. Back in Adelaide, Symon told journalists that Lloyd George was a 'a miracle of cheery optimism'; you had to meet him, 'to understand the buoyant and magnetic personality which inspired England in the darkest days of the war'. Lloyd George never lost faith in the 'unconquerable soul' of the British race. 'In politics even the strongest Minister is liable to sudden fall, but when I left England there was no apparent menace to Mr. Lloyd George's tenure of power.'[12] Within a year Lloyd George was out of office.

Symon did not tell the journalists about one of his activities while in the United Kingdom. Late in July he left Kilmeny in London to spend part of his holiday travelling in Scotland. He stayed for a few days in Oban in the Firth of Lorn, the birthplace of the late Allan McLean, Symon's former Cabinet colleague. Lachlan Macquarie was born on the Isle of Mull eight miles across the inlet. Symon used some of this time in Oban to confide his thoughts in two letters he sent to Kilmeny.[13]

In the first, dated 31 July 1921, Jo realised he was the most senior living recipient of a KCMG in Australia. Symon felt he deserved promotion to GCMG for 'my services in the Senate, in the Commonwealth government, & particularly my public services during the war amply justify my claim'. He did not wish anyone to think he based his war contribution merely on his money donations. Admittedly, Governor Sir Henry Galway had said he expected subscriptions sufficient to present at most three motor ambulances. Symon's gift of £500 to purchase the second one so stimulated the movement that the Governor could offer something like ten or twelve. Symon wanted to emphasise his public services to aid recruiting and his support of the 'Yes' vote for conscription when he addressed meetings all over the country. These activities for which he gave up all professional work cost the Commonwealth or the State 'not one farthing'. Jo could not name any KCMG in Australia who was more entitled than himself for elevation. Moreover, advancement was not unusual. For example: 'Bonython was first an ordinary Knight, that is Knight Bachelor, then he solicited Deakin who got him a CMG, then a year or two ago he was advanced to KCMG as the result of persistent applications, and all for what?' Symon finished by saying he had never before asked for recognition.

Jo wrote again to Kilmeny on 3 August. Noting that Prime Minister Hughes was currently visiting the United Kingdom, Jo asked his daughter to write to Robert Garran as Hughes' Secretary seeking an interview in London for 'a few minutes'. Kilmeny should explain to Garran that her father was not immediately available because he had an invitation to stay with Lord Novar for a few days. Jo wanted Kilmeny to keep any appointment for him and explain to the Prime Minister why he wished to see him. On returning to London, Symon would wait upon Hughes if necessary, 'though I am loath to encroach as I am very conscious how greatly occupied he is'. Jo added more information about his 'public & patriotic service' he had forgotten to include, especially the presentation to HMS *Commonwealth* of the shield and plate for which he raised money, spoke at meetings, organised committees and decided designs. 'I never was more proud of anything than having the honour of making that presentation in the name of Australia as one of the functions incidental to the Coronation.'

Nothing of substance followed this letter until Symon met Hughes for half an hour in Melbourne on 1 December 1921. He told Kilmeny that Hughes was 'genuinely pleased' to see him and, on listening to his arguments, agreed that Symon had a case for promotion. Hughes discussed the problems arising out of the State complaints that 'Federal

'Not a sign or whisper of discontent anywhere'

people' were interfering with State recommendations. Symon said that distinctions like KBEs and OBEs were scattered about in South Australia while 'Commonwealth men like myself were ignored'. Hughes thought that Symon constituted 'a special case' and promised to write to Churchill as Colonial Secretary and 'to make a personal matter of it, to nominate Symon for a GCMG'. If Hughes 'is as good as his word' Symon had grounds to hope for a promotion in the King's Birthday list of 1922.[14]

Jo told Kilmeny of another approach he had made in Melbourne, and of the letter he subsequently sent to Sir Joseph Cook on 22 January 1922. He had chatted with Cook in the Queen's Hall of the Victorian Parliament Building on the day Cook was appointed High Commissioner to London.[15] Symon showed him copies of Chamberlain's letter of December 1900 and of his reply to the Colonial Secretary. He told Cook what he had done in the 21 years since his appointment as KCMG and said he was 'a little disappointed' that his political, ministerial and war services had not been recognised. Symon was 'quite frank' with Cook. As quoted earlier in Chapter 11, he felt entitled to a 'step-up' to a GCMG or to be sworn of the Privy Council like Justice Isaacs 'who occupies a seat on the High Court I should have had – but I have no regrets in that respect'. Jo told Kilmeny in April 1922:

> As to the other matter of recognition of my public & war services, I don't count on it at all. I don't put much trust in Hughes or Cook, altho' they both profess the highest esteem & regard for me. However great one's services may have been, when one is out of the arena & no longer to be feared, they go unrewarded.

In the following July, Jo reported to Kilmeny: 'I have not even had an acknowledgement from Sir Joseph Cook of my letter re GCMG, but I have little faith in either his or Hughes' protestations & promises.' On learning in August that Kilmeny had met Lady Cook, Jo hoped his daughter had told her 'you expect her husband & Hughes to do their duty by me as to the GCMG at the earliest opportunity, or a Privy Councillorship'. Symon never did receive a 'step-up'.[16]

During 1922 Symon was looking forward to the publication of an article he had written in the wake of the High Court decision in the *Engineers Case*. In 1921, the editor of the *Journal of Comparative Legislation and*

Sir Josiah Symon KCMG KC

International Law had commissioned him during Symon's visit to London to write the article. Symon prepared it on the ship returning to South Australia during September 1921. As he explained to Kilmeny, it was hard work writing without access to his papers. The 'abominable' heat on a crowded vessel added to his frustration and so did working with typists, including Angel, who had difficulty with his handwriting.[17]

The High Court's decision had placed Symon in an awkward position. In 1897–1900 he was a leading exponent of the view that 'if Australia was fit to enact her own laws she was fit to interpret them'. He might then have envisaged himself as one of the five judges expected to sit on the High Court. Whether or not he was on the Bench, he probably accepted that the Court would make some decisions he did not like, but not of the kind which assaulted or undermined the balance of the Commonwealth-State relationship. The decision in the *Engineers Case* obliged him to rethink his position on appeals to the Privy Council. Symon felt he could not trust the High Court, as presently composed, to defend the rights and interests of the States. There was just one problem. The 'Chamberlain compromise' he had applauded in 1900 provided that no appeal to the Privy Council could be permitted on constitutional powers unless the High Court 'shall certify that the question is one which ought to be determined by Her Majesty in Council'. The High Court in August 1921 refused to grant a certificate to appeal its decision in the *Engineers Case*.

Symon was left to argue for the retention of appeals in the circumstances presently available. He began the article, published in November 1922,[18] by setting out the history of Section 74, highlighting his role in securing its original form which abolished almost all appeals and the last-minute changes made at the Melbourne Session in 1898 to widen the scope of access to the Privy Council. He had changed his mind about opposing appeals to the Privy Council because he now recognised that the underlying assumption of his original argument was 'fallacious'. He and the other Convention delegates assumed that they were creating a nation. In putting that argument 'we old Federalists' failed

> to take sufficiently into account that we were within the British Empire, under the same King and Flag, or to realize that this fact deprived the terms 'nation' and 'nationhood' of the sense and meaning necessary to

the argument. We rather confused British Empire nationhood – which we shared – with independent nationhood, which we did not possess.

The aim of the federalists like himself 'was to remove the vice of disunion among the States as much and as far as possible – not to cure or replace it by secession from the British Commonwealth'. The notion of striving for 'nationhood' was useful for winning support for federation but there had been no attempt to create a nation in 'a political sense'. In effect, Symon was saying that Barton's aphorism of 1897 – 'For the first time in history, we have a nation for a continent and a continent for a nation' – was misleading. It would seem that many Australians had been misled.

Symon proceeded to raise 18 points or subjects to show that retaining the existing system of appeals did not diminish Australian courts. In the process he adopted some of the arguments he had opposed in 1898. He also talked up the quality and standing of the Privy Council in relation to the House of Lords. Some of his reasoning appeared circular or even bizarre. For example, he denied there was anything anomalous about maintaining appeals from one unit of the Empire but, if it were anomalous, that was no reason to abolish them and, in any case, the British Empire harboured a number of anomalies. He detected no hardness of feeling against appeals to an external court; besides, would one in wartime want to deny an appeal to the external Royal Navy? If cost was a problem about approaching the Privy Council then cost issues should be tackled rather than access to an appeal court. Where it suited, Symon either pushed the argument that the Australian people had decided how to administer justice to themselves or claimed that most Australians – the workers – had no interest in a subject of more concern to the trading and commercial classes. While the appeal system was not essential to the maintenance of imperial unity, it did have symbolic value and appeals did promote legal uniformity within the Empire.

At no stage did Symon mount a cogent and coherent argument for the retention of appeals, probably because he did not dare state his real objections to the High Court as then composed. He did, however, finish on a stronger note. The High Court had decided in a case in 1906 that the Commonwealth did not have the power to interfere with State instrumentalities. The people in 1911 and 1913 had rejected the

Government's attempts in referenda to give the High Court the power it did not have, and in 1920 the High Court had decided it did have the power. 'Most people would have thought that was just the situation which fairly called for a reference to the Privy Council, but the Court of 1920 refused to certify so that an appeal might take place.' The States sought to appeal against this refusal or to invoke the Royal Prerogative to grant special leave. Whatever the outcome, 'three points clearly appear':

> first, one or other of the High Court decisions is wrong; secondly, the States do not undervalue the Privy Council Appeal, and hope to be able to avail themselves of it in this grave constitutional difficulty; and thirdly, the people will know whether their decision that the Commonwealth should not have the power sought is to be of no effect.

Symon posed the question – 'Is it an advantage for the system of appeals to be retained or a mischief to be excised?' His answer was straightforward: 'Let us therefore adhere to Clause 74 – the Chamberlain Compromise. It works quite satisfactorily. To throw it into the melting-pot again gives no promise of any practical gain for Australia.'

A *Register* editorial of 23 January 1923 said that Symon had made 'a valuable contribution' to Australian constitutional law and thrown 'powerful light' on a subject over which there had been a difference of opinion and some 'misunderstanding'. No one among the survivors of the Convention was better qualified 'to deal from the historical and constitutional standpoint with the evolution of the present system of appeal'. The editorial concluded with the observation that the article 'will prove of unusual interest and value' to the legal profession, students of the constitution and Federal politicians. The writer never mentioned that Symon had changed his mind, let alone asked why he did so.

Symon was pleased that Kilmeny had received a complimentary copy of the article. She had been connected with it from the start and been in contact with the editor. 'These are the considerate little things which are attended to amongst decent people in England, that are quite forgotten here.' On reflection, Symon believed his article 'accomplishes the object he had in view and reads very well; indeed, it is quite creditable'. He sent one of his complimentary copies to Federal Chief Justice Sir Adrian Knox and another to Chief Justice Murray of the South Australian

'Not a sign or whisper of discontent anywhere'

Supreme Court, although he doubted if the latter 'can rise up to the level of the subject'.

> I suppose it was my natural modesty and shyness which prevented my saying what I thought of the PC article in print. As you ask me I thought it devilish good – exactly what I wanted it to be, clear and straight and forcible without flourishes of rhetoric. And besides it sets right a bit of the history of Federation and our Constitution about which misunderstanding was evidently growing up.[19]

Neither the *Register* nor Symon really identified the source or nature of any 'misunderstanding', and it is unlikely that Symon's thoughts added very much to what had become a non-subject. It has a place in this biography because it shows how Symon, usually unbending in the defence of a principle, could make changes to suit different circumstances. At the end of the 19th century he appeared to be well ahead of his time. The loyalties enhanced by the Great War, and the position adopted by the High Court in 1920, obliged him to take a step back.

Sir Josiah Symon formally retired from the firm of Symon, Browne & Symon in June 1922. He insisted, however, he had not retired from the profession of law. Symon explained to the *Mail* on 5 August 1922 that while he had already curtailed some of his legal work – having taken no criminal briefs for two or three years – he could limit his load still further. Nevertheless, he needed work in order not to 'rust'. Symon was 'easing down, not going out'. He intended to mingle work with other forms of 'relaxation', such as the orchards and gardens at 'Manoah', overseas travel and Auldana. These forms of relaxation were not inconsistent with the work he would continue to undertake. The reporter asked how he explained his good health. Symon stood up to his six feet in height, threw out his chest and said,

> I attribute a great deal of it to the fact that I have always spent my Saturdays and Sundays at Upper Sturt working on the hillsides with my men and inhaling the health-giving ozone of Mount Lofty. I have never come to town on Saturdays unless under great emergency. A fine Scotch constitution and plenty of hard work all my life have also had much to do with my health.

Within a few years Symon began referring to himself as an old man. His eyesight had so deteriorated that by the end of the 1920s Nell and their daughters often had to read for him. He relied more on family or staff for dictation and typing. In March 1928 he tripped over a dog and banged his left side and shoulder hard against the corner of a table in the smoking room at Manoah. A slow recovery and occasional attacks of lumbago contributed to the steady decline in the pace of life toward the end of the decade.

16

'I have had no rest or peace but only worry'

Symon's world started to go seriously wrong during 1923. His two surviving brothers died: Jim, virtually an alcoholic, succumbed in that year and David, long resettled near London, in the following one. The death of an 'old friend', W.B. Rounsevell, in July 1923 caused a different and more prolonged grief. When making his last Will, Rounsevell wanted to give some of his pictures to Sir Josiah Symon. Jo already had enough pictures and suggested that Rounsevell might leave them to the Symon children. Rounsevell liked the idea. He bequeathed four pictures to the four oldest children who in order of seniority should each select one. After Rounsevell's death Frank Blamey, the manager and secretary of Bagot's Executor and Trustee Company, informed Sir Josiah by letter that Charles Symon had called on him. Charles said he was the attorney for Margaret and Kilmeny and believed he was the only person in Adelaide who could make decisions on the pictures. Charles assured Blamey that his powers of attorney gave him the authority. Margaret, Lenore and Kilmeny subsequently gave the Company their authority for Charles to make the decisions, and he had forwarded an indemnity to the Company. Charles and Blamey then agreed to inform Sir Josiah of the position. Rounsevell's generous gesture kick-started an unresolved feud between father and eldest son.

Jo did not know until receiving the Company's letter that Charles had taken steps to make the choice for his sisters. Tactfully, he told Blamey he assumed his son did not think of telling him and had overlooked the fact of his being the last in seniority with the right to choose. Less tactfully, he said it would be 'invidious' for his son to make decisions for his sisters.

Symon then delved a little deeper. Carril, a joint attorney for Kilmeny, had apparently renounced his duty in favour of his brother who was an interested party: why and how did this occur? Further, Lenore was present in Adelaide and could exercise her own second choice. When Jo showed her the document giving her a choice Lenore said she did not understand she was giving up second pick. Symon then raised legal questions in relation to the powers of attorney and suggested that the indemnity implied doubt about the authority. He wanted the four beneficiaries to appoint a disinterested party to take possession of the pictures and place them where the beneficiaries could freely exercise their own choices in order of seniority.

Symon subsequently sent copies of the above correspondence to Margaret and Kilmeny. He told Kilmeny on 1 November 1923 of Charles' 'gratuitous & dictatorial interference, & rudeness towards me behind my back'. Charles had also 'shown selfishness & ingratitude to me & I ought not to be surprised. I have written perhaps more fully to Margaret, but I say no more about it, except that such conduct fills me with sorrow.'

Within six weeks, Jo was writing to Kilmeny about another 'sorrow'. He began his letter of 11 December by responding to her comments concerning 'the not uncommon tendency of parents to discriminate in their gifts to children – giving more to boys than to girls'. Jo agreed with her assessment of inequality as 'wrong & unjust', while claiming 'there might sometimes be reasons for a difference being made'. He referred to the case of which Kilmeny was well aware; the gift to Charles and his brothers in 1916 of his 'cream' investments in shares to the value of over £20,000 pounds each. When handed over after December 1920 the capital sum yielded four net annual incomes of between £1200 and £1400 each in 1923. It was 'a fairly comfortable provision anyone would say'. Jo had made progress in building something like the same amount for the three older girls. Kilmeny, he wrote, would be surprised to learn that Charles wanted to treat his father's voluntary gift as though it were the repayment of a loan. He sought interest on the £20,000 from the end of 1916 until the capital sum was made available, thus claiming the income from the shares which his father had used to finance wartime allowances for his children. Instead of showing gratitude for the £20,000, '& all else I have done for him', Charles had demanded more.

'I have had no rest or peace but only worry'

Well that is not the way to get it from me. I am very sorry, but it may be of interest to you to know that while you are deprecating the boys getting more than the girls, the eldest son of the family takes another view, & looks his gift horse narrowly in the mouth.

Family problems were careering out of Jo's control. On 25 August 1925 Mary married an actor, Anthony Clark, in London. Jo suspected that the young man was looking for financial security. The marriage soon collapsed, probably because Clark was gay. Jo did not want to speak more about the pictures except to refer to Charles' rudeness and disrespect towards the secretary of the Bagot Company and to himself. He told Kilmeny that her brother had 'developed an unmannerly & overbearing habit toward his family & his treatment of Carril, culminating in his practically kicking him out of the firm, was shameful'. Carril was doing nothing at the moment and might never be able to do anything because of his deafness. Oscar was in hospital and 'on the brink of financial ruin', owing to his extravagance although Jo acknowledged that most of the outlay led to 'wonderful improvements on his properties'. Besides, Edgehill had been successfully sold. Yet Symon could not see any relief from the worry he had experienced since retiring from work and he had received 'no help from my sons or rather no sympathy or encouragement'. What he wanted was leisure for literary work 'but alas, I have had no rest or peace but only worry'.[1]

By the end of 1924, when Kilmeny had returned to Adelaide, Jo told her of his three main grievances about Charles. First, Charles had not paid the £1791/11/11 in previous earnings still owed to Symon. Secondly, Charles was claiming interest on top of the gift of a fortune which was now giving him an unearned annual income of about £1500 a year (worth $125,867.87 in 2020). Thirdly, Charles and his partner, Dr Browne, had not yet paid a penny of the agreed price for the business they had taken over in 1922. They had agreed on a purchase price of £3500; it will be recalled that Symon paid £5000 to Way for a much smaller firm in 1875. Perhaps Charles believed that different rules would or should apply to financial matters within families, and that a son should not have to pay for his inheritance. Jo had a very different view. As he once told his own brother, David, 'business matters between relatives should be conducted in the most strict business way – looseness only leads to rows & difficulty'.[2]

Sir Josiah Symon KCMG KC

Kilmeny tried to persuade Jo against taking strong action to recover what he felt was owed to him, and they exchanged many sharp words. Early in 1925, Kilmeny took another trip to Europe. On board ship she wrote to her father: 'Nothing you could do would ever shake my confidence in and affection for Chase [Charles].' Jo thought her statement 'quite uncalled for' because Kilmeny had implicitly accused him

> of having sought or threatened to do things to shake your confidence & affection in him & there is no truth in that. Such a thing never entered my mind. What concerns me was not your confidence & affection for him which seems capable of bearing a great strain but the fact that he has ruthlessly & wickedly destroyed my confidence & affection. You seem to think lightly of that towards a most generous & affectionate father of nearly 80 years of age.

Jo said he had not told Kilmeny about her brother's behaviour towards him until she 'made it imperative' that he should do so. When Kilmeny learnt that Charles had misappropriated money she said he would have to return it 'sooner or later'. Jo replied: 'Well he has had three years to do it & made no attempt.' Kilmeny advised Jo against trying to beat him down because her father would end his career with a 'blot' on it. Jo disagreed. He failed to see how he created a 'blot' on his reputation simply by publicly revealing 'my son's guilt of filial ingratitude & misappropriation of his father's money', especially given his father's voluntary gift of a fortune which had made him independent. If, however, Kilmeny was right about the 'blot', Jo felt 'no uneasiness. I can tread the winepress alone.'

The father was at once cross, upset and mystified by his favourite daughter's attacks on him. He felt she had taken sides against him, but he 'took no umbrage'. She had written 'impulsively & without knowing the facts'. He just could not understand how and why she placed 'another instrument of mischief' in her brother's hands by giving Charles a power of attorney and did so without informing the Company or her father. Her financial affairs were already being managed by the Executor & Trustee Company and the Company complained that Charles had used the power which Margaret and Kilmeny had given him in a way 'which embarrasses them as trustees for you three girls (Margaret, Lenore and Kilmeny)'. Jo noted how Kilmeny said, 'I make mistakes sometimes too', though he would have replaced 'sometimes' with 'often'. He asked his daughter to tell him the mistakes he had made 'in this wretched business'. Charles clearly made no mistake 'in practically putting his hand into my pocket & taking my money. If there was a mistake, it was in thinking that I would submit tamely to be robbed.'

Jo had trouble accepting Kilmeny's defence of Charles as the only one of his sons 'who is doing anything'. Charles was 'doing it with the lucrative business which I built up during fifty-five years & which I gave him the option to buy & which he did buy but for which amongst his other claims to your approving judgement he has not paid one penny of the price'. Jo felt he had two strong lines of attack: Charles had transgressed best business practice and was guilty of 'moral turpitude'. He had another argument which his daughter might ponder. Charles had not only hurt a generous father:

> He has almost broken my heart, & taken away the peace & happiness I hoped for in age & the chance I looked for of writing the books I had planned & which Lucas is in every mail writing me to get on with. I wonder what he would say if I told him why during the last three years my eldest son has made it impossible for me to do anything in the way of literary work, which would have been of great public value.

Jo concluded: Kilmeny must judge where to place her 'confidence & affection' and he had no wish to influence or try to influence her in any way. 'I shall never write or talk to you again on this subject, & I shall keep out of your way if that seems necessary to resist the temptation. With my love all the same[.] Father.'[3]

An overseas trip offered a useful escape. Jo and Lenore left Adelaide on 4 May 1925 to visit Canada and the United Kingdom. Symon had a brief to represent the University of Sydney at a conference of Empire universities. He had set out before learning that the conference had been erroneously listed for 1925 and not 1926. Symon was happy just to be absent from Adelaide and, as he told the press on this return, he enjoyed every minute of his holiday.[4]

Symon had nothing but praise for the railways of Canada and their large gauge. He regretted that South Australia had attempted development before building railways and had not followed Canada in extending railways to develop the country. Australia should take the trans-Canadian express as a model for the reorganisation of express traffic in Australia. Canada was going ahead by leaps and bounds, and was taking full advantage of its wonderful water resources both for transport and power development. He was also greatly impressed with the luxurious coaches on British railways, and said he travelled from London to Edinburgh without feeling the fatigue usually associated with long journeys.

In London Symon attended a debate in the House of Commons. Austen (a son of Joseph) Chamberlain, the Foreign Secretary in Stanley Baldwin's second Conservative Government, sought support for a Britain-France-Germany pact to promote peace on the Rhine frontier. Symon described Chamberlain's speech as clear and earnest with occasional eloquence but 'little magnetism'. He distrusted the effectiveness of the proposed pact. Symon believed it would not be supported by the Dominions and he clearly preferred the counter arguments of Labour's Ramsay McDonald and of his hero Lloyd George.[5] The pact was eventually approved as the Locarno Treaty whereby Germany, France, Britain, Belgium and Italy mutually guaranteed peace in Western Europe. Symon was proved right to be sceptical.

Lenore accompanied her father to a garden party at Buckingham Palace. As Symon explained to the press, he was commanded to attend Buckingham Palace to be presented to the King and the Queen. Symon reported that King George V recounted many episodes from his visits to Australia in 1881 and 1901, and with the dates 'at his finger-tips'. Lenore also accompanied Jo to three separate social functions, hosted respectively by the Duchess of Norfolk, Mrs Benjamin Guinness and Lady Weigall, the wife of the Governor of South Australia. Symon went to a farewell luncheon at the Royal Colonial Institute for Field Marshal Sir William Birdwood, Bt. just prior to his taking the position of Commander-in-Chief in India. In Scotland Sir Charles Lucas and Symon stayed with Sir Everard im Thurn, a former Governor of Fiji, at Cockenzie House in East Lothian. Back in England, Symon spent a weekend at Wallington near Leamington with Viscount St Cyres, the son and heir of the 2nd Earl of Iddesleigh. Jo was especially pleased to attend Oliver's admission to the Bar of the Inner Temple, even though his youngest son intended to practise at the English Bar rather than return to Australia.

'I have had no rest or peace but only worry'

Thus 'rejuvenated' by the company of the 'interesting' and the titled, Symon returned home and issued a Writ through the Supreme Court of South Australia. Dated 23 December 1925 it named Josiah Henry Symon as the plaintiff and Charles James Ballaarat Symon as the defendant. The statement of claim set out the terms of the original partnership of Symon, Browne & Symon of 7 May 1920. The net profits of the firm were divided between four sixths for Josiah Symon and one sixth each for the other two partners. Symon owned everything on the premises, including the law library, and Charles and Browne paid rent for their use. Should his father retire or die, Charles had the option of purchase for £3500 paid in six instalments between three and twenty-six months. In accordance with the partnership agreement, the plaintiff gave one month's notice in writing of his intention to retire on 18 June 1922. Charles agreed on 31 August 1922 to purchase the business for £3500, to pay interest on the final three instalments and to pay the value of the office and its contents. Charles had sacked Carril who had joined the firm in April 1921, Browne subsequently joined another partnership, and Charles moved onto a partnership styled Symon, Mayo, Murray & Cudmore. The statement of claim estimated that Charles owed his father £7185/15/0. which included the £1791/11/11 of the earnings owed to the plaintiff and two sets of interest payments. The claim also sought unspecified damages.[6]

Charles finally responded on 2 April 1928 denying 'each and every allegation' in his father's claim. He was now and was at all times ready to pay the plaintiff much of what he owed 'on the condition that the Plaintiff will account to the Defendant for the income of the Trust fund'. Charles claimed that his father owed him £5274/3/10, the sum received in interest from the money invested for Charles as his share of the wartime Deed Poll of 1916. His father had been released from tax liability by claiming the interest had been paid to Charles – which it had not (it had just been spent on him and his siblings).

The arguments between father and son, conducted by intermediaries, continued until a final settlement in April 1930.[7] Each complained about the methods of the other. Symon objected to his son finding ways of delaying progress – such as taking off for South Africa and being hard to find – and accused him of misrepresenting agreements. On 6 October 1928 Justice Richards[8] struck out paragraphs and sentences of Symon's counterclaim following Charles' complaint that they 'are unnecessary, scandalous and tend to embarrass[,] prejudice and delay the fair trial of the action'. The final settlement involved Charles agreeing to pay his father £1000 and seven per cent interest on what had been owed on 7 March 1929. Both sides agreed to pay their own costs and not to proceed with other actions. If Jo had wanted and needed his original demands to be met he would have been disappointed.

By 1930, he was no longer in personal contact with his eldest son except for accidental encounters at 'Manoah' or in the city. A meeting in the city was now unlikely because Charles had left the law and become a grazier at Mylor in the Adelaide Hills. If Charles needed any further indication of his standing with the family's 'tribal elder', it was brought home on 24 November 1931. On that day he married Margaret Craven, the daughter of Walter and Lily Craven of McLaren Vale. Whereas the engagement notice of June 1931 made no reference to Charles' parents, the reports of the wedding did identify the bridegroom's parents as 'Sir Josiah Symon, KCMG KC and Lady Symon, Upper Sturt'.[9] Jo, however, had no intention of attending the wedding or the reception. No matter what she felt in private, Nell could not, out of loyalty to her husband, be present. The bride's father was also absent, but he was ill. Two of Charles' sisters – probably Lenore and Angel – attended the wedding at St Cuthbert's Church of England in the Adelaide suburb of Prospect and the reception in the South Australian Hotel. If Jo and Walter Craven had attended the reception, they might have conversed on one of the few subjects they had in common: they both owned vineyards. On the surface, Charles and Margaret Symon had even less in common. Charles at age 45 was 18 years older than his wife, and the pair were aeons apart in terms of life experience.

At least Jo and Kilmeny had long rediscovered some of their common ground, and overcame additional political differences. Kilmeny had supported Herbert Morrison, a Labour candidate who won a seat in 1922 on the London County Council. She also supported R.H. Tawney, Labour's Christian Socialist and historian, who almost won Tottenham South in the general election of 15 November 1922. Jo described the election as 'certainly a crushing defeat for Lloyd George and a quite justifiable cause of rejoicing on the part of the Tory party'.[10] He need not have worried

'I have had no rest or peace but only worry'

about Kilmeny's deeper loyalties. The nine-day General Strike in Britain of May 1926 helped to reunite them.

Kilmeny wrote to 'My dear Papa' on 13 May: 'Happily the General Strike is over.' 'I am of course <u>strongly</u> opposed to General Strikes so was <u>firmly</u> supporting the Government tho' I doubt that Baldwin is up to the job.' Oliver had signed on as a special constable, armed himself with a truncheon and a bowler hat and worked on the docks. Oliver later wrote an account of his temporary career which Jo proudly passed on to others, including Sir Charles Lucas. Jo agreed with Kilmeny that 'the behaviour of the British people during the strike was wonderful, and it confirms the view I have always held, that the mass of the people of England are dead against anything revolutionary'. The family, however, was not all of the same mind. Kilmeny reported that her sister, Margaret, 'is an out-and-out Communist by now I think: a pity!' Jo was 'very sorry' to hear that.[11] Irrespective of whether she ever joined the Party, the Symon family continued to regard Margaret, and her sister Mary, as 'communists'.

Margaret had travelled her own road. After her appointment as a Justice of the Peace and leaving Australia for England, she sat on the Bench at Westminster with Cecil Chapman, 'the poor man's lawyer'. She studied and admired the probation system, spoke warmly of arrangements for foster parents and waifs and strays, attended conferences of justices and visited some of His Majesty's prisons. Commissioned by the South Australian Government to enquire into the appointment of women justices in England, Margaret reported that although there was still some resentment about women sitting on the Bench there was no question of the necessity and usefulness of women magistrates. She quoted Miss Margery Fry JP, the noted prison reformer: 'Women do their best work when they are allowed to do it, not as women, but as human beings.' Margaret once represented the Labour Party for election to the St Pancras Borough Council and, though unsuccessful, supporters urged her to re-contest the seat.[12] She returned to Australia in 1928, opened her own progressive nursery school and troubled Jo when she adopted a 15-month old baby girl, Perdita, who attended the school. Perdita grew up referring to 'Mossy' (Margaret) as her mother.[13]

Two events in 1927 took Symon back to his past, a trip he did not find at all agreeable. The first brought him to Canberra for the opening of the new Parliament House on 9 May. Symon always believed he played a key role in the selection of Canberra as the national capital. He kept the blue pencil which he used to record his vote on 6 November 1908 when the Senate voted 19–17 in favour of the Canberra-Yass site over Tumut for the national capital.[14] The Commonwealth Government invited Symon to visit Canberra in November 1926 to see 'whether the wonderfully beautiful natural site, which I had been instrumental in selecting nearly twenty years ago, was being made the most of'. Symon subsequently wrote two long articles, each published in the *Advertiser* and the *Register*.[15]

Symon wrote to Prime Minister Bruce on 7 March 1927 and enclosed copies of the press articles he had also sent to John Butters who chaired the Federal Capital Commission. He told Bruce of being shown 'everything' during the three days. 'Canberra will certainly be one of the finest and most beautiful capital cities the world has ever seen.' Symon later told Lord Novar that this visit to Canberra was 'a very arduous and fatiguing experience' but was of interest to him because 'the final selection of Canberra was mainly due to my influence in the Senate in 1907–8'.[16] Symon pointedly informed Bruce that he, Symon, was the sole living member who held an official position in the Convention. Bruce understood the message. In his reply of 10 March he referred to Symon as the surviving 'Representative leader of the Convention'. Symon responded with two cherished memories of the Convention: it was on his motion at an informal preliminary meeting that Barton was appointed leader, and 'I was the Leader of the State Rights Party, with John Forrest as my doughty lieutenant – although our conception of State Rights seems different from what is understood now'.[17]

Symon was unimpressed by the ceremonies and events surrounding the official opening of Parliament House on 9 May. He told Kilmeny on 16 August that 'the Canberra function was no means a success – It was badly stage-managed'. He blamed Bruce, who 'is not imbued with the history or spirit of Australian Union'. Bruce was probably a schoolboy when 'the great fight took place 30 or 40 years ago' and had not bothered to acquaint himself with what was done. Jo described Bruce as 'a man without imagination or impressive personality and certainly not a magnetic speaker'. Symon was particularly annoyed that 'the few surviving founders of Federation, only some 6 or 7, were practically ignored in the actual ceremonial'. Worse still, the delegates from the other 'dominions' – he cited Canada, South Africa and, curiously, India – were treated in much the same way, even 'humiliated'. 'However, it is all over now. Mama and I were, of course, special guests but with nothing to indicate it except that we were there.'[18]

The other event was the appointment in 1927 of a Royal Commission to 'enquire into and report upon the powers of the Commonwealth under the Constitution and the working of the Constitution since Federation'. The Commission was asked to recommend constitutional changes it considered desirable and to examine and report upon ten specific subjects 'from a constitutional point of view': aviation, company law, health, industrial powers, the Interstate Commission, judicial powers, navigation laws, new States, taxation and trade and commerce. Professor John Peden, the long-serving Dean of Law at the University of Sydney, chaired the Commission. The other six members included three non-Labor parliamentarians, a businessman, and two State Labor MPs. The Federal Labor Party had refused to participate.

Symon regarded the appointment of the Commission as 'a blunder of the first magnitude'. In effect it was 'a roving commission to pick holes, or discover defects, in the Constitution'. The Government had a duty to say what, if anything, needed changing and to initiate the existing procedures for amendment. To act properly and effectively, it should arrange for an elected convention of the people to make recommendations. Even the most ardent federalist, he argued, would not say that the Constitution must remain untouched but Symon issued a conservative's warning. He quoted the 'wise words' from Shakespeare's *King Lear* where the husband of Lear's eldest daughter, Goneril, tells her that 'striving to better, oft we mar what's well'.

Sir Charles Lucas encouraged Symon to give evidence: 'You have firsthand knowledge ... which is shared by very few others now alive in Australia.' Lucas also hoped that by giving evidence Symon would be motivated to resume writing his book.[19] As one of the few members of the Convention still living Symon assumed the role of champion and defender of 'the finest instrument of government ever framed'. His extensive notes in preparation for an interview indicate that Symon worked hard in defining what he saw as the issues and in determining his approach to them. His research included a careful study of the American Constitution. He also examined the statements made by H.S. Nicholas, Counsel for the Commission, and by Sir Robert Garran, the Solicitor-General as well as the Secretary of the Attorney-General's Department.[20]

Symon appeared before the Commission in Adelaide on 1 February 1928 ready to answer questions on the ten specified subjects. He might have left his session feeling disappointed. Although he was given the opportunity to speak in favour of a people's convention should the Commission recommend any revolutionary changes, he had no interest in doing more than recommending a greater use of the referendum option. Symon did manage to talk about what he called 'the original owners of the soil' who have suffered and endured cruelties, ill-treatment and want of care. In a few sentences he argued for the creation for 'an aboriginal State' where 'full-blooded aborigines should follow their own methods of life and live under their own laws and customs and usages'. He also believed that it would be 'a fine thing' if the Commonwealth should undertake care of 'half-castes'.[21]

Symon need not have worried about 'a roving Commission picking holes'. As Geoffrey Sawer observed, proposals for reform 'petered out in the anti-climax of the Royal Commission ... which produced a useful student's textbook and a minor alteration in the *Judiciary Act*.'[22]

Two activities in the post-war decade gave Symon immense pleasure. One was reading and writing but the rate of both slowed down during the late 1920s. Jo told Kilmeny on 8 April 1930 that he was 'struggling to get my article in vindication of the high standard of the Convention and the South Australian Delegation into order for publication'. He had experienced delay because of 'questionable health and particularly by my failing eyesight, which I am afraid is irrecoverable'.[23] Shakespeare's life and work remained a perennial concern and Symon publicised his contacts with Shakespearean scholars in the northern hemisphere. He supported the attempts of Allan Wilkie, the British actor-manager, to promote Shakespeare on the stage, recommending him to Prime Minister Bruce in 1923 for an honour for his efforts 'to uphold and strengthen one of our greatest links of Empire – Shakespeare'.[24] Symon's own literary career culminated in 1929 when he published his three lectures on the

'I have had no rest or peace but only worry'

Bard in a single book entitled *Shakespeare the Englishman*.[25] He added thousands of words to the original versions while echoing his heroes, notably, Sidney Lee and Jean Jusserand, the long-serving French Ambassador to the United States, in expressing worship and admiration of Shakespeare.

Symon paid £219/7/8 to print five hundred copies, twelve of which were leather bound. The book sold for fifteen shillings each, of which Symon estimated his out-of-pocket production costs amounted to ten shillings a copy. It is not known whether this estimate took account of the dozen or more copies sent for review or of the flow of gifts to friends around Australia and in the UK and to institutions such as the State Library of South Australia, the Commonwealth Parliamentary Library, the library of the Royal Empire Society and the Museum and Art Gallery of NSW. The book received enthusiastic reviews in Australia, mostly written by those who happened to be enthusiastic about Symon.[26] Jo told Kilmeny on 3 July 1930 he had collected and printed nine or ten Australian press reviews and placed them in a pamphlet for distribution. He now wanted to introduce the book to British readers 'through some London booksellers of standing and repute'. Jo proposed to send Kilmeny 25 copies which she might place with booksellers, and he would send copies to a publisher/bookseller of his acquaintance. He told his daughter that he was 'not ambitious about it exactly', but he wanted the book 'to take its place amongst the literary output in England'.[27] Symon soon discovered that it was one thing to have an almost second-to-none knowledge of Shakespeare and his English world in Australia; it was another to make a mark in England with a book which added nothing much to local knowledge and did not attempt a re-interpretation of Shakespeare's plays or poetry.

Symon's other activity – distributing some of his largesse – occurred on a much smaller scale than Robert Barr Smith and Langdon Bonython. Nevertheless, Symon handed out many sums in the decade following the Great War. They included the following: £1000 to the University of Sydney for a literary scholarship; the Sir Josiah Symon Scholarship for a pupil of Stirling High School to attend a Scottish university; £1000 to Scotch College, Adelaide, for an English literature scholarship; a stained-glass window and funds to the Stirling Baptist Church in 1927; five guineas to the Moray House Club which was celebrating its Jubilee Year in 1928. In 1930 he sent 'some money' to Laura Symon, the widow of Jo's late brother William and herself now a grandmother.

In a major venture in the 1920s Symon gave the University of Adelaide £10,000 to establish what became the 'Lady Symon Building' which housed the University Women's Club. Symon originally wanted to establish a women's residential college. He had become very interested in women's education, no doubt under pressure from Margaret, Lenore and Kilmeny who regretted their lack of a formal education of the kind provided to four of the boys. Angel and Mary were given opportunities denied to their older sisters who had to settle for governesses. Trips to the art galleries, concert halls and theatres in the United Kingdom and Europe provided some compensation. Symon had come to recognise the need to right the gender balance in education. Nell also pressed him. Why should women not be eligible to apply for Rhodes scholarships? Jo sent Nell a letter from England in 1921 saying he liked her idea of Rhodes Scholarships for women. If he got the chance he would take it to 'useful ears'.[28] Nothing seemed to happen with that idea but Symon pursued his ambition to establish a women's college at the University of Adelaide.

In April 1923 he contacted Sir William Cullen, Chancellor of the University of Sydney, and Sir John McFarlane, the Chancellor of the University of Melbourne; he knew them both but the latter much better.[29] Symon wanted to know what their respective institutions had done or were doing in respect of residential colleges, hostels or halls for women students. In his letters to Cullen and McFarlane, Symon referred to the meeting over which the Bishop of Adelaide had presided and at which he and Prime Minister Bruce were the speakers. Symon moved the resolution that a women's residential college should be established and it received 'much approval and applause'. Symon wanted to know if there was sufficient interest in South Australia and learnt that there was little. Most young women who went to the University of Adelaide enrolled in the Teacher's Training College. The Women's Non-Party Association and the Liberal Women's Union were keen. When a notice was placed at the University seeking the names of interested women, a graduate student was the first to sign. Apparently she was to be 'avoided at all costs'. No names were added.[30]

'I have had no rest or peace but only worry'

Unable to secure support for a residential college Symon agreed that the money should be spent on premises to be used by the University Women Students' Union for a women's club. Sir Josiah Symon laid the foundation stone in October 1927 for the Lady Symon Building which was opened by him on 25 March 1929. The Chancellor, Chief Justice Sir George Murray, and the Vice-Chancellor, Professor Sir William Mitchell, led a group of dignitaries – among them, Dr Helen Mary Mayo, the second female medical graduate from the University, who had strongly supported Symon in his campaign for a women's residential college.

In 1927 Symon gave £1,500 to the Australian Inland Mission to build and establish a nursing home to be called 'The Eleanor Symon Nursing Home' at Innamincka.[31] Sir Sidney Kidman, whose pastoral stations were almost as great in area as the State of Victoria, thanked him on 25 July 1928 because the hospital was 'a great necessity'. Symon purchased the land and had given all the assistance he could to the Rev. John Flynn, the Presbyterian minister who had founded the Australian Inland Mission and the Flying Doctor Service. Symon replied to Kidman on 30 July: 'I have always had a tender spot in my heart and a deep sympathy for those, particularly the women, of the great outback who have in many cases faced the isolation and hardships of the wilderness.' He knew that Kidman had done much himself and was pleased to follow in his footsteps, 'particularly as I always recall with pleasure that many years ago I became for a time a kind of Godfather to some of your family after your mother's death'.[32]

In 1928 Symon told a former Moray House classmate that he had given the land and financed the building of a nursing home for new mothers and their babies, and for expectant mothers. It was named after 'my very great friend' Lady Northcote.[33] Lady Hore-Ruthven, the wife of the Governor of South Australia, formally opened Northcote Home in June 1928. Situated in a coastal suburb about seven miles from Adelaide it offered pleasant views and a relaxed atmosphere. Symon later paid for extensions to the building.

Sir Josiah Symon was a generous man, and by the mid-1920s was sufficiently well-known for his generosity to receive appealing letters from strangers. He sought advice from Langdon Bonython after one approach in June 1926. Bonython assured him he used to receive hundreds of such letters, perhaps innocently saying that Symon was far from the first port of call among the cadgers. Bonython had recently received an appeal from the UK for £100,000. He gave Symon some good advice: do not reply. Symon did make one 'mistake'. He ignored Christ's injunction as reported in St Mathew's Gospel: 'when thou doest alms, let not thy left hand know what thy right hand doeth.' In the 1920s Symon was forever giving friends and even casual contacts the details of his gifts to charitable causes.

Jo was selective when he decided which members of the family constituted a charitable cause. With the Depression under way in 1930, he gave Jim's youngest daughter, Miriam, £1000 of Commonwealth Government Inscribed Stock at six per cent to assist her trip to Australia. As mentioned earlier, he helped Eric, Miriam's elder brother, with substantial gifts during and after the Great War but had to reduce the sums to meet Oscar's soaring expenses. Despite Jo's strong advice to forgo plans for emigrating to South Australia to take up farming, Eric and his wife and family did emigrate. They bought a farm they could afford which was too small and susceptible to drought to be viable. Eric appealed to his uncle for financial help as the Depression added to his distress. Jo felt under no obligation, having warned his nephew against emigration. If Eric ever mentioned previous gifts to his family, or his uncle's advice, he did not feel at all indebted for past acts of generosity when mocking Jo in one of his poems. The final stanza read:

> *It always worked until the time*
> *The firm came down with a crash*
> *We took Josiah out to lunch*
> *And tried to raise the cash*
> *The poor fool said, 'NO' at once*
>   *And now we're in a mess*
> *Because I am the nephew of Josiah Henry S.*[34]

17
'I feel it all as a deep personal grief'

In October 1929, the Bruce-Page Government lost a division by one vote on the Maritime Industries Bill in Committee. If the Speaker, Sir Littleton Groom, had agreed to vote with the Government, the vote would have been tied and the Chairman of Committees could have exercised the casting vote and supported the Government. Groom declined to enter the Chamber on the ground that Westminster traditions required the Speaker to remain impartial. Symon sent him a telegram on 17 October expressing 'admiration and sympathy' for his actions which accorded with the 'best traditions' of the speakership. Littleton Groom said he preferred defeat to ending 'a career of service to the nation by an act of dishonour'. The Government obtained a dissolution of the House of Representatives and James Scullin led Labor to a sweeping victory in the election of 12 October 1929. Bruce lost his own seat in the Labor landslide. Groom lost Nationalist Party endorsement and the seat of Darling Downs he had held since 1901.[1]

Symon was not unduly troubled by the arrival of a Labor government. He had long been critical of Bruce's policy of heavy borrowing to finance development and sympathised with Scullin who had taken power just as Australia was entering the Great Depression. Lady Novar was perhaps unaware of Symon's negative view of Bruce when she commiserated with him on the Government's defeat. Referring to the electoral hiding of Baldwin's Conservative Government in May 1929, she remarked that Australia had followed 'our bad example' and returned 'a Socialist Government with two Irishmen at its head'.[2]

For Symon, worrying signs came soon enough. Speaking in Condobolin, NSW, on 8 January 1930, Arthur Blakeley, Minister for Home Affairs and the Territories, said that a referendum would probably be held later in the year seeking power to abolish State parliaments. If the people adopted the proposal the federal parliament would have complete control of national affairs leaving the administration of local matters to shires, municipalities and provinces.

Symon declared the proposal 'unpractical, revolutionary, and unnecessary'. Blakeley's ideas rested upon an entire misconception of the Constitution which placed definite limits on the powers of the Commonwealth. The rights of the States as then existing should be maintained, except for powers transferred to the Federal Government. 'I am confident', Symon said, 'that the people of Australia would not have accepted the Constitution on any other footing'. He could accept some changes. Symon thought one of the two State chambers should be abolished; and a party which won government in a general election 'should have the power to introduce and carry legislation which will give its policy the force of law'. Symon also opposed the notion that State Governors should be appointed from Britain. Local citizens could equally exercise the duties. Nevertheless, he did not support making changes to the appointment of a Governor-General. As for Blakeley, he 'should pack his fantastic schemes of unification in his old kitbag, with any other political troubles, and go home smiling'.[3]

Symon might abruptly dismiss Blakeley but knew he must remain on guard in defending what was achieved in 1897–1900. He emphatically opposed unification and the abolition of State parliaments. The so-called 'thorough conservative' described the South Australian Legislative Council as 'a costly and useless encumbrance',[4] and repeated his call for the abolition of all State upper houses and for the principle that elected governments should be free to implement their programs. He might, of course, have to adjust his thinking if those programs included policies he found abhorrent – as he did about appeals to the Privy Council after the High Court changed direction on constitutional interpretation in the *Engineers Case*. On two other matters, however, he was immovable: the integrity of the federation and the role of the monarch in the Australian Constitution. He had two additional obligations: one, reinforced by the Great War, to maintain Australia's place and status within the framework of King and Empire as accepted by the Australian Constitution; and the

'I feel it all as a deep personal grief'

other, to stand by the Australia as federated in 1901 in opposition to the secessionist movement in Western Australia.

Western Australia presented a threat in 1930–35 as internal opposition mounted to continued participation in the federation. The secessionist movement and its ultimate failure is not of prime concern here but it is relevant that Symon's decline in health did not prevent him from taking a role in opposing it. On 13 August 1930, the *Advertiser* published his response to a letter that Sir James Mitchell, the Premier of Western Australia and leader of the Nationalist-Country coalition, had published in the London *Times*. Mitchell argued that his State had suffered for joining the federation and Symon countered that while the smaller States had fared poorly this in itself was no argument for secession.[5] Symon said he wrote as one of the few survivors of the Convention where he led 'the States' Rights party'. The States were supposed to be protected by the Senate which had been turned into a party House. Symon's letter was then either reproduced or summarised in the country papers throughout Australia.

Within a few months Symon felt bound to enter the fight to protect the existing practice of appointing Governors-General. Sir Adrian Knox resigned as Chief Justice on 30 March 1930 upon learning he was a residuary legatee of his friend John Brown, the 'coal baron', shipowner and horse breeder. Three days later, Sir Isaac Isaacs was appointed Chief Justice. Symon telegraphed his warm congratulations. Isaacs replied: 'Sincere thanks for kind message greatly appreciated.'[6] Various Australian newspapers carried a story on 23 and 24 April 1930 that the Scullin Government intended to recommend Isaacs' appointment as Governor-General to succeed Lord Stonehaven, whose term of office expired in December 1930. Conservative newspapers,[7] the Australian Women's National League and the Australian branches of the Royal Empire Society expressed anger or dismay. They claimed that an Australian appointee was bound to be partisan, that the King would be insulted by having a candidate thrust upon him and that ties with the Empire would be threatened. John Latham, who had succeeded Bruce as Leader of the Nationalists, spoke out against 'this gratuitously unfriendly gesture'. Isaacs' appointment would 'sever an important link with what the great majority of Australians are still proud to call "the Mother Country"'.

Latham observed that the 1926 Imperial Conference defined the position of Governor-General as representative of the King, and not of any government, British or Dominion.[8]

Scullin rebuked Latham.[9] The Prime Minister said it was regrettable that rumours about a possible successor to Lord Stonehaven should become an excuse for public controversy. Moreover, the 'bandying of names and stirring up of party passions were disrespectful to whoever might be offered the appointment to the high office of Governor-General'. Scullin wondered about Latham's 'weird conception of Empire' when a suggestion about appointing an Australian to the high office meant for him 'a weakening of the Empire'. Symon added his own comment to this last point: 'Nobody says anything so absurd.'[10]

Sir Josiah Symon rose to Latham's defence. On 25 April he sent him a long telegram strongly supporting his denunciation of what Symon called the Government's 'humiliating' and 'grotesque' proposals regarding the appointment of a Governor-General. The Government's position was 'opposed to the letter and spirit of [the] Constitution' and should first have been submitted to Parliament and, if approved, sent to the people in a referendum. He also considered that the proposal was 'lacking in courtesy to His Majesty and the Imperial Government' because neither the King nor his advisers had the opportunity to express dissent. The telegram concluded: 'Will do utmost personally and as President of [the] Adelaide Branch Royal Empire Society in protest and opposition.' Latham telegraphed his reply, saying he 'greatly appreciated' Symon's stand, adding that the Government wanted to establish a new system without engaging in any discussion.[11]

The Prime Minister's comments on Latham's objections did not bury the controversy. Loyalist organisations in Victoria formed the Council of Combined Empire Societies in May 1930.[12] Symon stayed busy, though out of sight. In July he met W.H. Irvine in Adelaide. Irvine, a former colleague in the Federal Parliament, had been Attorney-General in Victoria and Victorian Premier prior to his election to the House of Representatives in 1906 as an Anti-Socialist. Irvine supported the Fusion, served as Attorney-General in the Cook Ministry, and soon after his re-election in 1917 accepted appointment as Chief Justice of the Victorian Supreme Court. Symon considered that Irvine's arrival in Adelaide 'deserves

'I feel it all as a deep personal grief'

to be included in the catalogue of angels' visits'.[13] The two men began corresponding on imperial and domestic political questions. Latham's trip to Adelaide in September had a similar outcome.

The story of Scullin's efforts to appoint Isaacs Governor-General has been told in several places.[14] Although the Federal Labor Party began falling apart in 1930 Scullin felt emboldened to take on a very reluctant King George V because of his party's almost unanimous commitment to appointing an Australian Governor-General. There were several outstanding issues: who should advise the King, should the advice offer him a choice of names, was the appointee primarily his representative or should he be the one acceptable to the relevant Dominion government? The Imperial Conference of 1926 had ruled out a role for British ministers in making the choice while leaving open the question of whether a Dominion government was entitled to recommend several names or just one. Prime Minister Scullin held out for Isaacs and refused to budge. The King would like to have appointed Birdwood and was reluctant to appoint Isaacs on the ground he did not know him. Prompted by Baron Stamfordham, the King's Principal Secretary, the King relented and agreed to appoint Isaacs. Instead of the traditional formula for an announcement in the Government Gazette beginning 'the King is pleased to appoint', the announcement of Isaacs' appointment was sent to Australia House in the following form: 'The King on the recommendation of Mr. Scullin had appointed Sir Isaac Isaacs to be Governor-General.' George V had made his displeasure very clear.

The press in Australia reported the Isaacs appointment on 3 December 1930. Latham spoke in the House of Representatives two days later. He pointed out that this method of appointment made the Governor-General the nominee of the Government of the day and not the personal representative of the King. He claimed that this method 'would tend to diminish the prestige of the Governor-General' and 'goes far to diminish the reality of the bond of empire which resides in the Crown'. His additional point was that judges, appointed to interpret the Constitution, should have nothing to hope for or fear from the Government. The promotion of the Chief Justice had infringed that principle. If judges could now look to further promotion there would be suspicion about their decisions which favoured the Government. Latham stressed that his criticisms related to the method of appointment and not to the individual appointed.

Symon sent Latham a letter on 12 December for his 'most able, indeed a noble and incisive criticism of what has happened'. He added his own point. The *Times Weekly* intimated that as long ago as 1 May Scullin had offered the post to Isaacs. If the report was accurate then, before consulting the King, 'Scullin had been trafficking with Isaacs and *vice versa* for the submission of the latter's name to the Sovereign for the appointment'. Scullin and Isaacs had never denied the paper's intimation. Instead, Scullin evaded the issue by switching to his 'weird notion' point. If such an offer had been made 'any Judge of right principle' would have spurned it. Instead the Chief Justice 'made himself a party to gaining what no doubt he regarded as a prize or reward from the Government under whom he holds his judicial office'.[15]

On the day he congratulated Latham, Symon published a letter in the *Advertiser*, the first of five he later reprinted and sent to friends and contacts throughout Australia and the United Kingdom. In his letter of 12 December he argued that Scullin had no authority 'to override or invite the King to set at naught' the Australian Constitution. He cited Clause 3 which stipulated that the Queen and her heirs and successors 'may appoint a Governor-General for the Commonwealth'. Neither Scullin nor the King could repeal or qualify that provision. The people alone could alter it and they had not been consulted or given their consent to Scullin's action which had placed the appointment of a Governor-General 'within the whirlpool of party politics'. Every 'sane person' would regard that as 'lamentable'.

Latham replied to Symon's personal letter on 16 December. He had found it difficult dealing with the issue for fear of misunderstanding and misrepresentation. Latham was nonetheless pleased that Symon thought his statement 'satisfactory'. He felt that the present Government 'has weakened every tie that binds us to the Mother Country and that holds the Empire together, and that it is also making Australia unpopular throughout the world'. (Latham's definition of 'the world' was obviously narrow; it is hard to imagine the people of Uganda being unduly disturbed.)[16]

Symon published his second letter in the *Advertiser* of 17 December. He repeated his opposition to Scullin's actions but now switched his focus

'I feel it all as a deep personal grief'

to an argument closer to one of his long-term objectives and to Latham's additional point. Symon had always believed in the absolute separation of executive and judicial functions, and held that view over and above his specific objections to the ubiquitous late Chief Justice Way. Hence he supported clause 8 of the *Judiciary Act 1903–1910*: 'A justice of the High Court shall not be capable of accepting or holding any other office or any other place or profit within the Commonwealth, except any such judicial office as may be conferred by or under any law of the Commonwealth.'

According to Symon, Isaacs should have informed the Prime Minister that he was ineligible to accept the offer of appointment as Governor-General. He knew of the prohibition having moved the amendment in the House of Representatives which eventually became clause 8 of the *Judiciary Act*. After Isaacs introduced his amendment another Victorian said it would almost amount to an infringement of 'the spirit of the Constitution' if the Chief Justice should at any time become the Acting Governor-General. In the Senate Symon had successfully moved a further amendment to preclude any judge of the High Court from occupying an executive position such as the Acting Governor-General. The House of Representatives, of which Isaacs was still a member, accepted the amendment. In his letter Symon noted how the future Justice O'Connor of the High Court was unequivocal in supporting Symon's position. Symon concluded his letter with a quotation from the 5th Duke of Newcastle, the Colonial Secretary, who in 1862 sent the following advice to the Governor of South Australia: 'To separate the functions of a Judge from those of a Governor is one of the first precautions which society adopts in order to secure itself from injustice, when it becomes capable of political and judicial organisation.'

Convinced that clause 8 would bar the Isaacs appointment Symon wanted his letter published outside of Adelaide. Dr E.S. Cunningham, the legendary editor of the Melbourne *Argus*, agreed to publish it. The *Argus* gave the letter considerable prominence on 18 December and Symon's reliable friend the *Barrier Times* of Broken Hill did the same two days later. The main newspapers in the other States either ignored it or preferred to publish critical replies to a letter they reduced to one or two sentences.

Symon's Melbourne friends rallied in support. Brudenell White wrote on 18 December on Melbourne Club notepaper to congratulate him on the letter which appeared in the *Argus*. The 'fateful deed' had been done, but Symon's words 'will strengthen the right minded and bring nearer the day of the adjustment of such affairs'. Symon's letters had been 'most favourably discussed in business circles here today'. Irvine also wrote to Symon on 18 December telling him that his two letters,

> must, coming from you, carry great weight, and, though the immediate mischief has been already done, will go far towards forming a sound public opinion on these vital constitutional matters. Your letters not only carry the authority of one of those who took a foremost part in framing our Constitution but they are a very eloquent appeal to the deep seated loyalty which, I am convinced, will again assert its power when all this froth that is born of rebellion and weak sentimentalism has been blown away.[17]

Meanwhile, despite his very limited contact with public opinion, Symon felt he could tell Lord Novar in a letter on 17 December that 'the people of Australia are still agitated by the extraordinary proceedings' regarding the selection of Isaacs as Governor-General. He spoke even more authoritatively in writing to Sir Edward Wallington on the following day:

> The people of Australia – except the political Labour Party – have been seething with disapproval and resentment because of Scullin's unconstitutional actions and procedure … the feeling of resentment is intense because the mass of the people regard what has happened as a discourtesy, in fact, an affront to the King and the bitterness against Scullin is deepening amongst all well-informed people.

Symon did not have to tell Wallington what he might do with this information. Sure enough, Wallington told Symon in reply that he had taken the letter to the King at Sandringham House.[18]

The *Advertiser* published several responses to Symon's second letter. An Adelaide 'leading counsel' argued that clause 8 did not debar a judge from becoming Governor-General, provided he resigned his judicial office before taking the position. Sir William Harrison Moore, Emeritus Professor of Law at the University of Melbourne, made the same point, as did James Fenton, the Acting Prime Minister (Scullin was still overseas).[19] Symon

'I feel it all as a deep personal grief'

responded to these comments in his third letter which the *Advertiser* published on 22 December. He dismissed these 'opinions' as 'not so much narrow as shallow', mere quibbles which evaded his 'grave and serious point'. Symon listed statements by prominent individuals as well as newspaper reports referring to Isaacs' 'appointment'. That is, Isaacs had accepted the 'appointment' while he was Chief Justice of the High Court. Clause 8, Symon wrote, should be 'printed in letters of gold, enacting, as it does, one of the fundamental principles of the Constitution, framed to secure the complete separation of the judicial from the executive'.

Symon felt he needed to make one more point to secure his argument that Isaacs had violated clause 8 of the *Judiciary Act*. In his fourth letter, published by the *Advertiser* on 24 December, he looked at the process which had taken place. Scullin offered Isaacs the appointment as long ago as 1 May; Isaacs left Scullin with the impression that he was agreeable; Scullin then gave the King no choice and, as Isaacs' friend and agent, accepted the King's commission on Isaacs' behalf; Scullin's receipt and possession of the commission 'were in law receipt and possession by Sir Isaac and conclusive of his appointment to and acceptance of the office'. At the moment, therefore, Isaacs occupied two offices but could not perform the duties of a Governor-General because he could not swear himself in and take the oath because he had infringed clause 8 of the *Judiciary Act*.

At a personal level, Symon felt shattered. He told Irvine on 24 December that 'I feel it all as a deep personal grief'. Symon wrote to Mrs George Chirnside on the same day: 'The situation is critical and most dangerous and it fills me with grief as one who was and is proud of the part he took in the establishment of this great free Commonwealth under the British Crown.'[20] At the same time, he entered the Christmas period feeling confident about his case. Symon soon learned, however, that some presumed allies did not regard clause 8 as their chief weapon; worse still, some of them had abandoned the battle.

He discovered that Latham was not altogether 'reliable'. Latham wrote to him on 24 December.[21] He agreed that anyone who holds office as a justice of the High Court 'is incapable of being appointed to the position of Governor General'. Yet Latham thought any difficulty arising out of the King having made such an appointment could be 'evaded' by making a new appointment after Isaacs' resignation from his office on the High Court. He further thought it would be 'interesting to see what the Government will do in the matter'.

Symon replied to Latham on 30 December. He did not believe that the King would lend himself to 'such trickery'. To appoint Isaacs anew as Governor-General 'would be too tragically disgraceful'. Nor did he think the King would 'condone a breach of a fundamental law of the Constitution. It would be too flagrant a blot.' A resignation from the High Court, taken after his appointment as Governor-General with the intention of either 'patching up or reappointing would certainly be playing fast and loose with the situation and be an indelible stain on Australia and on the exercise of the Royal Prerogative'. Yet Symon believed that 'Scullin, Isaacs and their friends will stick at nothing and we can only wait and see what they attempt'. Symon's own proposal was to take proceedings to the High Court where, presumably, Isaacs and the new Labor judges[22] would not sit on this issue. The Court could then declare the appointment of Isaacs null and void under clause 8. 'That would probably make them think and might be otherwise effective.' Importantly, the High Court must deal with a situation which required judicial attention.

On 31 December, Symon wrote another letter to Latham. He was now more strongly of the view that 'the evasion' Latham feared 'is not possible'. An infringement of clause 8 cannot be remedied because the disqualification is complete. No resignation with the object of 'whitewashing Sir Isaac' could restore the *status quo ante*. The King was now '*functus officio*' (he had no further official authority) and cannot make another appointment unless the present appointment was declared vacant or void. The maxim – 'the King can do no wrong' – merely means he is not personally responsible. Ministers are responsible and ministers also countersign such orders or appointments made by the King. Symon wondered whether Scullin had countersigned and was acting as Isaacs' friend or agent. His 'strong opinion' was that the whole question should go before the High Court to determine whether the appointment followed constitutional and invariable usage and method, whether it was *ab initio* unconstitutional and invalid. Scullin had issued a statement in London saying the King, on Scullin's recommendation, had appointed Sir Isaac Isaacs as Governor-General. In Symon's view, the appointment was really Scullin's, made in concert with Isaacs before he went to England. Importantly, the appointment was not the King's, for which Scullin and his ministers were responsible. Symon specifically noted the words: 'The King on the recommendation of Mr. Scullin had appointed Sir Isaac Isaacs to be Governor General.'

Symon said he was sorry to trouble Latham any further but emphasised that the High Court was the 'only constitutional resort' available and no time should be lost in getting proceedings before that tribunal. 'Nothing less will satisfy the thinking people of this country' unless Isaacs should retire from the post and the process could start again. 'I cannot believe that the King would reappoint him especially if there were strong popular representations against such a course from here.'[23]

Initially, Symon was delighted when the Combined Empire Societies briefed two senior Melbourne barristers – Sir Edward Mitchell, KC and Wilfred Fullagar[24] – for an 'opinion' of the Isaacs appointment. He also liked the line they took. Mitchell argued that Australian ministers had no power or authority to advise the King and therefore Isaacs' appointment was unconstitutional and invalid. Fullagar separately said if it could be shown that a British minister had advised the Crown to make the appointment then, and only then, would the appointment be constitutional and valid.[25]

Symon telegraphed Mitchell on 10 January after reading the Mitchell-Fullagar opinion: he entirely concurred. He sent a letter the same day rejoicing 'in its clear and definite terms', and adding that the issues to be examined included the questions raised in his own letters about the effect of clause 8. Symon approved of the idea of Isaacs consenting to friendly proceedings before the High Court, 'the interpreter and guardian of the Constitution'. It was 'unthinkable' for Isaacs to be sworn in before these issues were settled. In constitutional matters 'there is no necessity for any hostility and unfriendliness'. Unless this position was maintained Scullin and his Government would adopt the attitude that the whole matter was about the 'spite' of their political opponents and would attempt to 'bullock' the thing through.

Symon telegraphed Mitchell again on 12 January saying he understood there might be an attempt to evade disqualification under clause 8 by

Isaacs resigning and then seeking a fresh appointment by the King. It was critical to 'checkmate this by issuing and serving process before resignation'. Symon also sent Mitchell a letter on 12 January in which he noted the press references of the day revealing that 'the Scullin-Isaacs set are quaking in their shoes'. Symon called their decision to postpone the swearing-in an admission there is 'something rotten in the State of Denmark'. Symon thought it critical to frustrate any attempt to evade the consequences of an invalid appointment. He saw two options: serve a process by 15 January 1931, the date according to the press when Isaacs would submit his resignation, or arrange with the Government or with Isaacs to postpone the resignation and the swearing-in until there was a determination on his incapacity or otherwise for appointment as Governor-General. Above all,

> [t]he purity of the Constitution must be maintained and every attempt made to escape from or get round its obligations must be nipped in the bud. Forgive my troubling you but as loyal subjects of the King and free citizens of the Empire we are all interested. Our rights as well as our reputation are in jeopardy.[26]

Mitchell replied by hand on Australian Club notepaper in Melbourne on 14 January.[27] He explained he was acting as counsel and therefore was unable to do anything on matters where his clients had not sought advice. He and Isaacs 'did an immense amount of successful work at the Bar together – and I have always been on friendly terms with him' – although Mitchell was critical of some 'disastrous' judgements on constitutional matters. He agreed with everything Symon said on upholding the Constitution, and Mitchell had done what he could by publishing articles.

Symon was plainly unhappy about Mitchell's approach. He wrote an urgent letter to him on 19 January.[28] Like Mitchell, Symon had 'always been on good terms' with Isaacs ever since they had met in Adelaide when Isaacs was on his honeymoon and attended a case where Symon was engaged as counsel for the plaintiff. Isaacs had also been a member of the Convention, 'though perhaps not popular', but was not on the Judicial Committee of which Symon was chairman. 'Personal considerations', however, should not affect 'the grave constitutional issues now disturbing the people of Australia'. There was a serious question relating to the validity of the

'I feel it all as a deep personal grief'

appointment. Was the arrangement with Scullin justified under 'our own democratic Constitution? Was it in accordance with the methods and principles the King must follow in making such an appointment? And there was the question of clause 8. Isaacs was incapable of accepting the office and was now disqualified from being sworn in.

> It seems to me as vital and important and as profoundly affecting the validity of the appointment as the constitutional points you so ably deal with. It would indeed be a very sad thing if the great purpose of Clause 8 in not only securing the purity of the Bench and the spotless reputation of its judges were to be lightly treated. It would be lamentable to weaken or whittle away the lofty motive of that Clause with which or its effect neither the King nor his Imperial Ministers are concerned.

He recognised that counsel's opinion was usually given on the basis of the precise questions submitted. Yet Symon thought it fair for those acting for the Combined Empire Societies to have their attention drawn to clause 8 as being 'of equal importance with those you have so ably dealt with'. The validity of Isaacs taking office cannot be determined without considering the effect of clause 8 and the provisions cannot be ignored. 'Forgive my offering these respectful submissions but as one of the Founders of Federation and framers of the Constitution I feel that the appointment of Isaacs will be a permanent blot upon it and our reputation as a free and self-governing people.'

Mitchell wrote to Symon on 20 January after meeting representatives of the Combined Empire Societies and the Citizens' Defence League. He thought their application must fail.[29] Mitchell agreed with Symon about the effect of clause 8 though not on the suggested procedure. Until Mitchell saw the terms of the Isaacs appointment he could not give definite advice but could now be certain on one point. Whether the appointment of Isaacs was valid or not, without a change in the Constitution the federal ministry 'cannot lawfully act as the proper responsible advisers to His Majesty as to the appointment of a Governor-General'. If, after seeing the terms of appointment, Mitchell still thought it wrong in law he would give advice on possible action. Mitchell included a paragraph 'in strict confidence'. He had advice from a reliable source about the communists in Melbourne and more so in Sydney and probably Adelaide planning organised violence. As a result, civilians in Melbourne were taking urgent action to deal with threatened attacks on vital services.

Mitchell had just written the above when Symon's letter of 19 January arrived. Mitchell agreed about the importance of the issue. He observed that the Commonwealth was the most frequent litigant before the High Court and every justice would be aware the Government could offer a £10,000 a year gift if a vacancy in Yarralumla should occur. The people will not give the justices credit for being superhuman. He was nonetheless obliged to Symon for making him appreciate the importance of clause 8, apart from his own view about 'the probable difficulty of curing it so as to avoid its illegality'. Nonetheless, he now thought there were more important issues than changes in the appointment of Governors-General under the Constitution, namely, the actions of outside bodies in fettering or coercing actions of MPs and ministers.

Events had overtaken Symon. Sir Isaac Isaacs was sworn in on 22 January 1931 in the Legislative Council Chamber of the Victorian Parliament. Latham was in attendance. So were many former Deakinite liberals who had served with Isaacs in the House of Representatives. Sir Josiah and Lady Symon were not present. They had received an invitation but declined to attend.

Symon and Mitchell continued to write to each other with arguments about abstruse subjects such as 'the King can do no wrong' and the relationship between the Royal prerogative and statutory law. Symon now wanted to argue that the effect of clause 8 was to prevent a judge from taking any appointment other than a judicial one. Reading and re-reading the clause easily lent itself to such an interpretation. In any case, a resignation before the swearing-in 'does not get rid of his initial incapacity by law to accept or hold the office'. When the press told the Prime Minister of Symon's view, Scullin replied that Isaacs presumably knew as much about the Constitution as Symon did. If that was so, Isaacs ought to have known better than to lead Scullin into 'this mess'. Unfortunately, for Symon, 'the people of Australia' or even the 'right-thinking' ones seemed unaware of 'this mess' or were simply not bothered about it.[30]

Symon received some consolation in the form of Wallington's letter on Buckingham Palace notepaper sent to him on 20 January 1931. Wallington

'I feel it all as a deep personal grief'

thanked him for the first two letters published in the *Advertiser*. He was forwarding them to Sandringham for submission to the King. 'I have had many talks with His Majesty on this subject, and fully realise that Scullin has acted in a most indecent and unconstitutional manner.'[31]

It was sometimes difficult to persuade some supporters to focus on the main issue. Former Senator Thomas Glassey, a Presbyterian, sent Symon a 'VERY VERY PRIVATE' letter on 20 March.[32] While he placed Symon on a high pedestal 'as a big and great lawyer and a far seeing Statesman', Glassey did not think he had grasped the real meaning of Isaacs' appointment. Glassey thought the 'real originator of the scheme is that keen scholarly Anti-Britisher Arch[bishop Mannix]'. The section of the population led by this 'clever person' want to weaken the British Empire, and their first step in destroying its liberty was to appoint Isaacs.

Symon wrote again to Wallington on 7 May to say public opinion 'is overwhelming against Scullin and Isaacs particularly the latter' over the appointment to Governor-General. Symon now saw it as 'a conspiracy', with Isaacs as the 'chief instigator'. He never identified what the 'conspiracy' was about, and it is hard to imagine that Symon had slipped so far from reality to espy a 'Jewish plot' or envisaged Isaacs aligning himself with Mannix. Perhaps the 'conspiracy' was aimed at the King's prerogative? Whatever the aim, Symon now had another approach. He prepared a motion for a South Australian senator to enable the Senate to register a protest.

> The Senate desires to place on record its deep regret disapproval and protest against the unconstitutional and irregular methods and proceedings adopted by the Prime Minister Mr. Scullin in bringing about the appointment of the Right Hon. Sir Isaac Isaacs to the Governor-Generalship of the Commonwealth and without the authority or consent of the people of Australia or their Parliament or the States or their Parliaments and in violation of Clause 8 of the Judiciary Act – a law of the Commonwealth.[33]

Symon told Wallington he was not optimistic there would even be a vote on the issue. He was right. The Government and the Parliament were too absorbed with the consequences of the Great Depression.[34]

Sir Edward Wallington was well informed about the political situation in Australia in 1931. Two wings of the Labor Party left its caucus. One led by Joseph Lyons joined the Nationalists and Independents to form the United Australia Party (UAP) and Lyons replaced Latham as Leader of the Opposition. The other wing voted with the Opposition when Scullin lost a vote in the House of Representatives and obtained a dissolution. Wallington wrote to Symon on 30 November: 'I sincerely trust that the forthcoming election may result in the defeat of Scullin's government.'[35] Wallington (and probably the King) would have been pleased with the result on 19 December. Joseph Lyons and the UAP were swept into power. Bruce regained his seat of Flinders and Symon sent him a message of congratulations.

In February 1932, Bruce, Pearce, Gullett and Charles Hawker refused to attend the Governor-General's customary dinner on the opening of the new Parliament. They disapproved of 'the irregular method of his appointment'. Symon passed this information on to Lord Novar on 24 February 1932. He wished something of this kind had been done sooner and he hoped that now 'by proper and constitutional steps Isaacs will be recalled and the old and time-honoured method of appointment will be restored'. Symon sent letters congratulating Gullett, Pearce and Hawker on their stand, telling each man he would be more pleased if constitutional steps were taken to have the appointment recalled and a new appointment made in the customary way. He received no more than promising replies.[36]

Symon was not finished. When Latham, the Minister for External Affairs, was on his way to Geneva in February 1932 Symon suggested that he might have an opportunity to ascertain 'the view of men of light and leading in England as to the unholy circumstances and methods of appointment of our present Governor[-]General who should I think be recalled and the old and constitutional order flouted by Scullin and his government be restored'.[37] Sir Josiah Symon often refused to move on from a dead political issue.

He received his last rebuff when Western Australia voted for secession in April 1933. In no physical state to enter the campaign Symon exchanged letters and telegrams with Lyons, Latham, Hughes and Pearce in the lead-up to the vote. He asked Hughes to pass on his 'love' to the miners with whom he had fought for federation against Perth and the seaboard.

'I feel it all as a deep personal grief'

He sent a letter to the Chairman of the Federal League in Perth addressed to 'my Friends the Men and Women of Western Australia' warning that they were 'threatened with great humiliation and disaster at the hands of certain unthinking and misguided fellow-citizens'. If Western Australian senators had failed their State 'it is good reason for calling them to account but not for bringing about a revolution in this country'. This letter was published in the *West Australian* on 1 March 1933.[38] Sixty-six per cent of the electorate voted for secession on 8 April, yet on the same day replaced the pro-secession Mitchell Government with the anti-secessionist Labor Opposition. Symon was not all gloom. As he had told Pearce, the union would not be dissolved or even impaired by a majority secession vote. The secession movement itself drifted away after Symon's death in 1934 when the Imperial Parliament decided it could not intervene, and disappeared soon afterwards. It did not revive until 40 years after Symon's death.

18

'scandalous, offensive and defamatory'

Sir Isaac Isaacs' only sister died on 12 December 1933. Sir Josiah Symon sent a letter of condolence to the Governor-General at Yarralumla who warmly thanked him: 'Such a letter helps greatly.' In his reply Isaacs noted there were just four of them left from the Convention, but he had heard from others all were 'in good condition'.[1]

Symon's correspondence slowed down in the early months of 1934. There was no let-up, however, in Symon's approach to the issues which mattered to him. He exchanged views with Frederic Eggleston over constitutional change, saying 'we [at the Convention] provided amply for all amendments and alterations as occasion arose'. Symon told Eggleston that Parliament could provide the States with larger grants and that South Australia's great financial disability stemmed in part from the Commonwealth's failure to honour its agreement to finish the North-South railway 'within a reasonable time'. Completing it would help relieve unemployment.[2]

As English friends kept writing to him, Symon dictated letters in response. He maintained regular contact with Pam Lister in Stratford on Shakespearean subjects, a contact lasting more than two decades. Symon had grown very fond of L.S. Amery, the former Colonial and Dominions Secretary, who shared his enthusiasm for Empire, naval defence and Sir Charles Lucas. Both were saddened by Lucas's death in May 1931 and Symon contributed to the cost of the bust of Sir Charles placed in the Colonial Office. Symon told Amery in February 1934 that Prince George (the future King George VI) would be welcome when he arrived for the celebrations of 150 years since 1788, 'though many of us think it is a matter

'scandalous, offensive and defamatory'

of regret that the Earl and Countess of Athlone were not chosen'. He was more enthusiastic about Prince George in a letter he sent later to Lady Novar: 'All Australia is looking forward to the arrival of Prince George'. He nevertheless added his personal regrets about the non-selection of Earl and Countess of Athlone.[3]

In mid-March 1934, the Upper Sturt locality endured fearsome bushfires, possibly wilfully lit. More than 400 firefighters fought the blazes which at one stage threatened 'Manoah' and the Upper Sturt school and post office.[4] Sir Josiah Symon was safe throughout the crisis as he lay seriously ill in his Buxton Street home with an enlarged prostate and chronic thrombosis. Lenore cared for him. His condition steadily deteriorated until he died at around 7.45 am on Thursday 29 March 1934. He was aged 87 and had outlived all seven of his siblings and all the other South Australians who attended the 1897–8 Federal Convention. He was survived by his wife of just over 50 years and ten of their children.

The next day, Symon was cremated according to his wishes. Canon Slaney Poole, Symon's longest-standing friend in South Australia, officiated. The Commonwealth Government offered the family a state funeral which took place on Tuesday afternoon 3 April. A procession, 'more than a mile long',[5] formed outside Symon's home in Buxton Street and proceeded to St Peter's Cathedral. Lieutenant-Commander (ret.) Oliver Symon, the youngest of the five sons, carried the urn containing Symon's ashes into the Cathedral attended by the pall bearers: Sir George Murray, the Chief Justice, Sir William Mitchell, the Vice Chancellor of the University of Adelaide, Sir Henry Newland, Adelaide's senior surgeon, and Sir Walter Young, a businessman and adviser to the State and Federal Governments. The Dean of Adelaide and the Precentor of the Cathedral led a short service. The choir sang the 23rd Psalm, followed by a lesson, a prayer and a hymn – Frederick William Faber's 1854 creation 'Pilgrims of the Night' – whose opening line, 'Hark, hark, angelic songs are swelling', prefaced the hope of the final stanza and the refrain:

> *Angels sing on, your faithful watches keeping.*
> *sing us sweet fragments of the songs above,*
> *till morning's joy shall end the night of weeping,*
> *and life's long shadows break in cloudless love.*

Sir Josiah Symon KCMG KC

Refrain
Angels of Jesus, angels of light
Singing to welcome the pilgrims of the night!

The Free Church of Scotland and the Baptist past were not directly represented but there was an ecumenical presence. Father Faber had been born into a strict Calvinist and Huguenot family. Ordained as an Anglican priest, he followed John Henry Newman into the Catholic Church taking with him the tradition of community singing and the hymns of Charles Wesley which influenced his own compositions.

After the service, the cortege proceeded to the North Road Cemetery where Canon Poole conducted the burial service. Prominent citizens from politics, business, education, the services, the law and the fourth estate, as well as personal friends, joined the procession. Representatives of the Governor-General, the State Governor, the Prime Minister and the President of the Senate were among those carrying entrance cards to the enclosure at the cemetery. In addition to Oliver, members of the immediate family – Margaret, Charles, Oscar, Angel and Mary – were among the chief mourners. Lenore and Kilmeny were probably looking after Nell while Romilly's disability excluded him from public occasions. Carril was absent from Adelaide though he did organise a wreath of rowan berries and yew, the emblem of Clan Fraser to which his father had belonged through membership of a junior branch. The Governor-General, the Chief Justice, the Council and the various unions of the University, Minda Home, Northcote Home, the Royal Empire Society, the Justices' Association, Scotch College and the Auldana Vineyard all contributed wreaths.[6] Symon's ashes were interred in a plot already occupied by the remains of the two babies who died soon after their birth and would later accommodate the remains of Lenore and Carril.

Most South Australian newspapers reported the fact of Symon's death, offered some details of his life and covered the funeral. The *Recorder* of Port Pirie of 31 March offered a succinct assessment of Symon's career and influence:

> one of the State's most notable men, and one who had rendered South Australia much valuable service. He was an eminent lawyer,

'scandalous, offensive and defamatory'

a most eloquent and successful pleader and a great statesman. [It] will be remembered that he played a big part in the preparation of the Commonwealth constitution.

The metropolitan newspapers of the other States generally reproduced shortened versions of the accounts published in Adelaide. Symon could never have expected to receive the massive attention given to Kingston's death in 1908 but would have been disappointed that Sir Richard Baker's death in 1911 gained many more column inches than he did in 1934. The mistake of those unable to curb their vanity is to live for too long after their floreat years. Many of Symon's distinguished contemporaries of his best years were also of a humble origin. There was nothing very special about his rise to the front rank, although he was distinctive in rising so far in so many fields. Labor papers were more likely to retain a vivid memory, and were generally much kinder to former opponents than to 'Labor rats'. Symon would not have been displeased by the *Australian Worker*'s reference to him on 11 April 1934: 'Symon belonged to the old Tory school of politics' but 'frequently his outlook was broad – and occasionally democratic.'

On the day after the State Funeral, the Full Court of the Supreme Court and senior legal figures paid their own tribute to Sir Josiah. The Bench comprised the Chief Justice and Justices Parsons and Richards. The Attorney-General, the Crown Solicitor and three KCs sat at the Bar Table and nine other lawyers were in attendance. Sir George Murray began: 'The death of so distinguished a member of the legal profession as Sir Josiah Symon cannot be allowed to pass unnoticed.' The Chief Justice recalled the names of other leaders of the profession when he joined the Bar: Downer, Mann, Kingston and Nesbit. They, too, were 'men of remarkable ability', in many ways no less gifted than Symon, but as a tireless worker and with his attention to detail, forensic strategy and mastery of legal principle he surpassed them all. No one in South Australia 'ever had a more triumphant career'. Adding the private and political accomplishments to his legal achievements, Murray saw Symon as 'an outstanding man in any company, a man of dominating personality, and a man to be listened to and reckoned with'. The Chief Justice accepted the reality that in 1934 'Sir Josiah Symon was only a name' but claimed it would long be remembered 'as that of a very learned lawyer and a truly great advocate'.[7]

Sir Josiah Symon was becoming 'only a name' in another place. George Pearce of Western Australia was the one remaining senator in 1934 who had joined Symon at its first sitting in 1901, and Pearce and Patrick Lynch of Western Australia were the only senators still sitting in the Senate in 1934 who had served with Symon. Observing the then custom, three senators spoke on 28 June: Pearce for the Government, John Barnes for the Labor Opposition, and Alexander McLachlan for Symon's State.[8]

Pearce moved the motion of condolence, briefly listing the main facts of Symon's political career and then offering an assessment:

> By the death of Sir Josiah Symon, another member has been removed from the ranks of that fast disappearing band of distinguished jurists and statesmen who participated in the conferences which led to the establishment of the Commonwealth.
>
> ... I well remember the distinguished band of South Australian representatives in the first Senate. They were men of outstanding ability amongst all the members of the first Federal Parliament, and none of them ranged higher than Sir Josiah Symon. He possessed exceptional gifts and a remarkable personality, and, during the time he was a member of the first Senate, he made a mark in the history of Australia that will endure. I esteem it a great privilege to have been associated with so great a man, and to have seen the qualities which he displayed in those early days of federation.

Senator Barnes (Vic) had first entered the Senate in the 1913 election which saw Symon's departure. A stalwart of the AWU, he said those who were acquainted 'with some of the great work' done in the early days of federation by 'that great jurist, the late Sir Josiah Symon' will remember he was a very important figure in Australian politics at that time. His death would be felt, not only by his family but by the people of his State. Senator McLachlan, the Vice-President of the Executive Council, said he had known Sir Josiah Symon for almost 40 years. He spoke of Symon's 'unrivalled eminence' in courts of law in South Australia, his forensic abilities, his mental powers which were enriched by his knowledge of literature and of his important part in the framing of the Commonwealth 'scandalous, offensive and defamatory'

Constitution. McLachlan concluded: 'Although he was not born in this country, his sentiments were entirely Australian, and we all lament the passing of one whom we may fittingly term a great Australian.'

Five MPs spoke in the House of Representatives on 28 June.[9] Joseph Lyons and Charles Hawker were the most fulsome. Lyons ranged over Symon's career in State and Federal politics, his prominent role in drafting the federal constitution, his literary attainments and ability as a lawyer. 'We number him among the great Australians, and recall with pride the valuable service he rendered during a period of many years.' Hawker called Symon 'one of the most brilliant and forceful citizens which South Australia has ever produced'. Hawker emphasised Symon's broad outlook which encompassed his State, the Commonwealth and the Empire; Symon wanted to advance all three communities. James Scullin said Symon left 'a great mark on the history of the Commonwealth' while Earle Page (Country Party) referred to Symon's readiness to assist new members on legal questions and 'Jack' Beasley (Lang Labor) delivered his condolences in one brief perfunctory sentence.

No one in either Chamber referred to Symon's time as Commonwealth Attorney-General or to his commitment to free trade. Hawker alone came close to mentioning, albeit indirectly, Symon's enduring allegiance to the Senate as the States' House. What had mattered to Symon, hardly mattered in the Australia of the 1930s.

Joseph Lyons, Sir Isaac Isaacs, Sir Brudenell White and the Justices of the Supreme Court, among many others, sent letters and messages of condolence to Lady Symon. Brudenell White told her Symon was 'a Great Statesman, a Great Lawyer and a Great Man'.[10] The former Labor, National Labor and Nationalist Senator, Hugh de Largie, the Secretary of The Association of Members of the First Parliament, addressed a distinctive message to Lady Symon: 'We have lost a much esteemed colleague, and Australia, one of the most valuable Citizens who did much useful services in setting up the Federation of this Country, which none appreciates more than our Members who were associated with him in the Senate.'[11] On 12 April 1934, the Rev William Charteris of the Stirling Baptist Church sent a letter of sympathy to Lady Symon. The Church, he wrote, 'had lost an illustrious son – a loyal friend and a generous benefactor' who was 'a noble gentleman – a great Christian and an unfaltering disciple of our Lord Jesus'.[12]

Symon made several Wills and signed several deed polls during his lifetime, but the extant documents at his death were the Will dated 22 October 1931, a First Codicil of 14 July 1932 and a Second Codicil of 7 April 1933. The executors of Symon's Will – Elder's Trustee and Executor Company, Lenore and Carril Symon, and Kilmeny Symon, the literary executor – filed an affidavit with the Supreme Court on 18 July 1934 in support of an application for probate. The affidavit stated that 'certain words' of the Will 'appeared to the [executors] to be scandalous, offensive and defamatory regarding the persons about whom they were written, and that other words appeared not to affect the dispositions of the Will'. The Full Court of Chief Justice Murray and Justice Napier saw fit to support the executors and, in granting probate as requested, ordered that specified portions of the Will be omitted, kept sealed and made available for inspection only by leave of the Court or a judge.[13] In ordering the suppression of parts of the Will, Chief Justice Murray reportedly said the Court had decided to accede to the terms of the executors' motion.

As stated in the Preface, Sir Josiah Symon had left a real and personal estate valued at £220,026/10/2, worth $22,256,580.86 in 2020 according to the Reserve Bank's *Pre-Decimal Inflation Calculator*.

Jo made no 'special pecuniary provision' for his wife and children. Nell had already received investments of about £40,000 and Symon wanted her to have continued use of 'Manoah' and all its contents and of the Packard car. Sir Josiah expressed the wish that 'Manoah' should be retained as the family home during Lady Symon's widowhood, after which his trustees should use their influence to prevent the home and its estate being sold for not less than £18,000. Symon wanted 'my dear wife' to have 'Manoah' as her residence and a place where her married and unmarried children (except Charles) may come to stay.

> I do not consider that it will be for the peace and happiness of the family for my said wife to permit my son Charles to occupy temporarily or otherwise or to stay at 'Manoah' as one of the family during her life[.] And in order to avoid the ill consequences to or difference with the other members of the family I therefore earnestly desire and entreat her not to do so[.]

'scandalous, offensive and defamatory'

Symon declared he had made 'liberal provision' for all the children in his lifetime. The house in Buxton Street, presently held in trust for Romilly and available for Nell's use, would ultimately pass to Margaret and Lenore. Under the Will, Oliver should have all licences or grants of arms of which his father was the registered holder in the College of Arms London and to which he was entitled. Symon revoked this clause in a codicil and gave the licences or grants to Margaret, Lenore, and Kilmeny, to be disposed of as they thought fit.

Jo's silver cups and trophies, and the gold, silver, and bronze trophies and medals won by 'my Auldana Vineyard' were to be divided as equally as possible among his children (except for Charles and Romilly). Lenore should receive £500 to be applied, at her absolute discretion, towards the upkeep of Northcote Home or to be used for other charitable purposes. Symon expressed his desire that Nell and Kilmeny should co-operate in all matters relating to the publication of any records of his professional or political career or to the 'Federal Union of Australia', or his part or share in the 'union'. To assist them, he gave each an annuity of £100 during the time they were engaged on this work, and provided that all expenses incurred should be paid out of the residuary estate.

In addition to several gifts of paintings and artefacts to institutions, Symon made bequests to selected members of Symon's broader family. The original Will gave the Rev. Dudley Symon, MA (Oxon), headmaster of Woodbridge School, Suffolk, England, the sum of £1000, reduced to £500 by the Second Codicil. Dudley was Jim Symon's eldest son. The gift probably represented Jo's approval of primogeniture and his final thank-you present to the brother who had been his mentor and early benefactor. Symon left £500 to each of the sons of his sister, Elizabeth, and £1000 to Isabel May ('Maisie'), the youngest daughter of his late brother, David, who had captured Jo's attention. He provided Mrs Alice Evers an annuity of £50 for life in recognition of her 'affectionate care' of Jo's cousin, Caroline Sutherland. Symon added a gift of £25, free of death duties, for his chauffeur, Horace James Gillard, 'in recognition of his long and faithful service to myself and my family'.

The Will attempted to wind-up what had become the draining and complicated business of Auldana. Symon held practically all the shares in Auldana Limited and was 'the Governing Director thereof with absolute powers'. He directed the trustees to act as soon as reasonably possible after his death to arrange with and, if necessary, require Auldana Ltd to cease its operations as a manufacturer of wines. The trustees should require the company to restrict its operations to the culture and sale of grapes pending the winding up of the entire operation. The trustees were given power to postpone the sale at their discretion but must not employ any additional capital from the estate. While they may delay the final sale to a more opportune time, and should clear all of Auldana's debts before proceeding to sell everything, they should proceed as they saw fit after first giving Carril, Oscar and Oliver the option to buy the estate at 50 per cent of an independent valuation.

Symon quickly remedied what he knew to be a risk. While Oscar had no prospect of raising funds to enter the field as a single buyer, he might persuade one or both brothers to include him in a joint ownership and give him access to funds he would squander. Symon was already thinking that to give his 41-year old son a weekly allowance of £2 was a waste of money. He used the First Codicil to remove Oscar's option to buy into Auldana. Oscar's name was also removed as a beneficiary of the pictures in the billiard room at 'Manoah'. Oscar was also excluded from the general clause, as Charles and Romilly had been, which gave Jo's pictures and curios to 'all' his children.

Jo had made another last stand over Oscar, and this one survived. He decided to act upon learning of his son's drunken behaviour at Auldana. After dining and drinking together, Oscar and another man and two women arrived at Auldana in the early hours of 24 March 1932. Oscar woke the caretaker, demanded he open the cellar door and allegedly threatened him with instant dismissal if he did not keep his mouth shut. The four ate poached eggs provided by the caretaker and drank champagne before returning to town around dawn carrying at least five bottles of champagne. Oscar went to the flat of one of the women, rang Melva his wife but refused to go home. She contacted Jo who sent a car for him in the evening. Next day Jo dismissed Oscar as manager of Auldana. Oscar considered this action 'unjust'. His father had taken the word of a servant and not given Oscar an opportunity to explain himself.[14]

There was another important change. The trustees were given full power to sell Auldana shares, but they must retain an overriding

'scandalous, offensive and defamatory'

vote while Auldana Limited remained in existence. The Second Codicil removed the option for Carril and Oliver to buy the estate and, instead, left one half of the shares and all money derived from them to Carril with the other half being divided between the five daughters in equal shares as tenants in common.

It is not immediately apparent why his father removed some, though not all, of Oliver's inheritance. Symon, it will be recalled, had returned to the Supreme Court in 1928 and proudly presented his son for admission as a practitioner of the Court. Perhaps in 1933 he felt sorrier for Carril whose war-related deafness had rendered him unemployable and therefore more deserving. Of the three sons who with Charles had inherited substantial funds from the 1916 deed, Carril seemed better able to handle money. Perhaps the father realised that for all he had done to assist Oliver's naval career, his youngest son had reached his ceiling as a lieutenant commander when he should have risen to the higher rank attained by able, ambitious and driven officers. Why should he have access to or control over a grant of arms awarded to a man who had risen to be a knight of the realm?

Symon introduced the subject of Charles in Clause 25 of the Will: 'I DECLARE that it is my intention that my son CHARLES JAMES BALLAARAT SYMON shall be and is excluded' from all share interest or benefit, direct or indirect, under the Will. Charles, hitherto 'most generously treated', had repaid his father 'with ingratitude[,] rapacity and insult' but Symon hoped he will have the grace to repent 'and say with the Prodigal Son "Father I have sinned and am no more worthy to be called thy son"'.

Clause 26 began with an explanation. Symon thought 'it only right and fair for the information of my executors and family and to prevent misunderstanding' that he should put on record 'the constant and generous liberality and kindness' with which Charles had been treated, and which he 'repaid with the greatest ingratitude and unredeemed selfishness and misrepresentation'. The father knew he must show that his action against his son was 'not a mere whim but the appropriate expression of feelings' forced upon him by Charles' conduct. There followed 17 paragraphs, some consisting of one sentence and others quite long, all contributing to the most substantial clause in the original Will.

Jo constructed a chronological narrative beginning with sending his boy to St Peter's College. The young man was then sent to Magdalen College, Oxford, where he remained for the full term of four years with allowances but 'never did or achieved anything of mark'.[15] During his time in Oxford, Charles had a holiday in France with his mother and other family members, for which his father had paid. When Charles left Oxford, Symon sent him to the Inner Temple with a liberal allowance to work in the Chambers of an eminent Equity Counsel. Called to Bar, Charles travelled to America for a holiday and then home to Australia, all at his father's expense. Symon travelled to Sydney to meet Charles on his return, procured his admission as a practitioner of the Supreme Court and took him into a partnership on generous terms. He concurred with Charles' trip to Tasmania to make up his mind about enlistment, arranged for him for to receive his full share of the firm's profits while overseas in the British Army and to be entitled to a credit up to £300. On 26 September 1916, on the eve of his 70th birthday and in 'the blackest period of the war', Symon settled by deed poll almost all his first class investments to the value of £120,000 on his four enlisted sons. The capital would be transferred to them six months after the war was over. In the meantime, the interest would be paid to Symon to cover wartime expenses including the rest home he acquired in Buckinghamshire for Kilmeny and for which he paid all expenses. On his return to Australia, Charles asked for an advance on the capital grant of £1,100 to buy a house in North Adelaide. He eventually received a £31,000 capital grant like each of his three returned brothers, and 'has never had the grace to acknowledge or thank me for the gift'. At no time in the period after the Great War did Charles make any claim to the interest earned as income under the deed trust.

Paragraphs 13 and 15 of clause 26 dealt with the matters covered in the *Symon v Symon* battle of the latter half of the 1920s: the failure to pay anything of the much-reduced price of the firm at £3,500, the failure to hand over Symon's earnings of £1,791/11/11 and to pay the valuations of the office furniture. Paragraph 14 referred to Charles' refusal to allow Carril, his brother, to remain in the business, notifying him in writing to clear out of the office.

Symon concluded that his eldest son had behaved without merit or honesty. 'His conduct to me poisoned and embittered the closing days of my life. For these reasons and on these grounds I have excluded him

'scandalous, offensive and defamatory'

from any benefit under my Will.' This section of the Will was completed in October 1931 and was not amended by either of his two Codicils; that is, Jo had decided to exclude Charles from the Will after abandoning his legal action in the wake of a settlement unfavourable to himself and just before Charles' marriage.

Reading the Will, three of Jo's executors – Lenore, Kilmeny and Carril – decided to protect their brother from a savage public denunciation. Very probably, they also wanted to save their father from what Kilmeny in 1925 saw as a potential 'blot' on his reputation. Hence they sought to suppress certain words in the Will which were 'scandalous, offensive and defamatory'.

The intriguing question is why did Jo 'punish' his eldest son when he was so forgiving and patient with Oscar. One simple answer is that he gave in to Nell's soft spot for Oscar. A more complicated and plausible answer is that Jo believed Oscar could not help himself whereas Charles chose to be greedy and graceless. Jo had seen enough of Oscar at Oxford to know he was a drinker, a spender and a liar. He had long known of Oscar's 'absolute lack of a serious view of life, & incorrigible indolence', and long doubted that 'he will ever do much good on his own'.[16] He hoped he had been mistaken, wanted to believe his promises of reform and saw good signs in Oscar's results at Roseworthy, in his wartime record, in his marriage which at first stabilised him and in his commitment to farming. Jo always had higher hopes and expectations for Charles. He was the first-born male, the natural heir and successor. Jo's investment in him, moral as well as material, was much more substantial than anything laid out for Oscar or the other sons. Oscar angered Jo, but Charles hurt him.

Epilogue

On 20 September 1928, the Federal Government Gazette announced that a new Canberra suburb – 'Symonston' – would commemorate Sir Josiah Symon KCMG KC as one of the 'Founders of the Australian Constitution'. The names of the more celebrated 'Fathers of Federation' – such as Parkes, Griffith, Barton, Deakin and Kingston – adorn prominent and salubrious suburbs in Canberra. Symonston is neither prominent nor salubrious. One of its boundaries does extend to within eight kilometres of Canberra's City Centre and Symonston is the second largest suburb in the Australian Capital Territory (ACT). Yet much of it is designated as rural land, largely unused. The 2016 Census recorded a population for Symonston of 559; at the same time the ACT recorded a population just under 400,000. Unlike other Canberra suburbs, Symonston does not have any local shops or schools. Instead, there is a temporary remand centre, a periodic detention centre, a waste management centre, three caravan parks and other government buildings. Symonston is perhaps best known among Canberrans who want to feel good while making a relatively inexpensive addition to their household; the suburb contains the ACT's main dog pound which has an abundance of 'rescue dogs'.

It was probably fortunate that Symon did not live to see what became of 'his' suburb. At least the Commonwealth had acknowledged his contribution to this country's history, even if very few Canberrans now know why the suburb was so-named. There are some reminders in South Australia of Symon's earthly presence. Among them, 'Manoah' still exists, and a notice at the entrance acknowledges that it was once the property of Sir Josiah Symon. An unexplained fire destroyed all save one section

Epilogue

of the main building in 1974.¹ It has since been rebuilt, without much care for good taste. The Lady Symon Building still stands in the grounds of the University of Adelaide, and the Sir Josiah Symon Library is incorporated in the State Library of South Australia.

Symon's name, however, is not memorialised in Adelaide's streets or gardens. The names of many of his contemporaries adorn plaques along North Terrace: for example, Baker, Robert Barr Smith, Bonython, Charles Hawker, Kingston, Napier, Nesbit, Thomas Elder and Samuel Way. The Symon family had not nominated their chieftain for a plaque. It may have been galling for Symon to see what could be done. On 17 November 1924, Sir George Murray unveiled a statue of Sir Samuel Way on what one newspaper called 'a choice site' on North Terrace. Within a few days, Sir Langdon Bonython had raised the necessary funds from 15 of his business associates, thereby avoiding the necessity of a public appeal. Symon attended the unveiling ceremony. Perhaps while looking at the sculptor's creation of a very tall, stately and imposing figure, he recalled his own depictions of Way as 'a hasty impatient, noisy little animal' and 'our little friend the CJ'.

One annual event does commemorate Symon's name. It will be recalled that he had tried to interest the University of Adelaide in establishing a women's residential college. In 1939 Kilmeny joined the original Executive Committee which founded the women-only St Ann's College. Kilmeny was a member of the College Council (1944–64) and was present in 1965 when Lady Casey, the wife of the Governor-General, opened a building largely financed by funds previously donated by Lenore Symon who died in 1963. Lady Casey spoke of the Symon family's contribution to education and called them 'faithful and loving friends'.² The College library later benefited from Kilmeny's Will. Lenore and Kilmeny also left money to the College on the understanding that it would on 27 September of each year – their father's birthday – honour his memory with a gathering at his grave. A holly wreath should be placed there, a poem recited and a prayer delivered. The gathering should toast his memory with 'a wee tipple of Old Pulteney Scotch Whisky' (distilled in Wick), adjourn for a thanksgiving service, return to the now co-educational College for drinks and a dinner followed by a concert.³

Symon would have been disappointed though not surprised that his carefully crafted Will prompted two court actions. After all, for more than fifty years Symon's legal partnerships collected substantial fees from such contests. The first contest was probably necessary in order to endorse Symon's intentions. Nine of his children were represented in court at the end of 1934 seeking clarity about the trust fund. Charles, Carril and Oliver were represented together, Oscar had separate representation and one lawyer appeared for all five daughters. Justice Napier gave his reserved decision on 4 December 1934. He determined that, notwithstanding the settlement Symon made in 1891 and six subsequent dispositions of property, Symon retained the power to revoke and to make dispositions. Symon had validly excluded his sons from the trust fund in November 1916 and the fund was now held in trust for his daughters as tenants-in-common under the final deed of September 1930.[4]

Oscar's actions after his father's death would not have surprised anyone. As always, he needed money. Sensibly, he began by approaching Nell as the weakest link. She always defended him when her 'big husband' took one of his many final stands. Oscar probably knew that Nell had privately funded the boarding fees of his two sons until Jo insisted that such funds should be paid by the Trustee Company. Oscar wrote to 'My dear Mater' in October 1934: 'Are you in a position to let me have a few pounds please? If so the earlier the more useful it will be. – Don't believe what you may be told about me. The thing is absolutely wicked ... Wouldn't you like to see Booby [sic] and David again? [Oscar's two children] ... They have always wanted to see you. – that it is what hurts me most of all.'[5] Whether 'Mater' fell for this line is unknown.

Justice Napier's judgement had closed off Oscar's access to the trust fund. In 1935 Oscar applied to the Supreme Court for assistance from his father's estate under the *Testator's Family Maintenance Act*.[6] His action entailed risks; he was seemingly incapable of staying sober, holding down a job, telling the truth or paying his bills. Oscar's own lawyer said he had been treated fairly generously by the Trustee and Executor Company. Oscar wanted the Court to accept that his problems stemmed from strain which caused recurring bouts of his neurasthenic condition and they in turn led to occasional drinking to excess and hospitalisation. He said it would cost between £15 and £20 a week to support him, his family and a maid in the manner to which they were accustomed. Oscar would

Epilogue

have needed much more if he ever thought of paying off his debts. He acknowledged that his father had been generous and loving, making no distinctions between his children. Jo was also a forgiving father until he and Charles fell out just after Charles kicked Carril out of the firm in 1923. Usually Jo was just, but at times he would sentence without a hearing. Oscar cited the Auldana visit of March 1932 as one such occasion.

In court Oscar faced his father's former partner, E. Erskine Cleland KC, counsel for the five Symon daughters and a formidable cross-examiner. Cleland had the benefit of Kilmeny's four-page statement.[7] She said Oscar was well provided for financially in his father's lifetime, receiving more than each of his brothers. His inability to manage his affairs stemmed from extravagance; Oscar could never keep money and was unable to work continually at a job. 'His ill-health is largely due to intemperance.' Oscar's sisters had offered him a weekly allowance in 1934 which he refused, apparently because he wanted a larger sum and because the sisters laid down conditions which they were prepared to discuss but not while under threats. Kilmeny wrote that Oscar adopted the wrong approach. Within a few days of his father's death, he consulted a solicitor to see what he could get out of the estate, exhibiting 'an utter want of feeling and lack of thought as to what he knew were my father's wishes or what he intended'. Kilmeny concluded with a charitable understatement: 'Oscar is not very truthful: he cannot help that.'

At the end of July 1935 Justice Richards ordered the parties to confer in private. Meetings failed to resolve anything. Oscar kept trying to obtain more money from the trust fund held by his sisters. In August 1939 Kilmeny asked the manager of Elder's Trustee and Executor Company 'to request Mr O S Symon to refrain from writing her further letters'. She said the trusts could not be altered.[8] Where Oscar was concerned the daughters, unlike their father, could stick to a final decision.

Nell was not a party to either legal action. She conducted some of her late husband's business, remaining a Vice President of the Adelaide Branch of the English Association and attending at least one branch meeting. Nell corresponded with Pam Lister on Shakespearean subjects. She agreed to open Jo's library of the eight thousand books he bequeathed to the State Library. A family friend described her speech on 27 September 1935 (Kilmeny had suggested the date) as '[t]erse, pointed, and as beautiful as if it had been modelled on the Gettysburg Address'. The friend also spoke of Kilmeny being 'a tower of strength in carrying out her father's wishes'.[9] Buckingham Palace remembered Lady Symon. By the command of King George VI she received a certificate and a medal to wear in commemoration of the Coronation of 12 May 1937.[10]

Diagnosed for some years with arteriosclerosis Nell suffered a cerebral haemorrhage on Christmas Eve 1944. She died four days later at the Buxton Street residence where she spent most of her final years. Her Will sworn in April 1935 shocked and puzzled the Symon family. Nell had instructed that after cremation her remains should be removed to Melbourne and buried alongside her father in the Boroondara Cemetery in Kew. She requested that the remains of her favourite brother Ernest, who died in 1922, be disinterred from the Symon plot in the North Road Cemetery and placed alongside those of her father and herself. The request relating to Ernest was not met. Nell never explained why she wanted her final resting place to be next to her father rather than her husband. Two of the possible explanations were hardly flattering: she may have wanted to be free of Jo at last and may have wanted to remind the Symons that she was, first of all, a Cowle. If it were Nell's decision to add her name on the side of Jo's headstone, and for her inscription to refer to Jo as her husband, the removal of her remains to Melbourne may have been characteristically quirky rather than dismissive.

Charles Symon died suddenly of a heart attack at Mylor on 3 February 1941. He was aged 55. Overweight and a heavy drinker, he was no longer the young man who won the Military Cross. Charles left behind a widow, and a son and two daughters under the age of ten. Oscar died on 31 December 1950 in the Repatriation General Hospital, Springbank, alone and close to destitute at the age of 59. Romilly, aged 61 and suffering from chronic nephritis and diabetes, died on 8 April 1951. Carril drank heavily until his death in 1964 when aged 71. Oliver lived longest of the Symon sons, dying aged 84 on 11 August 1979. Jo had seen Carril and Oliver as inseparable when they were boys. A female friend of Carril observed them long after Jo's death sitting uncomfortably alongside each other during a cricket match at the Adelaide Oval. They did not exchange a word. With justification, Carril believed that Oliver had tricked him out of inheriting ownership of 'Manoah'.[11]

Epilogue

Kilmeny was right: the four fit boys of the family achieved very little, given their advantages and opportunities. Jo had been acutely aware of this, and Kilmeny told Cleland she believed that her father never intended to give any of his sons more money after his death. Jo was proud of his daughters and appeared relaxed about their slip-ups. He never publicly admitted any error in not providing the three older ones with a good formal education while Nell seemed content when Margaret, Lenore and Kilmeny took over the household and managed the younger children.

Perdita Eldridge adored her 'mother', Margaret, and grew close to Angel but came to look upon all five sisters as 'little old ladies' who had 'vast amounts of energy' and sufficient independent means yet without enough outlets to consume their drive. It might have been different if their father had given them some of the educational opportunities he lavished upon four of his sons. Even so, Perdita could include the five daughters in her discovery that the Symon children had been all over Europe, and visited cathedrals, galleries and museums (for theatre, a language barrier limited them to the United Kingdom). She found that the children 'were basically inculcated with (their father's) love of the arts and particularly books'. Every single member of the Symon family had libraries of their own.

Margaret went on to study child psychology in London and established the Inn Nursery School in Lower Mitcham, the first progressive nursery school in Australia. Her aim was to foster an environment where the child 'was encouraged to question, to express himself, act on his own initiative and to think for himself and others'. Lenore served on the Board of Northcote Rest Home for Mothers and Babies for ten years. She made donations to the Home but was largely held back by ill-health and often confined to bed.

Kilmeny appeared to family members and to outsiders as the one most like her father: 'legally minded, although not trained, not even academically trained.' For someone considered to be shy, her forte was knowing 'everybody in Adelaide and having contact with anybody who came from Britain'. Her friends and contacts included Sir John Downer's son, Alexander ('Alick'), a minister in the Menzies Government, and Douglas Pike, the author of *Paradise of Dissent* and the first general editor of the *Australian Dictionary of Biography*. Perdita Eldridge, who described

Mary as 'snappy', conceded she 'wasn't vitriolic like ... one of the other aunts, Aunt Kilmeny'.[12] Kilmeny did unnerve some of the children of the next generation. She could appear formidable and sometimes 'terrifying'.

In the 1920s, Angel was the secretary and publicity officer of Allan Wilkie's Shakespearean company and took walk-on parts in productions. After Wilkie's company collapsed during the Depression Angel frequently travelled to Britain and Europe to visit theatres and attend opera and concerts, all the time collecting programs, books and ephemera. She bequeathed her collection to the Barr Smith Library at the University of Adelaide in the name of Allan Wilkie and his wife, Frediswyde Hunter-Watts. She went to live with her sister Mary at the latter's property, 'Stringys', at Echunga. After Angel died in 1976 as a result of a car accident, Mary retained a portion of Angel's collection, added to it and donated $10,000 to assist the cataloguing of the collection. Following Mary's death in 1988 the whole collection including Angel's correspondence was transferred to the Barr Smith Library.

Mary Arden Clark died on 28 June 1988 just before her 88th birthday. Kilmeny thought her a 'genius'; others saw Mary as 'indomitable'. Her hearing loss presented her with more of a problem than a brief and failed marriage. The youngest daughter and the only one to enter holy wedlock may well have decided that one brief marriage was enough and that her sisters, influenced by Nell's innate indifference to marriage, were right in not seeking to marry. Mary remained an ardent theatre-goer, kept horses to ride and to race and collected art, books and pottery. Up until she died in her sleep, the last living child of Jo and Nell, Mary drove a tractor, tended her garden, read weekly newspapers posted from England and America and continued to 'strap' her horses at the races.

The daughters were a credit to their upbringing but could do little to enhance the Symon name. Unlike Sir John Downer, Symon did not create a political dynasty, and his name soon ceased to resonate in Adelaide's legal circles. His story has all but disappeared from public memory and his record in so many fields is not widely known. Nevertheless, Symon did leave his mark on the Australian Constitution. His contemporaries around Australia saw him as a formidable political figure, someone they respected and occasionally feared though rarely loved. The lawyer was an even more formidable figure, respected and feared. In his prime, barely

Epilogue

a week would pass when his name did not appear in the Adelaide press with reference to the law, politics, Auldana wines, literature, travel or philanthropy. There were also regular references to him in newspapers in Melbourne and Western Australia, whether he was in the country or travelling abroad. The important point is that whether they liked him or not, or thought his failures mattered more than his successes, Symon's contemporaries knew they were burying a titan when they formed a long cortege behind his cremated remains on the day they were borne to the North Road Cemetery.

Bibliography

Official
Commonwealth Parliamentary Debates
Commonwealth Parliamentary Papers
House of Assembly and Legislative Council (South Australia)

Personal Papers: National Library
Sir Edmund Barton
Sir Joseph Carruthers
Alfred Deakin
Elizabeth Dyer
Patrick McMahon Glynn
Sir George Pearce
Sir George Reid
Sir Josiah Symon
Symon Family Papers

Privately-held Papers
Elizabeth Dyer

Newspapers and magazines
Adelaide Express
Adelaide Observer (later, Observer)
Age
Argus
Australian Christian Commonwealth
Barrier Times
Border Watch

Bibliography

Bulletin (Sydney)
Coolgardie Miner
Critic
Daily Telegraph (Sydney)
Evening Journal
Express and Telegraph
Kalgoorlie Miner
Kapunda Herald
Labor Call
Mail
News (Adelaide)
Northern Argus
Observer
Quiz and the Lantern
South Australian Advertiser (later, *Advertiser*)
South Australian Chronicle and Weekly Mail (later *South Australian Chronicle* and then *Chronicle*)
South Australian Register (later, *Register*)
Southern Cross
Sydney Morning Herald
United Empire
Weekly Herald (later, *Herald* and then *Daily Herald*)
West Australian

Josiah Symon publications

Life, Essay read to Bible Class, Baptist Church, Stirling, 1861, Learmouth, Stirling, 1929
Some Scottish Poetry, L. Henn & Co, Adelaide 1884
'Tis Sixty Years Since, Vardon & Pritchard, Adelaide, 1897
Shakespeare Quotation, E. Mackay, Stirling (SA), 1901
Why I am a Free Trader, Cobden Club, Cassel, London, 1901
Shakespeare at Home, Hussey & Gillingham, Adelaide, 1905
Poetry and Its Claims, Bodley Head, London, 1911
Shakespeare the Englishman, W.K. Thomas, Adelaide, 1915
Symon, Sir Josiah, 'Australia and the Privy Council', *Journal of Comparative Legislation and International Law*, vol 4, no. 4, 1922
Governor-Generalship of Australia: Appointment of Sir Isaac Isaacs, Publishers Ltd, Adelaide, 1931

Sir Josiah Symon KCMG KC

Speeches, Publishers Ltd, Adelaide, 1932

The Hon. Sir Josiah Symon, KCMG, KC (edited and annotated by D. I. Wright), 'The Dawn of Federation: Some Episodes, Letters and Personalities and a Vindication', *South Australiana,* vol. 15, no. 2, 1976

Memoirs

Deakin, Alfred, *The Federal Story: The Inner History of the Federal Cause,* Robertson & Mullens, Melbourne, 1944

Pearce, George, *Carpenter to Cabinet: Thirty-Seven Years of Parliament,* Hutchinson & Co. Ltd, London, 1951

Reid, G.H., *My Reminiscences,* Cassell, London, 1917

Wise, B.R., *The Making of the Australian Commonwealth, 1889-1900* Pitman, London, 1909

Biographies

Bannon, John, *Supreme Federalist: The Political Life of Sir John Downer,* Wakefield Press, Adelaide, 2009

Bolton, Geoffrey, *Edmund Barton,* Allen & Unwin, St Leonards, 2000

Brett, Judith, *The Enigmatic Mr Deakin,* Text Publishing, Melbourne, 2017

Cowen, Zelman, *Isaac Isaacs,* Oxford University Press, Melbourne, 1967

Crowley, Frank, *Big John Forrest 1847–1918: A Founding Father of the Commonwealth of Australia,* University of Western Australia Press, Nedlands, 2000

Dyer, Elizabeth Symon, *The Bank Manager and his Family,* Peacock Publications, Adelaide, 2012

Glass, Margaret, *Charles Cameron Kingston: Federation Father,* Miegunyah Press, MUP, Carlton, 1997

Gorman, Zachary, *Sir Joseph Carruthers: Founder of the New South Wales Liberal Party,* Connor Court Publishing, Redlands Bay, 2018

Henderson, Anne, *Federation's Man of Letters: Patrick McMahon Glynn,* Connor Court Publishing Pty Ltd, Redland Bay, 2019

Heydon, Peter, *Quiet Decision: A Study of George Foster Pearce,* Melbourne University Press, Carlton, 1965

La Nauze, J.A., *Alfred Deakin: A Biography,* 2 vols, Melbourne University Press, Carlton, 1965

McMinn, W.G., *George Reid,* Melbourne University Press, Carlton, 1969

Murdoch, Walter, *Alfred Deakin: A Sketch,* Constable & Co., Ltd, London, 1923

O'Collins, Gerard, *Patrick McMahon Glynn: A Founder of Australian Federation,* MUP, Carlton, 1965

Bibliography

Rickard, John, *H.B. Higgins: The Rebel as Judge*, George Allen & Unwin, Sydney, 1984

Symon, David, *A Life of Eric Symon: 1894–1948*, New Age Publishers Pty Ltd, Sydney, 1991

Secondary

Austin, A.G. (ed.), *The Webbs' Australian Diary*, Isaac Pitman, Carlton, 1965

Bennett, J.M., *Keystone of the Federal Arch: A Historical Memoir of the High Court of Australia to 1980*, Australian Government Publishing Service, Canberra, 1980

Bridge, Carl, Bongiorno, Frank, and Lee, David (eds), *The High Commissioners: Australia's Representatives in the United Kingdom 1910–2010*, Department of Foreign Affairs and Trade, Canberra, 2010

Castles, Alex C. and Harris, Michael C., *Lawmakers and Wayward Whigs: Government and Law in South Australia 1836–1986*, Wakefield Press, Adelaide, 1987

Coleman, William Oliver, *Their Fiery Cross of Union: A Retelling of the Creation of the Australian Federation, 1889–1914*, Connor Court Publishing Pty Ltd., Redland Bay, 2021

Crisp L.F. (ed. John Hart), *Federation Fathers*, Melbourne University Press, Carlton, 1990

Denning, Warren, *Caucus Crisis: The rise & fall of the Scullin Government*, Hale & Iremonger, Sydney, 1982 edition

Donovan, Peter, *The Trial of Mary Schippan*, Donovan & Associates, Blackwood, 2004

Emerson, John, *First Among Equals: Chief Justices of South Australia since Federation*, University of Adelaide Barr Smith Press, South Australia, 2006

Emerson, John, *History of the Independent Bar of South Australia*, University of Adelaide Barr Smith Press, South Australia, 2006

Galligan, Brian, *Politics of the High Court: A Study of the Judicial Branch of Government in Australia*, University of Queensland Press, St Lucia, 1987

Grant, Peter R., *Philanthropy and Voluntary Action in the First World War: Mobilizing Charity*, Routledge, New York, 2014

Hirst, J.B., *Adelaide and the Country, 1870–1917: Their social and political relationship*, MUP, Carlton, 1973

Hirst, John, *The Sentimental Nation: The Making of the Australian Commonwealth*, OUP, South Melbourne, 2000

Huschke, Richard, *The Towitta Tragedy: The True Story of the Bertha Schippan Murder*, Richard Dutches, Alfredton, 2017

Irving, Helen (ed.), *The Centenary Companion to Australian Federation*, Cambridge University Press, Oakleigh, 1999

Kelly, Paul, *The End of Certainty: Power, Politics & Business in Australia*, rev. edn., Allen & Unwin, St Leonards, 1994

La Nauze. J.A., *The Hopetoun Blunder: The Appointment of the First Prime Minister of the Commonwealth of Australia December 1900*, Melbourne University Press, Carlton, 1957

La Nauze. J.A., *The Making of the Australian Constitution*, MUP, Carlton, 1972

Martin, Robert, *Under Mount Lofty: A History of the Stirling District in South Australia*, 2nd edn., District Council of Stirling, South Australia, 1960

Rickard, John, *Class and Politics in New South Wales, Victoria and the Early Commonwealth, 1890–1910*, ANU Press, Canberra, 1976

Rickard, John, *H.B. Higgins: The Rebel as Judge*, George Allen & Unwin, Sydney, 1984

Souter, Gavin, *Lion and Kangaroo: Australia: 1901–1919 The Rise of a Nation*, Fontana, Brisbane, 1978

Sumerling, Patricia, *The Noon Lady of Towitta: A mystery*, Wakefield Press, Adelaide, 2010

Sutherland, George, *Our Inheritance in the Hills: Being a Series of Articles by a Special Correspondent*, W.K. Thomas & Co., Adelaide 1889

Warburton, Elizabeth, *The Paddocks Beneath: A History of Burnside from the Beginning*, Corporation of the City of Burnside, Adelaide, 1981 (Richard House: Extended Index, Burnside Historical Society, 2012)

Wilcox, Craig, *Australia's Boer War: The War in South Africa 1899–1902*, published in association with the Australian War Memorial, Oxford University Press, South Melbourne, 2002

Wilkie, Benjamin, *The Scots in Australia 1788–1938*, Boydell Press, Woodbridge, Suffolk, UK, 2017

Articles, chapters, lectures, entries and papers

Craven, Greg, 'Heresy as Orthodoxy: Were the Founders Progressivists?', *Federal Law Review*, vol. 31 (1), 2003

de Garis, B.K., 'The Colonial Office and the Commonwealth Constitution Bill', in A.W. Martin (ed.), *Essays in Australian Federation*, Melbourne University Press, Carlton, 1969

Dermody, Kathleen, 'The 1897 Federal Convention Election: Success or Failure?', Papers on Parliament, No 30, November 1997

Gageler, Stephen, 'When the High Court Went on Strike', *Melbourne University Law Review*, vol. 40, no. 3, 2017

Bibliography

Lyons, Graham, 'Symon the Barrister: The Schippan Murder Case', New Heritage, June-August 1994

MacKenzie, John M., 'Essay and Reflection: On Scotland and the Empire', *International History Review*, vol. 15, no. 4, 1993

McMinn, W.G., 'The High Court Imbroglio and the Fall of the Reid–McLean Government', *Journal of the Royal Australian Historical Society*, vol. 64, Pt 1, June 1978

Mason, Sir Anthony, 'The High Court of Australia: A Personal Impression of its First 100 Years', *Melbourne University Law Review*, vol. 27. no 3, 2003

Priest, Susan, 'Archives, the Australian High Court and the "Strike of 1905"', *University of Queensland Law Journal*, vol. 32, no. 2, 2013

Reid, R.L., 'The South Australian Influence on the Proposals for Federation', *Proceedings of Royal Geographical Society of Australasia, South Australian Branch*, vol. 58, 1956–57

Richards, Eric, 'Varieties of Scottish Emigration in the Nineteenth Century', *Historical Studies*, vol. 21, no. 85, 19851957

Rubinstein, Hilary L., '"A Gross Discourtesy to His Majesty": The Campaign within Australia, 1930–31 against Sir Isaac Isaacs' Appointment as Governor General', *Australian Jewish Historical Society Journal*, vol. 14, part 3, 1998

Stimson, A.J, 'Sir Josiah Symon and the Railways Commissioner', *South Australiana*, vo. 24, no. 1, 1985

Taylor, Greg, 'The Judicial Incompatibility Clause – or how a version of the Kable principle almost made it into the Australian Constitution', 38 *Adelaide Law Review*, 2017

Williams, John M., '"Swelling the Ranks of the Peripatetic Unemployed": The First Decade of the High Court of Australia', High Court of Australia Public Lecture Series, 8 June 2011 (PDF 279k) (RTF 188k).

Williams, John M., 'South Australia and the Constitution: A mere provincial contribution?', J.C. Bannon Oration, 31 August 2021, https://www.johnbannonoration.com.au/

Wright, D.I., (ed.) The Hon. Sir Josiah Symon, KCMG, KC), 'The Dawn of Federation: Some Episodes, Letters and Personalities and a Vindication', *South Australiana*, vol. 15, no. 2, 1976

Wright, D.I., 'Sir Josiah Symon, Federation and the High Court', *Journal of the Royal Australian Historical Society*, vol. 64, Pt 2, September 1978

Wright, D.I., 'Symon, Sir Josiah Henry (1846–1934)' *ADB*, vol. 12, MUP, Carlton, 1990

Wright, D.I., 'Symon, Sir Josiah Henry (1846–1934)', *Biographical Dictionary of the Australian Senate*, vol. 1, 1901–1929, MUP, Carlton South, 2000

Sir Josiah Symon KCMG KC

Works of Reference

Australian Dictionary of Biography

Biographical Dictionary of the Australian Senate, vol. 1, 1901–1929, MUP, Carlton South, 2000

Craven, Greg (ed.), *Official Record of the Debates of National Australasian Convention*, 6 vols, Legal Books, Sydney 1986

Hughes, Colin A. and Graham, B.D., *A Handbook of Australian Government and Politics 1890–1964*, ANU Press, Canberra, 1968

Jaensch, Dean (ed.), *The Flinders History of South Australia: Political History*, Wakefield Press, Adelaide, 1986,

Prest, Wilfrid (ed.), *The Wakefield Companion to South Australian History*, Wakefield Press, Adelaide, 2001

Quick, John and Garran, Robert Randolph, *The Annotated Constitution of the Australian Commonwealth*, reprint of 1901 edition, Legal Books, Sydney, 1976

Sawer, Geoffrey, *Australian Federal Politics and Law 1901–1929*, MUP, Carlton, 1956

Williams, John M., *The Australian Constitution: A Documentary History*, MUP, Carlton, 2005

Notes

Preface

1. Reserve Bank of Australia, Pre-Decimal Inflation Calculator.
2. Don Wright of the University of Adelaide and of the University of Newcastle published four balanced articles which form a notable exception. See Bibliography.
3. L.P. Hartley, *The Go-Between*, Hamish Hamilton, London, 1971 edn., p. 9.
4. P.A. Howell, *South Australia and Federation*, Wakefield Press, Adelaide, 2002, pp. 182, 183–4.
5. Rosemary Laing, 'Richard Chaffey Baker and the Shaping of the Senate', annual Harry Evans Lecture, 2018.

Chapter 1 ~ 'a young man of considerable promise'

1. Wendy Robinson, 'Teacher Training in England and Wales: Past, Present and Future Perspectives', *Education Research and Perspectives*, vol. 33, no. 2, 2006.
2. For the above two paragraphs, see T.M. Parssinen, 'Popular Science and Society: The Phrenology Movement in Early Victorian Britain', *Journal of Social History*, vol. 8, no. 1, 1974, pp. 1–20.
3. Symon Papers, NLA, MS 1756/1/1.
4. The source for the above two paragraphs is Jo's letter sent from Mount Gambier to Jim Symon on 24 October 1867 in *ibid.*, 1/60.
5. *Ibid.*, 1/1.
6. For his 1863 and 1864 diaries, see *ibid.*, 2/3–4.
7. https://www.ed.ac.uk/education/about-us/maps-estates-history/history/maurice-paterson
8. Symon Papers, NLA, MS 1736/1/15–16.
9. *Ibid.*, 1/1 and 10.
10. Neil Heath (Rector, Alba Academy), 19 October 1864, *ibid.*, 1/8–9.

Chapter 2 ~ 'Make good friends of the cook.'

1. The information relating to John Watson's Institution is based on the copy of Jo's letter recorded in the Sundays' section on 2 October of the 1864 diary. Symon Papers, NLA, MS 1736/2/58.
2. See the note of 29 April 1865 in 'Memoranda' at the end of the 1864 diary in *ibid.*
3. For the above paragraph, see ibid., 1/23–6. The Parish itself could trace its history to the 12th century and the territory once formed part of the ancient Kingdom

of Strathclyde. The Disruption of 1843 divided loyalties around Neilston but the parish minister, the Rev. Hugh Aird, did not join the Free Church.
4   For the motivations and opportunities for emigration, see Eric Richards, 'Varieties of Scottish Emigration in the Nineteenth Century', *Historical Studies*, vol. 21, no. 85, 1985, pp. 473–94.
5   *Register News-Pictorial*, 21 August 1929.
6   Personal communication: Elizabeth Dyer.
7   For Devitt & Moore see Basil Lubbock, *The Colonial Clippers*, James Brown & Son, Glasgow, 1921, pp. 176–9 and Captain A.G. Course, *Painted Ports: The Story of the Ships of Devitt & Moore*, Hollis & Carter, London, 1961.
8   *Adelaide Express*, 17 September 1866.
9   Symon Papers, NLA, MS 1736/2/3.
10 'Diary of a Voyage'; for the handwritten version, see *ibid.*, 2/1–60; for the typed and more complete version, see *ibid.*, 2/2–56.
11 Josiah Symon (JHS) to Jim Symon (JSS), 24 September 1866, *ibid.*, 1/38. Throughout his life, Symon drew upon a widely-held stereotype in his occasional and private references to a 'Jew' or 'Jews'.
12 JHS to JSS, 24 September 1866, *ibid.*, 1/39.

Chapter 3 ~ 'this momentous step in my life'

1   *Census of South Australia, March 1866: Summary Tables*, Government Printer, Adelaide, 1866, pp. 1, 3 and 67.
2   See Robert Dare in Wilfrid Prest (ed.), *The Wakefield Companion to South Australian History*, Wakefield Press, Adelaide, 2001, pp. 257–8.
3   JHS to JSS, 24 and 28 October 1866, Symon Papers, NLA, MS 1736/1/39.
4   Mary Kitson, admitted to legal practice in October 1917, was South Australia's first female to take advantage of the *Female Law Practitioners Act* of 1911.
5   'Articles of Agreement', Symon Papers, NLA, MS 1736/5/1. On the back of the document Justice Boothby of the Supreme Court certified that he was 'satisfied' that Symon met the academical requirements and was of the required moral character. Boothby never met Symon; James Sutherland persuaded him that Symon more than met the classical and general requirements. Boothby was 'amoved' from office in July 1867 for repeated 'misbehaviour'.
6   Caroline, and a 'Miss McCallum', described in a letter to Jim of 20 July 1867 as 'a very good looking girl', were the only 'eligible' women mentioned in Jo's Mount Gambier letters.
7   For the above three paragraphs, see JHS to JSS, 25 January 1867, Symon Papers, NLA, MS 1736/1/43.
8   For the above three paragraphs, see JHS to JSS, 24 October 1866, 21 February 1867, late September 1867, 25 March 1868, *ibid.*, 1/39, 44 and 68.
9   In 1868 he might have admired 'universal suffrage' even less had the suffrage been sufficiently 'universal' to include females.
10 *Border Watch*, 4 September and 27 November 1867; JHS to JSS, 2 February 1868, Symon Papers, NLA, MS 1736/1/65; Diary, 23 November 1867, *ibid.*, 2/58.
11 *Border Watch*, 30 January 1868; JHS to JSS, 2 February 1868, Symon Papers, NLA, MS 1736/2/65.
12 For the above three paragraphs, see JHS to JSS, 5 April 1867 and January–February 1868, *ibid.*, 1/47, 64–5.
13 *South Australian Register*, 1 June 1868; *South Australian Law Reports*, vol 3, 1869, pp. 96–121.

Notes

14 For Way, see A. J. Hannan, The Life of Chief Justice Way, Angus & Robertson, Australia, 1960 and J. J. Bray, 'Way, Sir Samuel James (1836–1916), *Australian Dictionary of Biography (ADB)*, vol. 12, MUP, Carlton, 1990.
15 JHS to JSS, 23 April 1868, Symon Papers, NLA, MS 1736/1/70. For the Ward case, see *Border Watch*, 18 April 1868.
16 Andre Parkinson, 'The Regret of Sir Samuel Way', *Australian Journal of Legal History*, vol. 1, 1995, pp. 239–57.
17 Samuel Way to JHS, 16 February 1869, Symon Papers, NLA, MS 1736/1/90.

Chapter 4 ~ 'I can address a jury as effectively as the best of them.'

1 For the above three paragraphs, see JHS to JSS, 19 June 1870, Symon Papers, NLA, MS 1736/1/118.
2 JHS to JSS, 7 July 1870, *ibid.*, 1/119.
3 JHS to JSS, 13 August 1870, *ibid.*, 1/121.
4 JHS to JSS, 8 November 1870, *ibid.*, 1/127.
5 'Assignment of Articles of Clerkship', *ibid.*, 5/4 and 5.
6 Son of German-born parents, von Doussa later served briefly in the House of Assembly and the Legislative Council, and held the portfolios of Attorney-General and Education in the Jenkins Liberal Government 1903–4. He practised in every South Australian jurisdiction and in the High Court, but only occasionally crossed Symon's path as von Doussa was firmly settled in Mount Barker. See Wray Vamplew's entry in the *ADB*, vol. 12, MUP, Carlton, 1990.
7 JHS to JSS, 8 September 1872, Symon Papers, NLA, MS 1736/1/158.
8 For a warm appraisal, see D. Bruce Ross, 'Stow, Randolph Isham (1828–1878)', *ADB*, vol. 6, MUP, Carlton, 1976.
9 JHS to JSS, 22 April 1873, Symon Papers, NLA, MS 1736/1/177.
10 For the above paragraph, see *ibid.*, 1/230–235.
11 *Ibid.*, 1/249.
12 For the above three paragraphs see JHS to JSS, 25 February, 15 and 17 March 1876, *ibid.*, 1/236–7, 241–3.
13 *Ibid.*, 5/34.
14 *Ibid.*, 5/35.
15 Gwynne and Stow were so distressed and angered by the Way appointment, they refused to speak to him outside of their judicial duties.
16 JHS to JSS, 18 May 1876, Symon Papers, NLA, MS 1736/1/257–61 and 5/18.
17 See Way's handwritten memorandum listing some final points of the agreement in *ibid.*, 5/33. Hannan, *Way*. p. 94.
18 JHS to JSS, 18 May 1876, Symon Papers, NLA, MS 1736/1/257–61.
19 JHS to JSS, 16 July and 10 August 1876, *ibid.*,1/268–9 and 271.
20 JHS to JSS, 19 April and 17 May 1879, *ibid.*, 1/399 and 403–4. In this letter Jo reported on his efforts to introduce Bill to many people and his arrangement with the Attorney-General to make Bill an honorary member of the Adelaide Club.
21 *Ibid.*, 1/357.
22 *Ibid.*, 1/340; *Evening Journal*, 22–4 April and *Express and Telegraph*, 23–5 April 1879.
23 See Robin Millhouse, 'Bundey, Sir William Henry (1838–1909)', *ADB*, vol. 3, MUP, Carlton, 1969; Peter Bartlett, 'Downer, Sir John William (1843–1915)', *ADB*, vol. 8, MUP, Carlton, 1981.
24 JHS to JSS, 13 June 1878, Symon Papers, NLA, MS 1736/1/343.
25 JHS to JSS, 5 October 1878, *ibid.*, 1/352.
26 *Ibid.*, 1/299.

27 *South Australian Register*, 28 July 1879. An 'utter' barrister was allowed to practise while still studying.
28 JHS to JSS, 6 September 1879, Symon Papers, NLA, MS 1736/1/403–4.
29 *South Australian Chronicle and Weekly Mail*, 24 January 1880.
30 JHS to Bill Symon, 8 April 1880, Symon Papers, NLA, MS 1736/1/430.

Chapter 5 ~ 'your dogged determination to succeed did most of the climbing.'

1 Nell to JHS, the second half of 1881, Symon Papers, NLA, MS 1736/1/539.
2 For Jo's time spent in the United Kingdom and on the Continent in 1880–1 see the letters Jo wrote to Bill and his sisters in *ibid.*, 1/425ff.
3 Peter Howell, 'Constitutional and Political Development, 1857–1890' in Dean Jaensch (ed.), *The Flinders History of South Australia: Political History*, Wakefield Press, Adelaide, 1986, p. 110.
4 *South Australian Advertiser, Evening Journal*, 9 April 1881.
5 John Bannon, *Supreme Federalist: The Political Life of Sir John Downer*, Wakefield Press, Adelaide, 2009, p. 29. The *South Australian Register*, like the *Evening Journal* a Symon supporter, reproduced the paragraph on 8 June 1881. It will be recalled that in 1879 Symon told his brother that he intended to make an application for 'silk'.
6 For Nell's letters, see Symon Papers, NLA, MS 1736/1/519–34, 536–7; 539–57 and 561; Elizabeth Symon Dyer, The *Bank Manager and his Family*, Peacock Publications, Adelaide, 2012, pp. 46–50.
7 *Ibid.*, p. 49.
8 *South Australian Advertiser*, 8 December 1881.
9 House of Assembly, *Parliamentary Debates*, 22 August 1883, pp. 878–85.
10 *Ibid.*, 27 February 1884, pp. 2191–2201.
11 *Express and Telegraph*, 28 February 1884.
12 For Sowden, see Carl Bridge, 'Sowden, Sir William John (1858–1943)', *ADB*, vol. 12, MUP, Carlton, 1990. Sowden became one of Symon's strongest supporters as editor of the *Register* from 1899–1922.
13 *South Australian Register*, 27 March 1884.
14 *Kapunda Herald*, 20 June 1884.
15 *South Australian Register*, 2 July 1884.
16 *Evening Journal*, 5 July 1886. According to Don Wright, Symon in 1886 declined the offer of a safe Tory seat in the UK. Wright, 'Symon', *ADB*, vol. 12.
17 The Parnellites, led by Charles Stewart Parnell (1882–91), were members of the Irish Parliamentary Party which supported Home Rule.
18 For the above two paragraphs, see *Evening Journal*, 28 February 1887.
19 *Express and Telegraph*, 7 March 1887.
20 The practice of 'plumping': where two or more candidates were to be elected for the same seat, voters were entitled to discard their second vote and cast one vote for their preferred candidate. Of the 154 votes cast for Symon in Mount Gambier, 100 were 'plumpers'.
21 Livingston fell ill in the following year and died aged 48 on 30 September 1888. Krichhauff first won a seat in the House of Assembly in 1857, held his Victoria District seat from 1884 to 1890 when he transferred briefly to the Legislative Council. He died in 1904 at the age of 79.
22 Symon Papers, NLA, MS 1736/1/613/14–16; author not identified: 'Auld, Patrick (1811–1886)', *ADB*, vol 3, MUP, Carlton, 1969; Merrily Hallsworth, 'Mazure, Léon Edmond (1860–1939)', *ADB*, supp. vol., MUP, Carlton, 2005.
23 JHS to JSS, 2 December 1889, Symon Papers, NLA, MS 1736/1/613/309.

Notes

24 Bob did have some success. According to the 1881 Census, he employed three people in his printery and in 1886 he married Jane Williamson, aged 36, in Edinburgh. After she died six years later he moved to Somerset where he died in 1911 and was buried in the Frome Dissenters Cemetery.
25 Symon Papers, NLA, MS 1736/1/602.
26 Laura Symon to JHS, 6 April 1889, *ibid.*, 1/606.
27 William Symon to JHS, 2 April 1889, *ibid.*, 1/605.
28 David Symon had arrived in Western Australia in c. 1881, and lived in Fremantle where he became an ironmonger, shipping merchant, a senior partner in a firm of merchants and was a member of the Perth Stock Exchange and a JP. He was elected in 1890 for South Fremantle in the Legislative Assembly. David resigned in 1892 and returned to the UK to reside in Chiswick and worked as an auctioneer and general merchant.
29 Symon Papers, NLA, MS 1736/5/944d and e/951.
30 *Ibid.*, 5/968–1005, 1007–1027.
31 For a good press coverage of the case, see *Evening Journal*, 6–7 June 1889.
32 JHS to JSS, 17 February 1890, Symon Papers, NLA, MS 1736/1/613/318.

Chapter 6 – 'There is a first place and you alone occupy it.'

1 *Adelaide Observer*, 23 April 1892.
2 JHS to Kingston, 19 and 20 March 1891, Symon Papers, NLA, MS 1736/1/825/71–4.
3 For Jo's letters to Nell on this trip, see *ibid.*, 1/617ff.
4 *Advertiser*, 23 May 1892.
5 Playford to Kingston, 10 February 1892, Symon Papers, NLA, MS 1736/8/30. Jo wanted Nell to persuade Bakewell to ask Kingston what Playford might have said in his letter to Kingston.
6 Jim, when aged 51, had married Sarah Dottridge in 1886. She was blissfully unaware until they married that Jim was 30 years older than her. By 1892 the couple had three children; they were to have two more. Sarah died soon after delivering their fifth child in June 1901.
7 *South Australian Register*, 15 April 1892.
8 *Advertiser* and *South Australian Register*, 30 December; *South Australian Chronicle* and *Adelaide Observer*, 31 December 1892.
9 It appears that Kingston refused to pay more than £10, a figure Symon considered 'hardly adequate'. On 24 August Symon told Kingston he had reduced the bill to £15 because Kingston had asked him to lower it, but he could not take it down further. JHS to Kingston, 21 and 24 August 1893, Symon Papers, NLA, MS 1736/1/825/631 and 635. It is not known how this matter was resolved.
10 The 9th Earl of Kintore succeeded to his titles in 1880, sat with the Conservatives in the House of Lords and took his appointment for what he believed was a five-year term.
11 Edward Milner to JHS, Symon Papers, NLA, MS 1736/1/824–5.
12 *Evening Journal*, 1 April 1893.
13 Adams to JHS, 3 May and Price to JHS, 5 May 1893, Symon Papers, NLA, MS 1736/8/46–7.
14 Millhouse, 'Bundey', *ADB*, vol. 3. For a draft of the letter, see Symon Papers, NLA, MS 1736/8/116–17.
15 For the drafts, see *ibid.*, 8/101–116 and the final version, *ibid.*, 8/92–7.
16 Kintore to JHS 24 July 1893, *ibid.*, 8/86.
17 *South Australian Chronicle*, 4 November 1893.
18 *Express and Telegraph*, 1 November 1893.

19 JHS to Justice Bundey, 25 July 1894, Symon Papers, NLA, MS 1736/1/828.
20 For three lectures on Shakespearean quotations, see *Evening Journal*, 14 September 1894 and *Advertiser*, 19 July 1895 and 9 July 1897.
21 *South Australian Register*, 8 September 1893, 13 January 1894.
22 *South Australian Chronicle*, 24 November 1894.
23 Disraeli: 'men who are the friends of every country save their own'. Perhaps Symon thought that the early 19th century Foreign Secretary George Canning was too remote for 1894: 'A steady friend of the world alone; the friend of every country but his own.'
24 Reid's Free Trade Ministerialists won 61 seats and an Independent Free Trade supporter took one; the Protectionist Opposition secured 41 seats, Labor 18 and Independent Labor four. For Symon's letter, see Symon Papers, NLA, MS 1736/1/825/329.
25 For a convincing explanation of Reid's ambivalence over federation, see W.G. McMinn, *George Reid*, MUP, Carlton, 1989, ch. 14.
26 *South Australian Register*, 1 May 1896.
27 *Advertiser* and *South Australian Register*, 27 February 1896.
28 Rob van den Hoorn and John Playford, 'The Adelaide Hospital Row', in Jaensch (ed.), *Flinders History: Political*, Appendix to ch. 6.
29 *Adelaide Observer*, 25 July 1896.
30 JHS to JSS, 31 March 1896, Symon Papers, NLA, MS 1736/1/885/587.

Chapter 7 ~ 'it is for the people to say how they shall be governed.'

1   *South Australian Register*, 9 February 1897.
2   *Advertiser*, 1 March 1897.
3   *Advertiser* and *South Australian Register*, 16 February 1897.
4   *Quiz and the Lantern*, 18 February 1897.
5   *Northern Argus* (Clare), 19 February 1897.
6   *Chronicle*, 13 February 1897.
7   *Advertiser*, 2 March 1897.
8   For the overall final figures, see *Adelaide Observer*, 20 March 1897. See also Kathleen Dermody, 'The 1897 Federal Convention Election: a Success or Failure?', Paper on Parliament no. 30, November 1997.
9   Alfred Deakin, *The Federal Story: The Inner History of the Federal Cause*, Robertson & Mullens, Melbourne, 1944, pp. 59–60, 72.
10 JHS to Barton, 29 November 1894, Symon Papers, NLA, MS 1736/1/885/184; Barton to JHS, 4 December 1894, *ibid.*, 8/165.
11 *Ibid.*, 8/826.
12 Geoffrey Bolton, *Edmund Barton*, Allen & Unwin, St Leonards, 2000, p. 142. For a very negative appraisal of Barton, see William Oliver Coleman, *Their Fiery Cross of Union: A Retelling of the Creation of the Australian Federation, 1889–1914*, Connor Court Publishing Pty Ltd., Redland Bay, 2021, pp. 104–119.
13 Symon Papers, NLA, MS 1736/1/831.
14 G.H. Reid, *My Reminiscences*, Cassell, London, 1917, pp. 133–4; Deakin, *Federal Story*, p. 75.
15 *Argus*, 10 and 20 January 1920. See also, The Hon. Sir Josiah Symon, KCMG, KC (edited and annotated by D.I. Wright), 'The Dawn of Federation: Some Episodes, Letters and Personalities and a Vindication', *South Australiana*, vol. 15, no. 2, 1976, pp. 116–19.
16 The *Evening Journal*, 22 March 1897 reported that the Victorians sat on the ministerial benches; there was some confusion among the press on the first day.

Notes

17 Deakin, *Federal Story*, pp. 73–4.
18 *Express and Telegraph*, 24 March 1897.
19 For the brilliant 'Prince of Bohemia' Nesbit, see Graham Loughlin, 'Nesbit, Paris (1852–1927)', *ADB*, vol. 11, MUP, Carlton, 1988.
20 J.A. La Nauze, *Making of the Australian Constitution*, MUP, Carlton, 1974 edn., p. 121. For Symon's speech, see Greg Craven (ed.), *Official Record of the Debates of National Australasian Convention*, Adelaide 1897, vol. 3, Legal Books, Sydney 1986, pp. 125–41.
21 Deakin, *Federal Story*, p. 59.
22 *Ibid.*, pp. 59, 60 and 72; La Nauze, *Making of the Australian Constitution*, p. 104.
23 Judiciary Committee, Minutes of Proceedings, National Archives of Australia (NAA), R214/1; La Nauze, *The Making of the Australian Constitution*, p. 130–32.
24 Samuel Griffith, 'Notes on the Draft Federal Constitution Framed by the Adelaide Convention of 1897', June 1897, in John M. Williams, *The Australian Constitution: A Documentary History*, MUP, Carlton, 2005, pp. 621–3.
25 La Nauze, *Making of the Australian Constitution*, p. 169.
26 *Ibid.*, p. 142.
27 For the Deakin, Symon and Isaacs speeches, see *Official Record of the Debates*, Adelaide, vol. 3, pp. 506–15, 515–22 and 542–6.
28 For the lobbying preceding the vote, which began on the visit to Broken Hill, see La Nauze, *Making of the Australian Constitution*, pp. 141–6.

Chapter 8 ~ 'the finest instrument of government that ever was framed'

1 McMinn, *Reid*, pp. 137–8.
2 *Advertiser* and *South Australian Register*, 22 May; *Chronicle* and *Adelaide Observer*, 29 May 1897.
3 Wright, 'Symon', *ADB*, vol. 12.
4 *Quiz and the Lantern*, 27 May and *Adelaide Observer*, 29 May 1897.
5 John M. MacKenzie, 'Essay and Reflection: On Scotland and the Empire', *International History Review*, vol. 15, no. 4, 1993, pp. 714–39.
6 Symon Papers, NLA, MS 1736/9/28–30. For Carruthers, see Zachary Gorman, *Sir Joseph Carruthers: Founder of the New South Wales Liberal Party*, Connor Court Publishing, Redlands Bay, 2018.
7 Sir Joseph Carruthers, Autobiography, NLA, MS 5136, pp. 23–3.
8 La Nauze, *Making of the Australian Constitution*, pp. 179–80.
9 Craven, *Official Record of Debates*, Sydney, vol. 2, pp. 21–8.
10 John Quick, and Robert Randolph Garran, *The Annotated Constitution of the Australian Commonwealth*, reprint of 1901 edition, Legal Books, Sydney, 1976, pp. 183–93.
11 Craven, *Official Record of Debates*, Sydney, vol. 2, pp. 253–67; John Rickard, *H.B. Higgins: The Rebel as Judge*, George Allen & Unwin, Sydney, 1984, p. 94.
12 Craven, *Official Record of Debates*, Sydney, pp. 288–303.
13 Appointed Regius Professor of Modern History at Oxford University in 1882, Freeman was a prolific historian best known for his six-volume History of the Norman Conquest.
14 Craven, *Official Record of Debates*, pp. 491–2.
15 Quick and Garran, *Annotated Constitution*, pp. 189–93.
16 Quick and Garran noted that the smaller and larger colonies were generally aligned against each other. Yet McMillan and Walker (NSW) and Fraser and Zeal (Vic.) voted with the former on the Symon amendment; Gordon, Glynn and

Sir Josiah Symon KCMG KC

Kingston (SA) Hackett (WA) and Henry (Tas.) sided with the latter. For the division list, see Craven, *Official Record of Debates*, vol. 2, p. 728.
17   *Ibid.*, pp. 589-97.
18   *Ibid.*, p. 592.
19   *Ibid.*, pp. 682-3.
20   *Ibid.*, pp. 949-53; John Playford, 'Cockburn, Sir John Alexander (1850-1929)', *ADB*, vol. 8, MUP, Carlton, 1981.
21   Craven, *Official Record of Debates*, vol. 2, pp. 953-6.
22   For the Melbourne session, see Quick and Garran, *Annotated Constitution*, pp. 194-206.
23   For the Melbourne debates on rivers see *ibid.*, pp. 194-7; for the development of what became s.100, see *ibid.*, pp. 879-94; for a summary of proposals and amendments, see Craven, *Official Record of Debates*, vol. 1, pp. 549-52.
24   *Ibid.*, vol. 4, p. 32.
25   For the main Symon arguments, see *ibid.*, pp. 72-80.
26   *Ibid.*, p. 79.
27   La Nauze, *Making of the Australian Constitution*, pp. 208-211. He was writing before the Tasmanian Dam Case of 1983.
28   For the Abbott and Symon speeches, see Craven, *Official Record of Debates*, vol. 4, pp. 2286-2309.
29   *Ibid.*, pp. 2326-35.
30   *Ibid.*, pp. 2341-2.
31   Greg Taylor, 'The Judicial Incompatibility Clause – or how a version of the Kable principle almost made it into the Australian Constitution', 38 *Adelaide Law Review*, 2017, pp. 351-73.
32   Carruthers, J.H., Autobiography, Manuscript, NLA, pp. 22-3.
33   Craven, *Official Record of Debates*, vol. 4, pp. 2507-9.
34   For the implications of their successes, see John M. Williams, 'South Australia and the Constitution: A mere provincial contribution?, J.C. Bannon Oration, 31 August 2021, https://www.johnbannonoration.com.au/
35   Craven, Greg, 'Heresy as Orthodoxy: Were the Founders Progressivists?, *Federal Law Review*, vol. 31 (1), 2003.
36   *South Australian Register*, 5 April, *Weekly Herald*, 9 April 1898.
37   *Critic*, 16 April 1898. Watts was a farmer accused of murdering his sub-tenant, Thomas Lort, after the two men had engaged in a long drinking session some 30 miles from the town of Eudunda, north-east of Adelaide. Symon, appearing with Charles Kingston, successfully defended Watts by simultaneously elevating him to near-sainthood and identifying the key witness, the third member of the drinking session, as a liar, a coward and possibly the real culprit. *Advertiser*, 7 December 1891.
38   For Reid's speech and the changing reactions to it, see McMinn, *Reid*, pp. 148-54.
39   *South Australian Register*, 19 April 1898.
40   *Advertiser*, 15-16 and 20 April; *Chronicle*, 23 April 1898.
41   *Observer*, 11 June 1898.
42   McMinn, *Reid*, p. 155.
43   Symon Papers, NLA, MS 1736/9/89.
44   For the Deakin letters, see *ibid.*, 9/96, 100, 107.
45   *Advertiser*, 5 August and 13 August 1898. It would take 120 years before a State Premier, without necessarily having access to verifiable incriminating evidence, could pronounce, 'We believe you'.
46   A.G. Austen (ed.), *The Webbs' Australian Diary*, Isaac Pitman, Carlton, 1965, pp. 104-6.

Notes

Chapter 9 ~ 'a great paean of triumph in the closely knit union of the race.'

1. For these decisions and some of their implications, see La Nauze, *Making of the Australian Constitution*, pp. 242–7.
2. McMinn, *Reid*, pp. 165–6.
3. *South Australian Register*, 4 February and *Express and Telegraph*, 8 February 1899.
4. For Symon's well-received visit, see *Kalgoorlie Miner*, 2 April, *Coolgardie Miner*, 3 April and *West Australian*, 6 April 1900.
5. Published in the *Chronicle*, 29 July 1900. For accounts of the 1899 trip, see *Express and Telegraph*, 28 November 1899 and Dyer, *The Bank Manager*, pp. 60–1.
6. *Express and Telegraph*, 28 November 1899.
7. For the above four paragraphs, see Symon Papers, NLA, MS 1736/1/920/22–3, 472–6 and 9/124–46, 180; Bolton, *Barton*, pp. 202–3. Some 'alms' were delivered to Barton for his wife and the education of his children; this author is unaware of the specific figure. See Martha Rutledge, 'Barton, Sir Edmund (Toby) (1849–1920)', *ADB*, vol. 7, MUP, Carlton, 1979.
8. Symon Papers, NLA, MS 1736/1/920/484–5.
9. B.K. de Garis, 'The Colonial Office and the Commonwealth Constitution Bill', in A.W. Martin (ed.), *Essays in Australian Federation*, MUP, Carlton, 1969, p. 117.
10. Deakin Papers, NLA, MS 1540/11/142 and 152.
11. *South Australian Register*, 13 January 1900.
12. The NSW Labor Party had shifted its allegiance to defeat the Reid Government 75–41 on 7 September 1899. The Governor rejected Reid's proposals for a prorogation or a dissolution and the Lyne Protectionist Government took office on 14 September.
13. For the memoranda Symon sent to Selborne, see Symon Papers, NLA, MS 1736/9/163–70 and 185–92.
14. *Ibid.*, 11/157.
15. La Nauze, *Making of the Australian Constitution*, pp. 249–50. New Zealand sent two representatives to the 1891 Convention but had played no direct part in the federation movement thereafter.
16. For Symon's letters to Sowden, see Symon Papers, NLA, MS 1736/1/920/24–5 and 36–7.
17. JHS to Kaufman, 18 April 1900, *ibid.*, 1/920/123.
18. *Ibid.*, 1/895.
19. *Ibid.*, 1/920/27–9.
20. For the London story, see Deakin, *Federal Story*, ch.21; La Nauze, *Making of the Australian Constitution*, ch. 16; de Garis, 'The Colonial Office and the Commonwealth Constitution Bill'; Williams, *Australian Constitution*, pp. 1160–71.
21. Symon Papers, NLA, MS 1736/9/250.
22. Deakin, *Federal Story*, p. 141; *South Australian Register*, 15 June 1900.
23. Deakin, *Federal Story*, p. 155; Symon, 'Dawn of Federation', p. 138. Wright decided on the basis of Deakin's account that Symon's version was wrong.
24. For the clause, see La Nauze, *Making of the Australian Constitution*, p. 266 and the two notes on that page.
25. *Advertiser* and *South Australian Register*, 16 May 1900.
26. *South Australian Register*, 26 June 1900. For the subsequent exchanges, see Symon Papers, NLA, MS 1736/1/443–51.
27. For the above letters, see *ibid.*, 9/338/345/364/386.
28. For the subsequent Baker-Symon exchanges, see *Advertiser*, 17–23 May 1900.
29. Symon Papers, NLA, MS 1736/9/429.

30 The *Advertiser* on 16 May 1900 explained it did not have the space for the third piece. As it had opposed Symon on the appeals question the *Advertiser* had been generous.
31 Hannan, *Way*, p. 185.
32 Sowden to Symon, 26 March 1930, Symon Papers, NLA, MS 1736/1/4077. For Symon's response, see *ibid.*, 1/4083-4.
33 *Express and Telegraph*, 19 May 1900.
34 *Advertiser*, 21 September 1900. The lecture was subsequently published in 1905 and Jo would soon share the fate of many authors. He told Nell on 11 August 1909 – she was in the UK at the time – that he had received 'the magnificent sum of £2/13/-' for sales in Melbourne of *Shakespeare at Home*. Nell might invest the money or keep it as 'a memento of the profit of this literary venture'. Symon Papers, NLA, MS 1736/1/1476.
35 For Symon's letters to Hamilton, see *ibid.*, 1/920/31, 34, 48, 56, 72, 88, 112-14, 139, 142, 346-7, 395, 455, 462, 473.

Chapter 10 ~ 'I am jealous of the rights of the Commonwealth'

1 Chris Cunneen, 'Lyne, Sir William John (1844–1913)', *ADB*, vol. 10, MUP, Carlton, 1986.
2 Bannon, *Supreme Federalist*, p. 179.
3 Kingston to JHS, 28 November 1900, Symon Papers, NLA, MS 1736/9/507 (a more legible typed version in 9/509); Symon, 'Dawn of Federation', p. 146.
4 For a copy of the reprinted and distributed version of the speech, see Symon Papers, NLA, MS 1736/10/6.
5 *Ibid.*, 10/17.
6 *Ibid.*, 10/13.
7 *Critic*, 16 March 1901.
8 Bannon, *Supreme Federalist*, p. 183.
9 See Symon Papers, NLA, MS 1736/10/5 and 20ff.
10 The Archbishop changed his name from 'O'Reilly' to save time and labour in signing documents'. M. French, 'O'Reily, John (1846–1919)', *ADB*, vol 11, MUP, Carlton, 1988.
11 For the above two paragraphs, see Symon Papers, NLA, MS 1736/10/71, 86-92.
12 Lady Symon and her three eldest daughters received invitations to the ceremony and to the evening reception to meet the royal visitors.
13 N.D. Walker to JHS, 14 March 1901, Symon Papers, NLA, MS 1736/10/81-4.
14 *Ibid.*, 10/194-6.
15 For the above paragraph, see *ibid.*, 10/94, 96, 101-3.
16 *Register*, 16 August 1901.
17 Clemons attended Launceston Church Grammar School, graduated in law at Oxford, was called to the English Bar, practised law in Launceston and became a businessman. Clemons was keen to protect the States from Commonwealth intrusion and became Symon's closest friend and ally in the Senate. Joan Rydon, 'Clemons, John Singleton (1862–1944)', *Biographical Dictionary of the Australian Senate*, vol. 1, 1901–1929, MUP, Carlton South, 2000.
18 *Advertiser* and *Register*, 22 August 1901.
19 Peter Donovan, *The Trial of Mary Schippan*, Donovan & Associates, Blackwood, 2004, pp. 6–12. See also, Graham Lyons, 'Symon the Barrister: the Schippan Murder Case', *New Heritage*, June–August 1994, pp. 16–18; Patricia Sumerling, *The Noon Lady of Towitta: A mystery*, Wakefield Press, Adelaide, 2010; Richard Huschke,

Notes

The Towitta Tragedy: The True Story of the Bertha Schippan Murder, Richard Dutches, Alfredton, 2017.

20 Evidence of the public and press interest may readily be obtained from Adelaide-based newspapers. See also Donovan, *Mary Schippan*, and especially pp. 46–8, 52–3, 57, 59.
21 *Ibid.*, p. 50; Symon Papers, NLA, MS 1736/5/1418–1520.
22 For the summings-up and Way's summary, see *Register*, 11 March and *Advertiser*, 12 March 1902.
23 *Evening Journal*, 12 March 1902. Donovan described the result as 'another triumph for the eloquent and flamboyant Sir Josiah Symon, at least as far as he was concerned'. Donovan did not appear to consider the impact of a relentless cross-examination. See Donovan, *Mary Schippan*, p. 121.
24 For Reid's letters, see Symon Papers, NLA, MS 1736/10/142–3 and 151.
25 Martha Rutledge, 'Neild, John Cash (1846–1911)', vol. 10, *ADB*, MUP, Carlton, 1986; Craig Wilcox, 'Neild, John Cash (1846–1911)', *Biographical Dictionary of the Australian Senate*, MUP, Carlton South, 2000.
26 For the above exchanges, see Symon Papers, NLA, MS 1736/10/152–3, 158–61, 174(a), 178, 180, 184, 187. For Neild's continuing stand, see his article in the *Daily Telegraph*, 27 November 1907.
27 Martha Rutledge, 'O'Connor, Richard Edward ('Dick') (1851–1912)', *ADB*, vol. 11, MUP, Carlton 1988.
28 Symon Papers, NLA, MS 1736/10/259–61, 263.
29 *Ibid.*, 10/79, 104–7.
30 Way was Acting Governor for the period between the end of Lord Tennyson's term as Governor and Sir George Ruthven Le Hunte's arrival (July 1902-July 1903).
31 Bolton, *Barton*, pp. 280–2.
32 For the above paragraphs, see Symon Papers, NLA, MS 1736/10/229, 234–6, 238–44, 150. The *Advertiser* reported that Symon did not attend the gala event on which the press duly feasted. See *Advertiser*, 18 and 20 April and *SMH* 20 April 1903.
33 J.A. La Nauze, *Alfred Deakin: A Biography*, vol. 1, MUP, Carlton, 1965, p. 289.
34 *Commonwealth Parliamentary Debates*, (*CPD*), Senate, vol. 15, pp. 2920–47.
35 *Ibid.*, 5 August, pp. 3074–6.
36 For South Australian commentary, see *Register* 1, 14 September, *Observer*, 19 September 1903.
37 *Observer*, 16 October 1903.
38 An unhappy Downer, whose drinking as well as Barton's desertion of his friend may have cost him an appointment to the High Court, had already decided not to contest the election for the Senate on 16 December 1903.
39 For Way's unflattering comment on the caravan and its inhabitants, see John M. Williams, '"Swelling the Ranks of the Peripatetic Unemployed": The First Decade of the High Court of Australia', High Court of Australia, Public Lecture Series, 8 June 2011, p. 19 (PDF 279k) (RTF 188k).

Chapter 11 ~ 'he is not fit to be Prime Minister.'

1 For some accounts, see W.G. McMinn, 'The High Court Imbroglio and the Fall of the Reid–McLean Government', *Journal of the Royal Australian Historical Society*, vol. 64, Pt 1, June 1978, pp. 14–31; D.I. Wright, 'Sir Josiah Symon, Federation and the High Court', *Journal of the Royal Australian Historical Society*, vol. 64, Pt 2, September 1978, pp. 73–88; Susan Priest, 'Archives, the Australian High Court and the "Strike of 1905"', *University of Queensland Law Journal*, vol. 32, no. 2, 2013, pp. 253–64; Stephen Gageler, 'When the High Court Went on Strike', *Melbourne University Law Review*, vol. 40, no. 3, 2017, pp. 1098–1141.

Sir Josiah Symon KCMG KC

2 Sir Anthony Mason, 'The High Court of Australia: A Personal Impression of its First 100 Years', *Melbourne University Law Review*, vol. 27. no. 3, 2003, p. 868.
3 *Ibid.*, p. 867.
4 Symon Papers, NLA, MS 1736/11/3 and 6.
5 McMinn, *Reid*, pp. 210–211.
6 Symon Papers, NLA MS 1736/11/8, 13–14, 16, 18, 23, 25ff.
7 *Ibid.*, 11/25ff.
8 *Ibid.*, 11/20.
9 *Argus*, 4 November 1904.
10 'Re High Court Organization and Expenditure', Symon Papers, NLA, MS 1736/11/456–76.
11 Williams, 'Swelling the Ranks of the Peripatetic Unemployed', p. 28.
12 When Symon enquired of the associates' qualifications, Garran informed him on 27 April 1905 that E.A Barton had been called to the English Bar and H.E. Manning (O'Connor's associate) to the Sydney Bar. E.P.T. Griffith 'is not a barrister'. Symon Papers, NLA, MS 1736/11/312.
13 Attorney General to the Justices of the High Court, 29 July; Barton to Attorney-General, 2 August; Justices of the High Court to Attorney-General, 19 August 1904, *Commonwealth Parliamentary Papers* (*CPP*), 1905, no. 26, pp. 1–2.
14 *Ibid.*, 11/146-146a.
15 *CPP*, 1905, no. 26, pp. 2–3. See also Symon Papers, NLA, MS 1736/11/149 for the letter where JHS wrote 'I was not aware'
16 *CPP*, 1905, no. 26, pp. 3–4. McMinn, 'High Court Imbroglio', pp. 15–16.
17 Symon Papers, NLA, MS 1736/11/161.
18 *Ibid.*, 11/163–5.
19 *Ibid.*, 11/162.
20 McMinn, 'High Court Imbroglio', p. 16.
21 JHS to Reid, 1 March 1905, Symon Papers, NLA, MS 1736/11/236.
22 *Ibid.*, 11/239.
23 *Ibid.*, 11/425–6.
24 For Garran's attempts to persuade Symon of the necessity for associates and tipstaffs see Garran to JHS, 15 March 1905, *ibid.*, 11/531–4.
25 For letters and documents on the strike, see *ibid.*, 11/539–65. See also 'Mr. G.H. Castle, Principal Registrar, High Court of Australia (Correspondence Relating to Charge of Neglect of Duty)', *CPP*, No. 20, 16 August 1905.
26 Symon Papers, NLA. MS 1736/11/318, 323–7.
27 *Ibid.*, 11/353–4.
28 *Ibid.*, 11/352.
29 *Ibid.*, 11/387 (e-r).
30 *Ibid.*, 11/387 (a).
31 *Ibid.*, 11/395–8.
32 *Ibid.*, 11/416–18.
33 Symon appeared for the Adelaide and Suburban Tramway Coy; Nesbit represented the State Government. The case extended for an initial eight days. Symon went to Sydney a week later than expected. In April-May 1905, Symon had a substantial private caseload.
34 Ever alert to transgressions, Symon did not think it odd that he showed confidential documents to Clemons.
35 Symon Papers, NLA, MS 1736/11/102–4.
36 *Ibid.*, 11/105.

Notes

37 *Ibid.*, 11/449.
38 *Ibid.*, 11/611–13.
39 The three points: travelling expenses should be determined retrospectively as from 1 January 1905; allowances should be paid on a daily rate in addition to fares; while the judges reside in Sydney their travelling expenses while holding sessions in Melbourne shall be allowed on same basis as if they resided in Melbourne and had to travel to Sydney to attend court. See *ibid.*, 11/477.
40 *Ibid.*, 11/616–18.
41 McMinn, 'High Court Imbroglio', pp. 27–8.
42 La Nauze, *Deakin*, vol. 2. p. 385 and Priest, 'Strike of 1905', p. 2013.
43 Gageler, 'When the High Court went on Strike', pp. 1129–30.
44 Symon Papers, NLA, MS 1736/11/668.
45 *CPD*, vol. 25, Senate, pp. 133–4.
46 McMinn, 'High Court Imbroglio', p. 22 and endnote 42; JHS to Crouch Batchelor, 29 June 1917, Symon Papers, NLA MS 1736/53/173–7.

Chapter 12 ~ 'this combination has set me free from party'

1 *Herald*, 2 June 1906. James Henderson of the defence team had died in the meantime.
2 Hannan, *Way*, p. 209.
3 *Ibid.*
4 *Australian Christian Commonwealth*, 30 March 1906.
5 *Quiz*, 22 June 1906.
6 *Register* (two articles), 28 August and editorial *Australian Christian Commonwealth*, 31 August 1906.
7 Clemons to JHS, 9 October 1906, Symon Papers, NLA, MS 1736/10/479.
8 La Nauze, *Deakin*, vol. 2, p. 416 and endnote 24.
9 See, *Express and Telegraph* and *Advertiser*, 8 October; *Register*, 13 October 1906.
10 Dobson to JHS, 12 October 1906, Symon Papers, NLA, MS 1736/10/480.
11 *Ibid.*, 1/2505–6.
12 McMinn, *Reid*, ch. 23.
13 Reid to JHS, 10 November 1906, Symon Papers, NLA, MS 1736/10/481.
14 Joseph Vardon had founded a substantial printing and publishing company, served as a minister in the Jenkins and Butler ministries and was president of the Liberal Union (1910–13). See Malcolm Saunders, 'Vardon, Joseph (1843–1913)', *ADB*, vol. 12, MUP, Carlton, 1990; and Suzanne Rickard, 'Vardon, Joseph (1843–1913)', *The Biographical Dictionary of the Australian Senate*, vol. 1, 1901–1929, MUP, Carlton South, Vic., 2000.
15 See *Register*, 15 November and *Herald*, 17 and 24 November 1906.
16 Symon Papers, NLA, MS 1736/10/436.
17 Vivien Stewart, 'Tucker, Charles (1857–1928)', *ADB*, vol. 12, MUP, Carlton, 1990.
18 Symon Papers, NLA, MS 1736/10/449. See also *ibid.*, 10/510–21.
19 Hughes, Colin A and Graham, B.D., *A Handbook of Australian Government and Politics 1890–1964*, ANU Press, Canberra, 1968, pp. 299 and 545.
20 For Millen's and McLean's comments, see Symon Papers, NLA, MS 1736/10/462 and 486.
21 The above six paragraphs draw upon Symon Papers, NLA, MS 1736/10/482, 493, 498, 503–04, 510–14, 517–18. See also *ibid.*, 1736/1/110–11.
22 For their overseas trip, see Dyer, *The Bank Manager*, pp. 67–79.
23 *Ibid.*, p. 68.

24 *Daily Telegraph* and *SMH*, 17 July 1907.
25 Symon Papers, NLA, MS 1736/5/1865–70, 1894.
26 For Way and Rounsevell, see *ibid.*, 1/2002–3.
27 *CPD*, Senate, vol. 40, pp. 4708–23.
28 *Ibid.*, pp. 4797–81.
29 For the above three paragraphs, see Symon Papers, NLA, MS 1736/10/526, 529, 531, 547–8, 553–4.
30 For accounts of Reid's departure and of the meeting, see *Daily Telegraph*, 27 November 1908 and La Nauze, *Deakin*, p. 535.
31 *West Australian*, 9 March 1908.
32 Dyer, *The Bank Manager*, pp. 79–92, 95–8.
33 JHS to Nell, 1 June 1909, Symon Papers, NLA, MS 1736/1/1311.
34 *West Australian*, 9 June 1909.
35 Clemons to JHS, 17 June 1909, Symon Papers, NLA, MS 1736/10/566.
36 For the circular and Symon's reply, see *ibid.*, 10/567 and 569.
37 JHS to Nell, 29 June 1909, *ibid.*, 1/1463 and 1463(a).
38 *CPD*, Senate, vol. 39, pp. 682–4. On 16 July 1909, the Fusion Government survived a no-confidence motion in the House of Representatives by 34 votes to 27. Sawer said the debate on the non-confidence motion 'was the last great political inquest of the pre-World War period'. Geoffrey Sawer, *Australian Federal Politics and the Law 1921–1929*, MUP, Carlton, 1956, p. 77.
39 *CPD*, Senate, vol. 39, pp. 878–908.
40 *SMH*, 8 July 1909.
41 Symon Papers, NLA, MS 1736/1/1490 and 91.
42 *Ibid.*, 1/1466–6.

Chapter 13 ~ 'I am really sick of politics & want rest.'

1 *Register*, 9 April 1910.
2 *CPD*, Senate, vol. 58, pp. 4975–95.
3 *Advertiser*, 11 April 1911.
4 *Advertiser, Register, Daily Herald*, 22 April 1911.
5 *Advertiser*, 29 April 1911.
6 *West Australian*, 26 October 1911.
7 *Ibid.*
8 Quoted in I.R. Hancock, 'The 1911 Imperial Conference', *Historical Studies Australia and New Zealand*, vol. 12, no. 47. 1967, p. 366.
9 *West Australian*, 26 October 1911.
10 Jo's letters to Kilmeny (1897–1933) are to be found in Elizabeth Dyer Papers, NLA, MS 10369/1; letters to and from Carril will be found in Symon Family Papers, NLA, MS 10061/2/1–15.
11 JHS to CHNS (Carril Hector Nicholson Symon), 7 November 1912, *ibid.*, 10061/2/1.
12 T. Herbert Warren to JHS, 19 April 1909, Symon Papers, NLA, MS 1736/1/1298.
13 T.H. Bromley to JHS, 6 May 1909, *ibid.*, 1/1302.
14 *Ibid.*, 1/1490.
15 JHS to Manager, Bank of Adelaide, London, 21 November 1911 and 31 January 1912, *ibid.*, 1/1527/381 and 1/1685/6. Jo paid Oscar's Oxford and Magdalen fees separately.
16 JHS to CHNS, 24 April and 15 May 1912, Symon Family Papers, NLA, MS 10061/2/1.
17 Students taking 'Greats', the colloquial rendition of *Literae Humaniores*, Oxford's classics course, could take Pass Moderations for five terms or Honours

Notes

Moderations for seven. 'Greats' in 1912 remained the prestigious undergraduate option.
18 JHS to CHNS, 13 June 1912, Symon Family Papers, NLA, MS 10061/2/1.
19 CHNS to JHS, (no date) 1912, *ibid.*, 2/10; JHS to CHNS, 13 and 25 June 1912, *ibid.*, 2/1.
20 JHS to Parkin, 10 March 1913, *ibid.*, Symon Papers, NLA, MS 1736/1/1687/139–40.
21 *Ibid.*, 1/1685/417–8; 1/1687/10–11.
22 JHS to CHNS, 18 September 1912, Symon Family Papers, NLA, MS 10061/2/1.
23 JHS to LKS, 25 April and 2 May 1912, Elizabeth Dyer Papers, NLA, MS 10369/1.
24 The Liberal Union: Constitution, Rules and Political Platform, 1912, Symon Papers, NLA, MS 1736/12/2.
25 *Ibid.*,12/15–17.
26 *Ibid.*, 12/26. For a similar statement delivered to Vardon, see *ibid.*, 12/92–3.
27 See Symon's letters of April-May 1912 in *ibid.*, 12/43 and 45–9.
28 *Ibid.*, 12/49.
29 *Ibid.*, 12/51.
30 *Ibid.*, 12/20–1.
31 *Ibid.*, 12/91–2.
32 *Ibid.*, 12/49.
33 *Ibid.*, 1/1660.
34 *Ibid.*, 12/39 and 42. *ibid.*, Box 42.
35 *Ibid.*, 12/15 and 31–2.
36 *Advertiser*, 5 June 1912.
37 While the plebiscite was under way, the South Australian Parliament at a joint sitting elected John Shannon, a Liberal, by 32 votes to 21 to replace the Labor Senator, William Russell, who died on 28 June 1912.
38 *Advertiser*, 17 August 1912.
39 Symon Papers, NLA, MS 1736/12/104–5.
40 *Ibid.*, 12/108. For the many letters, pleas, regrets and offers to help, see *ibid.*, Box 42, files 12/1–3.
41 *Ibid.*, 12/154.
42 *Register*, 13 May 1913.
43 See, for example, *Advertiser*, 15 May 1913.
44 *Daily Herald*, 21 January 1913.
45 *Advertiser* and *Register*, 26 April 1913.
46 Symon Papers, NLA, MS 1736/12/171, 184, 187.
47 *Ibid.*, 1/1694 and 12/704–06.
48 For press clippings before and after the election, see *ibid.*, 12/10–12.
49 *Daily Herald* and *Register*, 26 June 2013.
50 Symon Papers, NLA, MS 1736/1/1718.
51 For Smith, see Martha Rutledge, 'Smith, Arthur Bruce (1851–1937)', *ADB*, vol. 11, MUP, Carlton, 1988 and Coleman, *Their Fiery Cross*, pp. 119–24.
52 Smith to JHS, 16 June 1913, Symon Papers, NLA, MS 1736/1/1712.
53 *Ibid.*, 1/1716.

Chapter 14 ~ 'My boys & girls are all in all to me.'
1 JHS to LKS (Kilmeny), 15 May 1914, Letters JHS to LKS, Elizabeth Dyer Papers, NLA, MS 10369/1.
2 War duties intervened. The Prince was recalled to his regiment and served in France. In line with other Royals, he relinquished his German titles in 1917 and his

Sir Josiah Symon KCMG KC

brother-in-law, King George V, appointed him Earl of Athlone. Symon regarded the Earl and his wife, Alice, as special friends.

3 The German-born Prince Louis followed the Royals in 1917 by anglicising his name to 'Mountbatten'. His second son, Louis Mountbatten, also became First Sea Lord, the last Viceroy of India, a mentor of Prince Charles and a victim of an IRA assassination in 1979.

4 JHS to LKS, 14 August 1914, Elizabeth Dyer Papers, NLA, MS 10369/1.

5 *Ibid.*

6 JHS to LKS, 3 September 1914 and 12 January 1916, *ibid*. Way's mistress, Susannah Gooding, died in 1888. In April 1898 Way, on his 62nd birthday, married Katharine Gollan, late Blue, née Gordon, a 44 year-old widow with a grown-up family. She died in May 1914.

7 For some of Symon's letters, see Symon Papers, NLA, MS 1736/1/2019/32–5 and 38.

8 *Ibid.*, 1/1916/214–15.

9 For these letters, see *ibid.*, 1/1916/214ff and see also a succession of later letters mentioned in Jo's letters to Kilmeny early in 1915. Colonel Seely (later the 1st Baron Mottistone) a former Conservative MP, a Liberal since 1906 and Winston Churchill's good friend, had fought in the Second Boer War and spent much of the Great War on active service enhancing his reputation for bravery and insubordination. Seely had been forced to resign as Secretary of State for War in March 1914 though he remained a member of the Committee of Imperial Defence.

10 JHS to Dr Cormack, 30 January 1915, *ibid.*, 1/1916/345.

11 JHS to Greenwood, 26 April 1915, *ibid.*, 1/1916/402–4.

12 For Oliver's account of the *New Zealand*'s involvement in the sinking of the *Blücher* during the Battle of the Dogger Bank on 24 January 1915, see Symon Family Papers, NLA, MS 10061/3/1.

13 Symon Papers, NLA, MS 1736/1/2019/98ff and 126–7. Jo met a similar response when he tried in 1915 to reverse a decision to assign Oliver to a torpedo boat.

14 NAA: B 2455, 8097688.

15 Symon Papers, NLA, MS 1736/2104/82.

16 *Ibid.*, 1/2019/473.

17 *Ibid.*, 1/2104/221.

18 Quoted in Dyer, *The Bank Manager*, p. 111.

19 Peter R. Grant, *Philanthropy and Voluntary Action in the First World War: Mobilizing Charity*, Routledge, New York, 2014, pp. 130–131.

20 CJBS to JHS, 30 July 1917, Symon Family Papers, NLA, MS 10061/3/1.

21 For Symon's correspondence on this subject, see Symon Papers, NLA, MS 1736/1/2019/357–8 and 1/2010.

22 *Ibid.*, 1/1766–7.

23 *Ibid.*, 1/1916/236.

24 *Ibid.*, 1/2104/90–3.

25 JHS to LKS, 11 December 1914, Elizabeth Dyer Papers, NLA, MS 10369/1.

26 For the above two letters see, Symon Papers, NLA, MS 1736/1/2019/152–3.

27 *Ibid.*, 1/1757.

28 JHS to J. S Leslie, 21 September 1914, *ibid.*, 1/1916/174–5.

29 Prest (ed.), *Wakefield Companion to South Australian History*, pp. 224–5, 628–9.

30 *Advertiser*, 9 April 1916.

31 Sir Sidney Lee had edited the *Dictionary of National Biography* since 1891. His death on 3 March 1926 ended for Symon over two decades of 'a valued and intimate friendship, personal and literary'. He sent copies of his tribute to Lee, published in the *Advertiser* on 27 March, to friends in Australia and the UK.

Notes

32 *Daily Herald*, 8 May 1916.
33 JHS to Denny, 5 January 1916, Symon Papers, NLA, MS 1736/1/2019/135.
34 *Ibid.*, 1/2019/276–9. H. Crouch Batchelor in England and Symon often corresponded despite their fundamental disagreement; Crouch Batchelor believed that Francis Bacon wrote all the works attributed to William Shakespeare.
35 *Ibid.*, 1/1985. For the Lynch reply, see *ibid.*, 1/1987–8.
36 *Advertiser* 19 October 1916.
37 *Express and Telegraph*, October 1916.
38 Symon Papers, NLA, MS 1736/1/1992. The article was published in the *Sun* (Sydney) on 22 October 1916.
39 Symon Papers, NLA, MS 1736/1/1989 and 1992.
40 'Bill' Denny, a lawyer and a pro-conscriptionist State Labor MP for an Adelaide seat, served in the AIF, was awarded an MC and was a minister in State Labor governments before and after the Great War. See Merrilyn Lincoln, 'Denny, William Joseph (1872–1946)', *ADB*, vol. 8, MUP, Carlton, 1981.
41 For the 'the Little Doctor', see Geoffrey Serle, 'Maloney, William Robert (Nuttall) (1854–1940)', *ADB*, vol. 10, MUP, Carlton, 1986.
42 *Register*, 30 October 1916. See also JHS to CHNS, 2 November 1916, Symon Family Papers, MS 10061/2/5.
43 *Express and Telegraph*, 10 November 1916.
44 JHS to Sir William Irvine, 1 April 1917, Symon Papers, NLA, MS 1736/1/2104/114–15.
45 JHS to Crouch Batchelor, 29 June 1917, *ibid.*, 53/173–7.
46 JHS to Serjeant Gillen, 26 November 1917, *ibid.*, 1/2104/270.
47 JHS to CHNS, 23 December 1917 and 31 March 1918 Symon Family Papers, NLA, MS 10061/2/6 and 7.
48 JHS to LKS, 30 March 1918, Elizabeth Dyer Papers, NLA, MS 10369/1.
49 For the above three paragraphs, see Symon Papers, NLA, MS 1736/5/439–72.
50 *Ibid.*, 5/716, 729–33.
51 *Observer*, 13 April 1918.
52 For Bulpett's relations with the late 19th century courtesan, La Belle Otero, see Karen Blixen, *Out of Africa*, Putnam, London, 1946 edition, pp. 224–5.
53 Selous was the model for Rider Haggard's fictional hero, Alan Quartermain. Boyes allegedly bought Mount Kenya from a Kikuyu headman for the price of four goats. In 1911 Bulpett presented Symon with a copy of *John Boyes, King of the Wa-Kikuyu*. For Bulpett's letters to JHS, see Symon Papers, NLA, MS 1736/1/1574 (1911) and *ibid.*, 2141–4 (1918).
54 Nesbit to JHS, 26 November 1918, *ibid.*, 1/2225.

Chapter 15 ~ 'Not a sign or whisper of discontent anywhere'

1 Povey was the more qualified member of the new partnership but Blackburn VC, South Australia's first Victoria Cross winner and a State MP, provided the recognition.
2 JHS to Eric Symon, 1 and 8 April 1919 and 8 January 1920, Symon Papers, NLA, MS 1736/1/2277/204, 217 and 431; JHS to James Nicholson, 14 April 1919, *ibid.*, 1/2227/221.
3 JHS to LKS, 6 March 1920, Elizabeth Dyer Papers, NLA, MS 10369/1.
4 JHS to LKS, 6 April 1919, *ibid.*
5 JHS to Oscar, 24 February and 2 March 1922, Symon Papers, NLA, MS 1736/2684/137–8, 140.
6 *Observer*, 16 July 1921.

7   *Chronicle*, 11 October 1919; *Register*, 8 January and 10 August 1920.
8   *Register*, 8 January 1920.
9   *Amalgamated Society of Engineers v Adelaide Steamship Co Ltd*, (1920) 28 CLR 129. Chief Justice (Sir) Adrian Knox and Justices Isaacs, Higgins, Rich and Starke formed the majority with Justice Gavan Duffy dissenting. Isaacs read the joint majority judgement while Higgins contributed his own.
10 Symon Papers, NLA, MS 1736/1/2318–9.
11 JHS to Nell, 4 July 1921, *ibid.*, 1/2388.
12 *Advertiser* and *Register*, 25 October 1921.
13 JHS to LKS, 31 July and 3 August 1921, Elizabeth Dyer Papers, NLA, MS 10369/1.
14 When Hughes visited Adelaide on 4–6 December 1921 he left the train from Melbourne and had breakfast at 'Manoah' before driving into the city with Symon. *Mail* (Adelaide), 3 December 1921.
15 Symon Papers, NLA, MS 1736/1/2505–6.
16 JHS to LKS, 10 April, 30 July and 14 August 1922, Elizabeth Dyer Papers, NLA, MS 10369/1.
17 *Ibid.*, 11, 17 and 20 September 1921.
18 Sir Josiah Symon, 'Australia and the Privy Council', *Journal of Comparative Legislation and International Law*, vol 4, no. 4, 1922, pp. 137–151.
19 JHS to LKS, 5 February 1923, Elizabeth Dyer Papers, NLA, MS 10369/1.

Chapter 16 ~ 'I have had no rest or peace but only worry'

1   For the above five paragraphs, see in particular Frank Blamey to JHS, 23 October; JHS to Blamey, 27 October 1923; JHS to LKS, 1 November and 1 December 1923 and 6 March 1924, Elizabeth Dyer Papers, NLA, MS 10369/1.
2   JHS to David Symon, 3 January 1893, Symon Papers, NLA, MS 1736/1/491–2.
3   JHS to LKS, 25 April 1925, Elizabeth Dyer Papers, NLA, MS 10369/1.
4   For his comments on the trip, see *Advertiser* and *Register*, 20 October 1925.
5   See his letter of 22 June published in the *Register*, 28 July 1925.
6   Copy in the author's possession.
7   Copies of these exchanges are in the author's possession.
8   (Sir) John Richards (1869–1957), born and first educated in South Australia completed his education at the Methodist Shebbear College, Devon (Sir Samuel Way's *alma mater*), and obtained a Doctor of Law at London University. Returning to Adelaide, Richards spent two years as the managing clerk in Symon & Rounsevell and became Way's associate. Appointed Crown Solicitor, he took silk in 1921 and joined the South Australian Supreme Court in 1927.
9   *Advertiser*, 27 June, 25 and 26 November, 9 December 1931.
10 JHS to LKS, 18 December 1922, Elizabeth Dyer Papers, NLA, MS 10369/1.
11 Symon Papers, NLA, MS 1736/1/3092 and 3107; JHS to LKS, 1 July 1926, Elizabeth Dyer Papers, 10369/1.
12 *News* (Adelaide), 7 June 1928. For Margaret's report on women in the justice system, see *ibid.*, 26 April 1928.
13 Interview: Perdita Eldridge, 23 March 2007, NLA, ORAL, TRC 5785, pp. 3–4, 6; interview: Perdita Eldridge, 11 May 2021.
14 The original vote was 18-all but James McColl, who won Echuca in 1901 and 1903 as a Protectionist and took a Victorian Senate seat in 1906 as an 'Anti-Socialist', changed sides in a second ballot. Simon Fraser, the one Victorian Free Trader in the Senate, voted for Canberra-Yass on the first ballot. Symon believed that the Free Trade Opposition defeated the combined Labor-Protectionist parties on this issue.

Notes

15 *Advertiser* 28 February and 3 March; *Register*, 1 and 3 March 1927.
16 JHS to Lord Novar, 25 March 1927, Symon Papers, NLA, MS 1736/1/3305–6 and 3353–4.
17 For these exchanges with Bruce, see *ibid.*, 1/3285–6, 3291–2 and 3300–1.
18 JHS to LKS, 16 August 1927, Elizabeth Dyer Papers, NLA, MS 10369/1.
19 Lucas to JHS, 19 February 1928, Symon Papers, NLA, MS 1736/1/3483.
20 *Ibid.*, 15/30, 38–53.
21 A copy in the author's possession.
22 Sawer, *Australian Federal Politics and Law*, p. 326.
23 JHS to LKS, 4 April 1930, Elizabeth Dyer Papers, NLA, MS 10369/1.
24 JHS to Bruce, 27 August 1923, Symon Papers, NLA, MS 1736/1/2643–4. For Wilkie, see John Rickard, 'Wilkie, Allan (1878–1970)', *ADB*, vol. 12, MUP, Carlton, 1990.
25 Josiah Symon, *Shakespeare the Englishman*, Register Newspapers, Adelaide 1929.
26 See, for example, S. Talbot Smith, *Register News Pictorial*, 12 September 1929.
27 Elizabeth Dyer Papers, NLA, MS 10369/1.
28 JHS to Nell, 5 May 1921, Symon Papers, NLA, MS 1736/1/2383.
29 *Ibid.*, 25/1–2.
30 *Ibid.*, 25/8–24.
31 Symon first promised £1500 in 1924 to the Australian Inland Mission for the building to be named after Nell and Lenore. See *Register*, 25 March 1924. Some later reports suggested the building might be named after a prominent JP, the Symons' eldest daughter Elizabeth (Margaret). Launched in 1929 as the Eleanor Symon Nursing Home, the Mission subsequently accepted a change of name to the Elizabeth Symon Nursing Home to meet Jo's desire to commemorate his mother.
32 *Ibid.*, 27/6 and 7.
33 *Ibid.*, 1/3435.
34 Symon, David, *A Life of Eric Symon: 1894–1948*, New Age Publishers Pty Ltd, Sydney, 1991, p. 28. For Jo's gifts to Eric, see *ibid.*, p. 13 and Symon Papers, NLA, MS 1/2019/489, 1/2180–1. Eric eventually joined the Communist Party. One of his sons, Peter Dudley Symon, served in senior posts in the original Communist Party, the short-lived Socialist Party of Australia and the recycled Communist Party of Australia. An ASIO report in 1972 said Peter 'can only be described as "a nice bloke"'. https://www.adelaidenow.com.au/news/south-australia/never-before-seen-asio-reports.

Chapter 17 ~ 'I feel it as a deep personal grief'

1 Symon Papers, NLA, MS 1736/1/3841 and 43. Littleton Groom regained Darling Downs in 1931, joined the United Australia Party in 1933, retained his seat in 1934 and died in 1936.
2 Lady Novar to JHS, 11 November 1929, *ibid.*, 1/3872. Scullin was born in Australia of Irish-born parents and Ted Theodore, the Treasurer and second in seniority, was born in Australia of an Irish mother. Frank Brennan and Joseph Lyons, third and fourth respectively in seniority, were both Australian-born and of Irish descent.
3 *Advertiser*, 10 January and *News*, 20 January 1930.
4 *News* (Adelaide), 17 July 1930.
5 *Advertiser* 13, 15 and 21 August and 1 September 1930.
6 Symon Papers, NLA, MS 1736/1/4080.
7 See, for example, the Melbourne *Argus* editorial of 24 April 1930.
8 *Argus*, 25 April 1930.
9 *News* (Adelaide), 25 April 1930.

10 Handwritten note attached to *The Times Weekly Edition*, 1 May 1930, Symon Papers, NLA, MS 1736/17/9.
11 *Ibid.*, 17/1 and 3.
12 Hilary L. Rubinstein, '"A Gross Discourtesy to His Majesty": The Campaign within Australia, 1930–31 against Sir Isaac Isaacs' Appointment as Governor General', *Australian Jewish Historical Society Journal*, vol. 14, part 3, 1998, pp. 425–58.
13 JHS to Irvine, 12 July 1930, Symon Papers, NLA, MS 1736/17/16.
14 For example: Christopher Cunneen, *King's Men, Australia's Governors-General from Hopetoun to Isaacs*, George Allen & Unwin, Sydney, 1983, pp. 172–82; John Robertson, *J.H. Scullin: A Political Biography*, University of Western Australia Press, Nedlands, 1974, pp. 285–8; Zelman Cowen, *Isaac Isaacs*, Oxford University Press, Melbourne, 1967, ch. 8; John Waugh, 'An Australian in the Palace of the King-Emperor: James Scullin, George V and the Appointment of the First Australian-born Governor-General', *Federal Law Review*, vol. 39, no. 2, 2011, pp. 235–53.
15 Symon Papers, NLA, MS 1736/17/23–4.
16 *Ibid.*, 17/30.
17 For the Brudenell White and Irvine letters, see *ibid.*, 17/40–1, 43.
18 For the letters sent to Novar and Wallington, see *ibid.*, 17/37 and 39.
19 *Advertiser*, 18 and 20 December 1930.
20 Symon Papers, NLA, MS 1736/17/55–6.
21 *Ibid.*, 17/57.
22 On 19 December 1930, the Government acted on a caucus decision and appointed Herbert Vere Evatt and Edward McTiernan to the High Court. Evatt was then the Independent Labor MP for the State seat of Balmain, and McTiernan, a former NSW State Attorney-General, was the Federal Labor MP for Parkes. Scullin and Attorney-General Brennan, who may have opposed the appointments, were overseas at the time.
23 For Symon's replies to Latham, see Symon Papers, NLA, MS 1736/17/62 and 65–6.
24 Mitchell (1855–1941) was a leading barrister in constitutional and equity law and had led for the States in the *Engineers' Case*; Fullagar (1892–1961) was appointed to the High Court in 1950 and was held in the highest regard.
25 *Argus*, 8 and 19 January 1931.
26 For Symon's messages to Mitchell, see Symon Papers, NLA, MS 1736/17/74–79.
27 *Ibid.*, 17/92.
28 *Ibid.*, 17/102–3.
29 *Ibid.*, 17/117–19.
30 For further exchanges, see *ibid.*, 17/123–4, 129–33, 146–51.
31 *Ibid.*, 17/105.
32 *Ibid.*, 17/182–3. Glassey had been a militant trade unionist and a Labor Party MP but was elected sixth as a Protectionist for a Queensland Senate seat in 1901. Defeated in 1903, he tried to be a Deakinite Liberal and settled for the Queensland Nationalist Party from 1917.
33 *Ibid.*, 17/185.
34 *Ibid.*, 17/198 and 203.
35 *Ibid.*, 17/225.
36 For Symon's letters, see *ibid.*, 17/228–31. Warren Denning, a Gallery journalist, described the boycott as 'an exhibition of bad manners which received the contempt it merited'. Warren Denning, *Caucus Crisis: The rise & fall of the Scullin Government*, Hale & Iremonger, Sydney, 1982 edition, p. 102.
37 JHS to Latham, 24 February 1932, Latham Papers, NLA, MS 1009/1/2278.
38 For Symon's correspondence, see Symon Papers, NLA, MS 1736/16/95ff.

Notes

Chapter 18 ~ 'scandalous, offensive and defamatory'

1. Isaacs to JHS, 4 January 1934, Symon Papers, NLA, MS 1736/1/5598. Five delegates were still alive: A.H. Henning (WA), Isaacs Vic.), James (WA), Lewis (Tas.) and Symon.
2. *Ibid.*, 1/5602
3. JHS to Amery, 8 February 1934, *ibid.*, 1/5613 and JHS to Lady Novar, 26 February 1934, *ibid.*, 1/5619. After serving as a Major-General in the British Army in the Great War, Athlone was Governor-General of South Africa (!924–30). The Countess (Princess Alice) was Queen Victoria's last living grandchild when she died in 1981.
4. *Advertiser*, 4 March 1934.
5. *Ibid.*, 3 April 1934.
6. *News* (Adelaide), 3 April and *Advertiser*, 4 April 1934.
7. *Advertiser*, 6 April 1934.
8. *CPD*, Senate, vol. 144, pp. 9–10. It was a crowded occasion because, among others, the Senate acknowledged the deaths of King Albert of Belgium, Sir Robert Gibson, the Chairman of the Commonwealth Bank Board and William Holman, the former Labor Premier of NSW who was expelled by the Party for supporting conscription.
9. *Ibid.*, pp. 17–18.
10. Symon Papers, NLA, MS 1736/32/9.
11. *Ibid.*, 32/19.
12. William Charteris to Lady Symon,12 April 1934, *ibid.*, 32/14–15.
13. For the Will of 22 October 1931, the First Codicil of 14 July 1932 and the Second Codicil, 7 April 1933, see *ibid.*, 21/178–210. For the published details, *News* (Adelaide), 7 August and *Advertiser*, 8 August 1934. The author holds a copy of the redacted pages.
14. *Advertiser*, 18 July 1935.
15. Charles graduated with a Third, Oxford's 'gentleman's degree', at a time when about 30 per cent of Oxford graduates received Thirds. Other Thirds included two British Prime Ministers – Stanley Baldwin and Sir Alec Douglas-Home – as well as W.H. Auden, Lewis Carroll, and A.A. Milne. Evelyn Waugh was awarded a Third in his final examinations but left Oxford without a degree because he had not fulfilled the required nine terms of residence.
16. JHS to LKS, 6 March 1913, Papers of Elizabeth Dyer, NLA, MS 10369/1.

Epilogue

1. Adelaide *News*, 29 March 1974.
2. *Per Litteras Lumen*, 1966, p. 11.
3. For the ceremony at the gravesite in 2019, see info@stannscollege.edu.au, click 'About Us'
4. *Advertiser*, 28 November and 5 December 1934.
5. Oscar to Nell, 23 October 1934, Elizabeth Dyer Papers.
6. *News* (Adelaide), 17 July; *Advertiser*, 18–19 July and 31 July 1935.
7. Symon Papers, NLA, MS 1736/21/273–7.
8. Elizabeth Dyer Papers.
9. State Library of South Australia (SLSA), PRG 240/16.
10. *Ibid.*,
11. Confidential information.
12. For the quotations in this paragraph, see Perdita Eldridge, 23 March 2007, NLA, OH-5785, pp. 6 and 30.

Index

A

Abbott, Joseph, 97–9, 100, 119–21, 133, 142, 144–5
Adelaide Bar, ix, 36, 48, 70, 74, 252
Adelaide Club, 36, 52, 55, 59, 168, 331, n. 20
Amery, Leopold, 302
Andrews, Richard, 63
Ash, George, 95
Ashburton, 5th Baron and party, 78
Asquith, Herbert, 207, 240
Atkinson & Way, 45
Auld, Patrick, 67
Auldana, vineyard and winery, 67–8, 77, 96, 97, 101, 167, 171, 175, 202, 259, 267, 304, 309, 309–11, 317, 321
Australasian Federal Convention, 1897–8, x, Adelaide, 100–107, Sydney, 112–18, Melbourne, 118–24
Australian Natives' Association/ANA, x, 86–7, 92, 97, 130

B

Baker, Richard Chaffey, 60, 81, 90, 94–6, 101, 105, 106–7, 112, 113, 115, 120, 121, 125, 132, 133, 137, 140, 142–3, 144–5, 150–1, 153–4, 156, 198, 305, 315
Bakewell, J.W., 36, 43, 45, 47–8, 54–5, 68–9, 71, 127
Bannerman, Campbell, 3
Baptist churches and preachers, 3, 7, 10, 11, 15, 127, 281, 307
Barr Smith, Robert, 36, 65–6, 281, 315, 320

Barton, Edmund, 88, 92, 97, 98, 99, 100, 101, 105, 106, 112, 113, 121, 122, 124, 126, 132–3, 134, 136, 140–1, 149–50, 151, 153, 154, 162, 163–4, 166, 174, 175–6, 176, 181, 193, 198, 203, 212, 256–8, 265, 278, 314, 334, n. 12; 337, n. 7; 339, n, 38; 340, n. 12
Berry, Graham, 115, 121
Birdwood ('Birdie'), William, 259, 274, 289
Blackstone, William, 33–4, 145
Blakeley, Arthur, 285–6
Blamey, Frank, 269, 271
Bonython, Langdon, 144, 153, 262, 281, 283–4, 315
Bonney, Albert, 70–3
Bonney, Johanna, 70–2
Bonney, Lillie, 70–2
Boothby, William, 43, 44
Boucaut, James, 42, 50, 71, 83, 95
Boyes, John, 253
Bray, John, 56, 58, 61, 80
Brook, James, 36, 37, 38–40, 48
Browne, Thomas, 255, 267, 271, 275
Bruce, Stanley Melbourne, 123, 278–9, 280, 282, 285, 287, 300
Buchanan, Alexander, 251, 253
Buckle, George, 260
Bulpett, Charles, 253, 345, n. 52 and n. 53
Bundey, William, 50, 52, 56, 63, 83, 85, 95, 127, 128
Burke, Edmund, 24–5
Butters, John, 278

C

Campbell, Colonel, 77, 78
Canberra, 277–8, 314, no. 14
'Carry-On', 256
Chamberlain, Austen, 274
Chamberlain, Joseph, x, 108, 120, 131, 133–6, 138, 140–1, 142, 145, 263, 264, 266, 274
Charleston, David, 95, 154, 194, 195, 197
Churchill, Winston, 201, 235, 263, 344, n. 9
Clark, Inglis, 75, 155, 166
Clark, Anthony, 271
Cleland, Erskine, 127–8, 171, 196, 233–4, 251–2, 317, 319
Clemons, John, 157, 161, 162, 172, 186–7, 193, 198–9, 204–5, 209, 210, 338, ch. 10, n. 17, 340, n. 34
Cobden Society, 64
Cockburn, John, 96, 113, 117, 121,
Colonial and Indian Exhibition, 1884, 64
Colton, John, 63
Commercial Bank of South Australia, 64
Conscription, xi, 233, 248, 249, 250, 262, 345, n. 40, 349, n. 8
Cook, Joseph, 194, 206, 207–8, 229, 263, 288
Corbin, Dr Thomas, 70–2
Cornwell, John, 242–3
'Corset case', 170–1, 173, 192
Cotton, George, 56, 57
Cowle, Charles, 58, 59–60
Cowle, Felix, 78
Cowle, Margaret ('Maggie'), 58
Cowle, Olive, 130
Culross. Rev., 7, 10, 11, 13, 15

D

Deakin, Alfred, 92, 96, 98, 99, 100–1, 102–3, 105–6, 121, 123, 126, 134–6, 140–1, 149, 150, 154, 155, 162, 165, 166, 167, 170, 171, 172, 176, 189–90, 193, 194, 197, 198. 201, 203, 205–6, 207–13, 215, 216, 229, 256–7, 262, 298, 314, 337, n. 23
Dendy, Dr, 59
Denny, William, 249, 345, n. 40
Dickson, James, 136, 140, 150
Downer, John, xi, 50, 57–8, 61–2, 65, 81, 82, 95–6, 97, 98, 99, 100–1, 105, 107, 112–13, 115, 116, 119, 121, 123, 129, 146, 153–4, 167, 171, 173, 192, 305, 319, 320, 339, n. 38
Drake, James, 166, 172

E

Edward, Prince of Wales, 222, 259–60
Eggleston, Frederic, 302
Elder, Thomas, 36, 315
Emden, Captain Müller, 245–6
Engineers' Case, 259, 263–7
E, S &A Bank, 58, 68
Errington, Thomas, 62–3
Executor and Trustee Company, 269, 271, 272, 316

F

Fawkes, Wilmot, 260,
Federal Council, 61–2, 75
Fenton, James, 292
Free Church of Scotland, 7, 8, 10, 15, 18, 127, 304, 329–30, n. 3
Forrest, John, 92, 105, 106–7, 108, 115–16, 121, 123, 126, 138–40, 143, 146, 150, 197, 206, 207–8, 229, 278
Free Trade Association, SA, 64, 173
Fusion, 207–11, 213, 214, 227, 229, 231, 232, 257, 288, 342, n. 38
Fysh, Philip, 98, 116, 136, 140

G

Galway, Henry, 243, 262
Garran, Robert, 106, 113, 116, 118, 150, 174, 180, 181–2, 262, 280, 335, n. 16, 340, n. 12 and n. 24
Gladstone, William Ewart, 3, 24, 28–9, 65, 120, 133, 207
Gladstonian liberalism, 144
Glassey, Thomas, 299, 348, n. 32
Glynn, Patrick, xi, 95–6, 102–3, 106, 113, 115, 116, 118, 121, 123, 124, 125, 147, 152, 153, 171, 192, 206, 335, n. 16
Gooding, Susannah, 35, 344, n. 6
Gordon, Adam Lindsay, 29, 33
Gordon, John, 95–6, 98–9, 106, 113, 118, 125, 129, 137, 145, 172, 251, 335, n. 16
Gould, Albert, 198–200
Graham, John, 6, 7, 11

Index

Great Boulder Proprietary Gold Mines Limited, x, 68, 130, 147, 175
Greene, Graham, 236, 237, 240
Greenwood, Hamar, 240
Griffith, Samuel, 98, 103–5, 121, 138–140, 140, 142–3, 145, 150, 152–3, 155, 166, 168, 169, 176–82, 183, 184, 185, 187, 190–1, 193, 256–9, 314, 340, n. 12
Groom, Littleton, 203, 285, 347, n. 1
Guthrie, Dr, 10
Gwynne, Edward, 34, 41, 45, 331, ch. 4, n. 15

H

Halsey, Lionel, 225, 259
Hamilton, George, 43
Hamilton, Richard, 147–8
Hanson, Richard, 43, 45
Harcourt, Lewis, 240
Harcourt, William, 65
Hawker, Charles, 300, 307, 315
Heath, Neil, 11–12, 16
Henderson, James, 171, 341, n. 1
Higgins, Henry, 103–4, 114–15, 116–117, 121, 166, 173, 176, 177–8, 193, 197, 346, ch. 15, n. 9
High Court, x, xii, 75–6, 101, 104, 105, 119–20, 123, 136, 140, 142, 145, 146, 155, 162, 165, 166–7, 167–8, 169, 170, 172, 174–91, 194, 198, 203, 204, 211, 212, 251, 258–9, 263–7, 293–5, 348, n. 22 and n. 24
Holder, William, 81, 82, 95, 96, 113, 124, 125, 132, 133, 134, 146, 149, 152, 153, 156
Hopetoun, 7th Earl, 149
Hopwood, Francis, 240
'Hospital row', 89–90
Howe, James, 95, 96, 100, 113, 117, 123, 124, 125, 151
Hughes 'Billy', 248, 250, 262–3, 300, 346, n. 14

I

im Thurn, Everard, 274
Ingleby, Rupert, 60
Inter-Colonial Convention 1883, 61
Inverness families, *St Vincent*, 18–19, 19–20
Irish Home Rule, 65, 120, 197, 207, 332, n. 17

Isaacs, Isaac, 105, 113, 121, 122, 128, 166, 190, 193–4, 263, 287, 289–300, 302, 307, 346, n. 9, 349, n. 1

J

Jellicoe, John, 259
Johns, Fred, 173, 228
Judicial Committee of Privy Council, 136, 165, 169, 176, 178, 233
Jusserand, Jean, 281

K

Kent Hughes, H., 33
King, Thomas, 49, 56, 62–37
Kingston, Charles Cameron, xi, 40–1, 61, 63, 75–6, 81–2, 83–5, 86–7, 88, 89, 89–91, 92, 93–4, 95, 95–6, 97–99, 100–1, 102, 103, 106, 108, 112–13, 116, 117, 124, 125, 126, 128, 129–30, 131–32, 136–7, 143–4, 145, 146, 149–50, 152–3, 154, 155, 163–4, 197, 305, 314, 315, 333, n. 9
Kingston, Sir George Strickland, 41
Kingston, Lucy, 41
Kintore, the 9th Earl, 81–2, 83–4, 333, n. 10
Knox, Adrian, 266, 287, 346, ch. 15, n. 9

L

Law, Bonar, 238, 240
Le Hunte, George and Caroline, 260
Lee, Sidney, 247, 260, 281, 345, n. 31
Levi, Lawrence, 17
Lewis, Neil, 106, 116, 121, 150, 349, n. 1
Liberal Union, 217, 225–32
Lloyd George, David, 207, 261, 274, 276
Louttit, Alexander, 15, 20–1
Loyal Orange Lodges, x, 154, 196–7, 220, 228
Lucas, Charles, 260–1, 273, 274, 277, 279, 302
Lynch, Patrick, 248, 308
Lyne, William ('Bill'), 115, 135, 149–50, 201, 203, 207–8, 210, 337, n. 12
Lyons, Joseph, 300, 307, 347, n. 2

M

McCay, James, 172
McDonald, Ramsey, 276

McGregor, Gregor, 154, 156, 191, 200, 215
McFarlane, Allan, 25
Mclean, Allan, 134, 135, 170, 171, 172, 181, 190, 191, 197, 210, 211, 261
McMillan, Northrup and Lucy, 253
McMinn, Winston, 170, 171, 177, 180, 190
Maling, David, 173
Maloney, William, 249
Mann, Charles, 43, 49, 58, 63, 71, 305
Mannix, Daniel, 250, 299
'Manoah', xiv, xv, 74, 82, 154, 167, 184, 201, 223, 228, 241, 245, 259, 267, 268, 276, 303, 308, 310, 314, 318, 346, n. 14
'Marlins', 244,
Mason, Anthony, 169
Mazure, Edmond, 67-8, 77
'Miller Case', 252, 253
Minda, 68, 304
Mitchell, Edward, 295-8
Mitchell, James, 287, 301
Moray House, 7-8, 10-11, 14, 51, 282, 283
Morgan, William, 56, 58
Morley, John, 65
Munro Robert, 240
Munro Ferguson (later Novar), Ronald and Helen, 239, 260, 262, 278, 285, 292, 300, 303
Murray, George, 171, 192-3, 238, 266-7, 283, 303, 305-6, 308, 315

N

Napier, Mellis, 255, 315, 316
Neild, John, 154, 161-2, 203, 204, 339, n. 26
Nesbit, Paris, 101, 140, 154, 171, 173, 196, 217, 253-4, 305, 315
Newland, John, 230, 231, 248
Nicholson, George ('Geordie'), 3, 80
Northcote, Henry and Cecilia, 190, 218, 219, 222, 260, 283
Northcote, Stafford (known as Viscount St Cyres), 274

O

O'Connor, Richard, 101, 105, 112-13, 121, 132, 146, 150, 157, 161, 162-3, 163, 166, 173, 175, 176, 181, 182, 187, 291, 340, n. 12
O'Loghlin, James, 152, 203-4, 231
O'Reily, John, 154, 338, n. 10

P

Parkes, Henry, 88, 92, 97, 98, 314
Parliament House, official opening, 277-9
'Parnellites', 65
Parr, J.H., 43
Paterson, Maurice, 10-11
Paton, William, 14
Playford, Thomas, 75, 75-6, 79, 81, 82, 154, 166, 197, 333, n. 5
Phrenology, 4-5
Povey, Edward, 255, 345, n. 1
Poynton, Alexander, 153
Prince Alexander of Teck (Athlone), 235, 303, 334, n. 2
Prince Louis of Battenberg (Mountbatten), 235, 344, n. 3, 349, ch. 18, n. 3

Q

Quick, John, 92, 106, 113-14, 116, 118, 121, 150, 172, 335, n. 16

R

Reed, Francis, 60
Reid, George, 74, 87-9, 92, 97-9, 100, 105, 106, 108, 113, 117, 118-19, 121, 124-5, 126, 126-7, 129, 160-1, 170, 171-2, 179-81, 182-9, 189-90, 191, 194, 197-8, 205-6, 210, 211, 212, 216, 218, 229, 234-5, 238, 240, 241, 257, 258, 334, n. 24 and n. 2; 337, n. 12, 342, n. 30
Rosebery, 5th Earl, 3
Rounsevell, W.B., 43
Rounsevell, H.V., 127-8, 204, 233, 234, 255
Royal Colonial Institute/Royal Empire Society, x, 80, 206, 261, 274, 281, 287, 288
Royal Family, Queen Victoria, x. 8, 75, 101, 108, 109, 146, 151, Edward VII, 8, George V, 274, Edward Prince of Wales, 222, 259-60, Prince George, 302-3
Royal Commission on the Constitution, 1927-9, 279-80

S

Scott, Walter, x, 17, 85, 108-9, 110, 111
Scottish education, 3-6
Scullin, James, 285, 287, 288, 289-90, 292-3, 294-5, 295-6, 297, 298-300, 307, 347, n. 2, 348, n. 22

Index

Secessionist campaign in WA, 287, 300–1
Second Anglo-Boer War, 131, 132, 151
Seely, John, 207, 239–40, 349, n.9
Selborne, 2nd Earl, 130–1, 135–6
Selous, Frederick, 253
Smith, Bruce, 232
Smith, Francis Villeneuve, 251, 252
'Snow Case', 250–1
Social Democratic Federation, 64
Solomon, Vaiben, 95, 96, 100, 113, 121, 124, 125, 131–2, 144, 153
Sowden, William, 62, 137, 144, 146, 227, 332, n.12
Spence, Helen, 95
State elections, SA, 1881, 56–7, 1884, 61, 62–3, 1888, 65–7, 1893, 82–3, 1896, 88–9
Stirling by-election, 142–5
Stirling, Scotland, ix, 3, 9, 10, 13, 15, 16, 40, 41, 51, 53, 55, 80, 130, 151, 218, 234, 244–5, 247
Stirling High School, 3, 6, 281
Stock, William, 56, 57
Stow, Jefferson, 63
Stow, Randolph, 40, 45, 50, 51, 63, 331, ch.4, n.15
Stuart, J.M., 81, 159
Sutherland: 1–2, David ('Uncle'), 2, 15, 23, 24, 33, James ('Cousin'), 2, 15, 23–5, 27, 29, 30–34, 35, 36, 37, 39, 52, Caroline ('Carrie'), 2, 25–6, 27, 51, 309, 330, n.6, Elizabeth, see below
Symon, Josiah's father (James), 1, 3, 9, 16, 42, 45, 51, mother (Elizabeth), 1–2, 9, 15, 42, 51, 53, 77, 79, 80, 130, 147, 151, 347, n.31
Symon, Josiah, siblings: James ('Jim'), 2–3, 8, 9, 15, 16, 17, 23, 24, 25–7, 28, 30, 31, 32, 33, 47, 38, 40, 41–4, 46–8, 50, 51–2, 54, 68, 69, 70, 73, 80, 90–1, 255, 269, 284, 309, 333, n.6, Esther, 2, 33, 51, 247, Margaret, 2, 51, 247, Elizabeth, 3, 80, 256, 309, Robert, 3, 9, 16, 68, 333, n.24, William ('Bill'), 3, 6, 9, 16, 28, 36, 42, 43, 44, 48, 51–5, 68–70, 71, 76, 128, 147–8, 331, n.20, David, 3, 9, 16, 70, 76, 234, 243–4, 269, 271, 309, 333, n.28
Symon, Eleanor ('Nell'), née Cowle, 58–60, 64, 68, 76–7, 79, 80, 130, 199–200, 201, 201–2, 206, 207, 207–8, 211–13, 217–18, 219, 221, 234, 241, 242, 245, 260, 268, 276, 282, 304, 308–9, 313, 316, 317–18, 320
Symon, Josiah and Nell: children: Margaret, 60, 64, 201, 202, 220, 221, 223, 234, 244, 245, 256, 269–70, 272, 277, 282, 304, 309, 319, 346, ch.16, n.12; 347, n.31, Eleanor (Lenore), 60–1, 64, 206, 207, 238, 242, 244, 245, 249, 261, 269–70, 272, 273, 274, 278, 282, 303, 304, 308, 309, 313, 315, 319, 347, n.31, Alison, 60–1, Kilmeny, 61, 64, 217, 220, 222–3, 230, 232, 234–38, 239, 240, 241, 244–5, 250, 261–3, 264, 265, 269, 270–3, 276–7, 278, 280, 281, 282, 304, 308, 309, 312, 313, 315, 317, 317–18, 319, 319–20, Charles, 28, 61, 201, 202, 207, 220, 221–2, 233, 234, 238–9, 241–2, 255, 269–73, 275–6, 304, 308–13, 316, 317, 318, 349, n.15, Una, 68, Romilly, 68, 76, 241, 245, 304, 309, 310, 318, Oscar, 28, 76, 201, 218, 220–1, 222–3, 224, 241, 255–6, 271, 284, 304, 310, 313, 316–17, 318, 343, n.15, Carril, 28, 87, 201, 206, 220, 221–3, 224, 232, 234, 235–8, 239–40, 241, 244, 250, 256, 270, 271, 275, 304, 308, 310, 311, 312, 313, 316, 317, 318, Oliver, 87, 201, 202, 207, 224–5, 234, 235–8, 239, 240, 244, 259, 274, 277, 303, 304, 309, 310, 311, 316, 318, 332, 344, n.12 and n.13, Angel, 206, 221, 234, 235, 236, 239, 244, 264, 276, 282, 304, 319, 320, Mary, 146, 206, 244, 245, 271, 277, 282, 304, 320
Symon, Josiah and his children: 77, 79, 234, 235, 236–7, 244, 245, encourages them in arts and books and learning languages, 220, 224, 282, 319, financial generosity 220, 233, 234, 241–2, 244, 270, 309, and to some children of siblings, 243, 255–6, 284, controlling careers 201, 220, 224–5, 235–8, 240, 308–18, relations with and opinion of Charles, 220, 221, 233, 234, 238–9, 241–2, 269–73, 275–6, 308, 310, 311–13, relations with and opinion of Oscar: 221, 222–3, 241, 255–6, 271, 310, 313, Kilmeny as confidante: 220, 222–3, 230, 232, 235–8, 241, 245, 250, 261–3, 266, 270–3, 276–7, 280–1
Symon, Josiah, narrative
 education, 3–7, pupil teacher, 3–4, critical of system, 6, Dux, 7, Moray

House, 7–12, primary school teacher, 1864–5, 13–14
voyage to South Australia, 15–21
legal career: articled clerk, Mount Gambier, 23–35, Adelaide, 37–9, initial self-doubt, 36, 38, 39–40, growing self-confidence, 37, 48, 50, Way & Symon, 40, Symon & Bakewell, 47, Symon, Bakewell & Symon, 52, Symon, Bakewell, Stow & Piper, 127, Symon, Rounsevell & Cleland, 127, Symon, Rounsevell & Symon, 233, Symon & Browne, 255, Symon, Browne & Symon, 255, Symon, Browne, Symon & Povey, 255, Symon, Browne & Symon, 255, opinions of, and relations with, Samuel Way, 35, 37, 43–7, 51, 63, 88, 89, 94–5, 104–5, 128, 140–3, 145–6, 152–3, 165, 291, 315, cases, 70–3, 157–60, 170–1, 173 and 192, 192–3, 196 and 198, 250–1, 252–3, 336, n. 37; reputation, ix, 50, 70, 127–8, 154, 201, 305–7, judicial appointment refused, 63, not offered, 166–7, 193–4, 238
political career, State elections, 55–7, 62–3, 65–7, campaign for federation x, 61–2, 75, 87–88, 92–4, key Convention interventions, 101–2, 106, 335, n. 27, 114–15, 115–16, 117–18, 119–21, appeals to the Privy Council, xii, 75, 76, 104, 118, 137, 140–1, 143, 145–6, 264–7, federation referenda, 75–6, 124–6, 130, 131, free trader, xi, 64, 150, 151, 152, 153, 156–7, 159–60, 161–3, 172, 173, 195, 204, 258, 307, 347, n. 14, Federal elections, 151–5, 194–8, 212–13, 225–32, appointment to office, 171–2, secures conciliation and arbitration Bill, 173–4, 'Ithuriel' assessment, 173, clashes with High Court justices, 174–82, clashes with Prime Minister, 182–9; rejected Fusion, 207–8, 208–11, 213, 214, 227, 231, 232, 257, rejected Liberal Union conditions, 223–30, loses seat as independent, 230–32
Great War: unnerved in 1914, anti-German, 242, 245–7, attempts to promote and protect sons, 235–8, contributions to war causes, 242–3, conscriptionist, xi, 233, 248–50, 262, hostility to Hughes, 248, 250,
exchanges with Kilmeny, pride in family, 242, 253–4, 256
post-war: two trips to the UK 260–1, 273–4, Prince of Wales visit, 259–60, pursuit of higher honours, 261–3, semi-retirement, 267, breakdown of relations with Charles, 269–73, 275–6, 308, 310, 311–13, Canberra opening 277–9, defence of the Constitution, 279–80, opinions of Bruce 278–9, 285, 300, writing, 258, 263–7, 273, 279–80, death and funeral, 303–4, eulogies, 304–7, Will and the consequences, 308–13, 315–17

Symon, Josiah, activities, beliefs, conflicts, connections, making and using, 36, 66, 55, 108, 222, 236, 238–9, 239–40, 259–60, 261, 312
free trader, xi, 64, 88, 150, 151, 153, 156, 157, 161–2, 172,
identities, xii–xiii, 93, 111, 162
importance of family, xiii, 9, 15, 24, 36, 38, 40, 41, 43, 44, 51–2, 53, 55, 61, 64, 68–70, 74, 77, 79–80, 127, 128, 130, 167, 201, 206, 207, 218, 220, 221, 223, 225, 230, 234, 236–7, 239, 240, 243, 244–5, 254, 255, 268, 271, 276, 277, 284, 308–13
independent conservative, xi–xii, 24–5, 86–7, 96, 143–4, 153, 156, 173–4, 204, 208, 209, 279, 286
intolerance of heavy drinking, 27–8, 68–70, 76, 147–8, 224, 310
loyal to Crown and Empire, xii, 8, 64, 109, 109–11, 120–1, 131, 151, 207, 234–5, 247, 259–60, 264–5, 273, 280, 286, 288, 296, 302, 304, 307
major public speeches, 56–7, 86–7, 92–4, 108–1, 142–5, 151–2, 165, 210–11, 215–16, 229–30, 247–8; assessments as a public speaker, 12, 38, 62, 94, 101, 102–3, 112, 121–2, 124, 154; in demand, 74, assessment of other speakers, 9, 10, 33, 35, 50, 65, 210–11, 257, 274, 278
philanthropy, 51, 242–3, 281–4, 309, 321
physical attributes: height, 7, 102, 267, eyesight problems, 7, 30, 268, 280, health, 8, 49, 55, 77, 260, 267–8, 280, 287, final breakdown, 303

Index

principles and values, 4, 7, 8, 11, 14, 20, 24–5, 28–9, 47, 97, 110, 111, 127, 150, 273, 307
racial attitudes, xi, xii, 78, 79, 109–10, 111, 121, 122, 131, 151–2, 234, 247, 261, 330, ch. 2, n. 11
religious affiliations, 7, 10, 59–60, 127, 281, 304, 307
Senate as the States House, xi, 105–6, 232
Shakespeare, Symon's publications, x, 323–4, lectures, 85–6, 128, 146–7, 247, contacts, x, 280–1, 302, 345, n. 34
sporting limitations, 29–30
State rights, xi, 76, 93, 123, 164, 191, 194, 195, 278
relations with Deakin, 103–4, 134–6, 140–1, 165, 166, 191,195, 201, 202–3, 205, 207–8, 209, 210–11
relations with Kingston, 41, 49, 61, 63, 75–6, 81–2, 83–4, 84–5, 88–9, 89–91, 94–6, 97–101, 102, 129–30, 132, 137, 140–1, 143–5, 149–50, 152–5, 163–4
relations with Reid, 87–9, 97–9, 100, 105–6, 117, 118–19, 121, 124–5, 126, 160–1, 170, 171–2, 177, 179–81, 182–90, 191, 194, 205–6, 210, 212, 238, 240, 257, 258
theatre, 30–1
wealth, ix, x, 36, 64, 67–8, 130, 167, 175, 270, 308–9, 309–10
work ethic: 8–9, 10, 15, 33, 37, 41, 42, 46, 48, 60, 64, 68–9, 75, 100, 127, 220, 233, 234, 267, 273, 279–80
Symon, Josiah, three familial obligations
Eric, 255, 284, 347, n. 34
Laura, 63–4, 69–70, 147, 282
Melva, 256, 310
Supreme Court, United States, 155, 176, 178, 188

T

Taylor, Robert, 49–50
Tennyson, Hallam, 131, 146, 163, 164, 339, ch. 10, n. 30
Thomson, Dugald, 172
Townsend, William, 56, 57, 62
Trustee and Executor Company, 269, 272, 308, 310, 316, 317

Tucker, Charles, 93, 196, 199
Turner, George, 99, 106, 108, 149, 150, 172, 181, 190, 211

V

Vardon, Joseph, 194, 195, 197, 198, 203, 204, 214, 227, 228–9, 230, 231, 341, n. 14

W

Walker, James, 103, 132–3, 156, 198–200, 203, 204–5, 211, 335, n. 16
Wallington, Edward, 108, 259–60, 292, 298–300
Waterhouse, Arthur, 27–8, 69
Watson, John, 170, 173, 174, 176
Way, Samuel, 34–5, 36, 37, 38, 39–41, 42, 48, 52, 54, 56, 60, 72, 73, 74, 83–4, 89, 157, 158–60, 163, 164, 166, 167, 168, 170–1, 192–3, 196, 204, 217, 238, 271, 331, ch. 4, n. 15; 339, n. 39, 344, n. 6, 346, ch. 16, n. 8
Symon's criticisms of, 35, 37, 43–7, 51, 63, 88, 89, 94–5, 104–5, 128, 140–3, 145–6, 152–3, 165, 291, 315
Way & Brook, ix, 36, 38, 40, 41, 45
Way & Symon, 40, 45, 46
Webb, Beatrice and Sidney, 128
Webster family, 71–2
White, Brudenell, 291–2, 307
Whitley, J.H., 261
Wigley, William, 57
Will, 308–18, 310–13, 315–18,
Williams, W.W., 30
Wise, Bernhard, 103–4, 117, 126, 146
'Wootten Lea', 36

Z

Zeal, William, 118, 154–5, 156, 335–6, n. 16

Wakefield Press is an independent publishing and
distribution company based in Adelaide, South Australia.
We love good stories and publish beautiful books.
To see our full range of books, please visit our website at
www.wakefieldpress.com.au
where all titles are available for purchase.
To keep up with our latest releases, news and events,
subscribe to our monthly newsletter.

Find us!

Facebook: www.facebook.com/wakefield.press
Twitter: www.twitter.com/wakefieldpress
Instagram: www.instagram.com/wakefieldpress

www.ingramcontent.com/pod-product-compliance
Lightning Source LLC
Chambersburg PA
CBHW051249300426
44114CB00011B/954